THE END OF THE SCHISM

THE END OF THE SCHISM

CATHOLICS, PROTESTANTS, AND THE REMAKING
OF CHRISTIAN LIFE IN EUROPE, 1880s–1970s

UDI GREENBERG

HARVARD UNIVERSITY PRESS
Cambridge, Massachusetts
London, England
2025

Copyright © 2025 by the President and Fellows of Harvard College
All rights reserved
Printed in the United States of America

First printing

Library of Congress Cataloging-in-Publication Data

Names: Greenberg, Udi, 1980– author.
Title: The end of the schism : Catholics, Protestants, and the remaking of Christian life in Europe, 1880s–1970s / Udi Greenberg.
Description: Cambridge, Massachusetts : Harvard University Press, 2025. |
Includes bibliographical references and index.
Identifiers: LCCN 2024016167 (print) | LCCN 2024016168 (ebook) |
ISBN 9780674248762 (cloth) | ISBN 9780674298767 (pdf) |
ISBN 9780674298774 (epub)
Subjects: LCSH: Catholic Church—Relations—Protestant churches. | Ecumenical movement—Europe—History—20th century. | Protestant churches—Relations—Catholic Church. | Christianity and politics—Europe—History—19th century. | Christianity and politics—Europe—History—20th century. | Christian life—Europe—History—19th century. | Christian life—Europe—History—20th century.
Classification: LCC BR735 .G745 2025 (print) | LCC BR735 (ebook) |
DDC 280/.042—dc23/eng/20240911
LC record available at https://lccn.loc.gov/2024016167
LC ebook record available at https://lccn.loc.gov/2024016168

CONTENTS

Introduction · 1

1. Anti-Catholicism and Anti-Protestantism
   in the Long Nineteenth Century · 24

2. Mutual Dreams of Order in an Unruly World, 1880s–1920s · 63

3. The Birth of Ecumenism from the Crucible of Nazism · 116

4. Grand Compromises at the Zenith of Christian Power · 172

5. Radical Ecumenism in the 1960s and 1970s · 228

Conclusion · 280

NOTES · 289
ACKNOWLEDGMENTS · 339
INDEX · 343

THE END OF THE SCHISM

Introduction

THROUGHOUT THE EXTREME tumult that transformed Europe in the twentieth century, Christianity was a rare source of continuity. As empires fell, revolutions upended political regimes, and cities were bombed into ash, the churches remained vital sites of social interaction. For many, confession embodied much more than just personal belief. It facilitated membership in a vast network of church-affiliated organizations, which allowed people across the continent to engage with each other and the world. Self-identified Catholic and Protestant political parties were central actors in European politics, often wielding considerable power. Confessional civil organs, such as labor unions and youth movements, offered believers venues to participate in the economy and to enjoy their free time. By launching public campaigns against pornography and persecuting same-sex relationships and abortion, Catholic and Protestant organizations fundamentally shaped many Europeans' understanding and expression of gender and sexuality. Christian missionaries—long crucial agents of European empires—helped Europeans develop new understandings of faraway places. Indeed, the churches undergirded not just their members' religious, political, and social habits, but also many aspects of European intellectual life. Catholic and Protestant publications sought to define how countless Europeans understood a time of rapid social change, revolutions, and wars. Christian political theorists, economists, marriage experts, and missionaries endlessly debated and explained what being Catholic or Protestant meant in concrete terms, and a gigantic apparatus of Christian research centers, presses, and popular magazines brought their ideas to a wide readership.

Yet even as the Catholic and Protestant milieus endured, the relationship *between* them changed in dramatic and unexpected ways. While the violent wars between the confessions had ended centuries earlier, at the dawn of the twentieth century the animosity between Catholics and Protestants remained a foundational feature of European life. It extended far beyond seminaries and theology departments: across national and linguistic boundaries, Christian political parties, labor unions, lay associations, and publishing houses were strictly Catholic or Protestant. Their leaders often portrayed themselves as locked in mortal competition with each other. Lay writers routinely blamed the other confession for every modern malady, from political subversion to economic backwardness and sexual perversity. The German Protestant sociologist Max Weber reflected these divisions when he claimed that capitalism emerged from the spirit of the Reformation, and lamented that Catholicism, with its absurd focus on superstition and papal infallibility, fostered resignation and destitution.[1] Catholics offered their own version of these arguments, decrying the Protestant rejection of clerical authority as opening the gates to nihilism and anarchy. As the French Catholic thinker Alfred Baudrillart explained in a large conference in Paris in 1904, Protestants were so possessed by the "fanatic" desire to undermine political authority that they had to be prohibited from holding public office.[2] While such sweeping generalizations concealed each confession's enormous internal diversity and tensions, they were not confined to enthusiastic polemicists. They circulated in countless works by respected theologians, social theorists, and politicians, and many considered such claims to be common sense. The popularity of these sentiments also had toxic repercussions. Anti-Catholicism and anti-Protestantism fueled a litany of political clashes, legal discrimination, and even violent state-led campaigns against confessional schools and orders. The overwhelming majority of Europeans took it for granted that peaceful coexistence was a pipe dream.

By the middle of the twentieth century, however, this reality had changed beyond recognition. Across Central and Western Europe, interconfessional cooperation swiftly eclipsed centuries of hostilities. In several countries, Catholic and Protestant parties gave way to explicitly interconfessional "Christian democrats," who came to rule their countries. These political transformations were followed by additional experiments, such as joint Catholic-Protestant economic think tanks, marriage and sex clinics, and interconfessional collaboration between missionary agencies. Perhaps most remarkably, this pragmatic cooperation was accompanied by a new intellectual campaign that described the two confessions as sharing a deep spiritual affinity. An army of writers labored to refute older stereotypes by claiming that all Christians agreed on how to translate the Gospel into concrete teachings: which economic policies to support, what gender and sexual norms to uphold, and how to define Europe's relationship to the Global South. As the prominent German historian Walther von Loewenich proclaimed in 1959, the two confessions were allies in "Europe's salvation."[3] Contemporaries named this innovative reconciliation "ecumenism," from the Greek term *oikoumene*, which referred to Christian unity in the time of the early church. This intellectual project was so successful that it received doctrinal confirmation in the 1960s, when both the Catholic Church and many of Europe's Protestant churches formally declared themselves "brethren in faith." Confessional distinctions and tensions never disappeared completely, but anti-Catholicism and anti-Protestantism dramatically weakened. In ways that would have shocked their predecessors, most Europeans came to view the two confessions as part of a broad, "Christian" camp.

What explains this surprising change of fortunes? After four centuries of inter-Christian hostility, with its legacy of persecution and violence, how and why did ecumenism develop? It is tempting to see this shift as a process of Christianity's opening to tolerance and pluralism. This, after all, is how Christian elites themselves explained it. As they sought to both justify and encourage the budding ecumenical revolution, Christian social theorists and theologians routinely described it as an expression of maturation. Living in the modern world, they claimed, required religious communities to grow out of the childish desire to achieve total hegemony in public life and learn to respect past enemies. As the widely read Swiss Protestant essayist Walter Nigg declared in 1953, "Sectarianism . . . is all too conductive to malice, and tends to blur one's vision of truth."[4] In this version of the story, World War II loomed large as the crucial turning point. As Christian scholars began to write the history of ecumenism in the postwar decades, they repeatedly claimed that Catholics and Protestants were brought together by mutual suffering and a realization that only peaceful engagement could prevent another catastrophe and achieve stability in a war-torn continent. The German Catholic theologian Johannes Hessen, a prolific proponent of reconciliation, reflected this widespread notion when he equated the quest for inter-Christian peace with Christianity's rejection of fascist authoritarianism. The path to "holy unity," he explained, opened because the "bitter experiences" of living under fascism fostered a new appreciation of freedom and solidarity beyond confessional boundaries.[5]

Comforting as this narrative may be, it is badly misleading. This book offers a new understanding of ecumenism's origins, nature, and consequences. To do this, it revises this earlier story in three important ways. First, even though Christian writers portrayed their engagement with each other as an egalitarian process, ecumenism was also deeply rooted in efforts to preserve hierarchies. Its conceptual groundwork was laid half a century before World War II, during both confessions' anxious and difficult encounters with modern life in the late nineteenth century. Like many Europeans, Christian elites understood the decades from the 1880s onward as a period of alarming instability. They worried that the millions who poured into the swelling cities, living in workers' slums and patronizing mass entertainment industries, had become detached from the meaning and spirituality that could only be found in communal life. What is more, a slew of new egalitarian ideologies proliferated throughout Europe. Socialist parties, which surged across the continent, rocked the economy with strikes and calls for economic redistribution, while budding feminist organizations offered new emancipatory visions. These ideas rattled many Europeans, but the anxieties they sparked had a special edge among Catholics and Protestants. This was in part because many persons and groups involved in these movements, especially socialist organizations, were openly atheist and aimed to diminish or eradicate Christianity's influence in public life; in France, some radicals went so far as to pursue these goals by murdering clergy. Though such extreme acts were exceedingly rare, they had a profound impact. They led many Christians to believe that egalitarianism always had a dark undercurrent, which could easily morph into anti-Christian violence.

In a response that would have far-reaching consequences for European life, both Catholics and Protestant elites conflated demands for equality with predatory secularism. In books and speeches, they described egalitarianism as a hubristic revolt against God's order that sought to free humans from all limitations and obligations and was bound to foster chaos. As the popular German Catholic writer Viktor Cathrein argued in 1890, "inequality is the necessary outcome of the natural development of man" and any effort to upend it required "external violence."[6] To prevent social disintegration, therefore, both confessions insisted on the necessity of inequality. In writing and public advocacy, Christian scholars, politicians, and activists sought to convince workers and women of the need to embrace one's given place in society, and to view it as the fulfillment of one's destiny. The Christian mission, so the logic went, was to bestow on them the respect for self-denial and self-control that an unequal and just society demanded. These beliefs also had an important colonial dimension as European empires expanded in Asia and Africa. Descending on local communities across the globe, Christian missionaries were vexed by colonial subjects' alleged lack of appreciation for hard work and inequality. Asians and Africans, they claimed, were easy prey for misguided religions, especially Islam, which falsely promised equality for all without toil or sacrifice. Christian missionaries therefore claimed that their main task was not merely religious conversion but also social and psychological training. Under European tutelage, communities overseas would learn how to work and live in the properly unequal order ordained by God.

Ecumenism was the product of this mutual desire to produce and maintain economic, gendered, and colonial hierarchies. Rooted in the anxieties that both confessions shared, it led some Catholics and Protestants to view each other, at least pragmatically, as allies against mutual enemies. Indeed, in ways that scholarship has not often registered, opposition to egalitarian causes helped inspire the first tactical collaboration between the confessions. In the late nineteenth and early twentieth centuries, Catholics and Protestants across Europe founded interconfessional and anti-socialist labor unions, which became important forums for labor activism. They cooperated in crafting innovative anti-socialist welfare legislation, such as pension and health insurance, that reshaped workers' relationship to their states. The two confessions also successfully worked together to mobilize against feminism and to restrict public expressions of sexuality beyond the heterosexual family, a process that radically expanded the state's regulation of the intimate sphere. These campaigns were echoed overseas, where Catholic and Protestant missionaries converged in efforts to sever colonial subjects' ties to local norms and cultures and acculturate them to European tutelage. The struggle to preserve inequality further expanded as the center of ecumenical cooperation after World War II. In the postwar decades, interconfessional parties and organizations sidelined Christian voices that called for egalitarian agendas (such as engagement with socialism) and poured enormous energy into crafting unequal welfare systems, sexist family laws, and paternalist training programs for Asians and Africans.

Yet it was not just these parallel efforts to legitimize inequality that fostered a sense of deeper unity. Understanding ecumenism as a project to perpetuate disparities entails a second significant revision of the standard narrative, one that obliges us to rethink ecumenism's timeline. The first large-scale and comprehensive efforts to reconcile the two confessions emerged not from the Christian confrontation with the violence of World War II but from an earlier, and darker, origin: namely, some Christians' enthusiasm for the Nazis in the 1930s. Often forgotten today, an important tenet of early Nazi ideology was its promise to bridge the historical divide between Catholics and Protestants. Like the tensions between classes and regions, the Nazis claimed that this historical religious enmity should give way to a new solidarity and unity in the racial body. Catholics and Protestants who supported this Nazi vision thus began to describe the two confessions as part of a broader "Christian" community. As they celebrated the Third Reich's aggressive anti-socialism, anti-feminism, and imperialism, which they hoped would permanently uproot the notion of universal human equality, they also emulated its call for Catholic-Protestant reconciliation. In the words of the Austrian Nazi sympathizer Alois Hudal, whoever "eliminates the religious division would render the greatest service . . . to the German race and Europe's entire cultural leadership."[7] This went further than earlier pragmatic collaborations to direct workers, women, and colonial subjects away from dangerous habits; for the first time, a large group of Catholic and Protestant writers across Europe claimed that the two confessions were part of the same community, and that they shared equal access to divine truth. It was under these conditions that Catholic and Protestant theologians launched pathbreaking efforts to identify conceptual similarities between their teachings and liturgies. In conferences and lectures, they claimed that all Christians recognized that divine grace operated through national and racial collectives, which made doctrinal differences over celibacy or divorce marginal.

Ecumenism was not the domain of Nazi sympathizers alone. Antifascist Christians also rushed to develop their own ecumenical theory. They claimed that the two confessions were united against biological racism and that divine grace required autonomy from the overreaching state. It would be easy to claim that this version of ecumenism emerged victorious after the war, when Christian democratic parties accepted pluralist democracy as the future of Europe. This acceptance, however, was facilitated by a broad process of historical revisionism, as anti-fascist

Introduction

ecumenists welcomed former fascist sympathizers in their efforts to build a broad Christian alliance. Indeed, Christian elites were eager to put aside their early disagreements. They were so alarmed by the expansion of communism, the dawn of the Cold War, and the wartime challenges to the patriarchal family that they actively shed ecumenism's association with pro- and anti-fascist ideologies and sought to place the inter-Christian alliance in the intellectual and social mainstream. Christian elites were convinced that only broad cooperation, accommodating all factions of Christian thought, could prevent the destruction of Christianity. This compromise meant that postwar ecumenism retained some characteristics of its unsavory origins. Explicit references to authoritarianism, racism, and anti-Semitism were repressed, but Catholic and Protestant cooperation often remained unforgivingly anti-egalitarian and combative. In fact, the most important legacy of the 1930s for postwar Christian elites was not the need to rethink their earlier priorities, but the realization that defending inequalities was best achieved through ecumenical cooperation. This was a lesson that clearly resonated. The surge in joint Catholic and Protestant organizations, events, and publications in the 1950s put ecumenism in the center of Christian thought and politics.

This process of convergence had its corollary in the missionary world. It took place in response to the anti-colonial revolts of the 1930s and the shocking advances of decolonization in Asia and Africa in the following decades. Missionary leaders and theoreticians shared a deep unease about Asian and African liberation movements. In Gandhi's and others' challenges to European hegemony they saw a direct threat to the missions, which often depended on imperial support for their operation, and which had long subscribed to notions of European superiority. Despite this near consensus, Christian elites also fiercely clashed over their initial response to anti-colonial movements. One group of Catholics and Protestants, who sought to reconcile Christianity with Nazi racism, argued that local cultures and norms were the expression of the races' different essence. One influential German writer argued in 1938 that primitive remnants, instead of being something that had to be removed, were the expression of "race consciousness" that missionaries had to protect.[8] In contrast, other figures from both confessions insisted that Christ's message was explicitly anti-racist. They proclaimed that missions must emphasize the universal qualities that bound together all humans and cultures. The collapse of Europe's empires, first in Asia in the 1940s and then in Africa in the 1950s and 1960s, ultimately led these two groups to put aside their differences.

If Christianity was to survive as a minority in a hostile world, new cooperation was needed between confessions and ideological inclinations. Motivated by this conviction, missionaries not only rushed to create innovative and interconfessional organizations. They also developed new missionary theories and practices that explained European tutelage as the protection and even empowerment of local traditions.

Recognizing these origins offers a third overarching revision to the standard narrative, which acknowledges ecumenism's contradictory nature: it entailed both revolutionary tolerance and harsh exclusion. Proponents of reconciliation often claimed that their project was premised on recognizing the universal desire for spirituality. The Protestant economist Georg Wünsch asserted, for example, in 1952 that Christian peace aspired to endow the whole world with the "spirit of grace."[9] In some respects, ecumenism was indeed emancipatory. It ended long traditions that had often led to very real discrimination. During the late nineteenth century, Protestants of different denominations and political convictions were united not only in their intense dislike of Catholics. In the Catholic Church, with its affiliated orders, schools, and charities, they saw a vast plot to bring down modern states and hinder social progress. For that reason, they often backed discriminatory measures against Catholicism. For decades—well into the twentieth century—they supported the expulsion of Catholic orders, the suppression of Catholic education, and in some cases the arrest and persecution of Catholic activists. While Catholics in Central and Western Europe rarely had the power to retaliate in the same way, some of them harbored similar fantasies of exclusion. When the French conservative writer Gaston Mercier called in 1901 for the suppression of "the Protestant spirit," he echoed widespread sentiments.[10] Ecumenism, in this regard, was a campaign against more than unpleasant prejudice. It successfully combated discriminatory realities and desires.

Yet the generosity that Catholics and Protestants began to show to each other in the twentieth century was not only juxtaposed against self-proclaimed secular actors, like socialists. It was also firmly confined to Christians. Even though some Christian writers questioned Christians' monopoly on access to divine grace and sought to open a new tolerance toward Jews and Muslims, proponents of Catholic-Protestant reconciliation mostly kept their distance from these efforts.[11] In fact, Christian ecumenism was often conceived in explicit *opposition* to those other projects. Some of the leading advocates for Catholic-Protestant engagement, such

Introduction

as German social theorist Alfred Dedo Müller, were openly anti-Semitic. Others, such as Swiss missionary Walbert Bühlmann, expressed Islamophobic sentiments and believed that Catholic-Protestant cooperation was needed to secure indirect European control over Africa. Such figures envisioned an inter-Christian alliance as a tool to maintain Christian hegemony over public life and *restrict* tolerance for non-Christians, both in Europe and overseas. It is therefore telling that a crucial feature of early ecumenical texts was their focus not only on tolerance but also on enmity. Advocates of interconfessional cooperation constantly described themselves as building defensive walls against a dark deluge of foes, employing apocalyptic metaphors of battle and destruction. The German ecumenist Johannes Hessen spoke for many when he characterized Christian peace in 1946 as a "brotherhood of weapons" in an existential war against mutual enemies. Ecumenism was therefore rife with exclusionary impulses. It was a form of religious pluralism that simultaneously removed some religious boundaries while policing others.[12]

Despite the profound limits of early ecumenical thought and action, there were important efforts to expand its boundaries. As protesters in the late 1960s and 1970s launched a blistering attack on so many aspects of European life, a new generation of Christian thinkers and activists worked to invest Catholic-Protestant relations with new meanings. Inspired by the New Left, a group of radical Catholics and Protestants claimed that the churches were wrong to fixate on hierarchies and stability. Christ's teachings, so the logic went, required siding with the weak against sources of power and inequality; Christians had to rise against capitalism and in favor of redistribution. This ecumenical vision also called on Christians to mobilize against the patriarchy and the Christian fixation on restricting sexuality to the family. Going far beyond earlier and anti-fascist critiques of natalism, its leaders endorsed radical feminism, abortion, and same-sex relationships. They also joined anti-colonial campaigns to end European paternalism and redistribute wealth and power from the Global North to the Global South. Like the New Left that helped inspire it, this radical ecumenism did not succeed in thoroughly remaking European life. Most Christian elites, church leaders, and communities remained skeptical of, and even hostile to, egalitarian Christianity, and stuck to the ideas that were crafted between the 1930s and the 1950s. Yet the failures of this reform demonstrate the triumph of the ecumenical project. Even those who radically rethought its ideological content took it for granted that Catholics and Protestants were part of the same intellectual camp and had to cooperate in pursuit of the same political and spiritual goals.

The End of the Schism thus tells the story of these broad changes across the "long twentieth century," from the 1880s to the 1970s.[13] As Catholics and Protestants confronted the transformations wrought by modern life at home and abroad, they also rethought their relationship to each other. This process, in which Christians constantly updated their teachings on theology, politics, economics, sexuality, and Europe's relationship to the Global South, was arduous and filled with contradictions. It was often controversial, generating bitter debates inside and between the confessions. Yet by its own measures, it was immensely successful. Through a series of convergences and compromises, Catholics and Protestants came to imagine and practice life together.

The Intellectual Worlds of Ecumenism

At its core, ecumenism was an intellectual project. Many of its main proponents assumed that changing how believers thought about each other was the necessary precondition for generating cooperation in the world of politics, institutions, or social activism. In this book I therefore reconstruct this intellectual journey by tracing the debates that defined Christian thought across countless magazines, books, and conference proceedings. This intellectual universe was not confined to the halls of seminaries and theology departments. Grasping the broad scope of Christian thinking and writing requires focusing on both clerical and lay figures, writers and thinkers who self-identified as either Catholic or Protestant, referenced Christianity as a source of legitimacy, and published in confessional presses. Many of the texts explored in this book were very popular—some were major best-sellers—and they were widely read, translated, and discussed by laypeople. They were part of the explosion of literacy and inexpensive print culture, particularly from the late nineteenth century onward. This panoramic view helps capture sensitivities that were often slow to register in texts of clerical authorities. Indeed, the notion that Catholics and Protestants could and should cooperate with each other circulated in lay works decades before it received clerical stamps of approval.[14]

Four kinds of thinkers were particularly important to the story of ecumenism; each chapter explores their writing, agreements, and disagree-

Introduction

ments. The first group was theologians. Theology's reputation today is that of an abstract and even esoteric form of knowledge, accessible to only a handful of specialists. Its history is often studied separately from the thinking of lay writers and politicians. But through much of the nineteenth and twentieth centuries, theology was a widely read field. In addition to focusing on sacred texts' implications for religious rites or ecclesiology, Catholic and Protestant theologians commented on politics, sexuality, and international affairs. They often did so in publications that were digestible and clear, at least to readers with rudimentary knowledge of Christian discourses. They were therefore influential voices among both clerics and laypeople; some were best-selling authors. Theology's importance, which historians of European thought have recently begun to recognize, was true also for the story of Catholic-Protestant relations.[15] Theologians crafted key concepts and narratives that explained why centuries of divisions were a mistake, and why sacred texts required new interpretations. They popularized such claims with booklets and pamphlets and institutionalized them by founding new lay organizations and associations. The chapters that follow reconstruct the theological innovations that both enabled and reflected the ecumenical revolution. They trace the broad political and intellectual forces that remade Christian dogmas.

Theologians, however, were far from the only participants in the transformation of Christian thought. Even more influential, at least for most lay readers, were economists and social theorists. Beginning in the late nineteenth century, both Catholics and Protestants wondered how to respond to the emerging conflict between the urban working class and the bourgeoisie. This question acquired a special urgency because it held religious consequences: Europe's growing socialist parties were anticlerical and even atheist, and openly sought to eradicate the churches' role in social life. In their efforts to arrest the rise of socialism, both Catholics and Protestants developed their own versions of social theory. They aimed to ameliorate industrialism's worst excesses while enshrining the inequality between workers and employers and convincing the two classes to live in harmony with each other. Economists and social scientists spent decades debating how this goal was best achieved, whether through voluntary associations, state interventions, or market competition. The evolution of this debate had important consequences for confessional relations. Early in the twentieth century, Catholics and Protestants could not agree on the best way to achieve the goal of harmonious and unequal class relations; they were particularly divided over the role of the state in mediating the economy. From the 1930s onward, however, they agreed that the state had to intervene in economic life and bind workers and employers through regulation and limited welfare programs. Because social theorists recognized this intellectual convergence, they were some of the most explicit and vocal proponents of ecumenism. Their writings endlessly celebrated the emergence of "Christian" economic thought, and the think tanks they led provided crucial spaces for interconfessional engagement.

The third group of writers and thinkers this book highlights are commentators on gender and sexuality. Debates about the proper roles of men and women, marriage, and sex were central to the evolution of modern Christian thought.[16] And they were not solely the preoccupation of theologians and church leaders; in the Catholic and Protestant milieus, a range of influential (and often self-declared) experts emerged, publishing popular marriage advice guides and sex manuals. Christian publishing houses and clinics were some of the most influential sites for European thinking about these topics.[17] Less recognized, gender and sexuality were also important for confessional relations. In the nineteenth and early twentieth centuries, confessional animosities were routinely laced with sexual anxieties. Whether it was Protestants' bewilderment about celibacy or Catholics' critique of divorce, commentators endlessly blamed the other confession as the source of promiscuity and sexual chaos. Yet as time passed, the two confessions progressively converged around shared concerns, particularly the preservation of a patriarchal social, familial, and sexual order. They cooperated in campaigns against feminism and sex reformers, and they radically expanded European states' regulation of family relations and sexuality. Between the 1930s and the 1950s, they also developed a shared understanding of marriage as a site of both reproduction and affection, a Christian alternative to feminist visions of liberation. These shifts encouraged several leading writers to talk about an ecumenical sex ethic, and even to condone interconfessional marriages.

The final group that merits attention in this story are missionary writers. Despite scholars' growing attention to missionaries, especially their complicated role in colonial governance, missionary theory has not been fully integrated into the history of European Christianity.[18] Most works on Christian thought and politics do not mention missionaries or missionary writers, and missiology is the least studied Christian body of knowledge. This is a strange omission, given that missionary journals, books, and conferences were major sites for Christian thought, especially about Asia and Africa. As European empires grew exponentially in the late nineteenth century and then collapsed in the twentieth, missionary writings on non-European cultures, ethnography, and race were important to European thinking about the Global South. They defined European efforts to discipline Asians and Africans into "modern" productivity as a spiritual task, a goal that resonated with and reinforced the Christian campaigns directed at workers and women at home.[19] Missionary writings were just as important for thinking about confessional relations. During the imperial period, missionary theoreticians had fed the flames of anti-Catholicism and anti-Protestantism by describing each other as threats to Europe's "civilizing mission." After decolonization in the 1950s and 1960s, fears that Christianity might be wiped out in Asia and Africa led missionaries to view each other as allies, a task that was helped by their parallel adoption of economic development as a new way to retain Christian influence and power in the Global South.

Exploring this broad array of figures offers an expansive view of Christian thought, both among and between Catholics and Protestants. It brings to the fore writers who have not always been the focal point in histories of European religion or thought, but were in fact influential, popular, and widely read. Crucially, exploring them together demonstrates how Christian thinking regarding theology, economics, sexuality, and mission was always intertwined and evolved in concert. Vocabularies and concepts that were coined in one sphere of knowledge often quickly began to define writing in another. Catholic and Protestant writers in the late nineteenth century, for example, regularly warned that the modern economy was dominated by "materialism," by which they meant capitalism and socialism's alleged reduction of human life to earthly and material gains. Almost immediately the term "materialism" appeared in writings against feminism and sex reform movements, which described a similar fixation with "materialist" pleasure at the expense of spirituality. The term "materialism" also appeared in the writings of missionaries, who claimed it captured the spiritual evils at the core of African religions, especially Islam. In the same vein, the thinkers who sympathized with the New Left in the 1960s and 1970s routinely mobilized analogous terms and frameworks when discussing different struggles. If the Gospel called on believers to engage in anti-imperialist uprisings in Asia and Africa, as many claimed, it was incumbent on them to also end the "imperial" domination that subjugated workers, women, and sexual minorities in Europe. Bringing together these different domains of Christian thought therefore does more than highlight the different actors who reimagined confessional relations. It illustrates the vast and intersecting set of concerns that constantly remade Christian thinking.

This choice of protagonists also offers a broad and fresh understanding of what constitutes Christian thought, both Catholic and Protestant. For a long time, scholars of Catholic thought focused on clerical texts, such as papal encyclicals or the doctrinal statements of the Second Vatican Council (1962–1965), as representing the Catholic mainstream.[20] But as recent scholarship has emphasized, popes and bishops were only one set of voices in the diversity that constituted "the Church." Especially in Central and Western Europe, where lay organizations and publication houses enjoyed considerable autonomy, proclamations were often either ignored or invoked instrumentally to support a preexisting agenda. Some lay groups even explicitly and openly challenged the church's nominal "center" in the Vatican.[21] Ecumenism was in fact a prime example of these dynamics. From the 1920s to the 1950s, Popes Pius XI, Pius XII, and their allies in the Vatican repeatedly condemned engagement with Protestants, only to be rebuffed by Catholic elites in Germany, France, and elsewhere. For that reason, in this book I analyze papal encyclicals and proclamations mostly when they were widely invoked and utilized by lay figures. This focus on more local actors helps to reconstruct the large-scale and rich intellectual universe of Catholic thinking.

Taking a panoramic view is equally useful to understanding European Protestants, who have received far less attention than Catholics. Because they never had an institution like the Vatican that claimed to speak on their behalf, scholarship on Protestants has often focused on a series of international congresses that brought together Protestant politicians, church leaders, and activists. It has also explored in detail the evolution of academic theologians.[22] Yet these insightful studies have often overlooked Protestants' enormous lay apparatus of knowledge production on everything from economics and sexuality to race. These writings circulated throughout Europe; social theory from Germany was read in Belgium, and texts from the Netherlands found audiences in France. I reconstruct this broader intellectual conversation by focusing on Lutherans and Calvinists (Reformed), who constituted the vast majority of Europe's Protestants. For both confessions, my focus is not on canonical figures, but on the conceptual and discursive strategies that a wide array of Christian elites developed to manage modern life, with all the tensions and contradictions this process entailed.

Introduction

Bringing together the broader history of the two confessions in a joint narrative also illuminates their prolonged and intense exchange. For decades, scholarship on Christianity was a niche project, written for and by members of religious communities. It mostly told their stories through a confessional lens, emphasizing their unique experiences and characteristics. Over the last two decades, as controversies over religion's place in the public sphere have rekindled interest in the history of Christianity, scholars beyond the churches' borders have begun to trace the churches' vital role in modern Europe. With a critical eye, they have mapped Catholics' and Protestants' impact on anti-Semitism, anti-communist mobilization, sexual norms, democratic reconstruction, and discourses of human rights.[23] Despite this change of perspective, however, even these innovative works have largely remained within confessional boundaries. Whether their focus is regional, national, or international, they often map either Catholic or Protestant networks and discourses. While this effectively highlights dynamics internal to each confession, Catholics and Protestants did not always develop independently from each other. They not only responded to similar events and anxieties but were well versed in each other's ideas. They routinely cited each other's writings and reflected on their similarities and differences. In fact, comparisons of Catholic and Protestant teachings were one of the most popular genres of the late nineteenth and early twentieth centuries. By tracing their parallel reflections on theological, social, gender, and missionary issues, this book examines the two confessions as part of a larger intellectual universe. It seeks to explain when and why they disagreed with each other, and what happened when they agreed.

The decision to tell ecumenism's story through the history of ideas requires some explanation. It is too easy to assume that Christian writers who called for reconciliation were mostly following shifting social realities. When theologians like the German Lutheran Wilhelm Stählin said that the two confessions were "spiritual brothers," were they not simply responding to the dramatic increase in Catholic-Protestant interactions in hospitals or the military during World War II?[24] When the Catholic Church formally announced in 1964 that it saw Protestants as "brethren," was it not merely acknowledging that Christian social milieus were weakening, and that their members now went to the same schools and movie theaters?[25] Social conditions mattered a great deal to Christian thought, but ideas did not simply reflect them. The first ecumenical theories emerged in the 1930s, many years before the dramatic increase in social interactions between the two confessions. The writers that crafted them were well aware that they were an intellectual vanguard: they put great effort into refuting anti-Catholic and anti-Protestant stereotypes, which they recognized were still prevalent among their readers. More importantly, social contact alone cannot explain why reconciliation became acceptable and even desirable for so many Christians. For this to happen, communities needed coherent conceptual justifications that drew on familiar traditions but explained them in new ways. By tracing the language and concepts at the center of the ecumenical revolution, this book aims to uncover a project that was both creative and surprising.

The creativity that enabled ecumenical engagement is especially important because its impact beyond the world of ideas was profound and far-reaching. My focus in these chapters is intellectual history, but I also chart the new political, institutional, and social realities that confessional relations helped inspire and legitimize. As the following pages show, each stage in the evolution of Catholic-Protestant relations had broad consequences for European life. The social vision that animated Catholic and Protestant elites since the late nineteenth century, with its focus on reciprocal and unequal alliance between workers and employers, underlay many countries' economic arrangements. Christian cooperation was central to the formation of new labor laws, workers' organizations, and revolutionary welfare regimes. Interconfessional action also powered far-reaching legislation on matters of gender and sexuality. Ecumenical mobilization encouraged new family laws, as well as state regulation of pornography, prostitution, and abortion. And cooperation between Catholic and Protestant missionaries facilitated one of Europe's responses to decolonization, in the form of economic development schemes. Catholics and Protestants, that is, insisted that their teachings about social order, intimate relations, and international interactions had universal applicability. They had to be enshrined in laws, policies, and institutions that regulated the behavior of all Europeans. Indeed, despite their increased attention to the regulation of religion by European states, historians have not always registered how many functions of modern governance were designed by religious actors who sought to secure the conditions they believed were necessary for virtuous life.[26] Christians' success in implementing their visions was always partial, and it was always heavily contested. But together, Catholic and Protestant activists, politicians, and thinkers influenced the lives of millions, including those far away from Christianity's orbit.

Introduction

The Contours of the Ecumenical Revolution

Ecumenism emerged in a broad, complex, and long process, but it had clear geographical contours. Germany was the most important country for its growth. It was the site of the earliest and most intense inter-Christian engagement, which was heavily influenced by the Third Reich. Its demographics, which included sizable communities of self-identified Catholics and Protestants, made their political cooperation unusually consequential. For that reason, Germany receives outsized attention in this book. The transformation of confessional relations, however, was not just a German affair. As the following pages show, ecumenism followed similar temporal and conceptual frames in France, Belgium, the Netherlands, Austria, and Switzerland. This was because Christian elites in those countries, despite their different histories and confessional demographics, also shared a similar set of experiences and concerns. Whether they debated how to regulate sexuality in the 1890s or how to adjust to Nazi hegemony in the 1940s, they routinely utilized the same terms and concepts. Those similarities became increasingly apparent to Christians themselves, who drew from and emulated each other throughout the nineteenth and twentieth centuries. Through translations, international gatherings, and multilingual organizations, they formed a coherent intellectual and political universe. I therefore chart the trends that brought together Christians in German-, French-, and Dutch-speaking regions. Throughout this book, these are the countries I refer to as "Europe" or "European."

This geographical and linguistic framework, especially when applied to a story that stretches over a century, does come at a cost. Some important local and national particularities inevitably get lost. Focusing on Central and Western Europe also obscures some of the broader networks that shaped Christian life. Thinkers and politicians in France, for example, often shared concerns and actively engaged with counterparts in Eastern Europe.[27] Yet when it comes to confessional relations, the countries at the center of this book had distinctive features and timing. This becomes evident when contrasted to other parts of Europe, where anti-Catholicism and anti-Protestantism lived far longer. In Southern Europe, where clerical authority was stronger, state authorities continued to discriminate against Protestants into the 1960s. Italy, for example, prohibited Protestant missionaries from working in the country, and Spain banned Protestant public worship, positions that generated vocal protest from Protestant organizations. In the north, Protestant-majority countries in Scandinavia similarly had little inhibition about discriminating against Catholicism, whether in denying funds to Catholic institutions or putting outright bans on Catholic orders. In Northern Ireland, confessional animosities fueled violence well into the late twentieth century. Confessional reconciliation, in short, was not a side effect of pan-European trends. It was the product of unique dynamics.[28]

This focus on Central and Western Europe also clarifies some of ecumenism's distinctive features. Around the same time that confessional reconciliation emerged as a coherent project in Europe, a new understanding of religious pluralism also became hegemonic in the United States. Alarmed by the rise of "totalitarian" Nazism and communism, which they understood as secular ideologies, many Protestants abandoned long-standing suspicions and called for cooperation with the Catholic and Jewish minorities. Many mused about the values of "tri-faith" or "Judeo-Christian" cultures, which they then sought to mobilize in Cold War Europe.[29] European ecumenists may have shared the anti-communism of their American counterparts, but their ideas had little to do with American influence. They had crafted their theories long before American postwar hegemony, and their goal was to solve a separate set of issues they believed to be endemic to European life, such as economic, family, and colonial relations. Indeed, European Christian proponents of interconfessional relations showed remarkably little interest in the words of North American Christians. With a few exceptions, they almost never cited publications by icons like theologian Reinhold Niebuhr, and they were even less interested in reconciliation with Jews.[30] American and European understandings of religious pluralism, that is, may have changed in parallel, but their causes and content were different.

To capture the confluence of events, actors, and intellectual convergences that brought about the ecumenical revolution, this book progresses chronologically through five key periods. Chapter 1 focuses on the era from the French Revolution to the early twentieth century and charts the intellectual and political world that ecumenism sought to demolish. This period witnessed a sharp upsurge of confessional hostilities in Europe. Across national and linguistic boundaries, anti-Catholic and anti-Protestant organizations proliferated, accompanied by a large body of popular anti-Catholic and anti-Protestant texts, producing what one scholar called a "second confessional age."[31] The reason for this intensity was that confession acquired new and expansive meanings. Much more than doctrinal difference, many Europeans saw it as the key for under-

Introduction

standing and navigating modernity. Both Catholics and Protestants, for example, often claimed that the other confession's teachings were behind the era's revolutionary politics. They blamed each other for the French Revolution's horrific violence, and for every revolutionary outburst that later rocked the continent. They also took it for granted that confession shaped economic and social behavior in the industrial and capitalist economy. Writers repeatedly claimed that their confession alone possessed the self-control and charity needed for prosperity, and warned that the other confession bred destitution and criminality. Such animosities also had important gendered and sexual dimensions. Seizing on old doctrinal differences, especially around clerical celibacy and divorce, the two confessions blamed each other for destroying the "healthy" patriarchal family. Meanwhile, missionary writers endlessly warned that the other confession was undermining Europe's quest to educate and discipline "lesser races." These sentiments were so widespread, and circulated in the works of so many prominent scholars, polemicists, and politicians, that their impact far transcended the world of letters. They also exploded in harsh campaigns of persecution and legal discrimination.

Chapter 2 explores the decades from the 1880s to the 1920s, when Catholics and Protestants developed a series of overlapping concerns about life in the modern world. In particular, it traces how each confession came to worry about workers, women, and colonial subjects, which Christian elites believed were falling victim to dangerous, nihilistic, and profoundly anti-Christian ideologies. The first and most important threat that Christians identified was socialism. Its critique of private property, they claimed, degraded the divine imperatives to work, control one's urges, and protect one's family through intergenerational inheritance. In an effort to enshrine a harmonious but unequal class order, both Catholics and Protestants established new and parallel workers' organizations, unions, and welfare programs; they even established a few interconfessional organizations. Elites in both confessions were also anxious about the emergence of organized feminism and sex reform movements, which expanded considerably at the turn of the century. Claiming that the heterosexual family was the foundation of society because it taught people self-denial and self-control, they launched parallel public campaigns to defend it and even cooperated in utilizing state power to craft anti-feminist legislation and expand the state's regulation of sexuality. Finally, Catholics and Protestants came to believe in Christianity's role in "uplifting" Asians and Africans in Europe's colonies, a project in which missions were important actors. They claimed that the missions' main priority was not conversion but training "modern" habits of self-denial and hard work. These parallel developments, and the occasional cooperation they fostered, did not end the suspicions that the confessions harbored toward each other, and most commentators continued to insist that only their confession could offer long-term solutions to Europe's challenges. They did, however, provide the blueprint for cooperation, which would be substantially expanded in the future.

Chapter 3 focuses on the birth of ecumenism amid the crisis of the 1930s. Alongside mutual fears of communism, the trigger for Catholic-Protestant reconciliation was the Nazis' promise to end the historic divisions between the confessions. Claiming that their movement was aligned with both Catholics' and Protestants' anti-socialist and anti-feminist teachings, Adolf Hitler and other senior Nazis asserted that both confessions should become equal members in the nation's unified racial collective. This innovation led many Catholics and Protestants who sympathized with fascism to view Catholic-Protestant cooperation as the order of the day, first in Germany and then in other countries. Echoing Nazi metaphors, they claimed that the two confessions were part of a unified and racially healthy body. What is more, thinkers in both confessions also adapted their earlier theories to fit with the project of fascism. They agreed that their long-desired anti-socialism was best achieved through an aggressive state management of production and labor relations. They claimed that the patriarchal and heterosexual family should be protected by the state, and should participate in the eugenicist scheme of producing healthy children (even though several writers rejected some Nazi policies, such as forced sterilization). They argued that Nazi racial ideology should inform proselytism in the Global South, where the missions were to support the "race consciousness" of Asian and African populations. These convergences were deeper than earlier ideas because they were based on more than mutual animosities. Catholics and Protestants now agreed that no confession should aspire to social hegemony alone. Together with the Nazi-inspired vision of interconfessional unity, these similarities led many Christian writers to view the other confession as more than a tactical ally, as it had been in previous decades. They were, as one German writer put it, "brothers."[32]

This cooperation, however, was controversial. Several anti-fascist Christians countered it with a different kind of ecumenism, which facili-

Introduction

tated a different set of intellectual convergences. For these Catholics and Protestants, the Nazi obsession with immutable race was blasphemy. It was akin to socialism, because it reduced human life to material, rather than spiritual, conditions. They claimed that cooperation between the confessions was premised on preserving human autonomy from totalizing "earthly" regimes. As the French Catholic theologian Yves Congar, the most important theoretician of this group, argued, the Christian community transcended any earthly boundaries like nations, because it represented Christ's wounded body.[33] Like their intellectual opponents, however, anti-fascist ecumenists relied on more than abstract theology. They were also helped by intellectual convergences that took place between the confessions. Both Catholic and Protestant anti-fascists claimed that the protection of "natural" hierarchies necessitated autonomous economic exchange beyond authoritarian state management. They argued that the family's legitimacy lay not in racial reproduction and health, but in fostering love and even sexual pleasure. Some of them even began to claim that Europe's "civilizing mission" should be replaced by an effort to empower indigenous cultures. Some anti-fascist thinkers seized on these similarities to explain why their ecumenism was more than a pragmatic alliance against the Nazi enemy. In their telling, it showed why Catholics and Protestants shared a deep and positive vision for European life.

Even though the Nazi experiment collapsed in a hurricane of apocalyptic violence, the vision of an interconfessional alliance did not die with it. Chapter 4 shows that ecumenism instead expanded in popularity in the postwar era. As they emerged from the war's devastation, Christians largely decided not to dwell on their disagreements. In part because of their mutual hostility to communism in the early Cold War, those who opposed fascism and those who supported it quickly came together and sought to forge a broad Christian consensus. Ecumenism was central to the forging of this new unity. In the field of politics, this compromise took the form of qualified support for democracy and pluralist politics that excluded communists from power. Catholics and Protestants also reached a broad agreement on the way to enshrine economic stability and class inequalities. With the failure of the authoritarian and statist experiment, they agreed on a combination of market competition and state-managed welfare. They resumed their quest to defeat feminism and enshrine patriarchy, but updated their reasoning: they claimed that the heterosexual family was the only site for "true" sexual pleasure and fulfillment. All these convergences released ecumenism from its strict association with Nazi sympathizers and anti-fascists, allowing it to facilitate broad consensus. They also helped make the postwar decades into a period of ecumenical breakthroughs: across Central and Western Europe, interconfessional parties became the dominant force in European politics, legislating Christian priorities. Indeed, postwar ecumenism was both qualitatively and quantitatively different from earlier efforts at cooperation. Unlike the first experiments of the late nineteenth century, it was accompanied by a vast chorus that talked about spiritual similarities and helped give birth to a range of ecumenical think tanks, publications, and parties.

Another important factor in ecumenism's breakthrough, also discussed in Chapter 4, was decolonization. Historians have recently begun to appreciate the extent to which the collapse of European empires from the late 1940s to the early 1960s changed the former metropole. The relocation of military forces, financial institutions, and labor from Asia and Africa to Europe brought changes to European policing, welfare programs, and the regulation of families.[34] In ways that have rarely been recognized, it also altered Christian thinking about the Global South.[35] Missionary writers and church leaders were deeply anxious that decolonization would bring about the destruction of Christianity in Asia and Africa. They especially feared that African states would follow the model of China, where communist authorities expelled all Europeans and North American missionaries in 1951. In an effort to forestall this scenario, Catholic and Protestant missionaries initiated unprecedented cooperation. They established new networks and organizations, in which Catholics and Protestants worked together for the first time to maintain Christian footholds in decolonized states. In particular, the two confessions cooperated on projects of economic development, which promised to implement new technologies and training programs. Through those projects, missionaries hoped to disassociate themselves from colonialism while preserving European tutelage and influence in the Global South.

Finally, Chapter 5 uncovers how a new generation of thinkers crafted a radical and progressive ecumenism in the 1960s and 1970s. As Europe was rocked by the rise of the New Left and protest movements, a cohort of Catholics and Protestants sought to break ecumenism's ties to hierarchical and paternalist projects. Through creative readings of early Christian texts, they claimed that Christians should mobilize in support of revolutionary socialism, radical feminism, sexual emancipation, and Third World liberation. For this purpose, they created new organizations, launched campaigns against long-held taboos such as abortion and same-sex relationships, and created international forums for anticolonial theory. Crucially, all those endeavors were explicitly ecumenical. In the minds of radical Christians, Catholic-Protestant engagement was not a tool against non-Christian enemies but instead the first step toward the churches' opening to new forces and ideas. Like the New Left that helped inspire it, this effort failed to achieve its objectives and did not transform Europe's churches into sites of egalitarianism. But it extended ecumenism to new spheres of Christian thought, making it the norm not only in the conservatively-inclined mainstream but also among protestors and reformers.

As this broad chronicle demonstrates, the birth and evolution of ecumenism is more than an obscure episode of church history. It is the story of believers' efforts to decide what it meant to be Christian in the modern world. As Christians across Europe sought to marry religious belief with social transformations, they forged new understandings of economics, sexuality, and international politics. This story also illuminates the consequences of those ideas, the possibilities they enabled, and the options they precluded. Catholic and Protestant publications helped inspire political mobilization, the creation of new civil associations, the polarizing public campaigns on sexual matters, and the formation of new missionary organizations. Above all, ecumenism's evolution is a story about the enormous conceptual innovations that were needed to bring former enemies together. It required reinterpreting sacred texts and redescribing familiar historical events, and it sprawled through many genres and fields of knowledge. These conceptual efforts offered new ways for believers to understand their place in the world. The result was both inclusive and exclusionary, blending hope and fury.

CHAPTER I

Anti-Catholicism and Anti-Protestantism in the Long Nineteenth Century

THE SPANISH CATHOLIC theologian Jaume Balmes seemed like an unlikely candidate to pen an international blockbuster. As a young man in the 1830s, his work mostly consisted of abstract reflections about consciousness and newspaper commentary on Spanish politics. In 1842, however, Balmes published the tome *Protestantism and Catholicism Compared in Their Effects on European Civilization,* which became a sensation. Though it is largely forgotten today, it fascinated nineteenth-century readers; it was translated into all major European languages in countless editions (twenty in French alone) and remained in print for five decades. According to Balmes, every aspect of European life was an expression of either Catholic or Protestant principles. Confession determined not only people's rituals and holidays but also their political beliefs, economic fortunes, tendency toward crime (or lack thereof), sexuality, and capacity to maintain an overseas empire. In Balmes's sweeping narrative, which spanned everything from historical reflections to commentary on family life, the two confessions constituted different civilizations, by which he meant divergent sets of informal norms, institutions, and mental dispositions. They also existed in profound opposition: Catholicism represented "morality," "order," and "charity," whereas Protestantism fostered "passions," "anarchy," and "ferocity." This was why their clash continued well after their violent wars ended in the seventeenth century. Catholic and Protestant teachings continued to fundamentally shape European life more than two hundred years later, and their conflict would end only with one side's complete triumph.[1]

To readers today, Balmes's claims can seem strange, if not downright comical. Was it not obvious that European life the nineteenth century was shaped less by confessional differences and more by modern developments, such as the spread of capitalism or the expansion of empires? How could one reduce diverse communities, with changing beliefs and habits, to homogeneous labels like "Catholicism" or "Protestantism"? Yet for many Europeans, Balmes's ideas were both familiar and utterly convincing. In fact, he was only one in a large Catholic scholarly phalanx that contrasted the two confessions and blamed Protestantism for dangerous modern phenomena, from the violence of the French Revolution to the spread of civil marriage. Nor were writings in this genre limited to Catholics; Protestants were equally enthusiastic participants. Turning Balmes's logic against him, Protestant commentators regularly attributed every modern vice to Catholicism and every blessing to the Reformation. This habit of investing one's confession with expansive meanings was widespread in Europe and stretched far beyond the circles of professional theologians. In a vast body of publications, political theorists debated whether one confession spread tyranny while the other brought freedom; sociologists measured the rates of Catholic and Protestant out-of-wedlock births and suicides; and leading economists debated the confessions' impacts on commerce and work ethic. Confessional logic, that is, was not restricted to extreme polemicists like Balmes. It was a central trope in European thought and culture.

If confessional thinking appealed to so many Christian writers and thinkers, it was because of its endless adaptability to new conditions. The "long nineteenth century," the period that began with the French Revolution and ended with World War I, brought unprecedented changes to European life. The rise of mass politics led to a series of revolutions and destabilizing new institutions, such as parliaments and parties. Nationalist movements advocated for new solidarities and demanded new nation-states. The spread of capitalism and urbanization upended work habits, family ties, and social hierarchies. Marriage and family life acquired new meanings, recast as sites of love and fulfillment. And Europeans began to radically expand the scope and depth of their colonial domination. Anti-Catholic and anti-Protestant writings offered powerful guides to these bewildering upheavals. They neatly explained them in familiar terms, and argued that such changes stemmed from, and could be understood through, existing doctrinal principles, such as Catholic reliance on clerical authority or the Protestant insistence on *sola scriptura* (personal interpretation of the Bible). Christian writers were especially adept at invoking the bloody history of confessional conflicts to explain the high stakes of contemporary events. If the French Revolution was a Protestant plot, as some Catholic commentators claimed, was it not bound to lead to new religious wars?

Confessional thinking and binaries, therefore, were not premodern leftovers that slowly faded with the advance of modernity. They were central frameworks for making sense of modern life and for shaping one's participation in it. Confessionalism was also integral to the emergence of modern fields of study, such as statistics and economic theory. Bureaucrats and social scientists mined government and parish reports to trace how confessional affiliation determined one's likelihood to commit crimes or achieve high-income employment. Confessional thinking proved so adaptable that it absorbed the emerging focus of many European elites on the alleged difference between "civilized" and modern conduct, premised on self-control and self-denial, and its undisciplined opponents. As one French Protestant writer wrote in 1854, Protestant teachings were the foundation of "civilization" whereas the Catholics' submission to papal authority condemned them to the "servility, laziness, and misery . . . of barbarism."[2] This intellectual flexibility in relation to modern conditions was partly the reason that the circulation of such texts increased over time. Aided by the spread of inexpensive print, confessional texts like *Protestantism and Catholicism Compared* became more numerous and widespread in the late nineteenth century, reaching enormous readership.

This malleability meant that both anti-Catholicism and anti-Protestantism enjoyed transnational reach. Europe's confessional demographics varied widely in the nineteenth century. Protestants were large majorities (roughly two-thirds) in Germany and the Netherlands but tiny minorities (less than 5 percent) in France and Belgium. But because confessional writings sought to explain trends that transcended national boundaries, from revolutionary politics to an increase in abortion, their circulation was similarly capacious. As was the case with anti-Semitic texts, anti-Catholic books from Germany appeared in France, while anti-Protestant pamphlets from the Netherlands circulated in Austria. To be sure, national differences mattered, and the intensity of confessional sentiments often shifted in response to local events. Anti-Catholic and anti-

Protestant publications tended to surge in concert with the flaring of national controversies or election campaigns. Nevertheless, the key qualities that writers attributed to a confession were shared across Europe. Anti-Catholicism and anti-Protestantism constituted a pan-European body of knowledge, with shared tropes and assumptions.[3]

To illustrate the creativity and intensity of confessional animosities, this chapter charts the key meanings that Catholics and Protestants attributed to each other. Through popular publications, it reconstructs how polemicists, scholars, and politicians employed confessional binaries to explain the destabilizing genesis of revolutionary and democratic politics in the late eighteenth and early nineteenth centuries; the evolution of the modern nation-states; the emergence of industrial capitalism and urban life; the ethos of loving marriage; and missionaries' participation in imperial expansion in Asia and Africa. In each and every sphere, writers relentlessly warned that the other confession was actively destroying people's "appropriate" behavior by denying them the capacity for self-improvement. Selectively mining each other's writings for proof, Catholics and Protestants reported with horror on vulgar rhetoric or violent actions, while dismissing similar examples from their own camp as unrepresentative. Even though historians have studied anti-Catholicism and (to a much lesser degree) anti-Protestantism, they have not often registered how writers from both confessions were locked in a cycle of mutual polarization. Each attack confirmed one's worst fears, and in turn legitimized retaliation.[4]

Though it's not always easy to gauge how such ideas registered with readers, it is clear that confessional thinking had a far-reaching impact on social and political life. Even though the churches were not as powerful as they were in previous centuries, their affiliated organizations, such as youth movements and reading clubs, remained crucial actors in European social and cultural life. Alongside nation, gender, or class, confession often determined one's political affiliation, choice of social surrounding, and children's education; confession, that is, was not simply a matter of private belief, but broadly structured European public life. As the nineteenth century progressed, the relationship between these emerging confessional milieus was marked by perpetual hostility. Even as Catholic and Protestant communities were internally divided across theological and political axes, they often united in campaigns against each other, which occasionally erupted in violence. Without waiting for directives from church authorities, activists and politicians sought to restrict the other confession's organizations (such as Catholic religious orders), education, or public ceremonies. Most notoriously, Protestant activists and politicians sometimes formed anti-Catholic coalitions with secular anti-clericals and occasionally Jews, who harbored their own animosities toward the Catholic Church.[5] In Switzerland and Germany, they helped mobilize state power to impose a series of repressive and discriminatory measures against Catholics.

The scope and depth of confessional animosities are important in their own right, but they are especially crucial for the story of ecumenism. When Catholic and Protestant writers began to call for reconciliation in the twentieth century, they were not responding to a slow and organic fading of confessional hostilities. The exact opposite was the case: as happened with anti-Semitism, in the previous century anti-Catholic and anti-Protestant stereotypes had acquired new meanings and new intensity. This meant that their swift disappearance in the twentieth century was hardly natural. It would require a sustained and prolonged effort, one that would need to dislodge powerful intellectual traditions.

Confession and Politics after the French Revolution

Among many things, the French Revolution was a religious event. Because the Catholic Church was so deeply tied to the old regime through a web of legal privileges, financial support, and special status as state religion, the revolutionaries assumed that their project of establishing popular sovereignty would require far-reaching church reforms. At first the changes brought by the National Assembly, which declared itself the center of French politics, mostly replicated the acts of other European monarchs. The delegates abolished the clergy's political privileges and granted free worship rights to non-Catholics. But once the Revolution became engulfed in war, and anxieties about internal enemies surged, the church became the target of radicalizing measures. With dizzying speed, the Assembly forced the election of bishops by citizens, the requirement that priests take a loyalty oath, and a ban on religious apparel. By 1793 and 1794, the Jacobins, the Revolution's most radical faction, moved to aggressively eradicate Christianity altogether, prohibiting public worship and shutting down churches (including Notre Dame cathedral, which they renamed the Temple of Reason and stripped of its carved-stone saints). Resorting to harrowing violence, the Jacobins also carried out massacres and executions of Catholic opponents, including the beheading of Carmelite nuns who refused to take a loyalty oath to the revolutionary state.[6]

Anti-Catholicism and Anti-Protestantism

These shocking events helped refashion and escalate old confessional hostilities. Was it not obvious, many Christian writers claimed, that the Revolution, for all its ingenuity, was the culmination of trends that began centuries earlier, during the wars of religion? In ways that may seem surprising in retrospect, both those who despised the Revolution and those who sympathized with it often claimed that its ideological principles flowed directly from confessional teachings. Male popular sovereignty, legal equality, a free press: all of those were depicted by writers as expressions of Protestantism or (less commonly) Catholicism. Though these ideas were not completely new, and had precedents in previous centuries, they now became central to Christian thinking.[7] For writers of both confessions, including prominent political theoreticians and polemicists, establishing those links helped make sense of disorienting realities and demonstrated their high stakes. The conflation of confession and politics proved so popular that it endured for decades, making anti-Protestantism and anti-Catholicism a key feature of European politics.

The first to articulate the link between the Revolution's political drama and confessional faith were its Catholic opponents. If the Revolution was so hostile to the Catholic Church, they argued, this could only be because it was the belated child of the Reformation. Joseph de Maistre, a prominent conservative Catholic, was one of the first to articulate this logic, claiming that Protestantism was "not only a religious, but a civil heresy as well." In *Reflections on Protestantism in Its Relations to Sovereignty* (1789), he claimed that by abolishing the clergy's authority and rooting the Gospel's interpretation with the laity, Luther and his followers fostered arrogance, leading the masses to believe they could rule without divine authority. In this telling, this theological disaster was the source of the Revolution. Once Protestants "unshackled pride against authority and replaced obedience with discussion," they could not constrain their most fanatic impulses. For De Maistre, who equated Catholicism with stability, Protestantism seemed like an inherently anarchic force. It was a "fatal ulcer which attaches itself to every sovereign power and eats away at them . . . the son of pride, the father of anarchy, the universal solvent."[8] The monarchist lawyer Christophe-Galart de Montjoie, who penned what was likely the Revolution's first history, similarly claimed that Protestants were responsible for the era's political catastrophe. The introduction of religious tolerance by revolutionaries, he prophetically warned in *History of the Revolution in France* (1791), was designed to bring about the end of the monarchy, a belief that was echoed by multiple pamphlets that mocked the Revolution as "reeking" of "Luther and Calvin."[9]

This association between revolutionary politics and the dreaded Reformation stemmed in part from internal Catholic debates. It was a tool in the clash between two Catholic factions, which had begun decades earlier but which the Revolution radically intensified. On the one side stood the "reformed Catholics," who sought to reconcile the Church with the principles of scientific inquiry. Its leaders, both lay thinkers and clergy, supported some political freedom, and called for the autonomy of local clergy from papal authority.[10] On the other side stood the "ultramontanes," who understood Catholicism as rooted in popular piety and opposition to the Enlightenment. They insisted on papal authority, which for them epitomized the Church's claim to absolute truth (the name *ultramontane*, "beyond the mountain," gestured to the Vatican's authority beyond the Alps). As De Maistre, whose *The Pope* (1819) was an especially vivid expression of ultramontane principles, put it, "There can be no public morality . . . without Catholicism; there can be no Catholicism without the pope; there can be no pope without the sovereignty that belongs to him."[11] Depicting the Revolution, and the Enlightenment more broadly, as the reincarnation of Luther's teachings was therefore especially popular among the ultramontanes. They mobilized this logic in an effort to delegitimize reformers as the tools of heretics. Both during and after the Revolution, ultramontanes believed that only their uncompromising posture could secure Catholicism's survival in a hostile world. Supported by a groundswell of popular piety, pilgrimages, and worship of saints, it increasingly marginalized Catholic reformers and became the dominant school of Catholic thought in France, Germany, Belgium, and the Netherlands.[12]

The battle waged by ultramontanes against reformers can help explain why the link between revolutionary principles and anti-Protestantism remained potent for decades after the French Revolution and the subsequent Napoleonic Wars. Ultramontane thinkers believed they had found a powerful polemic both against European liberals' continued advocacy for expanded rights and reformed Catholics' increasingly isolated efforts to support them. The French writer Felicité Lamennais, for example, whose *Essay on Indifference in Matters of Religion* (1817) sold tens of thousands of copies and was one of the early nineteenth century's most popular Catholic texts, lamented that Luther had replaced Catholicism's "principle of authority" with the principle of "inquiry." In doing so, he paradoxically ushered in both moral relativism and fanatical hatred of all authority, which fueled both sixteenth-century Protestant atrocities and the more recent Jacobin regicide. As Lamennais put it, "The fanaticism of religious liberty brings forth the fanaticism of political liberty."[13] The most elaborate and popular articulation of these ideas was Jaume Balmes's blockbuster *Protestantism and Catholicism Compared in Their Effects on European Civilization* (1842). According to Balmes, Catholicism's celebration of tradition and human dignity had always restrained political power. Even absolute monarchs, such as Louis XIV, recognized their subjects as worthy of divine grace and realized that they could not be subjected to "unjust and arbitrary regulations." Protestantism, however, with its "spirit of insubordination and rebellion," gave birth to a competing democratic ideal and sought to annihilate all forms of authority. Ironically, its zeal and hubris then birthed a tyranny much worse than the one it claimed to replace, leaving in its trail nothing but "a stream of blood."[14]

The link between confession and politics, however, was not restricted to Catholics. Protestants of different political inclinations similarly spent considerable energy reflecting on political events, but for different ideological purposes. This tendency was especially on display among liberal Protestants, whose prominence in social and intellectual life increasingly grew in the early nineteenth century in Central and Western Europe. Thinkers in this school conceived of Christianity as premised not on original sin, but on humans' capacity for self-improvement through reason and enlightenment. Often inspired by German theologian Friedrich Schleiermacher, they claimed that divine revelation was accessible to all who practice self-examination, and that God's grace was best expressed by the establishment of a free and reasoned society.[15] Members of this milieu, who were mostly urban and educated men and who joined civil organizations like the Freemasons, therefore sought to turn the ultramontane narrative on its head. The Reformation, they claimed, was indeed behind modern revolutionary politics, but this showed liberalism's divine origin, and why the realization of liberal principles still required fierce anti-Catholicism.[16]

One of the first prominent Protestant writers to update confessional thinking to the era's politics was French Charles de Villers, whose *An Essay on the Spirit and Influence of the Reformation by Luther* (1804) articulated dichotomies that would characterize liberal Protestantism for the next century. In Villers's narrative, which quickly appeared also in English, German, and Dutch, the Catholic Church was the agent of "stupor and apathy," whose obsession with the clergy's leadership fostered mindless acceptance of authority. This approach also spilled into the political sphere, where the church and its flock alike supported authoritarianism, accepting tradition as its legitimizing logic. The Reformation, however, breathed "new life and activity" into European life. By shaking the very notion of traditional authority and emphasizing the individual's ability to interpret the Bible, it opened the people's minds to reason, "an emancipation which was nothing but a natural and necessary consequence of the restoration of learning." This meant that the questioning of Church dogmas unleashed a parallel challenge to monarchs' political supremacy. Luther and his followers inspired the birth of liberal institutions, such as parliaments, a process in which "a return to liberty in religious affairs" became "a return to political liberty as well" and that culminated with the Revolution. De Villers conceded that some revolutionaries were excessively passionate in their politics, which led to unnecessary violence. This, he however argued, was not inherent to emancipatory politics, but a marginal deviation from the Reformation's message of egalitarianism and freedom.[17]

Like the Catholic story it sought to counter, Villers's narrative left as many questions as it answered. It never explained why it took centuries for the Reformation to mutate into the Revolution, or why many Protestant-majority countries, such as Prussia, remained firmly in the absolutist fold. Yet for liberal Protestants this story was appealing, because it helped dissociate them from the Jacobins' radical and anti-Christian violence. It was especially popular among French liberals. The French-Swiss writer Benjamin Constant, one of early French liberalism's leading lights, claimed in *Principles of Politics* (1815) that Protestant dogmas ushered in the separation of church and state, and more generally fostered tolerance. The "multitude of sects" that the Reformation helped produce brought about "complete and utter freedom of all forms of worship," which seamlessly translated into politics, nursing popular sovereignty and equality.[18] The influential politician and thinker (and future prime minister) Francois Guizot similarly complemented his writings on constitutionalism with historical reflections. His *General History of Civilization in Europe* (1828) mused about the Reformation's inauguration of political revolution for liberty.[19]

These narratives also proved popular in the German-speaking sphere, where members of the Protestant liberal milieu repeatedly equated liberal principles with anti-Catholicism. The liberal theologian Heinrich Gottlieb Tzschirner, for example, who was the rector of Leipzig University, declared that it was Luther, and not the Enlightenment, that replaced Catholic autocracy with individual judgment. In his popular *Protestantism and Catholicism in Their Relationship to Politics* (1822), he explained that Protestantism, with its focus on rational thinking, was the only source that could sustain free expression and judicial independence.[20] Heinrich von Sybel, a German editor and politician from Marburg, took those ideas even further, claiming that the Reformation introduced the modern demarcation between the private sphere, where religion belonged, and the public one, which was the state's domain. In *The Political Parties of the Rhine Region and Their Attitude to the Prussian Constitution* (1847), he explained that by establishing a direct link between believers and God, Luther helped make faith a personal matter, thus freeing the state to foster collective improvement. In Sybel's telling, it was obvious that the Catholic Church, in its insistence that education and family law should remain free from state intervention, was ultimately seeking "the extermination of the state." This conviction led him a few decades later to co-found the German Association (Deutscher Verein), an organization dedicated to persecuting Catholic ultramontanes in state and civil society.[21] Indeed, as liberal activism continued in the 1830s, 1840s, and 1850s, and even exploded in revolutions in 1848, liberal Protestants joined their secular counterparts in pushing for anti-Catholic measures. In Prussia they called for shutting down monasteries, while in Belgium they sought to restrict Catholic education.

The adaptation of anti-Catholicism to new political realities, however, spanned the divide of Protestant politics. It also defined evangelical Protestantism, an intellectual and political movement that emerged in the aftermath of the Revolution and remained a major intellectual and political force, especially in southern France, the Netherlands, Germany, and Switzerland. For the preachers, writers, and politicians who led this "Protestant Awakening," liberals were wrong to disregard the centrality of original sin. Humans' fallen nature meant there were always limits to their capacity to remake themselves or the world with reason; adherence to tradition and submission to God were necessary to prevent the coming of anarchy. For figures like the Swiss historian and pastor Merle d'Aubigné, for example, whose *History of the Reformation* (1835) was a pan-European best-seller, this meant that Protestantism could not be equated with liberal principles and certainly not with the French Revolution. What Luther taught was respect for tradition and hierarchies, which alone could produce "an enlightened [and] far-seeing prudence"; Luther's support for German princes who repressed farmers' rebellions demonstrated his recognition that stability was a precondition for piety.[22] While evangelical Protestants had diverse political inclinations, they all agreed on the need to tame revolutionary impulses. In Germany and the Netherlands, for example, they opposed liberals' desire to remove religious education from schools.[23]

Despite their disagreement with liberals, however, evangelicals shared the conviction that Catholicism was the ultimate force behind political instability. Few reflected this logic more forcefully than Guillaume Groen van Prinsterer, a Dutch preacher (and private secretary to King Willem II) who became one of his country's most prominent politicians. According to Prinsterer's *Unbelief in Revolution* (1847), which remained in circulation for decades, French Jacobins and nineteenth-century liberals had little to do with Luther's praise for order. Unlike the reformer, they forgot that any effort to organize society on human reason alone was hubristic and bound to breed chaos. Though this claim aligned with those of Catholic critics, Prinsterer also insisted that Catholicism, which he equated with ultramontanes, shared the Revolution's key assumptions. Like the Jacobins, Catholics replaced God with human (papal) authority, and like the murderous revolutionaries, they viewed any resistance to their power as heretical danger in need of subjugation.[24] Alarmed by the continued advocacy of both liberals and Catholics, Prinsterer later claimed to find a direct causality between them, and insisted that Catholicism was *responsible* for the French Revolution, the Napoleonic Wars, and the persistent agitation of liberals in the following decades. As he put it, by weaponizing God's words to legitimize human autocracy, the Catholic Church "sowed the seeds that shortly sprouted into novel opinions and caused the eruption that was the Revolution of 1789," bringing about a tyranny worse than any premodern monarchy.[25]

The potency of confessional thinking, and the political binaries it reinforced, were especially on display when they led to violence. The most extreme case, which received intense international coverage, was Switzerland, where years of agitation and clashes over the alleged incompatibility of Catholicism and republican politics exploded in acrimony. In the early 1840s, liberal and evangelical Protestants, in alliance with secular anti-clericals, led a campaign to diminish the Catholic presence by closing monasteries and convents. In response, Catholics in Luzern, one of the Swiss Federation's Catholic-majority cantons, invited the Jesuit order to open a branch there and participate in shaping education. Against an impending federal ban on the Jesuits, which was heavily propagated by politicians from Protestant-majority regions, Luzern joined six other cantons in founding a new coalition, popularly known as the Sonderbund, or Separatist League. Two years later, anti-Catholics won local elections and gathered enough votes in the federal Diet to declare the League treasonous. Its secession was not only a violation of constitutional arrangements, politicians like radical Ulrich Ochsenbein claimed, but also a tool of Catholic subjugation against the spirit of "freedom," "progress," and "authority." Armed hostilities followed, in what amounted to a Swiss civil war, as federal troops occupied the Catholic cities of Fribourg and Lucerne and smashed the Sonderbund resistance. In the new constitution written after the war, article 51 banned the Jesuit order from all clerical functions and teaching.[26]

By the middle of the nineteenth century, then, anti-Protestantism and anti-Catholicism had acquired new political meanings among the major camps of Christian thought. Ultramontane Catholics, liberal Protestants, and evangelical Protestants diverged on fundamental political principles, but they agreed that the Revolution and the subsequent spread of liberal ideologies and movements was a radicalization of earlier confessional hostilities. This association between confession and politics proved so powerful that it continued to define Christian thinking into the second half of the nineteenth century. It was repeated in countless books, articles, and sermons, and fed constant agitation from the 1840s to the 1870s. By that time, however, confessional hostilities acquired another dimension. As one French Protestant from that period commented, the goal of political life was not only freedom and order, but also "national greatness and unity."[27] Like many other Europeans, Catholics and Protestants increasingly conceived of themselves as part of the project of national rejuvenation. It was one in which faith played a major role, as did confessional animosities.

Confession and Subversion in the Age of Nationalism

The project of nation building, which in Europe accelerated radically from the 1840s onward, was always laced with anxieties. As they paradoxically sought to create the nations that they believed were timeless, nationalist thinkers and politicians constantly worried that the masses' national consciousness was undermined by apathy, foreign meddling, or active resistance. This was especially true after the uprisings of 1848, in which many nationalists' hopes to achieve national autonomy or create new nation-states were violently crushed by monarchical forces. As the Italian politician nationalist icon Giuseppe Mazzini ruefully commented after his short-lived uprising was defeated in Rome, the masses' inaction showed that "you can fight alone, but you cannot win alone."[28] Yet even later in the nineteenth century, when nationalism's appeal grew and nationalists scored major victories (as in the unification in Italy and in Germany), worries remained. As they observed the ethnic, religious, and linguistic diversity of their countries, nationalist politicians and scholars could not but worry that their cherished goal of unity was profoundly fragile. Thus, even as they optimistically sought to nationalize diverse populations through educational campaigns or the invention of new holidays, nationalists constantly warned against efforts to subvert their work. Communities with diasporic ties, such as Jews and Roma, were especially vulnerable to accusations of disloyalty or disobedience.

The tensions between Catholics and Protestants were quickly absorbed into these rising nationalist anxieties. Christian writers were so accustomed to viewing Christian creeds in political terms that they seamlessly conflated their own confession with national grandeur and the other confession with anti-nationalist zeal. Only one confession, so the thinking went, could undergird the spiritual emancipation and solidarities that nationalism required. Catholics in particular became the targets of intense nationalist vitriol. In Germany, Belgium, the Netherlands, and France, fears of their alleged support for "foreign" subversion helped fuel aggressive campaigns of discrimination and persecution, ones that sometimes surpassed anti-Semitic measures and often altered European states' regulation of religion. By the late nineteenth century the same logic also began to circulate among some Catholics. Especially in France, conservative commentators decried Protestants as the agents of foreign conspiracies and called for their exclusion from public life. Confessional animosities, that is, provided Christian writers with the framework to express their contradictory feelings about their nation. They explained both the nation's liberating potential and its perpetual weakness.

The new national meanings invested in anti-Catholicism and anti-Protestantism were in part the result of the confessions' growing centrality to social life. From the 1850s onward, Europeans increasingly participated in voluntary civil organizations, such as youth movements and civil associations. Substantially expanding on earlier precedents, these groups were meant to offer new forms of leisure, opportunities for self-improvement, and communal bonds. Christian activists were especially enthusiastic participants in this process, forming confessional clubs, publishing houses, and even orchestras. In their minds, civil associations were meant to make sure that from cradle to grave, one would be embedded in networks of support that would maintain one's faith. The result of this process was that in much of Central and Western Europe, Catholics and Protestants increasingly lived in separate milieus. Considerable parts of socialization took place within confessional boundaries. In the case of Catholics, this reality was translated also into politics, as the effort to secure communal interests (especially Catholic education, which was repeatedly attacked by secular and Protestant liberals) led to the foundation of political parties, like the Catholic Party in Belgium (in 1869) and the Center Party in Germany (in 1871).[29] Even though the emergence of social milieus was visible also among non-Christians, Catholic and Protestant polemicists often focused on one confession and warned that its civil groups were a proof of its alienation from the nation. This was especially true for Protestants, who believed that voluntary associations should popularize national sentiments. In their eyes, Catholic organizations were a perversity: they were organs that used civil society to subvert the nation that secured their freedom.

This linkage between nationalism and anti-Catholicism was further deepened by theological and ecclesiastical trends in the Catholic Church. During the 1850s and 1860s, the Vatican decisively put its weight behind ultramontanism, issuing several encyclicals that celebrated popular piety, hostility to liberalism, and a focus on papal authority. This process reached its culmination in 1870–1871, when bishops gathered in Rome for the First Vatican Council and embraced ultramontane principles as formal church dogma. In the statement *Pastor aeternus,* the council declared that the pope held "a world-wide primacy" to which all believers had to submit, and added further that his judgment was "infallible."[30] For dismayed nationalists around Europe, such declarations exposed the Catholic Church as the center of a global conspiracy. It confirmed their worry that Catholic allegiance lay with "foreign" authority in the Vatican.

The confluence of these different trends was especially potent in the German-speaking lands, where the Catholic minority comprised about a third of the population. As efforts to unify the region under Prussian rule unfolded from 1864 to 1871, both liberal and evangelical Protestants converged in panic over Catholic subversion. According to theologian Karl von Hase, whose *Handbook to the Controversy with Rome* (1862) went through multiple editions in that decade, Catholics sought to replace national authority with a foreign and ecclesiastical rule. When they requested Church autonomy in marriage and education, they were in fact asserting that the pope's will "takes precedent over civil law," and thus "menac[ing] the State with continual illegalities."[31] Liberal German politician Adolf Zeising was even harsher, claiming that Catholic bishops and priests were "slaves of the Roman curia" and thus anti-national agents. Sweepingly conflating the entire German Catholic population with clerical leadership, he argued in *Religion and Scholarship, State and Church* (1873) that Catholics betrayed their "political and national duty," and that until they formally renounced papal authority, they should not be allowed to vote, hold public office, or enjoy other political rights.[32] The senior politician Paul Hinschius went so far as to claim that the Catholic population could soon become the basis for an armed fifth column. In his *The Papal Infallibility and the Vatican Council* (1871), he warned that Catholic refusal to renounce papal authority constituted a "death sentence" against the new German state.[33]

Such panic may seem oddly inflated, given the pope's meager political or military might, especially after Italian troops took over Rome in 1871, annexed the papal states, and limited the Holy See's political authority to a few square miles in Vatican City. But both liberal and evangelical Protestants regularly declared that the pope held unlimited control over his flock, which he planned to use for sedition. A representative spokesperson for this conviction was the liberal Protestant economist Émile de Laveleye, who warned that Catholic voters and their parliamentary representatives lacked any sense of free will. As he put it in his booklet *The Clerical Party in Belgium* (1872), which had a circulation of more than two million copies and was widely translated, the Catholic "voters obey the priests, the priests obey the bishops, and the bishops obey the pope; hence the pope is king." In Laveleye's mind, it was a scandal that Catholics were allowed to abuse the freedoms granted to them by the state in order to ultimately subjugate its sovereignty to Rome. To counter such a threat, the state had to impose nationalist and anti-Catholic education on its Catholic population to make sure that Belgium became part of "the reformed nations."[34] Even more apocalyptic was the British prime minister William Gladstone, whose *The Vatican Decrees in Their Bearing on Civil Allegiance* (1874) was widely translated and became a reference point for polemics across the continent. A vocal anti-Catholic (he also wrote the introduction to Laveleye's texts in English), Gladstone warned of a future in which the pope would destroy national sovereignty and would rule over "the ashes of the city, and amid the whitening bones of the people" through his mindless and subversive subjects.[35]

The organization that best epitomized Protestant anxieties was the Jesuit order, historically the most ultramontane organ in the Catholic world. Drawing on a long tradition that linked Jesuits to conspiracies, both liberal and evangelicals decried the Jesuits as an infiltrating squad designed to undermine national loyalty.[36] The liberal French historian Jules Michelet, whose *The Jesuits* (1843) was a sensation across Europe (it appeared in ten editions within a year in France alone), claimed that Jesuit-run education sought to turn young souls against the French nation. "Unity, nationality, the nation," he wrote, are the principles that the Jesuits sought to "lower and to mutilate."[37] In Germany, evangelical Protestant historian Heinrich Wiskemann similarly blamed the Jesuits for "covert and overt violence" against the nation. Their missionary and educational work, he stated in *The Teaching and Praxis of the Jesuits in Religious, Moral, and Political Affairs* (1858), were only a cover for subversive propaganda, which encouraged Catholics to commit "atrocities of such magnitudes, the likes of which are seen only among the heathens."[38] These sentiments were replicated in hundreds of novels, pamphlets, and monographs across Europe, and were so intense that they translated into public advocacy. Together with secular liberals, Protestants helped pressure almost all European governments to expel the Jesuits for at least several years, from France (1845) and Switzerland (1847) to Sicily (1860) and Germany (1872). Norway went so far as to enshrine the Jesuit ban in its constitution.[39]

It was ultimately in Germany, which was formally constituted as a unified state in 1871, that the nationalist panic over alleged Catholic subversion received its most notorious and far-reaching political manifestation. Even though Germany's creation came on the heels of Prussia's spectacular military victory over France, both liberal and evangelical Protestants rushed to warn about its fragility. To secure the new nation-state, they claimed, Germany had to unleash a "culture war" (*Kulturkampf*), a massive campaign of anti-Catholic repression. The first measure came in December 1871, when the German Reichstag approved, and chancellor Otto von Bismarck signed, a ban on priests from discussing political matters in churches. In the following few years, it was the Prussian local parliament (Landtag) that largely took the lead, abolishing church supervision of schools (1872); requiring all clergy to be approved by the state through a series of state-run exams in German history and culture (1873); and allowing for the arrest or exile of any priest who held religious ceremonies without state approval (1874). Though these laws were applicable to all churches, in practice they were applied only against Catholics. In a clear violation of the state's claim to religious freedom, state officials (sometimes with the support of local vigilantes) shut down countless monasteries and convents, fired thousands of Catholic educators, and imprisoned or forced into exile many Catholic missionaries and activists. These measures were not always enforced systematically, and the national government loosened some restrictions in the 1880s, but the *Kulturkampf* had far-reaching consequences. Amplifying confessional mistrust and suspicion, it left deep scars in German political life. Efforts to formally grant Protestantism and Catholicism equal legal status were continuously defeated in the German parliament, and did not pass until after World War I.[40]

Though Germany was an extreme case, especially in its level of state-sponsored repression, Protestants elsewhere were eager to channel anti-Catholic anxieties into action. Throughout the second half of the nineteenth century, they mobilized civil associations and municipalities in efforts to diminish Catholic presence in the public sphere. In the Netherlands, liberal and evangelical Protestants put aside their disagreements over religious education and supported restrictions on Catholic processions (often enforced by popular violence).[41] In Belgium, Protestants spent the 1870s and 1880s supporting efforts to restrict Catholic teachings in schools, though these ultimately backfired and strengthened Catholic organizations.[42] In France, liberal Protestant educators like Ferdinand Buisson served as senior officials in the Third Republic's drive in the 1880s and 1890s to wrestle education away from the Catholic Church.[43] One of the most aggressive efforts at popular mobilization took place in Austria, where a group of Protestant German nationalists concluded that Catholicism was the main obstacle to unity between their country and Germany. Under the slogan "Away from Rome!," a group of activists and writers embarked on a multiyear drive to convert all German Catholics to Protestantism, organizing reading groups, publications, and sing-along events across the Austrian countryside. While "Away from Rome!" fell far short of its founders' ambitious hopes—only about 70,000 Catholics converted—German and Austrian state officials worried it would desta-

Anti-Catholicism and Anti-Protestantism

bilize their shared border. Ultimately, they moved to suppress the group through secret police infiltration and censorship.[44]

Even though anti-Protestantism never inspired political campaigns of such magnitude, it proved equally adaptable to nationalist narratives. This was the case in France, where the decades following the establishment of the Third Republic in 1871 witnessed growing polarization between anti-clerical republicans, who sought to diminish the Catholic Church's authority over education and family law, and the conservative camp, which deemed Catholic privileges integral to national cohesion. Building on the equation between Protestantism and revolutionary violence, conservative Catholics also began to argue that the tiny Protestant minority was a threat to France's "true" Catholic heritage. According to writers like Ernest Renauld and Julien Fontaine, the republic's efforts to secularize public life were not only an expression of Protestant anarchy, as anti-revolutionary writers had long argued. They were also a cover for an international Protestant conspiracy to undermine national sovereignty. In this telling, Protestants, with their inherent individualism and opposition to authority, could not tolerate the solidarities that nationalism required. Their overrepresentation in the republic's economic and political elites—at one point half of the cabinet members were liberal Protestant politicians—was therefore part of a scheme to break national institutions from within.[45] It was a desire, historian Jean-Baptiste Maraval claimed, that Protestants had harbored for centuries and that they were now on the verge of realizing.[46] As was the case with anti-Catholicism, no accusation seemed too absurd. The Catholic Pierre Froment's *Protestant Betrayal* (1899) was only one of many publications to claim that French Protestants were the servants of Germany and Britain and awaited the opportune moment to open the nation's borders to foreign occupation.[47]

Both the prevalence and the extremity of these ideas were on full display during France's most polarizing political controversy, the Dreyfus affair (1894–1906), when a Jewish officer was wrongfully convicted of treason. Today the affair is mostly remembered for the anti-Semitic sentiments it exposed and fueled, but it also had a strong anti-Protestant component. For even though the alleged traitor was Jewish, anti-Protestantism was so integral to the mindset of Catholic nationalists that many writers took it for granted that Dreyfus served the cause of Protestant infiltration. Few expressed these sentiments with the flair of Alfred Baudrillart, the rector of the Catholic Institute in Paris, the leading Catholic academic institution in France. According to Baudrillart's *The Catholic Church, the Renaissance, and Protestantism* (1905), the trial exposed Protestantism's intrinsic opposition to France's national ethos. Because Luther and the Reformation sprang up among "people of German race and language," it was always loaded with "exotic flavor of which it has never been freed." If Protestants remained a tiny minority in France, this was not a historical accident, and certainly not because of earlier persecutions. It was because the nation "felt instinctively" that Protestantism "was the great enemy of its national character." Indeed, Baudrillart was convinced that the Protestants' tiny numbers in France only masked their astounding potential for destruction. "Fired with fanaticism," he proclaimed, Protestants formed "a state within a state," which had to be dismantled, either through education or by denying Protestants political rights.[48] Such sentiments were common among radical nationalists, who viewed Protestants, alongside Jews and Masons, as existential dangers. Charles Maurras, leader of the authoritarian party Action Française, declared that "the Protestant spirit is our enemy."[49]

Both anti-Catholicism and anti-Protestantism, in short, proved to be crucial vehicles for nationalist thinking. In the second half of the nineteenth century, when nationalism was still new and its victory far from certain, confessional hatreds captured both nationalists' hopes and fears: they offered a powerful way to explain why the nation was at the same time powerful and fragile, a vehicle for spiritual awakening also exposed to relentless threats. Indeed, confessional hostilities hardly declined in this period. They instead seemed to intensify, fueling new calls for discrimination. If anything, as time progressed, writers seemed even more eager than before to divide their world into confessional dichotomies, attributing endless ills to one confession and benefits to the other. This tendency was perhaps more obvious in their thinking about economics and social order.

The Birth of Economic Theory from the Spirit of Confessionalism

Even though all European societies felt the rise of industrial capitalism in the nineteenth century, the depth and scope of its impact varied considerably across the continent. One of its fault lines was geographical: the continent's northern parts, such as the Netherlands, northern Germany, and Britain, experienced accelerated industrialization, while the continent's south, especially Italy and Spain, remained more heavily agrarian. In the era of inflated confessional hostilities, many scholars and commentators could not resist noting that this difference happened to overlap with confessional demographics. If the north was Protestant-majority and the south Catholic-majority, did this not mean there was an inherent relationship between confession and economics? This link between confession and economics also seemed to be confirmed by domestic disparities. In France, Germany, and the Netherlands, in particular, Protestants were more disproportionately represented in high-income professions like banking and law, whereas Catholics were more dominant in agriculture and labor. Whether they admired or disliked the modern economy, therefore, Christian social theorists across the confessional divide increasingly concluded that economic order was the product of certain mental dispositions, which in turn were the products of religion. Capitalism, they set out to show, was ultimately an expression of theological differences regarding clerical authority and divine grace. In fact, Christian writers increasingly insisted that confessional affiliation was responsible for almost all social phenomena, from crime rates to suicide. Armed with statistics, they sought to prove that either anti-Catholicism or anti-Protestantism was the key to a prosperous and stable social order.

The link between capitalism and confession was especially popular among liberal Protestants, who welcomed industrial capitalism as an expression of their vision of human betterment. In their mind, capitalism required discipline, self-denial, and rational thinking, allegedly modern qualities that could only come from Protestantism's emphasis on personal responsibility for interpreting the Gospel. One of the first to articulate this vision was the French pastor and writer Napoleon Roussel, whose *Catholic and Protestant Nations Compared in Their Threefold Relations to Wealth, Knowledge, and Morality* (1854) appeared in several languages and enjoyed considerable attention. Roussel set out to counter the works of anti-Protestants like Balmes through a series of juxtapositions between Catholic-majority and Protestant-majority countries, such as Austria and Prussia, or Belgium and Holland. After painstakingly demonstrating with charts of taxes, private investment, and commerce volume that "Protestant" countries were more prosperous, he attributed the difference to the two confessions' allegedly divergent approaches to work and education. In Roussel's telling, Protestants valued hard work, cherished prudence, and were mentally capable of adopting new technologies. Catholics, on the other hand, because of their blind obedience to the pope, were mired in a primitive mindset and lacked any desire for improvement. In what amounted to an anti-Catholic "culture of poverty" theory, Roussel even interpreted higher rates of savings among Protestants as indicators of moral strength and social responsibility. Protestants' larger bank accounts, he maintained, were an expression not merely of higher income, but also of their ability to postpone gratification and "their spirit of order," which Catholics tragically lacked.[50]

Such claims became enormously popular in the following decades. By rooting capitalism in dogmatic differences, commentators explained it not as a system mired in ugly class struggle or brutal competition but as the expression of divine moral teachings. This was the logic for French economist Armand Audiganne, who attributed confessional wealth gaps in French towns to differences in the two faiths' alleged capacity for self-control.[51] It was also the key for German historian and statistician Wilhelm Heinrich Riehl, whose popular *German Work* (1861) argued that the Reformation endowed work with dignity and facilitated capitalist ethics because it broke the medieval guilds' control over the professions.[52] By far the most famous was the Belgian economist Laveleye, who published *Protestantism and Catholicism in Their Bearing upon the Liberty and Prosperity of Nations* (1875) alongside numerous anti-Catholic political tracts. In this widely read and translated work, Laveleye claimed that the economic divergences between the different parts of Europe emerged from the Reformation's principle of *sola scriptura,* which encouraged individuals to find guidance in the Bible rather than in clerical proclamations. Catholics' spiritual life continued to revolve around sacraments, tradition, and papal edicts, while Protestants in contrast were driven to utilize and develop their critical capacities. This ethos, Laveleye maintained, instilled in Protestants a drive for "indefinite improvement." In the economic sphere, this drive was expressed as an endless appetite for innovation and entrepreneurship, the invention of new products and development of new technologies. In Laveleye's eyes, alongside the spirit of self-denial and hard work these qualities created the ideological cocktail of modern capitalism, which was akin to modernity itself. Catholicism, on the other hand, was obsessed with "puerile ceremonies," miracles, and pilgrimages, and thus was "outside the atmosphere of modern thought."[53]

All of this meant that by the time the German sociologist Max Weber published his famed *The Protestant Ethic and the Spirit of Capitalism* (1904), in which he claimed that capitalism's ethos of self-denial, constant saving, and hard work emerged from the Reformation, his innovation lay not in the link between capitalism and Protestantism, nor in the insinuation that Catholicism was inimical to the modern economy. Both of those notions had a long pedigree, and for many liberal Protestants, like Weber himself, they had acquired the status of truism. Where Weber broke new ground was in presenting a more indirect lineage, in which psychology, rather than formal dogma, was the true motor of capitalism. According to Weber, Calvin's notion of predestination put unbearable psychological pressure on his followers. Desperate to find signs that they were not condemned to eternal suffering in the next world, the early Calvinists turned to economics and convinced themselves that success in business and commerce showed their status as divinely chosen. This is why they were so willing to deny themselves earthly pleasures and instead put all they could into investments. Weber's famous work, then, put a more ambivalent twist on established genealogies, one that reflected his ambiguous judgment of capitalism. While he celebrated the capitalist system for its relentless drive for innovation, he also described it as the product of psychological desperation and irrational anxieties. This ambiguity was lost on many Protestant readers, who understood *The Protestant Ethic* as yet another version of a triumphalist trope. They were mostly enthusiastic about Weber's anti-Catholic arguments and his claim that confessional disparities were still alive in the twentieth century.[54]

Though the link between the Reformation and capitalism was a Protestant invention, it had a cross-confessional appeal. Many Catholic writers also embraced it, but claimed it demonstrated the difference between Protestant nihilism and Catholic charity. French writer Louis-Gaston de Ségur, for example, who wrote the first Catholic retort to Roussel, claimed that Protestants' hostility to spiritual authority led to an obsession with earthly pleasures and wealth. In his best-selling *Plain Talk about the Protestantism of Today* (1859), he claimed that Protestants embraced capitalism because it allowed them to live by the decadent motto "let us eat, and let us drink, and let's be merry!" Catholics, on the other hand, were tied to each other by charity and generosity, which Ségur measured by comparing donation rates to relief for the poor.[55] Another prominent anti-Protestant writer, the Belgian Jean-Baptiste Malou, similarly conceded that Protestants were more prosperous, but maintained that this was because they replaced spirituality and communal bonds with licentious selfishness. "Protestantism," he sneered, "can calculate only on material means. It amasses and expends strength in money" in a quest "for things earthly."⁵⁶ Like their Protestant equivalents, such claims continued to circulate in Catholic publications for decades, and well into the twentieth century. The German writer and politician Joseph Mausbach, in *Core Questions of the Christian World* (1905), maintained that Protestants were depraved profit-seekers and that Catholics fell behind in "the spirit of worldly business" because they privileged charity and care for their families and communities.⁵⁷

A different Catholic approach was to deny the entire Protestant genealogy. Rather than reject its moral implications, several Catholic writers who were more sympathetic to capitalism sought to offer a different confessional framework, claiming that the modern economy was in fact Catholic. The influential Belgian Catholic editor Prosper de Haulleville, for example, claimed in *The Future of Catholic Peoples* (1876) that allegations about Catholic failures to develop a work ethic and self-discipline were premised on faulty data. Producing his own charts, he claimed that in Prussia, the Reformation's birthplace, "the Catholic provinces of the Rhine, Westphalia, and Silesia are the richest and most prosperous of the whole kingdom, whilst the Protestant districts of Pomerania and Brandenburg are the poorest and most destitute, besides producing the largest number of emigrants."⁵⁸ In the following decade the French historian (and future member of the Académie française) Georges Goyau traveled to Germany to compare its Catholic and Protestant regions. Based on his observations, he concluded that the Protestant advantage was bound to fade and be eclipsed by Catholic wealth. This was because Protestants, in their nihilism, were likely to spend their fortunes, whereas Catholics, who believed in the principle of self-sacrifice, celebrated work's dignity and thus were able to resist the siren calls of hedonism.⁵⁹

Beyond their fixation with confessional dichotomies, all these popular works shared a belief that economic behavior was part of a broader universe of moral and mental dispositions. For most writers at the time, economic disparities between confessions revealed a much broader truth: each confession's ability or failure to sustain social harmony. Self-control in fact appeared to Christian thinkers as not simply a necessary quality for a functioning economy. It was the precondition for all social relations. For respectable scholars and polemicists alike, it therefore seemed obvious that confessional differences were responsible for all major aspects of social existence. Law and crime, peace or violence: all flowed directly from religious faith. The growth of modern information and statistics, which governments and research centers across Europe began to publish in the nineteenth century, only seemed to corroborate such assertions. In reports, numbers, and graphs, scholars claimed to find hard and "scientific" evidence for the confessions' different conduct. For contemporaries, that is, there was no tension between confession and modern knowledge. The latter only confirmed the pervasive significance of the former.

Few represented the efforts to link economics, modern science, social order, and confession more forcefully than the French Protestant Roussel, who was one of the first to link Protestantism to capitalism. By comparing Catholic-majority and Protestant-majority countries, Roussel aimed to expose more than differences in prosperity. More ambitiously, he claimed to have uncovered profound confessional differences in respect for law: in how Catholics and Protestants treated bribery, theft, and more than anything, violence. By mining national criminal records, Roussel claimed that "Catholic" countries were rife with crime and corruption. They were especially violent: in Spain, one table showed, there was one attempted or successful killing for every 4,113 inhabitants. In Naples, the number was one for every 2,750. In contrast, the lands blessed by the Reformation enjoyed serenity and lawfulness. There was only one murder for every 100,000 in Prussia, and one for every 270,000 in Scotland. The differences were similarly striking in other departments, such as theft or forgery. Catholics, Roussel calculated based on sporadic publications, were probably twice as likely as Protestants to be incarcerated, which clearly showed their moral failures. Roussel was particularly glib when discussing suicide, which he claimed was popular among Catholics. "The Roman doctrine that he who suffers may offer his troubles as a pleasing oblation to God," he claimed, perversely led many believers to find comfort in the hideous act of "self-murder."[60]

Even sympathetic readers noted how many economic, political, and social factors Roussel had to ignore in order to produce such sweeping judgments. But such critiques did not diminish the popularity of his approach; instead, anti-Catholic Protestants sought to counter it by adopting better statistics to prove their superiority. In the 1860s the German Lutheran Church began to collect and make public information on its members' marriage and birth patterns, in part in the hope that such data would shine a harsh light on Catholics. Scholars, both liberal and evangelical, quickly followed: the conservative Lutheran theologian Alexander von Oettingen, for example, published the groundbreaking *Moral Statistics and the Christian Ethics* (1868), which included hundreds of tables and graphs that compared rates of suicide, births, and crimes of all kinds (the book was so popular that new editions appeared throughout the 1870s and 1880s).⁶¹ In fact, the parallel surge in government records and the growing prestige of the social sciences opened ever new avenues for obsessive confessional comparisons. The German economist Martin Offenbacher, for example, made a splash with his *Confession and Social Stratification* (1900), a large-scale study of education, work, and economics in the confessionally mixed state of Baden. Comparing the two confessions, he concluded that Catholics were less capable of self-control, which was why they were less represented than Protestants in schools and in high-income professions. What was telling about Offenbacher's work was not so much that it provided fodder for polemical rhetoric. Rather, it was how much both he and his readers took it for granted that confession was the basis for one's capacity to learn and become a productive member of society.⁶²

The same logic informed the Catholic response, which both built on and expanded the anti-Protestant writings of earlier decades. If Protestants were so lacking in self-control, so the logic went, this had consequences not only for the economy but also for public peace. The French social theorist Ségur, for example, who was one of the first Catholics to study confession and economics, also claimed that many Catholic practices criticized by Protestants, such as the celebration of saints and public processions, were in fact the training ground for communal peace. By blending social gathering with worship, they fostered "the sentiment of eternal unions of souls with God and of solidarity of men among themselves," which in turn trained believers to obey the law and treat all with dignity. Protestants, whose opposition to these rites was on the rise in the 1850s and 1860s, thus wreaked havoc on their own moral capacity, leaving themselves at the mercy of selfish impulses. "Protestantism is cold, formal, naked, just like the walls of its temples," Ségur lamented, "for him who becomes a Protestant, no hope of control when passion rages," which inevitably led to theft and violence.⁶³ As these ideas continued to circulate in the following decades, Catholic scholars followed Protestants by seeking to bolster them with statistics. The German theologian and statistician Hermann Krose, for example, utilized reports from parishes to produce his much-discussed *The Influence of Confession on Ethics: Based on the Results of Statistics* (1900), which claimed to show that Catholics were less likely than Protestants to steal, murder, or fall into alcoholism.⁶⁴ A few years later, Catholic political scientist Hans Rost took a similar approach in his effort to combat other anti-Catholic stereotypes.

In his groundbreaking *Suicide* (1905), which drew on hospital and government records, he claimed to show that it was Protestants, and not Catholics, who were prone to take their own lives.[65]

Alongside being vehicles for national anxieties, therefore, anti-Catholicism and anti-Protestantism also became key sites to develop European thinking about economics and social order. As they sought to understand both the causes and the consequences of capitalism and modern life more broadly, Christian writers routinely explained them as expressions of binary and mutually exclusive dogmas, which allegedly structured an individual's entire social conduct. Despite their differences, however, writers from both confessions were united in their worry that confessional failures threatened more than social order. Both Protestants like Roussel and Catholics like Ségur dedicated lengthy tables and passages to comparing the rates of out-of-wedlock births. Indeed, all agreed that the same forces that shaped public order shaped the family, sex, and reproduction. As much as it shaped one's social conduct, one's confession structured the sphere of intimacy and desires.

Prying Priests and Divorcing Pastors: Confession, Family, and Sexuality

Since their inception, the theological differences between Catholics and Protestants extended deeply into the intimate sphere. Luther's abolition of clerical celibacy, his stripping sacrament status from marriage, and his approval of divorce (under certain conditions) were some of his most controversial acts, and the fault lines they created between the churches were as deep as they were enduring.[66] During the nineteenth century a legion of authors endeavored to make these doctrinal differences even more central to each confession's self-understanding. Writers insisted with growing urgency that the two confessions' approaches to politics, nation, and social order were deeply tied to their approaches to marriage and sexuality. These anxieties over Catholic or Protestant teachings were so intense that they eclipsed important similarities between the confessions. Like many other Europeans in the nineteenth century, family theorists and novelists in both confessions began to describe heterosexual marriage as a site of love for the couple (as opposed to an economic arrangement).[67] They also shared a gendered view of social functions, assuming that men presided over public affairs and that women's task was the rearing of children at home.[68] In the era's polarizing environment, however, any notion of resemblance would have struck writers as absurd. The other confession's sexual ethics were invoked only to explain the dangers it posed to the family.

The centrality of gender and sexuality to confessional animosities was further heightened by the drive of many states to arrogate control over marriage and family laws, which had been under the churches' authority. The process began with the French Revolution, which in 1791 and 1792 abolished celibacy as a requirement for clerical positions and allowed civil marriage and divorce. Many of those decisions were reversed after the fall of the Jacobins, but they continued to inspire reformers, especially liberals, who viewed the diminishment of clerical authority as an emancipatory goal and called for similar measures throughout the nineteenth century. Protestants, for whom marriage was not a sacrament, largely acquiesced to those calls. Catholics, on the other hand, especially the dominant ultramontanes, decried state intervention in the private sphere as a radical assault on ecclesiastical autonomy. Haunted by the memory of the French Revolution, they plausibly warned that legal reforms were destined to accelerate into violent de-Christianization. These conflicts were ultimately settled when liberal reformers managed to legalize civil marriages and divorce in the Austrian Empire (1867), Germany (1875), France (1884), and elsewhere, but the confessional divisions they exacerbated lasted much longer. In the minds of many commentators, the push for civil marriage exposed profound differences between Catholics' and Protestants' understanding of family life, social order, and the relationship between them. As one prominent French Catholic preacher argued in 1888, the divide over civil marriage showed that Catholics adhered to "divine and inviolable law" but Protestants embraced "moral decay" and "corrupt manners."[69]

Even more than civil marriage, however, it was the question of celibacy that captured the centrality of the relationship between confession and sexuality. The Catholic prohibition on clerical marriage (and, by extension, sex) had long been controversial, and philosophers in the seventeenth and eighteenth century often condemned it as an inhumane denial of "natural" sexual desires.[70] In the nineteenth century, both liberal and evangelical Protestants built on this tradition, and in a stream of popular writings warned that celibacy unintentionally increased sexual activity outside the family. The German novelist Otto Corvin, for example, claimed that celibacy was the invention of impotent clerics, who in medieval times enshrined their fears of the human body into dogma. In his best-seller *Historical Monuments to Christian Fanaticism* (1845), which continued to appear for three decades, he explained that these restrictions, because of their opposition to "the eternal law of nature," led Catholic clergy to engage in wild sexual transgressions, from "fornications with their mothers and sisters" to sodomy with "four footed animals."[71] The same belief, that repression backfired as excess, informed the French author Napoleon Roussel, whose comparative study of the two confessions dedicated lengthy sections to sexual matters. Poring over conviction statistics, he concluded that Catholic priests were disproportionally represented among rapists. "What an argument against compulsory celibacy!" he exclaimed, "Ecclesiastical discipline cannot reform human nature."[72] The sexually crazed priest was a key trope in nineteenth-century writing, one that Protestants shared with secular and Jewish thinkers. In both novels and scholarship, priests loomed as the epitome of sexual perversion.[73]

The popularity of such texts partly resulted from their vulgarity, but also reflected broader thinking and anxieties about the fate of the family in the nineteenth century. During this period, Protestant commentators invested new significance in marriage, describing it as a site of self-cultivation and improvement.[74] In their narratives, the priest emerged as its chief enemy. An indicative example for this version of family ethics was the Protestant Karl von Hase, whose aforementioned *Handbook to the Controversy with Rome* (1862) was one of the most popular anti-Catholic texts before and during Germany's *Kulturkampf*. According to Hase, marriage and affection were the necessary precondition for ethical and rational thinking. It provided men with sustained emotional support and an outlet for sexual desires, and enabled them to develop the capacity to engage with others selflessly and confidently (women, according to Hase, were in charge of the domestic sphere and thus did not need these qualities to the same extent). In Hase's telling, this arrangement was threatened by Catholic priests, who were denied "the confidence ... [that] a pastor and father of a family acquires." Overwhelmed by a sense of inferiority, they sought to compensate by preying on young women. For Hase, who dedicated half of his book to discussing family matters, Catholic priests were a threat to more than female chastity. They were an inherently destabilizing force, a tantalizing alternative to a life of self-control and social commitment.[75] The popularity of these ideas can be gleaned from the fact that they did not appear only in the writings of famous anti-Catholic polemicists. Even marriage manuals and theological guidelines routinely mentioned that the rejection of celibacy was the foundation of "healthy" marriage.[76]

The Catholic priest also loomed as a threat for Protestant writers because of his alleged challenge to the husband's authority. The sacrament of the confessional in particular sparked considerable anxiety, as writers wondered what transpired between women and their priests in a dark space closed to the world. A representative articulator of these fears was Charles Chiniquy, a French-Canadian writer whose *The Priest, the Woman, and the Confessional* (1874) was a sensation in Europe, appearing in nine languages and countless editions. According to Chiniquy, the confessional was dangerous, but not only because it offered priests a chance for sexual advances. Much worse, it enabled psychological control: by encouraging women to share their personal doubts and regrets, and then providing counsel, priests fostered an emotional dependency that should belong to the husband. Invoking military analogies, Chiniquy described Catholic priests as armies storming the female castle, seeking to "enslave and degrade" their minds. They in particular encouraged women to discuss their husbands' sexual failures, which allowed the priest to "visit all of [the woman's] most secret recesses and corners" and to become her "supreme master, for the surrender has been unconditional." The consequence, Chiniquy noted with a mix of disgust and envy, was that the husband's authority was shattered and married women were no longer committed to sexual monogamy. In the confessional, the married woman "has drunk the poisonous cup . . . of her prostitution" and will "henceforth delight in her spirit and secret orgies."[77] Chiniquy's background as a convert from Catholicism to Protestantism gave his writings high visibility, but similar texts appeared with increasing frequency in the 1870s, 1880s, and 1890s. By equating Catholicism with a threat to marriage, they helped explain why Protestants had to support its subordination to civil legislation.[78]

Because Protestant writers often linked marriage with social stability, they also could not resist conflating marital and political subversion. In their minds, disloyalty to the husband and disloyalty to the state fed on each other, as both undermined "natural" authorities. Roussel, for example, maintained that marriage, which provided training in selfless responsibility, was the basis of loyalty to the state. Because of their exclusion from marriage, priests were more likely to obey the Vatican's "foreign" commands, which they then instilled among their flock.[79] The liberal Prussian diplomat and scholar Christian Carl Josias Bunsen, in his best-selling *Signs of the Time* (1855), similarly explained that marriage was the foundation of civil loyalty. The Catholic insistence on celibacy was therefore part of its overall scheme of "treason."[80] The most comprehensive linking of the two spheres was produced by Johann Caspar Bluntschli, a Swiss-German legal scholar and later one of Germany's most prominent liberal politicians. In his *Psychological Studies of State and Church* (1844), Bluntschli claimed that the ideal relationship between state and church was akin to marriage. The male (state) had authority over public matters like politics and education, while the female (church) had authority over domestic issues like worship. The priests' preying on women, in this telling, embodied the Catholic Church's broader efforts to transgress its sphere and intervene in public affairs. Only by curtailing clerical and church authority could the state and church "understand and love each other, and their sublime marriage [be] accomplished." Such visions helped power Bluntschli's status not only as a scholar but also as a politician. After moving to Heidelberg in 1861, he helped found the Protestant Association (Protestantenverein), a civil organization dedicated to anti-Catholicism, and then participated in drafting anti-Catholic legislation during the *Kulturkampf*.[81]

There was something strange about this panic, given that Catholics shared many key assumptions with their Protestant detractors. The Catholic Church remained committed to celibacy and the indissolubility of marriage (efforts by reformed Catholics to abolish those in the 1830s were quickly extinguished by ultramontanes), but Catholic thinkers very much agreed with the understanding of marriage as a site of affection and self-cultivation.[82] Félix Dupanloup, for example, who was the bishop of Orleans and one of the continent's most influential commentators on family and education, claimed that marriages based on economic or status considerations were a betrayal of Christ's promise to his followers. In his widely read and translated *Christian Marriage* (1869), he declared that the purpose of partnership between men and women was "the guarantee of their happiness."[83] This focus on fulfillment and self-cultivation only increased with time, as marriage manuals and theological tracts alike described marriage as the site of emotional bonding. Jacques Marie Louis Monsabré, who from 1870 to 1890 was the preacher at Notre Dame in Paris, explained in a popular book that marriage is "the grace which perfects natural love," and allows spiritual affection to survive long after aging has dried up the fountain of sexual attraction.[84] For these and other writers, it seemed evident that this kind of marriage was also the training ground for social responsibility. With the love and support provided by their spouses, married people could gain the confidence to also interact with their fellow citizens.

Yet despite these similarities, what Catholic writers shared with Protestants was the narrow confessional understanding of marriage. If the family was constantly beleaguered, it seemed evident to social theorists and clerics that Protestantism was the ultimate threat. Central to this thinking was Luther's endorsement of divorce. According to Dupanloup, for example, marriage's capacity to provide happiness was premised on the couple's commitment to comfort each other for life. Without such a commitment, marriage was reduced to a temporary contract that could be abolished at will. Such commitment was especially important to protect women from male desires, which Dupanloup, like most Europeans at the time, assumed were especially strong. Without the promise of lifelong obligation, what was to stop men from divorcing after intercourse, which in essence would make marriage into a license for prostitution? In Dupanloup's telling, this was a dreadful consequence of the Reformation. By opening the doors for divorce, it destroyed the family's capacity to sustain love and instead made it the site of endless lust. For Dupanloup, the Reformation was therefore responsible for the persistence of vice in Europe, especially out-of-wedlock birth. It was also the trigger behind liberals' efforts to secularize the family by introducing civil marriage.[85] Dupanloup was hardly unique in such claims, and similar ideas were repeated by leading Catholic theologians and scholars across the continent.[86] As the German polemicist Franz Xaver Brors argued, by "laying of violent hands on so sacred an institution as matrimony," Luther unleashed a flood of "sin and disorder."[87]

This understanding of the Reformation meant that popular Catholic writers attributed to Protestants a wide variety of transgressions against the family. From sexual crime to the blurring of gender distinctions, Protestant communities seemed determined to replace conjugal reciprocity with selfish and self-harming practices. The Belgian Haulleville, one of the pioneers of using statistics for confessional polemics, claimed that Protestants' disrespect for marriage "lowered the tone and standard of morality" and encouraged extramarital sex. Calculating the rates of out-of-wedlock births to women in childbearing age (between 16 and 45), his book showed that Protestant-majority Prussia was a hellscape of immorality (the numbers were 39,501 out-of-wedlock births out of 2,983,146 women of childbearing age), whereas Catholic-majority Italy was a haven of chastity.[88] Perhaps because of their voyeuristic qualities, novels were a particularly popular vehicle for such ideas. Catholic readers, like their Protestant counterparts, showed an endless appetite for stories about sexual transgressions. In Germany their most popular supplier was Conrad von Bolanden (pseudonym for Josef Bischoff), who paradoxically described Protestants as both frigid and sex crazed. In *The Progressionists* (1872), for example, which depicted a mayoral election in a small Catholic town, the anti-Church candidate promised to legalize prostitution and make brothels "places of amusement authorized by laws," unleashing a wave of fornication that ends only when Catholic leaders reclaim authority.[89] In France, the conservative novelist Alphonse Daudet used his *The Evangelist* (1883) to tell the story of a sad Protestant mother and her heartless daughter, living in a broken family without male authority. The women surrounding them, all of whom had divorced their husbands, epitomized Daudet's anxieties by looking androgynous, losing any indication of their born sex.[90]

Like the anti-Catholics they sought to refute, Catholic social theorists drew direct links between the intimate sphere and social order. They insisted that the indissolubility of marriage provided the necessary basis for social stability, which Protestantism sought to undermine. The German writer Ludwig von Hammerstein, who was also an influential editor, maintained that a lifelong commitment in marriage fostered the capacity for political loyalty. While this was also the view of Protestants, Hammerstein added that by introducing divorce, the Reformation undermined the basis of political order and was responsible for instability.[91] The French writer François Martin employed a different logic, and claimed that the family was the model for reciprocal relationship between subjects and rulers. By fostering love and caring between parents and their children, citizens learned to respect political authority but also to demand autonomy and care in return. Protestants' disregard for family life, in this telling, created atomized individuals who lacked the ability to resist tyranny. This was why in Protestantism, "marriage has no other purpose than to produce citizens for the state, and it thus becomes an instrument of domination." Without parental love, "every child ... can, and sometimes even has to, be sacrificed" to political authority.[92]

Thinking in confessional binaries, in short, was so intuitive to many Christians that it informed their understanding of the intimate sphere. Breathing new life into old doctrinal differences, writers believed that one's basic desires, their management in the family, and their relationship to social order were all structured by confessional heritage. The struggle over conjugal happiness, however, was not restricted to Europe. As the French Catholic preacher Monsabré explained, it was also waged by missionaries overseas, who sought to redeem "the heathen."[93] For him, and for many others, the lands beyond Europe's shores were more than a site for missionary work and education. They were also the major battleground between the confessions, which acquired global proportions.

The Global Religious War: Confession in the Missionary World

The late nineteenth century was a boom time for missions. From the 1880s onward, in particular, missionary organizations mushroomed dramatically, sending thousands of workers to build new stations and schools on faraway continents. This growth, which was funded by European governments and a dedicated base of Christian donors, also helped drive a considerable expansion in missionary publications. Alongside popular magazines and pamphlets, which were widely read and provided a major source of income, missionary organizations in Germany, France, Belgium, Austria, and the Netherlands also launched academic journals and research centers. Missionary reports on life in newly colonized Asia and Africa fascinated European readers. Their explorations of foreign languages, family structures, and cosmologies were crucial avenues for European understanding of, and fantasies about, their empires. This was in part why, around the turn of the twentieth century, both colonial governments and church authorities moved to create new university positions in missionary studies. For them, as for many readers, missionaries were some of the most important reporters from imperial front lines.[94]

These trends benefited both Catholics and Protestants, who, as discussed in Chapter 2, were equally entangled in Europe's "civilizing mission" ideology. Yet in the age of growing animosities, missionary writings were characterized by an overwhelming sense of zero-sum competition. As happened in the spheres of politics, social theory, or sexuality, missionary writings were often organized around binary oppositions. When leading missionary writers and theoreticians described evangelization as the task of bringing salvation to faraway lands, they also warned of the other confession's nefarious plot to undermine it. Alongside feeding the colonial imagination, therefore, missionary writers helped European readers conceive of confessional divisions in new ways. In their writings, the conflict was global, with consequences far beyond Europe.[95]

Few epitomized these dynamics more powerfully than Gustav Warneck, an evangelical theoretician who emerged as Europe's most influential missionary thinker in the second half of the nineteenth century. A prolific writer, Warneck founded Central Europe's first missionary magazine and penned the hugely popular *Outline of a History of Protestant Missions* (1883), which went through multiple printings and appeared in all major European languages. According to Warneck, the late nineteenth century opened unprecedented possibilities for mass conversion. The colonization of vast territories in Asia and Africa, modern means of travel (especially the steamboat), and improved communication enabled missionaries to reach populations "hitherto inaccessible."[96] This exhilarating potential, however, was threatened by Catholic missionaries, who sought to recruit potential converts into the pope's armies. Driven by political ambitions and fanaticism, they were willing to sacrifice any pretense to spirituality: instead of spreading Christ's commands, Catholic missionaries lured Asians and Africans with alcohol, songs, and cheap entertainment. In Warneck's paradoxical telling, the efforts to foster blind obedience to Rome in fact made the commitment to Christianity weaker. The missionaries' superficial measures meant that non-Europeans quickly forgot them and then resorted to paganism. This was why centuries of Catholic missions failed to Christianize the globe. As Warneck rhetorically asked, "[Catholic] labors in the Levant, on the Frisian Islands, in Persia, Crimea, Egypt—what is left of them today? Scarcely a memento of their former existence."[97] For Warneck, what seemed like a contradiction between Catholicism's appeal and its failure was exactly what made it so worrisome. Catholic missionaries had a unique capacity to succeed and fail at the same time.

This contradictory understanding of Catholic missions was part of what made Warneck's work so popular among both liberal and evangelical Protestants. In the late nineteenth century, and well into the twentieth century, missionary leaders and theoreticians of diverse inclinations repeatedly contrasted their work with Catholics' alleged successes and failures. Carl Mirbt, one of Germany's most prominent liberal missionary writers, warned that Catholics, due to the Vatican's deep coffers, were far better funded and better organized than the Protestants. This allowed them to expand their reach, lure converts with food and clothing, and then transform them into obedient and mindless subjects.[98] Alexander Merensky of the Berlin mission similarly bemoaned Catholics' success in drawing Africans into their mission stations through promises of improved work and food. Where Protestants sought to instill in non-Europeans the values of love and self-control, Catholics offered license for hedonism.[99] In the Netherlands, too, anti-Catholicism was central to Protestant missionary theoreticians. François Daubanton, an influential evangelical missionary writer from Utrecht, blamed Catholics' desire to gain political power for their tolerance of blasphemous behavior in their congregations. In his *Introduction to the Protestant Science of Mission* (1911), the first handbook of its kind in Dutch, he decried Catholic missions for concealing immorality with "false outward appearance" and producing "fetishism with Christian veneer."[100] For these figures and others, it was evident that these tactics were all designed to counter Protestant work. As one German missionary leader explained, the Catholic goal was to "strangle" non-Catholic missions and secure "the glory of Rome."[101]

As also happened in the field of politics, these sentiments had considerable institutional consequences. During the 1880s, missionary leaders from across the continent launched an effort to establish permanent cooperation between all major Protestant missions, both liberal and evangelical. In a series of large international conferences, they began sharing knowledge and missionary strategies, a process that culminated in the establishment of the International Missionary Council in 1911, a permanent body (headquartered in Geneva) that coordinated Protestant missionary work across the globe.[102] Historians have sometimes described these efforts as the beginning of Catholic-Protestant rapprochement, but their purpose was the exact opposite.[103] Such institutional manifestations were largely motivated by the belief that cooperation among Protestants was necessary to counter Catholic supremacy. This was why Warneck was one of these efforts' most vocal proponents. As he explained in an address to a missionary conference in London in 1888, cooperation was necessary to counter "the enormous danger which threatens us from Rome."[104] Early gatherings and publications of pan-Protestant cooperation were peppered with anti-Catholic statements. The Dutch general and politician Menno David van Limburg Stirum spoke for many when he declared at one conference that Catholic missionaries committed harrowing "atrocities" and "intolerable" cruelties in their encouragement of ignorance among Asians and Africans.[105]

The prevalence of such sentiments among missionaries overseas is hard to measure, but evidence suggests that many shared these writers' assumptions. A case in point is the "Benedictines' controversy" that roiled the German colony in East Africa in the early twentieth century. Since their arrival in East Africa in the late nineteenth century, workers of the Berlin Protestant mission and the Catholic Benedictine order were locked in an intense competition. They especially vied for control over land, which the German colonial authorities violently seized from indigenous inhabitants and then redistributed to missions, who in turn used it to attract local farmers. In 1908, simmering tensions exploded when Protestant missionaries erected an outpost near Lake Nyasa, trying to make claims on Catholic-controlled land. Flooding colonial authorities with anti-Catholic propaganda, they claimed that establishing the outpost was an act of self-defense against Catholic subversives, who sought to undermine German rule and were, in the words of one figure, "enemies of the Gospel." For the next several years, the agitation continued, as missionaries demanded colonial intervention and restrictions on Catholic actions. Only the outbreak of World War I ultimately resolved this conflict, when East Africa was occupied by British forces and all the missionaries were expelled to Germany.[106]

Catholics, perhaps predictably, showed a similar preoccupation with Protestants. Extending common tropes from Europe to Asia and Africa, missionary theoreticians described their Protestant counterparts as hedonistic anarchists who were hell-bent on spreading chaos. An indicative example is Friedrich Schwager, a prominent administrator in German Catholic missions and longtime editor of their leading outlet, the *Journal of Missionary Studies*.[107] In several publications, Schwager claimed that Protestant missionaries could not be understood as mere competitors, like preachers of Hinduism or Shinto. Their hatred of authority, born in the Reformation's commitment to individual reading of the Bible, made them far more ambitious: their goal was to use their missionary schools to spread the spirit of revolution everywhere. Schwager insisted that Protestant missionary education was responsible for every political disorder that took place in Asia and Africa. Protestants therefore could not tolerate the Catholic presence: because Catholic missions sought to instill in their flock a sense of community and mutual responsibility, they were the Protestants' main opponents. Mirroring Protestant arguments, Schwager described Protestant outreach as simultaneously omnipotent (lubricated by bankers' donations) and meager, claiming it inflicted irreparable damage on its converts but somehow, at the same time, left no marks on them. But whatever the cause, one thing was clear: Protestantism posed a "very threatening danger for the Catholic missions."[108]

Schwager may have been extreme in his rhetoric, but his sense of a global and existential competition was widespread. It permeated missionary journals and reports across nations and languages. The French missionary (and later bishop) Joseph Dupont, for example, who coordinated Catholic work in Malawi, warned his readers about the "Protestant menace." As he bemoaned in 1892, Catholics' effort to bring industry and prosperity to Africa were undermined by Protestants' preaching of laziness and nihilistic pleasure.[109] Writers considered such sentiments a good sell with readers at home, and French missionary journals routinely explained their establishment of outposts as part of a global campaign against Protestant encroachment. One writer from Zambia pleaded in 1906 for funding for a new missionary station, proclaiming that it was needed "to forestall the Protestants."[110] The Vatican, as was often the case, was among the most hyperbolic, blending its enthusiasm for expanding missions to "countries hitherto accounted impracticable" with warnings against Protestants. In several encyclicals on the topic, Pope Leo XIII identified the Catholic missions' main opponent as "the alacrity and industry" of Protestants, "who strive to propagate the dominion of the prince of darkness."[111]

To be sure, the purpose of such inflated rhetoric was to mobilize readers in Europe, whose donations and volunteer work sustained missionary endeavors. But as was the case among Protestants, it reflected widespread sentiments among the missionaries themselves. This was the case in the French colony in Madagascar, for example, where confessional animosities boiled into an open conflict. Beginning in 1897, when Protestant workers from France's evangelical mission arrived in the colony, a competition erupted between them and a French branch of the Jesuit order. For several years both sides relentlessly pestered colonial authorities, claiming that they alone represented France's mission to pacify and "civilize" the natives. Catholics in particular warned that Protestants were a subversive element, fostering disobedience among the local population and cooperating with their British counterparts. The Jesuit Joseph Brucker, in one plea that was later published as a booklet, deplored Protestant schools as a spearhead "against France as well as Catholicism."[112] Such sentiments proved appealing to the colony's interim governor, who himself (like many high military officials in France) sympathized with the Catholics. Colonial authorities ultimately continued to fund and support Catholic schools, while the Protestants, for lack of funds, folded and returned home.[113] Confessional animosities, then, helped define many missionaries' participation in Europe's global expansion. In their eyes, and in the eyes of their readers at home, overcoming the other confession's designs on Asia and Africa was a central part of being Christian in the modern world.

BECAUSE ANTI-CATHOLIC AND anti-Protestant rhetoric was often so extreme, it can be easy to exaggerate its power. Animosity was never the only mode of Christian life, and throughout the nineteenth century, communities in confessionally mixed areas often lived in peace, practicing the tolerance that polemicists thought impossible. Even in places and periods of intense hostility, such as Germany during the *Kulturkampf*, members of the two confessions occasionally defied the warnings of the elites. Some attended each other's celebrations, spent leisure time together, and even intermarried.[114] To some extent, the vitriol of many writers stemmed from recognizing that their warnings were not universally resonant. At least in part, the urgency of their words was fueled by the sense that some Catholics and Protestants did not view each other as mortal danger. Occasionally some thinkers even sought to openly challenge mutual acrimony. In the 1870s the prominent Catholic theologian Ignaz von Döllinger called for a grand reconciliation, and even sought to convene interconfessional gatherings of theologians to resolve dogmatic differences.[115]

Yet if initiatives like Döllinger's failed—his planned conferences never took place, and Döllinger himself was ultimately excommunicated—this was not solely because of clerical resistance. The main cause was that anti-Catholicism and anti-Protestantism were all-encompassing: for countless writers, the differences between the confessions were not theological, but spanned politics, economics, sexuality, and missionary work. In fact, perhaps the most striking feature of confessional writing was their anemic interest in theology, beyond occasional gestures to issues like papal authority or celibacy. Confessional stereotypes were meant to explain nineteenth-century anxieties, whether about subversion of the nation-state or threats to modern marriage. They were intensified and reconfirmed by the rise of modern science and knowledge. In this ideological ecosystem, there was very little positive language to describe similarities between

Catholics and Protestants. Even in moments of brief cooperation, such as when Dutch Catholics and evangelical Protestants together fought to secure public funding for confessional schools in the 1860s, leaders justified their cooperation in pragmatic terms and continued to disparage their temporary allies.[116]

Equally important, the sentiments at the heart of anti-Catholicism and anti-Protestantism were popular. Like anti-Semitism, they did not originate from clerical proclamations, but appeared in countless lay writings, whether in social theory, racy novels, or missionary journals. The level of popular enthusiasm for such sentiments is hard to gauge, and changed over time and place, but it is clear that they resonated enough to sustain decades of best-selling publications. They also helped reinforce and legitimize social and political polarization: Europeans not only poured into confessional organizations, but many also backed large-scale campaigns of confessional persecution. All of this meant that the project of forging sustained peace between Catholics and Protestants was going to be a monumental intellectual and political undertaking. It would require thinkers and believers to reimagine their place in the world, a process that would begin when they would confront a new set of challenges.

CHAPTER 2

Mutual Dreams of Order in an Unruly World, 1880s–1920s

THE PERIOD FROM the 1880s to the 1920s brought about radical transformations in European life. As industrialization accelerated and urban centers swelled, a new socioeconomic order began to emerge. The bourgeoisie and the proletariat entered politics, eclipsing the authority of traditional elites while forming mass parties and envisioning bold new ways to distribute wealth and power. Equally far-reaching were changes propagated by movements seeking to redefine gender and sexual norms. Whether advocating for women's legal and labor rights, combating prostitution, or working to repress pornography, activists and organizations introduced new understandings of gender relations and sexual differences. These efforts were often intensified by the brutal expansion of European colonialism, especially in Asia and Africa. After military forces subjugated colonized populations, state authorities and charitable groups embarked on large-scale projects to map and "civilize" them. They often sought to impose new work habits and gender norms, both reproducing and transgressing norms from the metropole. While the scope of these developments was uneven across the European continent, World War I and the upheavals that followed dramatically accelerated them. From the ascendancy of socialist parties to the granting of women's suffrage and the establishment of new institutions of colonial control, many ideological projects developed in previous decades came to the forefront of European society.

On the surface, Catholic-Protestant relations seemed strangely untouched by these epochal changes. Confessional stereotypes remained widespread, proving adaptable to new realities. When Catholic and

Protestant writers expressed alarm at new trends, such as the rise of consumerism in cities, many were quick to ascribe blame to the other confession. Even World War I, which initially sparked euphoric talk in France, Germany, and elsewhere about "religious peace" between the confessions, proved to be only a temporary distraction, and familiar patterns soon returned. Deep into the 1920s, major works took anti-Protestantism and anti-Catholicism as an obvious starting point. In Paris, the popular *Defense of the West* (1927), by conservative Catholic essayist Henri Massis, recycled old tropes by blaming "the descendants of Luther" and their "murderous hatred" of order for fomenting the "chaos and irrationality" of German nationalism, Soviet communism, and anti-European sentiments in India, China, and Japan.[1] In Amsterdam, evangelical polemicist Gerhard Ohlenmüller led the International League for the Defense of Protestantism, which organized music festivals and publications for liberals and evangelicals alike to combat "vile Catholic propaganda" in the Netherlands and Germany.[2]

Yet despite this seeming continuity, Christian thought and politics underwent tectonic shifts during this period, with far-reaching consequences for relations between the confessions. As Catholics and Protestants of different inclinations responded to the new realities of the late nineteenth and early twentieth centuries, they developed three overlapping sets of concerns, about the social-economic order, sexuality, and missionary work. The first mutual worry that consumed Catholic and Protestant attention was the rise of European socialism. Both confessions became deeply anxious about the popularity of socialism's "materialist" worldview, which they believed anchored human experience and solidarity in purely economic, rather than spiritual, conditions. Especially alarming was the socialists' promise that a future classless society would entail the eradication of organized religion, which Karl Marx famously dismissed as the "opiate" that hindered the masses' revolutionary development. Because some socialists backed this promise with anti-Christian violence, many believed that socialism's triumph would bring back the radical secularism of the French Revolution. In response, both confessions developed a new social theory to defend inequality between employers and workers while seeking to instill in both a sense of solidarity. As one prominent Catholic writer put it, God "willed that the poor should respect the property of the rich, and that the rich should be beneficent to the poor," forging "a mutual bond."[3] These theories had important social and political consequences, as Catholic and Protestant elites launched similar workers' organizations and parties. In some cases, they even joined hands to form interconfessional anti-socialist associations. This emergence of anti-socialism as the main social mission of the churches introduced new organizations to European society, and in some cases led to the creation of new welfare regimes.

Catholic and Protestant leaders were equally concerned about the rise of feminism and Europe's burgeoning sex reform movements. Scholars have noted that proponents of patriarchy seem permanently anxious about its imminent disintegration, but the period between 1880 and the 1920s brought about new challenges to male dominance. Across the continent, women's activism surged, challenging male control over labor, politics, and education, and advocating for sweeping reforms in family law. Catholic and Protestant commentators, who had long linked the patriarchal family to social order, were equally anxious about these developments. In their eyes, those were another expression of the materialist mindset: the replacement of spirituality and divinely ordained differences with a selfish desire for earthly satisfaction, embodied most clearly in some reformers' effort to separate sex from procreation. In their effort to counter them, Christian elites developed similar vocabularies: in countless publications, theologians and self-proclaimed family experts of both confessions appropriated feminist rhetoric by claiming that *restricting* women's life to the family would lead to "true" freedom, and thus realize what one Catholic commentator called the "natural rights that God has assigned to them."[4] Equally consequential, the two confessions also converged in the belief that the heterosexual family was threatened by a new onslaught of temptations. In a new intellectual move, they called for far-reaching regulation of both male and female sexuality, whether censoring pornography or repressing prostitution, to enshrine the self-control that Christians believed was necessary for the family's survival. As in the social sphere, this conceptual agreement inspired new forms of activism and cooperation, from defeating feminist efforts and revising patriarchal civil codes to the formation of interconfessional "anti-vice" associations. In some cases, it successfully and radically expanded European states' regulation of sexuality.

Third and finally, the two confessions aligned in their work in colonial spaces. As briefly noted in Chapter 1, the brutal expansion of European colonialism in the late nineteenth century, especially in Africa, was followed by a rise in missionary activity. Catholic and Protestant missionary associations ballooned, played a key role in imperial governance (through missionary schools and hospitals), and spread knowledge about non-Europeans. Less noted by historians, Catholic and Protestant missionaries developed a similar understanding of their work during this period. Adopting the modern version of the "civilizing mission" ideology, both came to view conversion as a secondary goal, focusing instead on instilling in non-Europeans the qualities they associated with themselves: self-control, self-denial, and rational thought. In keeping with domestic priorities, these efforts mostly crystalized around economic and sexual matters. Catholics and Protestants agreed that one of the missions' top priorities was to foster hard work, which led to the creation of countless work-training centers across the world. They also exported their understanding of family ethics, particularly to combat polygamy. The links between domestic and foreign work were so strong that Christian writers used similar terms to describe them. Many claimed that the task of missionaries was to rescue Asians and Africans from the materialist focus on laziness and pleasure, which non-Christian beliefs allegedly fostered. As this overlap between the two confessions became increasingly clear in the early twentieth century, many missionaries claimed that Protestants and Catholics should unite against the perceived threat of Islam.

Joining these developments was the quest to rescue entire populations from the forces of chaos. Socialists, feminists, sex reformers, and colonial subjects: all seemed to Christian elites as mired in misleading ideologies that lured their followers with promises of immediate pleasure, discarded social solidarity, and were politically destabilizing. Indeed, Christian writers across different spheres of knowledge increasingly linked interiority and exteriority, conflating salvation with self-control and productivity. Christian teachings, in their mind, provided the only intellectual foundations on which social order could be built, and they therefore had to occasionally be imposed even on nonbelievers. This was why both Catholic and Protestant thinkers were also disturbed by the apparent disregard of socialists, feminists, sex reformers, and colonial subjects for existing social hierarchies. Even if they sympathized with some of these groups' demands, they insisted that a lasting emancipation required solidarity, and this required embracing one's assigned place in the world. During these decades, therefore, Christian leaders and activists endlessly sought to demonstrate that the world's hierarchies were natural and divinely ordained. Through social mobilization and legislation, they paradoxically sought to create the order they claimed was timeless. This was the approach that united their work in the social, sexual, and colonial spheres. In all of them, Christian books and speeches employed the same metaphors of the floods, storms, and invasions against which the churches sought to defend.

These worries were so widespread that they cut through the internal diversity and divisions of the different milieus. Conservative and reform-oriented Catholics could debate how to best recruit workers, and liberal and evangelical Protestants could disagree on which professions should be open to women, but they all shared the same worries about modernity's dangers. These overlapping sentiments meant that as Catholics and Protestants oscillated between confidence in their victory and anxieties of defeat, they also paid new attention to each other. As they listened to each other's reflections on what contemporaries called the "social question," the "woman question," and the "colonial question," writers and activists recognized their shared concerns and animosities. They also registered that their strategies in all those spheres were at times similar. And this, in turn, opened the door for cooperation, one that was at the same time hesitant and unprecedented.

Christian Social Thought and the Specter of Socialism

In the mid-nineteenth century, European social theorists became transfixed by a new subject: the male wage-earning worker. An army of commentators mapped the new world of the urban and industrial working classes and "discovered" their living conditions, experiences, and values. Like accounts of faraway lands, these texts combined alarm, disgust, and fascination. In reports, articles, and magazines, writers described lives of endless toil, filthy apartments, alcoholism, and despair. Without opportunities for education and self-cultivation, they warned, workers lacked the most basic capacity for self-control, which bred hedonism and social atomization. Perhaps most worrisome was the spread of socialism in workers' quarters. As socialist parties proliferated and demanded the abolition of class privileges, such as voting rights based on income and the domination of civil service by the upper classes, workers became synonymous with a radical challenge to social hierarchies. Their destabilizing power seemed especially ominous when mass strikes in mines and factories became widespread in the 1880s and 1890s. As militant actions spread through Europe's industrial centers—France alone experienced a thousand strikes a year—many grew violent, disrupting economic production and leading to bloody clashes with the military. A burning political question therefore emerged: How could workers be contained and pacified? From educators to urban planners, specialists debated how to prevent the working class from fulfilling Karl Marx's prediction that workers would become the final gravediggers of class difference. Contemporaries diverged in their approaches to the "worker question" or "social question" (the terms were often used interchangeably). But they agreed that the answer would determine Europe's future.

Catholic and Protestant theoreticians were among the most vocal participants in this discussion. This was partly because they overwhelmingly came from middle- and upper-class backgrounds and were thus inclined to view workers' militancy with a mix of suspicion and condescension. But they were also deeply alarmed by the socialists' anti-religious mobilization. One of the defining features of early socialist subcultures was a militant dislike of organized religion. Even as they formally accepted the right to worship and belief, socialist groups hardly hid their hostility to the "opiate" of the masses. In both Catholic- and Protestant-majority countries, socialist leaders encouraged workers to read popular anti-religious works, abandon church membership, and embrace non-Christian rituals such as secular weddings and cremation.[5] The most extreme case was the Paris Commune, which in 1871 briefly took over the French capital and established a radical socialist regime before the French military crushed it. After banning religious education and storming church property, some of the Commune's troops murdered prominent Catholic officials, including the city's archbishop.[6] One consequence of these atrocities, which for decades haunted Christian writers, was that Christians could for good reasons believe that socialism and its message of equality were direct heirs to the French Revolution and its traumatizing efforts to de-Christianize Europe. Commentators routinely bemoaned, as one Protestant journalist wrote in 1890, that workers lived in "sins of decadent paganism" and that their vision of a classless society would bring anarchy and violence.[7] The sense that socialism threatened the churches' very survival, just as revolutionaries did in the late eighteenth century, infused Christian commentary with anxious hyperbole. Pope Leo XIII spoke for many in his fiery encyclical *Quod apostolici muneris* (1878), when he described socialists and their opposition to inequality as a violent storm of "gathering evils."[8]

Both confessions therefore launched an effort to develop alternatives to socialism: social and economic theories to draw workers away from the revolutionary orbit. In the process, they produced remarkably similar vocabularies and visions. Catholics and Protestants alike sought to establish an order that would transcend class conflict and bring together workers and employers in harmonious cooperation. This intellectual project, which was rife with internal tensions and paradoxes, also inspired a practical political transformation. The two confessions founded new associations and organization for workers, from clubs and unions to political parties, that altered Europe's approaches to the management of labor, welfare, and economics. In fact, the promotion of an anti-socialist order was the very first sphere where interconfessional cooperation emerged. By the turn of the century and continuing long after World War I, some Catholics and Protestants experimented with interconfessional workers' unions and welfare legislation. To be sure, cooperation at this stage was limited, in part because Catholics and Protestants could not agree on the role of the state in economic relations. They endlessly debated whether the state should force employers to provide welfare, provide welfare itself, or leave class relations to autonomous associations. Still, even limited cooperation reflected a growing conceptual convergence between the confessions. After a century of blaming each other for economic injustice and social chaos, Catholics and Protestants took a crucial first step in a new direction.

By the last decades of the nineteenth century, fears about workers' adherence to socialism became a central preoccupation for Christian theorists. Some of the era's most influential anti-Catholic and anti-Protestant writers began to describe the socialists as a danger as urgent as the other confession. The Belgian liberal Protestant economist Émile de Laveleye, for example, whose popular writings in the 1860s and 1870s decried Catholicism as the worst hindrance to Europe's prosperity (while attributing modern enterprise to Protestantism), transitioned to anti-socialist analysis by the 1880s. Socialism, he explained in his widely read and widely translated *Contemporary Socialism* (1881), was Catholicism's twin in its hostility to individual freedom. The two shared a quest to subordinate the masses with "mystical hopes" of future redemption, and thus both had to be suppressed.[9] The German Jesuit Viktor Cathrein, one of Catholicism's most prominent anti-Protestant polemicists, took a similar approach, warning that socialism continued Luther's assault on natural hierarchies. His scorching book *Socialism* (1890), which appeared in dozens of editions and eight languages, explained that socialism's triumph would rob humans of their ability to enjoy the fruits of their labor and deny them the opportunity to engage in charity (since generosity could not take place without private possessions to share). What is more, socialism would eliminate the right of inheritance, thus dissolving a crucial bond between parents and their offspring.[10] Such dystopian proclamations circulated in thousands of essays, books, and speeches. As the Belgian Catholic labor organizer Antoine Pottier put it in 1889, socialism was "blasphemy against God as well as one immense curse against society."[11]

Historians have noted anti-socialism's growing significance for both confessions, but the similarities in the alternative visions they developed have received less attention.[12] Across the confessional divide, writers and politicians crafted parallel theories and vocabularies, seeking to steal the socialists' thunder by appropriating and subverting their claims. The earliest prominent Catholic figure to do so was Wilhelm Emmanuel von Ketteler, the reform-oriented bishop of Mainz and one of Germany's most renowned public thinkers. According to Ketteler's *The Worker Question and Christianity* (1864), a foundational text for future generations, Christians had to join workers in their condemnation of the modern economy. Capitalism and its relentless drive for profit were premised on materialism, an ideology that reduced human relations to economic exchange, denying the validity of morality, virtue, or grace. This was why, despite its promise to bring prosperity, capitalism fostered misery, exploitation, and the disintegration of social bonds. As Ketteler harshly put it, capitalism was nothing less than "new slavery." Yet Ketteler argued that socialism was just as oppressive. It, too, was a form of materialism: by fixating on class as the heart of all social relations, socialists disparaged noneconomic forms of solidarity, such as between members of the same family. Ultimately they left no room for spirituality. Like capitalists, they reduced labor to a transactional exchange instead of recognizing its inherent dignity. In a move that would become a trademark of Christian thought for the next century, Ketteler concluded that the warring ideologies of capitalism and socialism were two sides of the same materialist coin. Whether they celebrated individualism (which Ketteler equated with capitalism) or collectivism (which he equated with socialism), both resisted the natural differences in humans' skills and backgrounds, and between their desire for social relations that are not transactional. Both were thus bound to breed similar nightmares of social alienation and oppression.[13]

In Ketteler's telling, Catholicism's task was to arrest the spread of the materialist scourge by developing an alternative social order that would transcend class conflict. This order would be premised on a conceptual and psychological shift: individuals would define themselves not only by their economic role (as employers or workers), but also as members of multiple communities (families, professions, or neighborhoods) that had inherent value and were components of a "unified organism." Most importantly, Christians had to instill in both employers and workers a renewed sense of mutual solidarity, reminding them that they played complementary roles in God's order and shared human dignity. The wealthy, rather than treating workers as a commodity, should voluntarily provide better conditions, such as Sunday rest and cleaner factories. Workers, in return, should respect their employers' right to private property and the material inequality it entailed. While Ketteler's hopes for inter-class harmony mostly relied on changing people's thinking, he also sought to foster it through institutional experiments. For example, he envisioned workers' cooperatives, supported by donations from wealthy Christians, that would run small factories and set their own working hours and salaries. "It seems to me," he explained, "there could hardly be anything more Christian ... than a society for the organization of cooperative associations on a Christian basis."[14] After his effort to establish such cooperatives was not successful (they closed within a few years for lack of profit), Ketteler turned to supporting modest state regulations to ameliorate workers' harshest sufferings. In his widely read *Draft of a Catholic Political Program* (1873), prepared for the German Catholic Center Party, he called for capping daily working hours, establishing Sunday as a day of rest, and appointing inspectors to review factory conditions.[15]

For all its rhetorical and conceptual innovation, the most striking feature of Ketteler's theory was its internal tensions. If the Christian order of harmony and hierarchy was rooted in both human nature and divine imperative, how could employers and workers so easily ignore it? More importantly, even though his ideas promised to establish inter-class harmony and return dignity to labor, Ketteler also sought to preserve the very economic and social hierarchies that fostered class antagonism. After all, even though Ketteler condemned the growing capitalist economy as un-Christian, his work accepted as natural the vast inequality it created between employers and workers. The concessions he expected from the wealthy were very limited, but he hoped that workers would relinquish some of their core demands, such as limits on working hours and redistribution of property. In both rhetoric and content, Ketteler's work made it clear that the symmetry he observed between the capitalist and socialist branches of the materialist worldview did not in fact indicate that the two were equally dangerous. *The Worker Question and Christianity* mentioned employers and merchants mostly in passing but devoted dozens of pages to workers, offering multiple ways to lure them away from egalitarian politics (Ketteler particularly emphasized religious education). The purpose of conflating capitalism and socialism was to explain why socialism could not solve workers' fundamental pleas; their solution, the logic went, lay in spiritual, not material, considerations. Changes to economic conditions mattered only to the extent that they alleviated the most extreme miseries so that workers could regain a sense of self-control, which they purportedly lost in industrial society.

Ketteler's intellectual frame, which appropriated the socialists' anti-capitalist rhetoric while rejecting their main demands, proved enormously appealing to Catholics. Especially after the Paris Commune's spectacular anti-Christian violence, writers and theoreticians, both conservative and reform-oriented, railed against the threat of materialism and insisted that it must be countered with cross-class solidarity and acceptance of existing class differences. In Germany the reformist Franz Hitze, who was one of Ketteler's most important disciples and became a politician and a professor of social thought in Münster, helped popularize his teacher's language. In works such as *The Social Question and the Efforts to Solve It* (1877) and *The Essence of the Social Question* (1880), Hitze lambasted "materialist despotism," and called on Catholics to replace it with the spirit of mutual generosity and harmony.[16] In France similar ideas were popularized by the aristocrats Albert de Mun and René de la Tour du Pin, who read Ketteler's work during their brief captivity in Germany in 1870 (both served as officers in the Franco-Prussian War). As de Mun put it in *My Social Vocation* (1877), the Church's most urgent task was to overcome "the subversive doctrines" of materialism, ideally by resurrecting medieval guilds, where employers and workers managed production together.[17] In the Habsburg Empire, the conservative priest Joseph Scheicher made similar claims in *The Clergy and the Social Question* (1884).[18] These writers and others insisted on their equal hostility to capitalism and socialism, and often advocated for curtailing unregulated trade and labor relations. But their theories were also premised on the need to contain workers' radicalism by teaching them the need to accept economic inequalities as God's order.

This anti-materialist understanding of industrial society, with all its internal tensions, was codified by the Vatican's most important nineteenth-century statement on economic matters. That was Pope Leo XIII's encyclical *Rerum novarum* (1891), which some historians have described as a transformative moment in Catholic social thought but which mostly recycled ideas that had circulated in Catholic publications for decades. After bemoaning capitalism's cruel treatment of the working masses, the encyclical railed against socialism. In their hostility to private property and inequality, the pope declared, socialists were not only unjust but outright suicidal: by breaking the link between one's toil and its fruits, and by imposing equality between people of different talents and skills, socialism was destined to disincentivize work, which spelled economic collapse and anarchy. As an alternative to this dystopia, *Rerum novarum* envisioned an order based on mutual reconciliation, in which the two classes recognized their differences and codependence. As the pope mused, "Capital cannot do without labor, nor labor without capital," and only "mutual agreement" between them could bring about "the beauty of good order." Scholars have often highlighted the encyclical's embrace of some social measures, such as the call to mandate Sunday rest and limit child labor, but the text balanced those by making strict demands on workers. Workers were admonished to work as hard as possible for their employers' profit, never engage in disobedience or protest, and abandon their dreams of equality. Even as it sought to lure workers away from socialism, the Vatican could not resist scoffing at their ideas (in the process, emulating the socialists' disparagement of Christians). The socialists' militant demands for collective property, the encyclical declared paternalistically, reflected "foolish hopes which usually end in useless regrets and grievous loss."[19]

Even though the Vatican insisted on the Catholic origins of this antimaterialist vision, Protestants responded to Europe's accelerating industrialization and socialists' militant atheism with a remarkably similar rhetorical and conceptual arsenal. They, too, struggled to explain how to replace class antagonism with social harmony, while seeking to preserve inequality between workers and employers. An emblematic figure in this effort was the liberal German pastor Albert Schäffle, a leading economist and politician. In works such as *Capitalism and Socialism* (1870) and the multivolume *Construction and Life of the Social Body* (1875–1878), Schäffle maintained that society was an "organic" body, where all members and institutions were responsible for others' well-being. Christianity's mission was to defend this reciprocity against the materialist threat, which reduced human relations to economic transactions. To do so, Schäffle proposed new protections for workers: labor codes (especially hygiene standards in factories), insurance policies, and Sunday rest.[20] Even though these proposals implied a break from free-market orthodoxies, which liberal Protestants had long described as flowing from Luther's teachings, Schäffle's main concern was to neutralize socialism, which he considered a far more dangerous threat than capitalism. In two popular anti-socialist tracts, *Quintessence of Socialism* (1875) and *The Impossibility of Socialism* (1885), he explained that welfare policies had to go hand in hand with disciplinary measures. Through compulsory education, for example, young workers would develop the capacity to resist socialism's subversive ideas (a proposal that mirrored the socialists' own calls for compulsory education against capitalism and Christian teachings). Indeed, Schäffle insisted that economic competition was crucial for social life, because it allowed individuals to develop their "natural talents" and receive rewards for their uneven skills. In this telling, Christianity's mission was to help workers live in peace with this reality and accept their subordination as God's design.[21]

Because Protestants were as eager as Catholics to appeal to workers without giving in to their demands, these ideas resonated across Europe. Among both liberals and evangelicals, a new universe of Protestant scholarship and think tanks emerged, where specialists and politicians sought to defeat the materialist threat by creating and solidifying the order they considered natural. In Germany, Protestant economist Adolph Wagner and pastor Adolf Stöcker (who served as the emperor's court preacher) founded in 1890 the German Evangelical Social Congress, a think tank that included hundreds of prominent thinkers and leaders. At its annual conferences and in the pages of its affiliated journal, *Contemporary Evangelical-Social Questions,* liberal and evangelical members discussed proposals to weaken socialism's hold on workers, ranging from investing in public libraries to expanding public works projects.[22] In France the liberal Protestant pastor Tommy Fallot, who studied the difficulties facing urban workers in Paris and Wuppertal, claimed that the church's most urgent task was to reduce workers' resentment by introducing limited relief. In 1887 he joined lay figures such as the economist Charles Gide and the politician Jules Siegfried to find the Protestant Association for Practical Study of Social Questions, a think tank and publishing house for social reform. At multiple congresses and in essays, especially in its journal, *Review of Social Christianity,* the association called for the establishment of mutual aid societies, credit cooperatives, and affordable housing.[23] In

Mutual Dreams of Order in an Unruly World

the Netherlands, it was evangelicals who took the lead when the influential politician Abraham Kuyper, in his book *Our Program* (1879), announced a campaign against materialism and class conflict. Everywhere these grand ambitions starkly contrasted with the proposed reforms. Kuyper, for instance, declared only that Protestants would support shortened work hours and factory inspections.[24]

Even though these parallel campaigns against materialism were largely conceptual, their institutional consequences mattered. Animated by the specter of anti-Christian violence, business and political elites across the confessional divide sought to pacify class resentment by introducing new economic rewards. Some of the most famous Catholic benefits were found in workshops introduced by the French textile manufacturer Léon Harmel, which acquired a reputation as the model "Christian factory" in the 1880s. Along with providing sick funds and discounted food for workers, Harmel encouraged Catholic education and prayer. This effort was soon replicated in France's other industrial regions, in part because it increased employers' supervision of workers' health and free time.[25] Other Catholic politicians and social thinkers sought to popularize the anti-materialist spirit through special workers' associations. After reading Ketteler, for example, the French writer de Mun in 1871 launched the Society of Catholic Worker Circles, which organized meetings and discussions for Catholic clerics, officers, and workers. Its advocacy for improving labor conditions, particularly curtailing work hours and boosting pay, helped it gain traction among workers, growing within a few years to 375 branches and more than 40,000 members. Similar initiatives emerged in Germany and Belgium, where new clubs brought together workers and employers in joint associations. With memberships in the tens of thousands, they organized recreational activities, sponsored mutual insurance societies, and published anti-socialist texts.[26]

The same trends were noticeable among Protestants, where economic and political elites advocated for employer-run welfare schemes as the antidote to worker militancy. Education and psychology alone, the logic went, could not contain the workers' revolt against the "natural" order, nor could they give workers a sense of reciprocity with employers. Some economic and political measures were also required. The liberal French industrialist Édouard Gruner, for example, who was also the president of the country's Protestant association, introduced insurance against injuries and extreme illness in his factories. In an address to Protestant industrialists in Nimes in 1891, he explained that such measures were required if

"Christian responsibility" was to be a driving force in social life.[27] Other Protestants, such as French politician Jules Siegfried, believed that employers' best hope lay in building new housing for workers, where better air, light, and spaces for social recreation would neutralize radicalism. "Do we want to fight misery and Socialist errors at the same time?" he asked in 1889 in an opening speech to an international congress on workers' housing in Paris. "Then let us create workers' housing!" Siegfried's bill, which provided tax incentives to charities that built housing for workers, passed in the National Assembly in 1892, over protests by socialists that such housing would tie workers to specific locales and reduce their ability to strike.[28] Other thinkers and politicians sought to harness workers' energies by creating political organizations. In Germany, Stöcker and Wagner founded the Christian Social Workers' Party in 1878. Against the materialist siren song, it called for compulsory health and injury insurance and a ban on Sunday labor.[29] In the Netherlands, the politician Kuyper founded the Anti-Revolutionary Party, with an evangelical platform to combat both liberal capitalism and socialism. Advocating for compulsory health insurance and factory hygiene codes, the party sought to uplift humans away from their class identity.[30]

The tensions inherent in this paternalist outlook, which sought to tame workers' hostility to both capitalism and the churches without giving in to their demands, made the impact of Christian anti-socialist organizations paradoxical. Their profound suspicion toward the working class and socialism translated into a failure to win mass support from workers. Instead, their main support came from the workers' chief opponents: middle-class people and small business owners. The most indicative example is Austria, where Catholic clergy, reformers, and politicians founded the Christian Social Party in 1891, which promised to replace the materialist system of free competition and class conflict with a Christian economic doctrine. Under the leadership of the charismatic anti-Semite Karl Lueger, it forged powerful electoral machinery and won municipal elections in Vienna, the Habsburg Empire's center of power. The party's electorate, however, was made up not of factory workers but instead of a white-collar coalition of teachers, artisans, and bureaucrats. Once in power, the party primarily promoted only remarkably modest social initiatives, such as subsidized incomes for certain impoverished families and limiting public housing to the elderly; it enacted no significant policy regarding workers' conditions, payment, or health.[31] Similar dynamics characterized other confessional initiatives, whether employer-worker associations or political parties. They remained very small (the German Christian Social Workers' Party had meager support and was quickly dissolved) or attracted nonworkers (the Dutch Anti-Revolutionary Party relied largely on rural and middle-class votes). Rather than neutralizing socialist materialism, Christian writings and organizations merely gave voice to its anxious opponents.

This limited success in drawing workers inspired calls in both confessions to co-opt socialist demands in a new sphere: labor unions. This strategy was especially popular with reform-oriented Catholics and liberal Protestants, some of whom came to believe that social harmony would be achieved through empowered workers. This was the claim of German sociologist Heinrich Pesch, who studied workers' conditions in Britain and the Netherlands. According to Pesch's widely read books *The Social Teachings of the Church* (1890) and *Liberalism, Socialism, and Christian Social Order* (1893), the best way to defeat the materialist spirit was to accept a pluralist economy where workers could freely organize and engage in collective bargaining. In this telling, unions were not a capitulation to class conflict but a tool to transcend it. By improving their conditions, workers could gain dignity and forge voluntary solidarity with other classes.[32] Several Protestant theorists similarly began to argue that organized labor might be the most effective tool to combat materialism. As the German liberal politician Wilhelm Kulemann explained in his 1894 address to the German Evangelical Social Congress, mass mobilization and strikes could mitigate conflict because they improved workers' conditions and reduced the appeal of full-blown revolution.[33]

Catholics and Protestants both launched similarly frantic efforts to launch Christian labor unions. Establishing themselves as autonomous unions free of employers' supervision, these groups provided a home for workers who were alienated by the socialists' anti-religious fervor. The first Catholic unions appeared in Belgium in 1882 to advocate for collective bargaining. They were soon followed by Catholic unions in the Netherlands (1886), France (1887), Germany (1894), and Switzerland (1899), which gradually became more militant, even joining mass strikes that rocked Europe.[34] Similar efforts also took off among Protestants. In Germany the pastor Ludwig Weber founded Protestant workers' clubs, first in mining and then in other sectors. Modeled after Catholic equivalents— Weber published a detailed study of Catholics' social work, warning that Protestants must compete with them—the clubs advocated for better working conditions, boasting 50,000 members by 1889 and 140,000 two decades later.[35] The most politically successful of these efforts took place in the Netherlands, where evangelical Protestants seceded from the socialist-dominated labor union to found Patrimonium, a competing organization, in 1876. While it initially focused on combating the liberal government over religion's place in schools, Patrimonium directed its energies at weakening socialism through campaigns that supported workers' rights to unionize and strike. Its ranks swelled to 10,000, outnumbering the socialist national union three to one.[36] Because these organizations remained committed to the principle of cross-class cooperation and were less militant than their socialist counterparts (for example, they joined fewer strikes), they usually (with the exception of the Netherlands) did not draw as many members. Still, they became an important presence in Europe's social landscape.[37]

Ideologically and practically, the growing similarities between the two confessions' anti-socialism was increasingly apparent. Though they continued to view each other with suspicion, commentators began to praise the other confession's social theory, celebrate a shared commitment to social hierarchies, and even floated the idea of further interconfessional cooperation. The Catholic Pesch, whose theory emphasized pluralist engagement beyond the church's boundaries, commended what he described as Protestants' epoch-making evolution from individualism toward a socially oriented vision. Even though his earlier writings condemned Protestantism as inspiring greed, in 1900 he claimed that German Protestant thinkers were engaged in fruitful attempts "to break away from the predominance of individualistic self-love in the economic sphere, and to clear the way for a genuine social conception of the national economy."[38] Similar messages emerged from Protestants. The Dutch evangelical Kuyper, for example, praised the Catholic Ketteler for correctly identifying the materialist challenge to Christianity; he translated Ketteler's work into Dutch and routinely referenced it in his speeches.[39] Even more directed was the German liberal Protestant Schäffle, who devoted a lengthy section of his book *The Impossibility of Socialism* to the two confessions' mutual priorities. Was it not obvious, he wondered, that both "have a common interest in the positive overthrow of socialism?" Schäffle suggested that a joint struggle against socialism could end long-standing tensions between the confessions. Perhaps, he mused, they could even enrich each other through dialogue, "and this will give a powerful impulse towards peace."[40]

Such sentiments spilled beyond the sphere of ideas and inspired political experimentation. In confessionally mixed areas, some labor activists launched interconfessional labor unions, hoping that their combined power would counterbalance the socialists. In 1894, after socialists took over the mining union in Essen, the Catholic activist August Brust founded a competing organization, the Union of Christian Miners. With support from local Catholic and Protestant clergy, he declared the union open to both confessions, claiming that both shared hostility to atheist socialism and hoped for cooperation with employers. The union's early years were rife with disputes, especially about its approach to strikes, but its model appealed to many workers. Similar organizations developed in new cities and in other professions, in sponsored magazines and, in 1899, at a national congress in Mainz, where leaders formed an umbrella organization, the founding statement of which touted its embrace "of both Christian confessions." Within a few years, Christian unions swelled in size. In just one decade, their membership reached 340,000 members, especially among Catholics, who constituted the majority.[41] Similar models emerged in the Netherlands, where Catholic and Protestant textile unions, representing workers in one of the country's largest industries, decided to unite. In 1896 they founded the interconfessional Unitas, which in 1900 changed its name to the Netherlands Christian Textile Workers' Union and became the country's second largest labor organization. Within a few years the mining industry witnessed similar developments. In the Limburg district, new interconfessional mining unions sponsored mutual aid programs and publications. Interconfessional labor unions also emerged in Switzerland.[42]

Despite these experiments, interconfessional convergence in this period had limits. Even as Catholics and Protestants cooperated in anti-materialist campaigns, they remained suspicious of each other, and interconfessional organizations were a minority, dwarfed by confessional parties and unions. More substantially, Christians were often also divided along confessional lines over the state's role in managing the "social question." Sick pay, hygiene, rest time: Were these to be voluntarily provided by benevolent employers or imposed by state officials? Catholics, having spent much of the nineteenth century losing battles against European states over their autonomy, often worried that universal welfare would displace Catholic charities and youth organizations. Their social theorists and politicians claimed that the most "natural" social order was built on small-scale local organizations, such as employer-worker associations, cooperatives, and regional charities. Even writers who supported some welfare measures, such as Joseph Mausbach in Germany and Max Turman in France, qualified that state power was potentially corrupting and thus should be complemented by other organizations. In Turman's telling, it was consumers were most responsible to support worker welfare by purchasing only goods made by companies where employers were generous to workers.[43] The Vatican's pronouncements, such as *Rerum novarum,* similarly mentioned the state only begrudgingly and fleetingly, warning that its mediation in economic affairs must remain limited (restricted to regulating factory hygiene, for example).

Protestants, on the other hand, were often more open to state incursion into the social domain. While they categorically rejected socialist demands for large-scale nationalization of industry or deep redistribution, some Protestant intellectual and political elites believed that the state could mediate between the classes and actively contribute to forming an antimaterialist order. Liberal German Protestant economists such as Wagner and Schäffle claimed that only the state was strong and large enough to take on the disorder spurred by class conflict. The state alone, they argued, by sanctioning limits on work hours, prohibiting child labor, and initiating public works, could tame capitalism's enormous power and socialism's revolutionary impulses to secure equilibrium.[44] Dutch Protestants, both liberal and evangelical, similarly argued that the state should foster financial ties between workers and employers by funding joint disability accounts. While Protestant elites in France, where socialism was not as powerful as in Germany, did not believe such far-reaching policies were necessary, they still wondered if new welfare policy was called for. The French liberal politician Henri Monod, for example, claimed that the state had a duty to help realize the divine reciprocity between humans. It could do so by aiding the most unfortunate: the sick, the old, and orphans. In his two decades as the director of hygiene and public assistance, Monod and his supporters sponsored legislation that offered state protection to neglected children (1889), forced hospitals to provide universal care in return for public funding (1893), and imposed guidelines for hygienic public housing (1902).[45]

Both the similarities and the cleavages in confessional social theory were on full display during the creation of the nineteenth century's most ambitious anti-socialist policy, state-mandated welfare for workers, where Catholics and Protestants were both key players. The most far-reaching version of this welfare program emerged in Germany, where the socialist party expanded early and proved especially strong. In 1881 Chancellor Otto von Bismarck embarked on a campaign to blunt socialism's rise with new welfare programs. He sent the Reichstag a proposal to establish a national system of sickness insurance, drafted by the liberal Protestant Schäffle. The time had come, the chancellor proclaimed in a speech, to find "the cure of social ills not exclusively in the repression of socialists' excesses" (a reference to the government's efforts to suppress socialist activity), but by forging new economic programs "which are based on the ethical foundations of Christian national life."[46] While both the Catholic Center Party and Protestant-led conservative parties agreed to create mandatory insurance programs, paid for by employers and contributions from workers' salaries, they fiercely debated the state's role. After prolonged negotiations, they agreed that sick leave and medical care would be covered by privately owned insurance, which would be supervised by the state. These dynamics returned in 1884 after socialist candidates' electoral success in national elections facilitated further welfare expansion. The same interconfessional coalition introduced accident insurance, compensation for chronic injuries, and a few years later, old age and invalidity insurance, providing benefits to those deemed too old or weak to work. In all these schemes, Catholic and Protestant delegates agreed on the need to build financial ties between the classes, improve workers' conditions, and preserve inequality, but they endlessly debated how to balance the state's reach and the autonomy of privately run (and often confessional) organizations. These programs were not merely an expression of European states' growing intervention in economic affairs. They were also the product of the two confessions' convergence, their disagreements, and their compromises.[47]

The scope of Germany's social legislation may have been unusual, but a similar process also took place in the Netherlands. There, too, an interconfessional alliance forged a strategic compromise against socialism that both expanded and limited state authority, while breaking new ground in social policy. In 1888 the Dutch evangelical Anti-Revolutionary Party unseated the ruling liberals by forming an unprecedented coalition with Catholic delegates. Along with securing state funding for religious schools (a top priority for both confessions), the government, led by Calvinist Æneas Mackay, also passed the Labor Law, which set a minimum age (twelve) for workers, limited women's and young people's workday to eleven hours, and banned some forms of night work (all clauses that were far less extensive than what socialists demanded). In 1901 the same coalition—this time with Abraham Kuyper as prime minister—spent months debating whether and how to expand those measures. It passed the Workmen's Compensation Act, which, following the German model, blended state regulation with decentralized, privately run schemes. It mandated insurance for injured workers and created a national insurance board to regulate it, but also allowed employers to form their own associations to provide insurance under certain conditions. In the years leading up to World War I, the interconfessional coalition also sought to implement a national system of workers' insurance against disability, old age, and sickness, to be administered by joint committees of employers and workers. Propagated by Aritius Syb Talma, the former head of the Protestant labor union and the Dutch minister of agriculture, industry, and trade, it passed in 1913 against socialists' opposition.[48]

The two confessions' social theory proved resilient enough to survive the cataclysm of World War I and the ensuing upheavals. Catholics and Protestants were deeply alarmed by workers' parties' shocking march to power, first when the Bolsheviks seized the Russian capital in 1917, and then when socialists took over Germany and Austria and established new republics. Christians agreed, as French Protestant leader Élie Gounelle put it in 1925, that "atheistic Socialism" was not merely a flawed economic system, but also the destruction of human order and "the nemesis of civilization."[49] For all this hyperbolic rhetoric, however, strikingly little changed in Christian social theory and politics in the 1920s. Writers, politicians, and activists remained committed to the same approaches that failed to curb socialism's rise before the war: reminding workers that social hierarchies were divinely ordained, encouraging confessional workers' organizations, and advocating for limited welfare, preferably provided by employers. This was the case with the French Catholic Social Seminars, for example, where Catholic leaders and scholars had gathered since 1904 to discuss approaches to the "social question." Once Catholic leaders resumed these annual conferences after the war, they mostly reiterated their support for employers' health insurance and education. The meeting's final statement in 1922 asserted that employers had "the obligation of giving to their personnel a minimum allowance."[50] When hundreds of Protestant clergy, scholars, and politicians gathered in 1925 in Stockholm for a conference titled "Life and Work," their ideas, ranging from employer-funded family allowances to limits on child labor, sounded familiar. Belgian politician François Busé, who led his country's union of Protestant churches, spoke for many when he remarked that "the evangelical conception of labor and vocation" remained consistent in its response to Marxist egalitarianism.[51]

This persistent belief, that what failed before the war would succeed after it, carried over to relations between the confessions. Both remained largely committed to confessional unions, clubs, and political parties, insisting that these groups were best tasked with establishing an antimaterialist social order. There were some exceptions, especially in the war's immediate aftermath, when panic over socialist revolutions led several figures to float the idea of a "holy alliance" against materialism. The German Catholic politician Adam Stegerwald called in 1920 for the dissolution of confessional parties (including his own Center Party) and their replacement with a "popular bloc" against secularism.[52] He was followed by a small group of theologians who took on the task of outlining similarities in Catholic and Protestant dogmas. Led by the Lutheran writer (and convert from Catholicism) Friedrich Heiler, they launched the journal *One and Holy*, which aimed to "free the Christian spirit everywhere from confessional narrowness."[53] Both of these initiatives, however, quickly crashed on the shores of hostility. Both Catholic and Protestant elites dismissed the call for political unity, declaring, in the words of Catholic politician (and later chancellor) Joseph Wirth, that "the chasm between the confessions is still unbridgeable."[54] The Vatican, too, moved to suppress theological engagement, and in 1928 condemned engagement with Protestants as "a most grave error."[55] Lacking a broad base of social and political support, the discussions in Germany dissolved and *One and Holy* ceased its operations. Only in the Netherlands did sustained cooperation take place, when the Protestant Anti-Revolutionary Party and the Roman Catholic State Party formed a coalition in 1918, headed by Charles Ruijs de Beerenbrouck, the country's first Catholic prime minister. Yet even this was mostly justified in pragmatic terms; politicians described their alliance not as the realization of shared principles but as a necessary evil that would hopefully soon become unnecessary.[56]

The period from the 1870s to the 1920s, then, witnessed a growing convergence in Christian social theory. Anxious about a shared socialist enemy, Catholics and Protestants developed similar vocabularies and social visions, premised on social harmony and luring workers without accommodating their demands. Both the scope and the limits of these goals affected European social life. Christian labor unions and political parties helped introduce new private and state-run welfare programs, but also ensured that these programs remained modest and did not undermine capitalism's class differences. Yet the Christian campaign against materialism was not just economic. As the Protestant German prelate Jakob Schoell explained in his speech to the Stockholm congress, the modern industrial economy needed reform because it brought about "a radical change" to family structures and gender norms, fostering sexual nihilism and "the so-called doctrine of free love" among women.[57] Even though Schoell did not explain how economics led to promiscuity, the link was obvious to his listeners. For them, as for Catholics, the war on materialism was also about sex, and the "social question" was closely connected to the "woman question."

The Christian Family and Its Enemies

Luring male workers away from the socialist danger was not the only project in which Catholics and Protestants converged. During the late nineteenth and early twentieth centuries, they also shared anxieties about another restive group: women who demanded emancipation, whether in labor, law, or sexuality. As happened with socialists, feminists increasingly eclipsed the other confession as an existential threat to God's order, which in the sexual sphere was based on different roles for men and women. In journals, books, and sermons, Christian elites bemoaned feminism's allegedly corrosive influence on the family and paternal authority, which they considered the foundation of social relations. To be sure, the defense of heteronormativity, patriarchy, and marriage was nothing new in Christian thought. In the nineteenth century, it was the center of Christian teaching on loving and fulfilling marriage and was foundational to both anti-Catholicism and anti-Protestantism. Yet encounters with feminism in the late nineteenth century inspired new justifications for the family. Abandoning their initial insistence that women were inferior to men, writers and politicians appropriated feminist language to claim that preserving the social difference between the sexes advanced equality and emancipation. Only by limiting women's access to men's domains (such as work and politics) could women secure their "natural" rights. The conceptual and rhetorical similarity between Catholic and Protestant reflections on what contemporaries called the "woman question" was clear enough that it paved the way for political cooperation. Even as they continued to warn against celibacy or divorce, politicians from the two confessions joined hands to block feminist legislation, particularly in the realm of family law, and to safeguard sex-based inequality.

Christians justified their shared anti-feminist campaigns in the language of protecting tradition, but resisting change was hardly the only imperative. Instead, Catholic and Protestant relations were also increasingly defined by a new and overlapping quest to increase state regulation of sexuality, in ways that were truly unique to this period. Borrowing from their thinking on economic matters, Christian commentators of different inclinations described feminism as a materialist and hedonistic ideology that sought to replace communal duties with self-centered gratification. It was part of a broader drive to release sex from the divinely ordained sacrifices of procreation and parenthood, which manifested itself also in erotic publications and prostitution. As one prominent Catholic commentator exclaimed, all those temptations were part of "the materialist worldview" that was "devouring . . . civilized nations like cancer."[58] The belief that Europeans were threatened by such menacing enticements led Christian activists to go beyond moral condemnation and turn to public institutions. At the municipal, regional, and national levels, they joined hands to pass what contemporaries sometimes called "vice laws," allowing censorship of erotic materials, restricting access to prostitution and contraception, and limiting sexual activity between minors. Such laws entailed considerable challenge to laws regulating free speech and free publication that were enacted during the nineteenth century. They also substantially expanded state oversight on private conduct. Yet unlike the "social question," there was little disagreement between Catholics and Protestants over state involvement in sexual matters. All agreed that the state was a legitimate and necessary tool to produce the "clean" public sphere that the "natural" family required. The state, that is, was a dangerous tool when it sought to diminish economic inequality, but not when it helped restrict sexual emancipation.

Like the Christian campaign against socialism, efforts to solidify a "proper" gendered and sexual order were rife with tensions. Across the confessional divide, writers labored to explain why restricting women's capacity to make their own decisions was emancipatory. They similarly struggled to clarify why the "natural" order of conjugal love and purity was profoundly foreign to most Europeans, so much so that it required relentless exhortations, restrictions, and new regulations. Indeed, Christians' unprecedented expansion of state intervention in the sexual sphere paradoxically sought to produce the order they claimed was timeless. Yet in the minds of Christian commentators, the responsibility to control desires could not be left to believing individuals. Because the capacity for self-control and self-denial was the basis for all social interactions and order, the churches' teachings had to guide the life of all Europeans. This broad understanding of the "woman question" was shared by both Catholics and Protestants, and this in turn meant that the intense suspicion between them in the sexual sphere began to subside. By the 1920s their concerns were almost indistinguishable.

At first, overlapping Catholic and Protestant anxieties about women's shifting social roles focused on the working classes and socialism. Thinkers in both confessions worried that industrialization and urbanization not only fostered social unrest but also weakened the patriarchal family by encouraging female labor in mining and heavy industry, a worry that was reinforced by several prominent socialists' vocal support for feminism. The German Catholic Ketteler, for example, in his early reflections on the economy, argued that industrialization's most devastating consequence was the introduction of women's labor. Factory work, he claimed in an 1869 speech, distracted women from their "natural" duties as wives and mothers at home, undermined men's authority as breadwinners, and led to the neglect of children, and thus had to be prohibited.[59] Similar logic guided the French Catholic de Mun, who led a campaign to limit women's working hours. In an 1887 debate on women's labor at the National Assembly, he argued that women were "a feeble being par excellence," and that preserving their energies for duties at home was required for the "preservation of the family."[60] Worries about the consequences of women's factory work on the family structure, often cast as proclamations that the female body was inherently fragile, soon became a pillar of Catholic social activism. When Catholic politicians, economists, and social workers from across the continent gathered in Liège in 1886 for a Social Work Congress, one of their first resolutions was to ban night shifts for women and limit their work hours, goals that became central to national Catholic associations.[61] Similar concerns drove Protestants, who came to accept women's factory work as inevitable but insisted that it had to be limited to encourage women to focus on the family. In the 1880s and 1890s, all the major Protestant think tanks called for limiting women's work at night and during pregnancy.[62]

Women across Europe, however, soon ensured that the "woman question" transcended discussions of the working class. Organized feminism took off across Europe with renewed energy in the 1880s. Building on earlier efforts, feminist associations proliferated, seeking to challenge male dominance on multiple fronts. The struggle for women's suffrage drew the most attention, inspiring associations and campaigns across the continent. Other feminist campaigns sought to overcome women's material dependence on their husbands by ending restrictions on women's education or entry to skilled professions. Was it not obvious, asked feminists such as Auguste Schmidt in Germany and Maria Deraismes in France, that women's capacity as both citizens and mothers would be improved with access to schools, universities, and work? Still others focused on reforming patriarchal family laws, such as the husband's dominance over property and children's education. As the Dutch feminist activist Wilhelmina Drucker put it, "the state should not interfere with men or with women, nor invent a fictive competition between men and women. It should solely recognize people."[63] Like all broad and ambitious movements, feminism was diverse and rife with internal disagreement. Its leaders and theoreticians routinely clashed over fundamental questions and strategies, especially the desirability of women's labor. Taken together, however, these efforts posed a meaningful challenge to male supremacy and to a family structure organized around the man as the head of a household. Despite their modest initial successes, many feminists believed their triumph was imminent. The French feminist Theodore Stanton famously gushed in 1884 that the feminist movement was "like the incoming tide" that "has stirred an entire sex, even half the human race."[64]

While proponents of patriarchy have long been anxious about women's capacity to undermine it, the rise of organized feminism seemed unprecedented to contemporaries. As they began to devise their responses to it, Catholics and Protestants developed similar vocabularies. Initially, writers in both confessions dismissed this liberation movement by insisting on women's natural inferiority to men. The physical differences between the sexes, many argued, indicated a moral and spiritual hierarchy; women were prone to irrationality and lacked self-control, and thus had to lovingly accept men's authority. The Austrian Catholic writer Augustin Rösler, who was commissioned by the Austrian Catholic Society of Leo in 1892 to compose the first systematic Catholic reflections on feminism, had little doubt that women's chief duty was obeying her husband. "It is by nature that the woman is subordinate to the man," he claimed in his widely read *The Women Question from the Viewpoint of Nature, History, and Epiphany* (1893), "and as long as her nature is unsoiled, she follows the need of the man with love and devotion."⁶⁵ The liberal Protestant philosopher Friedrich Paulsen took the same approach, comparing women's status to that of children. Both groups, he wrote in *A System of Ethics* (1889), which went through twelve editions, enjoyed divine grace but were too immature to fully participate in public life. It was therefore logical that rights would be invested in the hands of fathers and husbands. "The inequality of rights," Paulsen concluded, "corresponds to an inequality of natural powers."⁶⁶ This was the reasoning that writers of both confessions used to counter feminists' calls for access to education and labor. If the destiny of women was their role as housewives and mothers, any prolonged departure from the home would hinder the fulfillment of their duties and would work against their nature. According to the Catholic Rösler, the chores that came with maintaining a household were enormously draining, requiring considerable perseverance. How could anyone expect women to also toil in schools and factories, he wondered, and still provide "a feeling of home" for her family?⁶⁷

Such harsh reasoning however soon came under fire within both confessions. Led mostly by women, several campaigns challenged the dichotomies of patriarchal thought and adopted some feminist demands, especially regarding access to work. The French Catholic Marie Maugeret, for example, who edited the periodical *Christian Feminism,* claimed that women could balance motherhood and labor. Their bodies were designed by God to sustain such toil, she wrote, which meant there could be "no restriction, no limitation, no regulation" to women's right to work.⁶⁸ In Germany the Protestant ethnographer Elisabeth Gnauck-Kühne went even further, arguing that working women were more dedicated to family duties thanks to their additional earnings. In a landmark address to the Evangelical Social Congress annual meeting in 1895, she drew on her studies of working women to claim that they "manage to fulfill their natural duties in home and family" even more than wealthy women, who relied on servants.⁶⁹ While these claims mostly reiterated the ideas of earlier feminists and, like them, paradoxically emphasized women's allegedly distinct qualities as mothers while demanding equal rights, they now were accompanied by institutional developments. As more Christian women envisioned expanded public roles, confessional women's organizations proliferated, advocating for improved legal rights and access to work. In France in 1896, Maugeret founded an organization that advocated for women's rights to work and to hold property. Five years later she launched the Federation of Joan of Arc, which organized national Catholic conferences to promote a woman's right to participate in politics.[70] In Germany, Gnauck-Kühne founded the German Protestant Women's League in 1899, which grew to 200,000 members within only a few years. After her surprising conversion to Catholicism, she launched the German Catholic Women's League in 1902, whose membership rose to 250,000. Similar organizations sprang up in Belgium, Holland, and Austria. By the turn of the century they had become a crucial constituency in organized Christianity.[71]

As Christian elites witnessed these developments, they devised a new approach for justifying inequality. Abandoning their insistence on female inferiority, they instead appropriated feminist language to claim that restricting women's rights would bring about "true" equality and self-realization. The French Catholic economist Charles Turgeon, for example, argued in *French Feminism* (1902) that feminists were right to complain about the persistence of gender discrimination. There could even be, he remarked, good reasons to consider supporting women's suffrage (in part because most contemporaries believed that women in France were more involved in Catholic life and thus more inclined to vote for Catholic politicians). Turgeon argued that the Catholic Church had always valued women as equal to men. Its celebration of Mary, for instance, reflected its vision of men and women as equal before God. And yet Turgeon insisted that feminists were wrong to try to realize this equality by seeking "formal" equality for women, whether through labor or equal legal rights in marriage. Instead, they were to recognize their true value through family life; "wives and mothers," he wrote, "those are the two functions of woman, the alpha and omega of her destiny."[72] The authoritative German theologian Joseph Mausbach expressed similar opinions. He argued in *The Position of Women in Life* (1906) that women's "true" freedom and self-realization were achieved by fulfilling their motherly functions.[73]

Both liberal and evangelical Protestants followed a similar trajectory. They, too, reconceptualized the difference between the sexes as a form of equality, whereby the gendered division of labor granted each sex its own set of rights. Friedrich Mahling, one of Germany's leading Protestant authorities on family and sexuality, dismissed claims of women's inferiority as profoundly un-Protestant. Writing in *Problems of the Modern Women Question* (1907), he reiterated that the Reformation taught that women were equal to men and thus free to read, think, and learn. But Mahling shared his Catholic counterparts' belief that women's dignity was best achieved not by entering the male world of work, but by presiding over children and the home. Rather than earning an independent income in factories and stores, women had to accept that being "wife and mother" was for them "life's most wholesome profession."[74] Through such framing, Protestant writers claimed to embrace the cause of female liberation while rejecting most of feminism's key demands, whether in matters of property or access to work and independent income. "The difference between the sexes," explained another Protestant commentator, was the basis of social order and "the prerequisite for all human civilization."[75] Dutch Protestant writers employed this logic to warn that feminism's quest for equality produced "unisexuality," thus robbing women of the capacity to feel happiness. The liberal sociologist S. R. Steinmetz explained in 1896 that married women's confinement to the home fostered not oppression but joy, because it channeled them from the "aberration" of labor and into "natural" motherhood.[76]

The emerging conceptual similarity between Catholic and Protestant anti-feminism had practical manifestations. Around the turn of the century, politicians from the two confessions began to cooperate on regulating gender. Just as with the "social question," they labored to produce inequalities that they also proclaimed were timeless. Nowhere was this more evident than in Germany, where Catholic and Protestant-led parties formed an ad hoc alliance against feminism. In 1896, after prolonged delays, the Reichstag began debating a proposed reform to the nation's family laws, which until then had largely been decided by local states. Drafted mostly by evangelical Protestant lawyers, the proposal was deeply patriarchal: it enshrined men's authority over joint property; granted men the right to determine children's education; and made divorce prolonged and difficult (though substantially easier for men to initiate). Feminists mobilized in force against the proposed laws. In multiple petitions and speeches, they lambasted the proposal as reactionary and unjust, while sympathetic Reichstag delegates—especially socialists—filed urgent requests for radical revisions. Delegates of the Catholic Center Party and the Protestant-dominated German Conservative Party, however, joined hands to defeat these feminist proposals. Their common votes ratified the code with only minimal revisions, and it went into effect in 1900, remaining in place for decades.[77]

Similar cooperation took place in the Netherlands. Around the turn of the century, Dutch feminists sought to reform long-standing patriarchal family laws. They introduced a series of bills intended to empower women, in part by granting them equal rights in matters of inheritance and authority in children's education. While evangelical Protestant and Catholic representatives occasionally expressed sympathy for Dutch women, they joined hands against feminists. Not only did a coalition of the Anti-Revolutionary Party and Catholic State Party vote together to block the proposed reforms; it also expanded fathers' authority over property rights, inheritance, and the education of children. The interconfessional bloc took the opportunity to also restrict women's ability to have families while participating in the workforce. In a series of laws, it barred married women from holding positions in the civil service, and later decreed that female teachers had to resign when they married.[78]

Married women were not the only target of Christian activism. Another important source of confessional cooperation against feminism was the status of unwed mothers and their children, whom contemporaries usually referred to as "illegitimate." Prominent feminists claimed that these mothers and children should enjoy the same financial support and inheritance rights that fathers were obliged to bestow on their wives and "legitimate" children. Léonie Rouzade in France and Helene Stöcker in Germany argued that "illegitimate," as a concept, served to subjugate women, making their well-being dependent on marriages to men while also freeing men of responsibility for their sexual behavior. Catholic and Protestant elites, however, united in insisting on the necessity of this inequality. "There is only *one* holy motherhood," wrote one Protestant commentator, and it existed within marriage; the "unwavering condemnation of irregular motherhood must always remain the foundation" of social order, and thus needed to be legally codified.[79] The Austrian Catholic Rösler agreed, and warned that dismantling the legal difference undermined "true" equality, because it would encourage women to stray from their "natural" function as mothers. A society that does not protect the married mother's unique position, he added in 1907, is "an unnatural one, stunted and destined to perish."[80] In both Germany and the Netherlands, Christian coalitions passed family laws that denied unwed mothers the same financial support that their married counterparts received (in Germany, the only concession to feminists was granting unwed mothers six weeks of support after birth). "Illegitimate" children similarly could not claim an inheritance upon their fathers' death, nor could they receive support for education.[81]

And yet defeating feminist drives for equality was hardly a cause for celebration in Christian circles. That was because Catholic and Protestant anxieties converged over a more worrisome development: feminist attempts to delink sexual activity from marriage, procreation, and the family. Writers such as Sweden's Ellen Key, whose blockbuster *Love and Marriage* (1905) appeared in almost every European language, argued that fulfilling sexual desires was an act of self-realization; a legitimate expression of love regardless of whether it led to marriage or procreation.[82] Such claims, which often went hand in hand with calls for the use of contraception, legalization of abortion, and the introduction of sex education in schools, reverberated in countless journals and books. Works such as Anna Fischer-Dückelmann's *The Sexual Life of Woman* (1900) in Germany and Madeleine Pelletier's *The Sexual Emancipation of Women* (1911) in France called for, in the words of one feminist, the "liberation of the female womb" from patriarchy.[83] No less radical was the emergence of sexual reform movements around the same time, with their prolific journals and sprawling research centers. Whether they were motivated by a desire to decriminalize same-sex relations, neo-Malthusian visions of limiting birth rates, or implementing eugenics, they all insisted on the need to rethink the ties between the sexual act and procreation. Even though radical feminists and sex reformers were hardly a unified group, and often disagreed on topics ranging from motherhood's significance to self-realization and the desirability of eugenics, they shared skepticism toward the churches' valorization of family and procreation. Christian ideas about family, writers in those movements claimed, were either damaging or irrelevant in the modern era.[84]

Christian commentators, who usually viewed these diverse movement as a homogeneous bloc, understood them as both feminism's logical conclusion and its most extreme consequence. By unleashing both men's and women's desires, they threatened to undermine not only gendered hierarchies but also the very conditions that made marriage and love possible. According to countless writers, sexual desire was a natural impulse granted to humans by God but was never designed for self-realization or fulfillment. Its goal was instead to lead men and women into conjugality to form a family and procreate. Indeed, the sexual drive acquired positive meaning if humans conceived of it as serving a purpose beyond themselves. Only after their bond was sacralized in religious ceremony, and only if marriage was initiated with the goal of child-rearing, could the sexual act be considered selfless and thus moral. For both Catholics and Protestants, even those who supported some rights for women, the quest to legitimize sexual activity beyond the family unit was therefore a narcissistic disregard for commitment to others. Gustav von Rohden, one of Germany's most prominent Protestant family experts, argued in 1911 that radical feminists and sex reformers claimed to fight for the oppressed but in reality sought to legitimize "animalistic" pleasure.[85]

If Catholics and Protestants subscribed to the same binaries, and viewed reciprocal and "selfish" sex as polar opposites, it was because they both understood sexuality as part of a broader struggle. Theologians and commentators on family across the confessional divide increasingly drew on the concepts that informed Christian economic thought to describe feminism and sex reforms as a materialist ideology. In this telling, separating sex from family was akin to the socialists' understanding of class relations. Both denied that dignity was achieved through communal giving and self-denial, and instead viewed human relations as transactional, geared only toward maximizing material and sensual benefits. As one Catholic commentator put it in a characteristic rhetorical embellishment, socialists, feminists, and sex reformers were branches of "the deepest evil ... [of] the gratifying, materialist spirit."[86] This ubiquitous conflation of social, gendered, and sexual matters helped explain why combating the new movements was seen as such an urgent task. It demonstrated how calls for sexual laxity would inevitably eradicate spirituality as such. Radical feminism and sex reform loomed so large in Christian writings that some blamed them for declining birth rates, a major source of despair for early twentieth-century Europeans. The Belgian Arthur Vermeersch, one of the continent's leading Catholic authorities on family affairs, warned in 1909 that tolerating nonreproductive sex made the inevitable sacrifices of family life unappealing, and thus threatened Europe's future existence.[87]

The consequences of this conceptual move were far-reaching. Around the turn of the twentieth century, Catholics and Protestants worked toward a new mission, into which anti-feminism was subsumed: combating anything that might unbridle carnal impulses outside the family, both for men and for women. The targets of this campaign were diverse and required different measures. They in particular included erotic publications and prostitution. To be sure, anxieties about erotic temptations beyond the family were not new to Christian thought, and had long permeated Catholic and Protestant writings. What was new, however, was the scope of Christian ambitions. Theologians, family experts, and politicians now aspired to reshape the public sphere: to regulate what people could read, what images they could purchase, and what they could see on the street. In their minds, new restrictions were necessary to prevent Europeans from succumbing to base instincts. Whether they followed Christ's commands on not, all Europeans had to follow the churches' principles of self-control to prevent social anarchy.

The person who most forcefully articulated this ambition was Hermann Roeren, a senior jurist and politician from Germany. In several publications Roeren warned that urbanization and new media had created unprecedented threats to sexual self-control. Wherever men and women walked in cities, he explained in *Public Immorality and How to Combat It* (1904), they were bombarded with sexual incitement: brothels offered sex for pay; stores sold erotic postcards and racy novels; pharmacies dispensed contraception. Roeren concluded that to prevent the triumph of materialism and the collapse of marriages, Catholics had to suppress some sources of temptation. In particular, they had to protect youth, whose capacity for self-control was not fully developed, by creating a public sphere fee from "vice."[88] These arguments resonated considerably, in part because they captured a meaningful shift in the public sphere. Due to the declining costs of printing and the expansion of readership, publications with erotic content (whether novels or postcards) were indeed more popular and visible than ever before. The worries that animated Roeren were therefore replicated in many works and inspired institutional mobilization. In the 1890s and 1900s, Catholic organizations against "public immorality" emerged in Germany, France, the Netherlands, and Austria. Populated by clerics, government officials, and activists, these groups published journals and pamphlets, organized boycotts of businesses that sold erotic texts, and demonstrated against "indecent" materials.[89]

A broad desire to "cleanse" the public sphere of materialist immorality also came to dominate Protestant thinking. As prominent Dutch theologian Herman Bavinck explained in *The Christian Family* (1908), selfless love in marriage had to be trained for and practiced daily; it would not survive amid the social legitimization of depravity.[90] Protestant publications sounded the alarm like their Catholic counterparts by conflating prostitution, erotic publications, and contraception. In some cases they also conflated those with violent and sensational stories on crime, which similarly threatened to strip impressionable readers of their capacity to self-control. The German pastor Ernst Schultze spoke for many when he claimed in *Trash Literature* (1909) that they all belonged to a hydra-like menace that needed elimination.[91] Protestants therefore mirrored Catholic activism by founding new associations of prominent lay scholars and politicians who pressured municipalities to shut down brothels and boycotted businesses that sold erotic and violent publications.[92] The conceptual proximity between economic and sexual issues was so common that several veterans of anti-socialist activism became the main protagonists of anti-vice campaigns. In France in the 1880s and 1890s, Tommy Fallot, the leader of Protestant outreach to workers, founded the Anti-Pornography League and the anti-prostitution Morality League.[93] In Germany in 1885, Ludwig Weber, who founded the first Protestant labor union, launched the Protestant Association for the Elevation of Public Morality. For these figures and for members of similar associations in the Netherlands, Belgium, and elsewhere, achieving social harmony and managing sexuality were closely connected. Both required the self-control, denial, and selflessness that modern culture and economic practices allegedly weakened.[94]

All this public focus on sexuality had ironic effects. Instead of reducing the public visibility of sex, which Christians claimed was their goal, anti-vice campaigns helped sustain desire's role in public discourse.[95] As they sought to explain what constituted "healthy" and "deviant" approaches to sexuality, Catholics and Protestants produced a growing body of guides designed for parents, teachers, and youth. Works such as the French Catholic Joseph Fonssagrives's *Advice for Parents and Teachers about Education for Purity* (1902) described in graphic detail (often with explicit illustrations) the anatomy of both sexes as well as various sexual acts.[96] Similarly, repeated warnings against "corrupting" temptations made them more present than ever. Readers of Iwan Bloch's widely translated book *The Sexual Life of Our Time* (1907), by one of Germany's most prominent Protestant experts on sexuality, included lurid depictions of homosexuality, pornography, sadism, and prostitution.[97] The campaigns of both confessions, that is, were premised on relentlessly highlighting the very temptations that allegedly undermined Europeans' self-control. As Bloch explained to his readers, "Anyone who wishes to understand modern love . . . must, in the first place, succeed in informing himself [about the dark threats to it]."[98]

Another irony of these anti-vice campaigns was that they helped transform how Christians legitimized "family values" that they claimed were unchanging. As they labored to explain how pornography and prostitution threatened civilization, Christian writers argued that marriage and the family were not only the basis of society and necessary for procreation, but also the key site for bringing sexual impulses under control.

The person who most eloquently articulated this notion was the Swiss writer Friedrich Wilhelm Foerster, whose *Sexual Ethics and Sexual Pedagogy* (1907), based on addresses given in Berlin to the German Association for the Struggle Against Sexual Sickness, appeared in five languages and was widely cited by Catholics and Protestants across the continent. According to Foerster, the core of human morality was overcoming the body's unyielding desire for satisfaction. Humans could realize their full potential only by taming their urges; otherwise, they are but slaves to their irrational whims and "subjective folly." The purpose of all traditions and moral teachings was to conquer people's inner desires, which Foerster argued was to achieve freedom. By endowing restraint with spiritual value, tradition allowed men and women to find meaning beyond themselves, and thus to "liberate" themselves from "the tyranny of the lower powers." For Foerster, this was Christianity's true genius. Through the figure of Jesus, it celebrated selfless love and self-denial as the center of human relations.[99]

According to Foerster, nowhere was this restraint more crucial than in the realm of sexuality, where passions were strongest. According to *Sexual Ethics and Sexual Pedagogy,* Christians were the first to view lifelong monogamy as the only legitimate site of sexual interaction, in contrast to earlier cultures that were polygamous or celebrated prostitution. By investing sex with sacred meaning, Christians took "an essential step towards the emancipation of the Eros," allowing men and women to "connect sexual love with all the higher interests and feelings of humanity." Following the intellectual trajectory of earlier anti-feminists, Foerster insisted that lifelong monogamy was not confinement but "true" sexual liberation. "If it rests with our 'individual' decision to contract union outside this permanent life-compact, or to dissolve this compact at will," he warned, "all too soon we should fall prey to changing erotic attacks and passions . . . sexual impulses and sensuous stimuli." In this framing, sex reformers limited people's freedom since they ruined the condition in which self-control could be practiced. Foerster thus celebrated monogamous marriage not so much for its realization of divine order but for its utilitarian function. This was also in part why he did not distinguish between Catholic and Protestant teachings; both, he argued, shared the same commitment to the spirit's taming of bodily impulses.[100]

Foerster's ideas, which were celebrated by many Catholics and Protestants, resonated for two reasons. First, they captured the growing new sense that the two confessions shared objectives in the sphere of sexuality.

Contemporaries recognized that their ambitions aligned, and anti-vice campaigns became central sites of sustained interconfessional cooperation. In France, the leaders of Protestant morality campaigns, such as Fallot and pastor Louis Comte, joined hands with Catholics like Marie Maugeret and Senator René Bérenger. In the nondenominational French League for the Improvement of Public Morality, they advocated for censoring pornographic literature, and despite internal disagreement, restrictions on prostitution.[101] In the Netherlands, Catholic and Protestant anti-vice activists also cooperated. Pastor Hendrik Pierson, who founded the country's first anti-prostitution organization, worked with Catholics in a series of local campaigns, which led multiple cities to outlaw brothels, notably Amsterdam in 1897.[102] The most sustained cooperation took place in Germany, where, in 1898, Catholic and Protestant activists in Cologne founded the Interconfessional Association Against Public Immorality, which quickly opened branches in many major cities. With a journal, various conferences, and a mobilization apparatus, its activists succeeded in shutting down brothels and restricting sales of erotic materials in multiple cities. According to one of its leaders, Franz Weigl, the mutual efforts of all Christians were the only path to "public decency."[103] Cooperation also expanded to the international sphere. In 1908, Christian delegations of both confessions gathered in Paris for the first international congress against pornography, where they shared experiences and mobilization strategies.[104]

Second, and equally important, Foerster's insistence that restricting sexual desire was the realization of freedom allowed Christians to propose a bold remaking of Europe's legal order. At the center of these anti-vice campaigns was the radical expansion of the state's regulation of sexuality. Across the confessional divide, Christian commentators claimed that the family could not rely only on moral awakening and voluntary action. Threatened by wild sexual stimuli, the family—and by extension, all of society—needed to be defended by state institutions that repressed "indecency" through censorship, fines, surveillance, and incarceration. In the eyes of Christians, if Europe's laws allowed prostitution, erotic publications, and contraception, this was not because they defended free speech or economic exchange, as defenders of these laws argued. Rather, it was because their goal was imposing materialism by limiting and even eliminating Europeans' ability to live in virtue. By this logic, imposing Christian norms on everyone, whether practicing Christians or not, was not overreach but liberating. This was why, in contrast to Christian discussions of economic relations, reflections on the sexual sphere almost universally described the state as the primary guardian of "harmonious" order. Not a single major thinker, Catholic or Protestant, warned that state regulation of family structures or sexual behavior could lead to tyranny or subvert "natural" social relations.

The consequences of these ideas made cooperation between Catholics and Protestants regarding the sexual sphere even more far-reaching than in their joint anti-socialist campaign. While unable to eradicate radical feminism and sex reform movements, interconfessional coalitions substantially expanded the state's authority to regulate sexuality. The most ambitious example was in the Netherlands. Building on cooperation in anti-vice campaigns, the ruling coalition of Protestant and Catholic parties enacted sweeping regulations. The 1911 "vice laws," as they became collectively known, took on Catholics' and Protestants' shared preoccupation. Among other things, the laws forced the closure of all brothels and criminalized pimping in an effort to eradicate prostitution. They banned the sale of pornography, restricted the sale of erotic texts, and empowered authorities to censor "indecent" works of art. They also prohibited advertisements for contraception. Finally, they increased already existing penalties on abortions and homosexuality. The laws hardly accomplished the high hopes that Christians pinned on them—"indecent" activities continued in clandestine forms, and sales of contraceptives did not decline—but they went a long way to restrict sexuality outside of the context of family and procreation. As the Protestant politician Anthony Brummelkamp proclaimed, "Marriage before God is protected from all violations and all sins against it, both before as well as in and outside of marriage. That is the only true and just starting point."[105]

The convergence of Catholic and Protestant activism had similar impacts elsewhere, even if not on the same scale. Christian organizations, sometimes in concert with other groups, enshrined their conception of sexual freedom by expanding the state's regulatory power. In Germany in 1900, after eight years of advocacy, Catholics and Protestants in the Reichstag amended the national criminal code. Over the protests of liberals and socialists, Germany's new laws criminalized pimping; allowed municipalities to restrict the sales of pornography; prohibited the sale of "filthy" materials to those under the age of sixteen; and banned advertisements for contraceptives. While writers of both confessions often lamented their inability to impose even harsher measures, such as blanket censorship of erotic materials and the abolition of prostitution, they continued to score successes at the regional level. In 1910, for example, following years of advocacy, the state of Baden shut down all brothels.[106] In France the coalition led by the Catholic senator Bérenger also won legislative victories. Its relentless advocacy helped bring about state restrictions on publications advocating prostitution (1895) and on sexual publications (1898), as well as the criminalization of private sales of pornography (1905).[107] Support for these restrictions was not exclusively Christian, and included groups with different agendas. Anti-prostitution in particular drew support from doctors, state officials, and feminists, who were animated by different concerns. For many contemporaries, however, the project of restrictions was mostly associated with Christian activism. German psychiatrist Richard von Krafft-Ebing, the era's most prominent sexologist, remarked in 1903 that there was "no doubt" that "Christianity is one of the most powerful forces favoring moral progress."[108]

Just like with Christian anti-socialism, interconfessional cooperation in anti-feminist and anti-vice campaigns survived the shock of World War I. If anything, the war's mass killing intensified Christians' fixation on procreation, and the belief that the child-giving family must be defended from feminism and non-procreative sexuality. In Germany and the Netherlands, for example, Catholic and Protestant political parties accepted female suffrage but quickly mobilized to defend other anti-feminist priorities. They preserved family laws that granted husbands authority over children and finances, and defeated the efforts of liberals and socialists to end inequality between married and unmarried women.[109] Anti-vice campaigns, which intensified in the 1920s, proved equally successful in forging coalitions against what the German Protestant Women's Organization decried in 1922 as "the dark flood" of sexual temptation.[110] In Germany, these campaigns culminated in 1926, when the Catholic Center Party and the Protestant-led DNVP passed a national censorship law against "trash and filth" materials. Overriding a constitutional right to free speech, the law empowered censorship panels to ban sales to youth of "indecent" movies, advertisements, and journals (fulfilling activists' desires, this also included publications with violent content).[111] In the Netherlands, where such laws were already operative, the focus was enforcement. Special vice squads were established in multiple police departments (the largest was in Amsterdam in 1924), which specialized in rooting out illicit prostitution, pornography, and contraception.[112] In France, Belgium, and Austria, Christian advocacy continued along similar lines. With varying degrees of success, Catholic and

Protestant politicians sought to shape how European understood, imagined, and practiced sex.[113]

The period of the late nineteenth and early twentieth centuries, in short, was a moment of meaningful transformation in Christian understandings of sexuality. In response to the rise of organized feminism, Catholics and Protestants articulated new and similar justifications for gender inequality and the role of the family, claiming that both empowered women against "irrational" or materialist aspirations. In response to sexual reform movements, they launched novel efforts to regulate European desires, which initiated new forms of interconfessional cooperation. Crucially, however, leaders in both confessions claimed that feminists and sex reformers were not just selfish and immoral. They also threatened what made Europe a unique place in the world. Indeed, in publications, sermons, and speeches, Catholics and Protestants routinely equated anyone who deviated from "proper" sexuality with Asian and African "savages." As the French Catholic writer Ferdinand-Antonin Vuillermet put it in 1925, feminist women who exposed their legs in public were like "pagans in their frenzied Saturnalia," lacking in European self-control.[114] If Protestants echoed this language, it was not only because they shared this understanding of gender. It was also because the two confessions had similar views of Christianity's role in "civilizing" overseas "barbarians."

Missions: Faith in Civilization

In the winter of 1884–1885, German chancellor Otto von Bismarck convened in Berlin delegates of the great imperial powers to negotiate their competing demands for dominance in Africa. In an effort to allay growing tensions between France, Britain, Belgium, and Portugal that he feared would destabilize Europe, Bismarck sought to secure peace by expanding the European balance of power on the "dark continent." Following extensive negotiations, these European states divided Africa into spheres of influence with the signing of the General Berlin Act. Inscribing Europeans' self-proclaimed right to rule over foreign subjects into an international treaty, the Berlin conference epitomized the era of "high imperialism," when European empires swelled and colonial violence reached frightening new heights. While the diplomats who sliced up the African continent were hardly interested in the spiritual salvation of the millions they planned to rule, focusing instead on economic extraction and geopolitical calculations, they nevertheless included a provision that detailed their responsibility to spread Christianity. Article 6 of the General Act granted Christian missionaries access to all territories and the special protection of colonial rulers, regardless of their nationality or confession. Alongside scientists and explorers, who were also granted these privileges, missionaries were to be the vanguard in "instructing the natives and bringing ... to them the blessings of civilizations."[115]

Christianity's inclusion in the treaty, as the result of intense missionary advocacy, was indicative of an important development in Christian thought and politics. It reflected and helped reinforce Catholics' and Protestants' growing embrace of the "civilizing mission" ideology, the quest to discipline and "uplift" Asians and Africans into the productivity, self-control, rationality, and refined manners that Europeans allegedly possessed. Even as they protested some features of European overseas domination, such as excessive violence or the spread of alcohol (which tended to follow European settlers), missionary leaders shared the logic that undergirded and justified colonial rule. In the late nineteenth and early twentieth centuries, they reconceptualized Christianity as a civilizational project, with the foundational tension this entailed: they described the Gospel as a set of norms that both distinguished white Europeans from racialized Others *and* were universal and thus had to be imposed abroad. Though this contrast between Christians and "barbarians" had a long history, in this period it acquired new specific meanings. Missionaries now claimed that their task was to bestow on converts the same qualities that defined their work at home: self-control and appreciation of social order. This was why missionary organizations, whose size and activity ballooned in this period, self-consciously developed close relationships with imperial authorities. They were often leaders in building the massive apparatus of schools and hospitals that provided colonial rulers with the necessary workforce for economic activity. Missionaries also ran research centers for ethnography, geography, and languages that provided vital knowledge for colonists. Some went so far as to claim that Christians were the civilizing mission's *only* true embodiment, free from the selfish profit considerations of most European settlers and bureaucrats. As the prominent missionary writer Gustav Warneck declared, missionaries were the ones who saw education as its own goal, and thus could confer Europe's "immense cultural superiority" on Asians and Africans.[116]

Scholars have painstakingly mapped the overlaps and tensions between Christian missions and the colonial apparatus, but much less noted is how the civilizing mission influenced confessional relations. As with social and sexual matters, Catholics and Protestants of diverse inclinations converged around similar beliefs and vocabularies in their thinking about European Christianity's place in the colonial world, or the "mission lands" as they were often called. In fact, in ways that historians have not always recognized, missionary theory and practice was heavily influenced by the evolution of anti-socialist and anti-feminist ideas at home. When church and mission leaders from both confessions described their goals with Asians and Africans, they echoed the same anxieties and hopes they had regarding workers and feminists. Like those unsettling European groups, "primitives" were lacking in self-control and needed to be disciplined to accept "proper" authority, work habits, and family relations. Africans, because they were considered the lowest in the civilizational hierarchy, were described as distant from God's "natural" social and sexual teachings and thus in need of forceful tutelage (why these natural teachings were so foreign to the majority of the world's population was rarely explained).[117] As with the anti-materialist campaigns in Europe, the conceptual overlaps between Catholics and Protestants in the colonies became substantial. Some missionary leaders and theoreticians even talked of a mutual Catholic-Protestant civilizational project, especially in a joint struggle against Islam. Such sentiments were still on the margins, and confessional hostilities persisted. But a mutual belief in Christianity's civilizing force facilitated a transition, where a sense of competition slowly morphed into ambivalence, and at times even into mutual interest.

The Catholic embrace of the civilizing mission began not with papal decrees, but with independent initiatives by missionary leaders and thinkers. One of the most prominent was Charles Lavigerie, the French bishop of Algeria and founder of the White Fathers missionary order. From the 1880s onward, Lavigerie insisted that Catholic missions were a civilizational force, by which he meant that their main concern was training local communities in modern trades and professions. "Christianity is not merely a matter of religious belief and practice," he claimed in 1886, "but is the foundation of the whole social order."[118] Similar dynamics could be detected in Germany, where Catholic missionaries adopted the language of civilizational hierarchies. The German Amandus Acker, who led the Fathers of the Holy Spirit order and chaired his country's Catholic missionary council, argued that Catholicism's main task was to "uplift" Asians and Africans from their passivity and ignorance by teaching them to use European technology. Warning that European influence might "contaminate" overseas communities with European "skepticism [and] materialism," he proclaimed that "in the colonies, we seek to endow a Christian civilization."[119] Even more emphatic was the German Catholic leader Andreas Amrhein, who claimed that Christian belief in salvation was the source of all material achievement. "Where the missionary works," he wrote, one could find "the hardest working laborers . . . the soil transforms into gardens, the population is decently dressed . . . and children finally grow up with discipline."[120] This departure from an emphasis on conversion, the purpose of missionary work earlier in the century, received the Vatican's stamp of approval. In an 1889 letter to Belgian missionaries in the Congo, Pope Leo XIII expressed his "ardent desire to see the savage peoples of Africa abandon the darkness of error for the Gospel's brilliant light and the . . . politeness of Christian civilization."[121]

Framing evangelization in civilizational terms came even more naturally to Protestants, who by the late nineteenth century were accustomed to equating themselves with productivity, scientific progress, and hard work. What was originally developed as an anti-Catholic trope was now employed in relation to non-Europeans: Protestants explained why Luther's teachings enabled Europe's global dominance and thus had to be exported everywhere. Carl Büttner, a director of the German Evangelical Mission Society, explained in *Colonial Politics and Christianity* (1885) that an inherent link between Protestantism and economic progress meant that the missions' main task was to integrate native populations into the modern production of coffee, tea, rubber, and palm oil. By doing so, he reasoned, missions would help "civilize the savages" and "uplift [them] . . . to ever higher cultural levels."[122] The missionary leader Carl Paul had reservations about European influence, which he worried might carry with it evils such as alcoholism, but in his book *The Mission in Our Colonies* (1898), he equated the Gospel with technological superiority. In his telling, Christianity's insistence on the universal nature of divine grace was what opened people's minds to the possibility of improvement. This was why "the blacks" needed "the guidance of the white men" in order "to raise the treasures that God has placed in the tropical landscape."[123] While Protestants often declared themselves more tolerant than Catholics toward indigenous traditions, especially because they more commonly administered rites in local languages rather than Latin, they assumed that European life was the embodiment of Christianity. The Norwegian Lothar Dahle, a prominent voice in Europe's missionary affairs, declared in a 1905 speech to the leaders of the major Protestant missions from continental Europe and Scandinavia that the missions' goal was to use "local languages and ideas" as a ladder toward "higher goals."[124]

For both confessions, conceiving of Christianity in these terms was appealing in part because of the legitimizing function it offered in Europe. It provided a rejoinder to an array of commentators who equated civilization, technical ingenuity, and scientific mastery over nature with secular and scientific thinking. This was especially true in France, where the republican regime from the 1870s onward described its civilizing mission in secular terms. French Catholic missionaries, in response, proclaimed that they were equal partners in this project. Bishop Lavigerie asserted in a fundraising pamphlet that if Europeans were "more farsighted, more industrious and more moral" than Africans, this was first and foremost because they were "Christian."[125] The French Protestant theologian Albert Réville argued that religion was the very source of civilizational difference, and thus integral to colonial uplift. In his hugely popular *Prolegomena of the History of Religions* (1881), he declared that "the only thing which explains the strange separation of the world's populations into civilized nations . . . and into nations incapable by themselves of attaining to civilization, is a primordial difference in the religious intuition."[126] But even beyond France, missionaries felt compelled to insist on the inseparable links between Europe's growing economic and technological might and Christianity, both of which they attributed to mental dispositions. The superintendent of the Berlin Mission, Alexander Merensky, argued that ancient Germans had been "extremely indolent" and "became the most industrious people in the world under the influence of Christianity."[127] In missionary publications, Christianity was routinely described in psychological terms, a force that led humans from the "childlike" state of confusion into a mature universe of self-awareness and industrious activity. A 1909 Protestant missionary exhibition in Amsterdam explained to visitors that the Gospel was the difference between the "lawlessness" of immaturity and the peace of productive self-control.[128]

As strategic as this civilizational rhetoric may have been, its adoption facilitated a far-reaching conceptual transformation. It introduced a new temporal dimension to Catholic and Protestant thought: commentators in both camps began to argue that missionary work was geared not toward near-term conversion, but toward a gradual educational process that would last for generations. Indeed, for all their insistence that civilization was rooted in religion, almost all commentators reversed the equation when it came to Asians and Africans. Employing common racial stereotypes, they claimed that "savages" were too irrational, passive, or unsophisticated to grasp the Gospel, therefore requiring decades of tutelage in European norms around work, education, and family life before they reached the capacity to become "fully" Christian. Some, such as German missionary to Sumatra Johannes Warneck, claimed in his popular book *The Living Forces of the Gospel* (1909) that certain races, namely Europeans and North Americans, were more biologically capable of comprehending the divine message, whereas others, especially Asians and Africans, would first need centuries of management.[129] Even though these ideas were at the extreme end on the spectrum of Christian thought—most missionaries rejected biologism because it raised doubts about the very possibility of conversion—Warneck's ideas reflected increasingly common sentiments. When the American missionary leader John Mott mused in the 1890s that the "opening" of Asia and Africa to Christian nations could spell "the evangelization of the world in this generation," most European missionary leaders dismissed his slogan as a naive misunderstanding of the missionary agenda. As one German Protestant bluntly remarked, "the savage must first become a human being and *then* a Christian."[130] This paternalist approach also conveniently explained why even if Asians and Africans were to convert in large numbers, Europeans would still need to maintain their leadership role over Christian missions and churches for the foreseeable future. When major Protestant missionaries gathered in 1910 at a conference in Edinburgh, their final statement mused that "it cannot be surprising that those who have received their knowledge of Christianity . . . from the vigorous . . . teaching of the European races, should be for a long time in bondage to European organizations."[131]

Few areas better illuminate the depth and scope of this approach than both confessions' growing fixation on labor in the mission field. Even as they envisioned their civilizing efforts continuing into the distant future, Catholic and Protestant missionaries were anxious to begin the process of disciplining native populations. Across different inclinations, orders, and denominations, writers agreed that this meant making non-Europeans into workers: subjects who were able to work long hours, accept instructions, and practice self-denial. In ways that echoed their anti-socialist theories in Europe, Christian writers and missionaries viewed the spread of the work ethic as central to their educational process. Their goal, as they saw it, was to help Asians and Africans develop the psychological habits that modern life required, and most importantly, to foster a Christian understanding of labor: to view it not as a transactional and materialist act that merely provided sustenance but as a vehicle for self-improvement and the fulfillment of one's role in a harmonious and unequal social order. Even as these ideals complimented the demands of capitalist employers, whose plantation and mines required a steady supply of trained and obedient workers, Christian writers insisted that this was not their primary agenda. Under the missions' guidance, they claimed, colonial subjects would learn to value labor for its own sake and acquire the self-control necessary for civilization and eventually Christianization.

For Catholics, the urgency of training non-Europeans for work seemed self-evident. If communities worked only to sustain themselves, rather than to produce surplus to be sold, was this not a mark of idleness and ignorance? The German Catholic missionary Norbert Weber, for example, explained that his order's main task in eastern Africa was to train local communities for a life of physical work. Through sweat and toil, they were to metamorphose from "the children of nature" into its masters, harvesting their environment through agriculture and learning better hygiene in the process.[132] The German missionary theoretician Amandus Acker added in 1908 that Catholic missionaries were the only Europeans who could fulfill this task. Unlike ideologies that linked labor to materialist calculations such as a desire for better clothing or housing, Christian thought recognized the obligation to work as a "divine duty," a value in itself that taught people self-control and abstinence.[133] Missionary writers were united in the conviction that the physical act of work, precisely because it was so unnatural to the "primitive races," would have a spiritual effect. In their minds, exteriority shaped interiority: physical challenges would train the soul for the principles of self-control, thus serving as the first step toward a higher existence.[134] In this conceptual world, hard work and Christian devotion became inseparable. As one Belgian missionary to the Congo explained, "besides the material well-being that work brings in itself, there is a spiritual good. The negro who works remains a good Christian, devoted to the practice of virtue, while an unemployed or idle one is vicious and often corrupt."[135]

This focus on labor and productivity was equally central to Protestants. As Réville put it, labor "is properly speaking the generator of civilization, is a moral fact, since it supposes effort, foresight, and self-control."[136] Protestant missionaries proclaimed that training colonial subjects in hard work was the core of their undertaking. Carl Mirbt, one of Germany's main missionary voices, reminded his readers, for example, that "Christianity is not the religion of dreams but of work." In his *Mission and Colonial Politics* (1910), much of which was devoted to the topic, Mirbt praised work programming in Africa, which helped transform the individual into a "useful and productive member of society."[137] It was a common refrain in missionary writing that endless physical labor was, paradoxically, the key to one's freedom. Berlin missionary leader Leopold Diestelkamp argued at the 1905 colonial conference in Berlin (where half of the presentations by missions were dedicated to labor) that it was work that gave workers a sense of purpose, enabled them to overcome difficulties, and expanded their capacity to appreciate their blessings.[138] Like their Catholic counterparts, Protestants enthused about overcoming slavery's legacies. In a spectacular display of circular logic, Mirbt proclaimed that if Africans continued to resent work, they had to be forced into it by colonial authorities, because only then would they regain the ethics of freedom.[139] For many, training for work was *the* convergence point between Christianity and the civilizing mission. As the director of Leipzig mission, Dietrich von Schwartz bluntly put it, "A lazy Christendom is worth nothing."[140]

This conception of labor as a spiritual task meant that thinkers of both confessions also shared the same logical tensions. Most glaringly, it led many missionaries to claim that non-Europeans needed to be trained against the conditions that Europeans had created. The Catholic Friedrich Schwanger, for example, bemoaned Africa's "luxuriant tropical" climate for rendering work unnecessary. Because fruits and vegetables were always plentiful, he reasoned, they simply fell into Africans' laps, making the sacrifices of work unimaginable. The Protestant Mirbt argued that the profound laziness he witnessed across Africa was the product not of inherent racial inferiority—a notion he forcefully rejected as un-Christian—but environmental conditions. Yet rather than explaining why European intervention in economic life was at all desirable, both Schwanger and Mirbt assumed it was beneficial. Europeans brought with them the technologies, management methods, and fertilizers that were designed for the allegedly more difficult conditions of Europe and that required a more disciplined approach to work. Europeans, in short, had to instill in Africans the psychological disposition they needed to fit the harsh realities that Europeans had brought.[141] Similarly tortured logic informed Johannes Warneck's claims that missionaries had to draw Asian and African animists to their compounds so they could be impressed by European technological superiority. In this telling, the primitive minds of heathens were mostly attracted to things that could make them work less, such as fertilizer, which Europeans could use to spark their interest in Christianity. Precisely what made them inferior to and different from European Christians, then, was to be the starting point of their process of conversion.[142]

These ideas did not remain in the realm of theory but had important implications for the missionary practices of both confessions. As their publications and reports never tired of touting, missions moved beyond religious education and medical care to include labor training as a major area of action. The fact that European empires did not apply their labor codes in the colonies meant that missionaries could impose long and punishing work programs. Missionaries thus founded thousands of work centers to propagate "the Gospel of work." In East Africa, for example, missionaries from the Catholic White Fathers order and Protestant representatives of the Berlin and Leipzig missions established local farms, where converts and converts-to-be toiled in the fields to cultivate cocoa, coffee, and yams. They also encouraged new crafts: young people learned (often in multiyear programs) to become carpenters, masons, and blacksmiths. In West Africa, missionaries of both confessions established training centers for construction workers and farmers. They took special pride in a program for locksmiths, which was considered one of the most sophisticated skills African trainees were capable of learning.[143] In the Congo, French and Belgian Jesuits and Dutch Protestants established farming on a commercial scale, and locals were trained to grow flowers, maize, and bananas and to work in factories that produced shoes, cigarettes, and furniture.[144] Similar centers appeared in Indonesia, India, and China. The motivation for these ventures was ideological but also practical. They provided missions with a key source of sustenance and income, and thus eased their reliance on donations. Still, labor was routinely linked with both salvation and psychological improvement. As one report from the German organization in Togo boasted, "the manual work" taught by missions was designed not to be profitable but to be "systematic and fruitful."[145]

Missionaries did not only seek to uplift local minds through labor. Another crucial part of the Christian civilizing mission around which the confessions converged was managing sexuality and family life. Their ire in this field was aimed at polygamy, the only topic to generate as much commentary as labor. As in Europe, Catholics and Protestants could not imagine a harmonious social order that was not predicated on monogamous commitment. In their eyes it was evident that allowing multiple sexual partners, even if united by formal marriage bonds, was bound to spark uncontrolled passions in men and women and thus lead them to materialism. Recycling the logic that animated Christian anti-feminism, missionaries claimed that the non-monogamous arrangements they encountered overseas were especially harmful to women. Polygamy, the logic went, gave men license to view women as sexual objects instead of lifelong partners. As Catholic thinker Josef Froberger remarked, with a common mix of disgust and fascination, polygamy "degraded" marriage into a permanent state of uncontrolled excitement.[146] The Protestant Gustav Warneck similarly equated polygamy with women's abduction and enslavement. By legitimizing jealousy between the wives of the same husband, which Warneck assumed was inevitable, polygamy disrupted "domestic peace" and reduced women's status to mere possessions. Missionary hostility to polygamy was not new, but now it was articulated in civilizational language, which depicted it as a materialist threat to self-control. The Belgian theologian Arthur Vermeersch, one of Europe's most prominent Catholic writers, reflected this approach when he described multiple sexual arrangements as different levels of cultural refinement. In his book *The Congolese Woman: House Servant, Polygamous Wife, Christian* (1913), a series of portraits written after his visit to the Congo, Vermeersch depicted missions as agents of emancipation: after African women moved from sexual slavery to polygamy, European Christians helped them reach monogamous marriage, in which men and women gained mastery over their passions.[147]

Sharing similar assumptions and reasoning, the Christian approach to polygamy often merged with its vision of labor. Missionaries of both confessions blamed non-monogamous arrangements for what they viewed as the scandalous habit of women working, which often involved physically demanding tasks. The Catholic Theodor Grentrup argued that polygamy's reduction of women to their physical functions led to their "perverse" habit of working. In his eyes, men's lack of training in sexual self-control resulted in laziness, thus shamefully leaving work to their wives.[148] Protestant commentators bundled polygamy and women's labor into the same problem. In their telling, polygamy reduced a woman's value to their bodily functions. Men therefore treated them like cattle, or a workforce to be exploited. As one liberal Swiss commentator bluntly put it, for "the negro" man, a woman "is there for him, and must work for him, and the more women he has, the more workers."[149] For many missionaries, combating polygamy was therefore the highest priority. When the leader of the German Rhineland mission, Franz Michael Zahn, gave the keynote address at the 1897 European missionary conference, he proclaimed that "the missionary influence on family life" had "decisive significance" for the future of global civilization.[150] Neither Catholics nor Protestants registered that local traditions and status considerations often prevented local populations from embracing European gendered divisions of labor. To the missionaries it was evident that there was only one correct social and gender order.

At times this hostility was compromised by practical considerations. Confronted with the persistence of local traditions, missionaries occasionally agreed to accept converts who maintained polygamous households. Missionary writers similarly reasoned that these relationships could be tolerated under certain conditions, for example, if divorcing a wife could lead to violence between tribes.[151] Yet as time progressed, the creeping dominance of civilizational reasoning put those who hesitate to emphasize monogamy on the defensive. Positive references to the Old Testament's many polygamists, which in the 1880s occasionally were used to justify tolerating alternative family arrangements, largely disappeared from missionary conferences and journals by the early twentieth century.[152] What is more, the misogynist belief that the sexual act was more morally compromising for women meant that tolerance was always restricted to men. Women with multiple partners were strictly barred from joining mission-led communities.[153] Missionaries routinely discussed how best to limit polygamy, especially by denying its practitioners participation in rites or a place in mission-run employment. They agreed, as one German theoretician put it, that "there is no doubt that polygamy ... [is] a socio-ethical evil that stands in contradiction to marriage's natural order."[154]

For all the self-confidence that this civilizational vision entailed, it was always laced with fears of its fragility. This was because Catholics and Protestants expressed a shared panic about Islam, which they imagined as a dark mirror-image of their own global aspirations. Viewing Islam as an existential enemy was nothing new to Christian thought, but building as it did on centuries of conflict, late nineteenth-century imperialism imbued it with new meanings. Echoing a trend among sociologists and scholars of religion, fields where missionaries played a significant role, Catholics and Protestants increasingly agreed that Islam's most cardinal problem was its opposition to civilization as they defined it: it encouraged resistance to work, self-control, and rational thinking. Hubert Hansen, the German Catholic missionary leader, argued that Islam's allure was its encouragement of laziness. This was why it also fostered opposition to European tutelage, and why its adherents were "anti-colonial, politically destructive vermin."[155] Josef Froberger, a leader of the White Fathers, similarly attributed Islam's spread outside of Europe to the fact it reinforced Africans' suspicion of studying or working. "We can say without exaggeration," he scoffed in a speech, "that Islam does not promote moral culture but instead hinders it [and] destroys it."[156] As was the case with anti-Catholic and anti-Protestant writings, these works' portrayal of Islam as superficial paradoxically also led to depicting its adherents as fanatics. The French Lavigerie explained that because they lacked the capacity for critical exploration and self-control, Muslims were prone to accept authority unquestionably and channeled their emotions into irrational devotion. This was why, he wrote in a public letter to Algeria's governor, they had to be driven "into the deserts, far from the civilized world."[157] (The governor, fearing Muslim violence in response to the insult, publicly renounced this message).

Steeped as they were in similar discourses and modes of thinking, Protestants also understood their competition with Islam in civilizational terms. This was the case with the Protestant Dietrich Westermann, a missionary to Tanzania who became one of Europe's most prominent scholars of Africa. Based on large-scale surveys conducted in Togo and Cameroon, Westermann maintained that Islam hindered the African continent's economic and technological development. It relied on abductions and human trafficking, throwing Africa back into the destructive slave trade. When data inconveniently contradicted such assessments, such as when the Haussa people in northern Togo presided over profitable agriculture and commerce, Westermann claimed that their conversion to Islam was superficial, merely an outward keeping of some ceremonies without accepting Islam's ethical teachings.[158] Others focused on polygamy as the source of Islam's perversity. The German missionary scholar Karl Meinhoff, for example, claimed that Islam's family ethics were "a form of prostitution," where sexual desire reigned supreme and refined love was extinguished.[159] For many, Islam was so alarming because it appealed to "primitive" people's instincts, all while channeling them to oppose the presence of Europeans. As the Dutch missionary writer Gottfried Simon explained in his widely translated book *Mohammedan Propaganda and the Protestant Mission* (1911), Islam's encouragement of laziness and sexual excess lured people away from Christianity, and then, lacking rational thinking, they were easily transformed into anti-Christian brutes.[160] In this telling, in which Islam fostered both passivity and fanatical activity, this religion was not merely the absence of Christian civilization but an active enemy with its own imperial aspirations. Julius Richter, who led Germany's Protestant missionary council and was one of its most prominent thinkers, articulated this logic when he chose "the danger of Islam" as the topic for his keynote speech at the 1905 colonial conference in Berlin. "Mohammadism," he thundered, was colonialism's chief antagonist, and "the danger is nearing like gathering clouds!"[161]

Islam, then, acquired the same meanings as socialism and feminism, depicted as the source and expression of uncontrolled subjectivity. By the early twentieth century these overlapping sensitivities among Catholics and Protestants were apparent enough that they generated hesitant talk of cooperation. As they read each other's publications and listened to each other's speeches at conferences, it dawned on some Christian thinkers and leaders that perhaps, despite vocal claims to the contrary, the two confessions shared important similarities. This was the case with Mirbt, who devoted considerable sections of his influential writings to the issue. Even as he expressed considerable suspicions about Catholics and their alleged desire to subject all converts to the Vatican's control, Mirbt bemoaned confessional divisions. For the pagans, after all, it made little difference if missionaries were one confession or the other, only that they brought with them schools, science, and the culture of work. Mirbt therefore suggested that the two confessions' differences paled in comparison to their mutual civilizational project. "The ecclesiastical differences between Protestants and Catholics," he explained, "become less important when measured against the great contrast between paganism and Christianity."[162] The Protestant missionary Erich Schultze similarly called on his Protestant readers to recognize Catholicism's contribution to the broader fight against Muslims overseas. The Catholics' "great resourcefulness and exemplary commitment," he exclaimed, made them an ally in the project of erecting "a bulwark against Islam."[163]

Similar voices could occasionally be detected among Catholics. The Bavarian capuchin leader Eustachius Nagel echoed his Protestant counterparts when he lamented that confessional hostilities overshadowed joint objectives in the mission field. If both instilled the spirit of work in non-Europeans, helped them develop proper family structures, and shared a mutual enemy in Islam, perhaps this could provide the basis for some reconciliation? In his speech at the 1905 colonial conference in Berlin, Nagel went so far as to express the hope that Asia and Africa would lead Catholics and Protestants to see their joint destiny. Working with cultures so far removed from themselves, he exclaimed, would remind them that "we all stand on the soil of Christendom," which in turn would lead them "to look at one another in a friendly manner . . . and even shake hands vigorously." Perhaps because Nagel's speech came after days of mind-numbing repetition, where speakers of both confessions reiterated their commitment to the same civilizing mission, the audience was unusually receptive to his message. The official minutes noted that the crowd welcomed his words with "heartfelt applause" and that some even stood to shout "bravo!"[164] In the Netherlands, too, several commentators pointed to similarities in missionary thinking. As the Dutch missionary scholar B. J. Esser explained in *Mission and Polygamy* (1905), the two confessions may have differed in their approach to sexual matters such as celibacy, but they agreed on the need to civilize heathens through monogamous marriage.[165]

Despite key parallels between Christian thinking about Europe and about colonial spaces, there were also crucial differences. Even as they attributed to socialists, feminists, and colonial subjects similar qualities and sought to discipline them toward similar goals, Christian elites, in both thought and practice, also developed distinct approaches to non-Europeans. Unlike European workers, for example, Asians and Africans were not considered potential sources of revolution, let alone atheism. Their main challenge to the "Christian" harmonious order was not radicalism but passivity, and therefore they did not require worker-employer cooperatives or welfare policies. Christian elites similarly took different approaches in the colonies when seeking to impose monogamous and heteronormative marriage as the heart of family ethics. While in Europe their primary vehicle was state laws and institutions, in most colonial spaces this was not an option, since European authorities left family matters to local communities and religious leaders. Missionaries and colonial governments clashed, for example, when missionaries protested divorce settlements in "mixed" interfaith marriages that gave authority over children to the non-Christian spouse.[166] In the mission lands, that is, the project of controlling human sexuality was restricted to Christian communities and work programs. Like the civilizing mission more broadly, it was assumed that its success would take decades, if not centuries.

These differences were part of the reason Catholic-Protestant cooperation in the missionary field was even more limited and marginal than it was with regard to social and sexual matters in Europe. Because thinkers and writers in both confessions envisioned Asia and Africa as existing in a different time, far behind Europe's stage of development, they were often more optimistic about their capacity to "uplift" the colonized peoples alone, without the strategic alliances that were necessary in Europe.[167] Indeed, for all the occasional talk of a mutual civilizational mission, there was no interconfessional cooperation on any meaningful scale in the missionary world. There was no sharing of resources between missionary outposts and training centers, and hardly any joint advocacy on matters of family law. In almost all of Asia and Africa, missionary organizations divided regions, counties, and towns between them, so they could avoid interacting with each other and reduce conflict over access to the same communities. This mutual sense that possibilities in the mission lands were different than in Europe proved important to the evolution of confessional relations. When the drive for a comprehensive Catholic-Protestant alliance began, it focused on Europe, only later turning its attention to the missionary world.

DESPITE WHAT THEIR critics often claimed, the European churches were not vestiges of premodern tradition. For all their claims to speak eternal truths, their understanding of the world constantly changed as they adapted to new pressures and developed novel vocabularies. In response to industrialization and the rise of socialism, Catholics and Protestants of different inclinations agreed on the need to establish a harmonious balance between the classes. Whether through paternalist associations, labor unions, or welfare programs, the goal was to foster in workers a new psychological disposition that embraced inequality. Thinkers in the two confessions also converged in their rethinking of gender and sexual norms. With new justifications for gendered difference and sexual control, which Christians described as emancipatory, they labored to legally distinguish the two sexes to reshape the public sphere. Their participation in colonialism was legitimized in similar terminologies. As with workers, women, and sex reformers, colonial subjects were to find their way to Christianity through psychological discipline, self-control, and self-denial. In each sphere, Christian thought inspired new forms of action. It produced new organizations, laws, and campaigns, which altered the lives of millions.

During this adaptation, Catholics and Protestants occasionally recognized their similarities. In a few cases they even joined hands; in ways that would have been unimaginable even a few decades earlier, in the midst of anti-Catholic and anti-Protestant agitation, activists and politicians formed interconfessional organizations and campaigns. To be sure, the depth or scope of Catholic-Protestant engagement from the 1880s to the 1920s should not be exaggerated. Cooperation remained largely practical and strategic, and almost no one talked about a deep similarity in theories of economic, sexual, or colonial order. Catholics and Protestants had mutual enemies, and at times they agreed on tools to defeat them, but that was rarely enough to spark talk of brotherhood or shared fate. There was still no positive language to articulate their shared priorities. Their convergence around similar worries, however, had consequences beyond this period. Their investment in social, gendered, and colonial inequalities would continue to define Christian politics for almost a century. Under new conditions, these spheres would also become the site of a deeper embrace that would relegate confessional tensions to the margins. All this would happen in the 1930s.

CHAPTER 3

The Birth of Ecumenism from the Crucible of Nazism

THE EVENTS of the 1930s and 1940s shook European Christianity. It could hardly have been otherwise: the calamity of the Great Depression, the meteoric rise of the radical right, and Nazi war and genocide meant that no movement or institution in Europe remained unaltered. Catholic and Protestant communities were no exception, and their thought and politics during the years of Nazi ascendance reflected efforts to navigate the realities of ever-increasing brutality. As historians have painstakingly shown, both confessions developed a wide array of strategies while encountering the Third Reich and its wartime collaborators across Europe. Theologians, church leaders, and lay theorists intensely debated the legitimacy of the right's harrowing measures in social policy, eugenics, and ethnic cleansing, and their responses crossed the spectrum from enthusiastic embrace to begrudging cooperation; only a small minority condemned the radical right as a pagan blasphemy that had to be resisted. In many ways, earlier divides, between conservative and reformed Catholics or liberal and evangelical Protestants, were either eclipsed by, or subsumed into, new internal debates about Christianity's relationship to fascism. The choices made by Christian leaders and believers alike would forever haunt the churches, especially when it came to their silence over, and sometimes support for, mass murder.

Less noted by scholars, these years also transformed the relationships between Catholics and Protestants. First in Germany, and then in other countries, a wide array of figures from both confessions undertook a bold campaign to forge a deep interconfessional engagement. Unlike previous efforts at cooperation, the projects of the 1930s and 1940s were not mere practical alliances against mutual enemies. Instead, a chorus of thinkers, writers, and activists, including those who had expressed anti-Catholic and anti-Protestant sentiments only a few years earlier, declared that the two confessions shared a positive outlook: they were brethren in the task of building a stable social, gendered, and international order. Nor were these novel efforts at cooperation limited to abstract theology; they generated new publications, exhibits, pamphlets, conferences, and other institutional endeavors. Proponents of interconfessional cooperation—an approach they called "ecumenism"—shared the conviction that they were ushering in the transformation of Christian life. The German Catholic philosopher Friedrich Muckermann spoke for many when he rejoiced in 1932 that "these times of crisis" seemed to bring about the "end of our religious wars."[1] Indeed, the ambitions of this movement meant that even its opponents perceived it to be too popular to openly confront. The Vatican, which as late as 1928 openly attacked Catholic-Protestant dialogue and forcefully disbanded a small interconfessional discussion group, remained silent on the expanding ecumenical project throughout the 1930s and early 1940s.

Two forces in particular sparked this shift in confessional relations. The first was increasing communist militancy. In 1928 Soviet authorities launched a wave of persecutions against churches and their leaders, rekindling the traumatizing memories of the French Revolution and the Paris Commune. When the devastation of the Great Depression emboldened communist parties across Europe, Christian elites weighed new alliances to counter what they understandably believed was an imminent wave of anti-Christian violence. While these sentiments mostly amounted to a more intense version of long-standing Christian anti-socialism, the second force behind confessional reconciliation was new. This was the Nazis' oft-forgotten promise to transcend the confessional divide. Adolf Hitler and his supporters espoused many ideas that sounded familiar to Christian ears. Nazi leaders insisted on the need for social harmony between unequal workers and employers and on solidifying the different roles of men and women as workers and mothers, respectively. Fulfilling many Christians' fantasies, they swiftly acted on those ideas, violently crushing organized labor and feminism. And yet in ways that were new, the Nazis condemned the strife between Catholics and Protestants as an obstacle to the formation of a unified and militarized racial community. The Nazi movement, they claimed, was a new synthesis that preserved the main teachings of the two churches, fusing them in a reborn "Aryan" body. In this ideological universe, confessional identities were not erased but subsumed to reach a higher destiny: protecting racial purity against its Jewish and Bolshevik enemies.

Though the Third Reich did not translate those ideas into state policy—its leaders lost interest in organized Christianity once their hold on political power was secure—the regime's initial successes helped popularize ecumenism. As Christian elites fiercely debated their responses to the Reich, and later to its emulators and allies across Central and Western Europe, many felt compelled to speak in an interconfessional key, developing new theologies and political theories in the process. The first were Christian supporters of the Nazi experiment. Parroting the Reich's rhetoric of corporal and racial unity, they claimed that Christ's body was composed of both confessions, and that its realization on earth required joint support for authoritarian politics. Such ideas, circulating in theological journals and best-selling booklets, facilitated new political experiments. Across the continent, confessional restrictions on social and political life were loosened and at times replaced by interconfessional organizations. Anti-fascist Christians, in response, also began to talk in interconfessional terms. They, too, claimed that Christ's body included both Catholics and Protestants but insisted that it transcended nations and races, forming a spiritual bond that was best served by a pluralist environment. For all their profound disagreement, the two sides of this debate shared the task of revising centuries of theology and dislodging entrenched anti-Catholic and anti-Protestant stereotypes. To do so, members of both churches reinterpreted sacred texts, coined new terms, and composed bold historical narratives.

Despite the conceptual innovations it entailed, ecumenism also carried the imprint of previous decades. In particular, theology and political theory were not the only manifestations of change. The economic order, sexuality and gender relations, and the missionary world, which had dominated Christian thought since the 1880s, inspired endless debates between sympathizers and opponents of the Third Reich about how old ideas should be updated and applied. In the process, these thinkers and church members forged new ways to envision Catholic-Protestant cooperation.

By far the most vibrant space for interconfessional thinking was social theory. Alarmed by the Great Depression, Christian economists and social theorists concluded that their previous efforts to foster harmony between workers and employers were clearly not enough in the new conditions. In an effort to update their anti-materialism to the era's massive dislocation, they developed two competing visions, both with interconfessional implications. The first, propagated by Christians who sympathized with the radical right, claimed that harmony was best achieved through authoritarian power. In this telling, Catholics and Protestants were to work together to help dictatorial state institutions radically intervene in economic life, even if that meant diminishing autonomy and space for Christian organizations. The pro-Nazi Lutheran economist Georg Wünsch argued in 1937 that by sponsoring public works and tightly regulating labor, the state could bring about "the fusion" of the two confessions into a unified "community of Christ," fulfilling mutual aspirations.[2] The second and competing vision, developed in response by opponents of fascism, insisted that anti-materialist harmony was best achieved through pluralist structures. It privileged civil society, voluntary organizations, and competitive economic relations as the basis for Christian grace.[3] Yet for all their disagreements with their opponents, the theorists and economists who articulated this pluralist vision all insisted on ecumenism. French Jesuit Yves Congar, one of Catholicism's most influential anti-fascist thinkers, exclaimed in 1937 that the two confessions were spiritual "brethren" in a struggle against the fascist "heresy."[4]

Similar dynamics characterized the two confessions' thinking on matters of gender and sexuality. There, too, Catholics and Protestants developed two competing interconfessional visions, both of which promised to continue the decades-long quest to protect "natural" heterosexual families while updating it for a new political era. The first camp, still concerned with the specter of feminism and sex reforms, believed the two confessions to be allies in the struggle to increase procreation within heterosexual family structures. Speaking in terms that overlapped with fascist discourses, its proponents claimed that the family should be premised on clear hierarchies between the sexes and on racially healthy children. The second camp was equally familialist and heteronormative, but worried much more about Nazi racism. Condemning Hitler's biological fixation as materialism devoid of spirituality, this camp's main proponents focused on conjugal love as the center of human intimacy. In their minds, Catholic and Protestant teachings were rooted not in natalism but in familial love. In a drastic revision of earlier Christian theories, they claimed that sexual pleasure inside marriage was legitimate and desirable even if it did not lead to procreation. Both of these groups drew on earlier discourses but also introduced new concepts and emphases to Christian family ethics. And while their focus on Catholic-Protestant similarities was less pronounced than was the case among social theorists, their intentional break with older stereotypes was crucial; in their writings, earlier confessional warnings about celibate priests or Protestant divorce were firmly rejected as misleading.

Finally, the upheavals of the 1930s also altered missionary thought, especially the missions' decades-long investment in the civilizing mission. The Nazis openly criticized the Christian missions, whose efforts at conversion and "uplifting" non-Europeans they considered inimical to racial determinism. Equally alarming to missionary elites, anti-colonialists in Asia also launched an intellectual campaign against Europeans' claim to set a universal culture to which all had to aspire. As they sought to respond to these critiques, Catholics and Protestants found both new divisions and convergences. One group, which included thinkers of both confessions, claimed that missionary work could happily coexist with racial and cultural segregation. Some went so far as to claim that this was its purpose: to enable each race and nation to worship God in its own distinct way. The other group, which also emerged in both confessions, condemned racism as a heresy. Like their opponents, however, its key thinkers insisted on differences: rather than impose European norms on the world, the missions' task was to help each nation to celebrate its own indigenous traditions (though in a Christian key). During this period these subtle adaptations to the civilizing mission did not yet lead to interconfessional cooperation, and missionaries expressed far less interest in ecumenism than did theologians, social theorists, or family experts. After World War II, however, these theoretical changes would become the basis for unprecedented and institutional collaboration.

The era of war, chaos, and genocide, then, had contradictory impacts on Christian life. On the one hand, it opened cleavages in Christian thinking. As cascading crises and radical political movements seemed to usher in a new era, Christian elites were torn by fierce debates about their role in the future. On the other hand, the 1930s and 1940s helped inspire reconciliation with old confessional enemies. Across multiple axes, writers began to argue that Christian participation in the modern world required Catholic and Protestant cooperation, which would realize the confessions' spiritual brotherhood. To be sure, like most revolutionary projects, Catholic-Protestant reconciliation was never uncontroversial, and confessional animosities did not disappear.[5] Ecumenism was also uneven: its key strength resided in Germany, Austria, France, Belgium, the Netherlands, and Switzerland. In those countries, Christian elites all lived under the Reich's hegemony (or in the case of Switzerland, in a center of anti-Nazi emigration). They responded to a similar set of concerns and, through exchanges and translations, borrowed from each other's interconfessional innovations. This contrasted with dynamics in Southern Europe, especially in Italy, Portugal, and Spain, where most Catholic leaders and clergy remained committed to confessional supremacy and continued to discriminate against Protestants. It also distinguished Central and Western Europe from Scandinavia, where anti-Catholic laws similarly persisted. Perhaps most importantly, visions of reconciliation at this time remained largely restricted to the sphere of ideas. Only in a few cases did Catholics and Protestants found mutual organizations. Still, where ecumenism did take root, change was considerable. For many Christians it offered an increasingly popular strategy to navigate a bewildering new world, and that strategy would have far-reaching consequences after the war.

The Pretext: Christian Anti-Communism and Nazi Ecumenism

The first shockwaves that helped remake confessional relations came from the Soviet Union. The Bolsheviks always considered Christianity a primitive remnant of unenlightened oppression and believed that its replacement with "scientific" atheism was essential for the future. Upon coming to power, they stripped the Orthodox Church of its privileges; transferred the administration of family law, burials, and education to secular state authorities; and founded the League of the Godless, which propagated atheism in conferences and exhibitions. In 1928, however, the Soviet anti-Christian campaign entered a radical new phase. As part of an ambitious five-year plan, launched to modernize the country's economy, Joseph Stalin and his followers sought to mold their subjects' minds, creating a "modern" and rational outlook by aggressively attacking Christian institutions, rituals, and beliefs. Soviet authorities issued a flurry of restrictive measures, from prohibiting Christian education to disbanding church charities, and applied them even to groups such as small Protestant sects that had previously been shielded from state persecution. In a decade of anti-Christian terror, communist leaders shut down thousands of churches, arrested tens of thousands of believers, and murdered or exiled countless individuals who were branded "servants of religious cults."[6] What is more, communist parties across Europe seemed eager to emulate this growing militancy, buoyed by instructions from Moscow and homegrown self-confidence. German communists, for example, unleashed a campaign of anti-Christian propaganda in 1929, claiming that any cooperation with Christian parties, such as that by moderate socialists, was a tool of "social fascism."[7] The level of militancy varied from place to place, but anti-Christian rhetoric was clearly on the rise in France, Belgium, and the Netherlands. When a civil war broke out in Spain in 1936, anti-clericalism exploded in terrifying violence, as communists and anarchists burned down churches and brutally massacred thousands of clergy and nuns.[8]

This surge of communist belligerency, which surpassed anything Europe had witnessed since the French Revolution, deeply shook Catholic and Protestant communities. Confirming Christians' most extreme anti-socialist fears, anxieties about the coming flood of anti-religious violence now consumed Christian thought and politics. The Vatican, for example, abandoned earlier efforts to negotiate a treaty with the Soviet Union and made anti-communist mobilization the center of its activities. In 1932 it founded the Jesuit Secretariat on Atheism in Rome, which organized exhibitions and charity events on the anti-Christian evils of communism; and in the widely advertised encyclical *Divini redemptoris* (1937), it condemned communism as "a satanic scourge."[9] Catholics elsewhere hardly needed the Vatican's encouragement as they launched anti-communist efforts. When German Catholic politicians and activists met for annual congresses in 1930 and 1931, speaker after speaker warned of "communist barbarism," leading to the founding of the Committee for the Struggle against Bolshevism to coordinate anti-communist research, publications, and exhibitions.[10] In France, the Catholic youth organization J.O.C. descended on working-class neighborhoods in an effort to stem the tide of worker radicalization. And the influential writers Robert Brasillach and Henri Massis issued a gushing report on the war in Spain, *The Cadets of Alcazar* (1936), which equated the struggle against communism with Christianity's epic battle with Islam (a comparison that was widespread in Christian writings, reflecting persistent ties between perceived enemies in Europe and overseas).[11] Responding to a growing wave of workers' strikes and demonstrations, Belgian and Dutch Catholic newspapers similarly reported on shocking outbursts of communist violence. As one Belgian leaflet exclaimed in 1932, "Communism threatens to overwhelm our countries [and] crush all civilization under its claws. Catholics ... eyes open. The hand on the sword!"[12]

Anti-communism was equally animating for Protestants. It powered liberals and evangelicals, who made it the centerpiece of their work, both separately and together. When Germany's Protestant association gathered for a large conference in Nuremberg in 1930, bringing liberals and evangelicals together, the organizing theme was the Christian response to Stalin's five-year plan. After lengthy presentations on communist atrocities, churches around the country launched charity drives for Soviet Christians, organized multiple anti-communist demonstrations, and published a flurry of booklets and pamphlets—many written by anti-Bolshevik Russian exiles—about the "the Bolshevik poison."[13] Deepening anti-communist sentiments also engulfed evangelical Protestants in the Netherlands, whose politicians and labor leaders spent the 1930s running on anti-communist tickets. Under the leadership of Hendrikus Colijn, the Anti-Revolutionary Party, the country's largest evangelical organization, scaled up its attack on communism's "godless" creed.[14] The international organization Life and Work, which was founded in 1925 to coordinate the cooperation of all major Protestant charities, churches, and parties, issued an urgent call in 1930 to combat communism. Even the International Union of Religious Socialists, which sought to redirect Protestant churches away from their anti-socialist agenda, felt compelled to voice anti-communist sentiments. In 1930 it ruefully announced: "We now know that the spirit of Bolshevism is [a] spirit of hate and contempt against all that smacks of religion and especially Christianity."[15]

Elevated Christian fears were an important impetus for Catholic-Protestant reconciliation. The social upheavals unleashed by the Great Depression were so extreme, and the prospects of imminent communist revolution so alarming, that many in both confessions scrambled to find new allies. Indeed, in 1930, when the General Council of the German Protestant Congress discussed the need for special prayers against Bolshevism, its members claimed that such prayers should also include Catholics, since the "current emergency" engulfed "all of Christendom."[16] In 1932, leaders of Catholic and Protestant youth organizations and charities gathered at a conference to discuss how to cooperate to effectively reach disaffected workers.[17] Still, as in previous decades, anti-socialism alone often failed to overcome ingrained hostilities. The two confessions, after all, had long recognized their mutual contempt for socialist organizations, which had not automatically translated to broader reconciliation. Some writers, in fact, continued to trace the communist misfortune to the other confession, recycling old stereotypes. The French

Catholic Hilaire Belloc, for example, in his popular anti-communist *Crisis of Civilization* (1935), claimed that the Soviet Union was the heir to Luther's idolatry and arrogance. Meanwhile, some Protestant polemicists continued to occasionally equate "Rome and Moscow" as twin enemies.[18]

Along with anti-communism, the second and more important force that powered ecumenism's birth was the rise of Nazism. In their formative 1920s and early 1930s, the Nazis routinely presented themselves as the churches' natural ally. While some leaders, such as the Nazi Party's unofficial philosopher Alfred Rosenberg, were openly anti-Christian, Hitler and others insisted that the party's ideas aligned them with Christian morality and traditions. This insistence went beyond the movement's employment of Christian concepts, such as the promise to bring about the "Thousand-Year Kingdom," or even their virulent anti-communism. The Nazis also echoed key tropes of Christian anti-materialist social theory. Nazi publications and speeches insisted that the movement would forge a new order beyond capitalism and socialism, whereby workers and the middle classes would live in harmony and realize their spiritual unity. Similarly, the Nazi approach to gender and sexuality resonated with many Christians' sensibilities. In the early 1930s, Nazi leaders such as Josef Goebbels insisted that their mission was to "restore" traditional gender and family order, in which men dominated work and politics while women oversaw child-rearing. As the years progressed, the Nazis began to lose interest in highlighting those similarities. They instead moved to criticizing some elements of Christian teachings, especially opposition to premarital sex, which the Nazis believed undermined their goal of increasing "Aryan" birth rates. But for several years the Nazis insisted that their economic, cultural, sexual, and racial project would realize the churches' mission. As Hitler put it in 1930, Christians should embrace the swastika as a "political sign that will unite the people who stand on the foundation of a non-Marxist, non-materialist . . . deeply idealistic worldview."[19]

The Nazis, however, did not merely parrot Christian ideas. They also sought to transform them with a revolutionary ecumenical framework, proclaiming an end to Catholic-Protestant conflict. Since its earliest days the Nazi movement had aimed to bridge the confessional divide. Its 1919 founding manifesto, the so-called "25 Points," declared that Nazism would promote "positive Christianity," a term the Nazis coined to signify Catholic and Protestant brotherhood. Hitler cared deeply about bringing together the two confessions. During his movement's early phase he decried the confessional divide as one of Germany's greatest woes, ascribing to it a variety of national failures the Nazis pledged to remedy. Long passages in his rambling *Mein Kampf* (1925), for example, were devoted to condemning the Protestant-led "Away from Rome" movement, which at the turn of the twentieth century sought to promote national unity by converting Austrian Catholics to Lutheranism. By elevating religious confession above ethnic and biological solidarity, Hitler bemoaned, the movement only alienated worthy "Aryans" from national unification, "made the fight [for national unity] impossible . . . and robbed it of many of the nation's best elements." Equally fateful, the confessional divide led to territorial divisions that plagued the German nation. After all, it was the key explanation for Catholic-majority Austria—Hitler's country of origin—remaining outside the Protestant-majority German state, a wrong the Nazis vowed to correct. The Nazis also blamed the confessional divide for Germany's tragic failure to construct a large and stable empire. In a major 1932 speech in Düsseldorf, Hitler mused that Christianity provided the spiritual "precondition of our people," by which he meant the ideological principle to sustain a military force. But "the shattering of this worldview" during the Reformation "meant a retreat of the entire German energy to the insides," hampering its capacity to capture necessary colonial possessions. In preparing for a new imperialist war, then, which the Nazis believed was inevitable, it was crucial for Protestants and Catholics to abandon their mutual animosities.[20]

In particular, the Nazis argued that confessional peace was integral to the mission of forging a unified and pure racial body. While preaching extreme biological determinism and attributing all human traits to an individual's racial composition, the Nazis also insisted on the importance of mental disposition. In their minds, it was not enough that one was born "Aryan"; it was also crucial to actively *think* about one's life as fulfillment of the race's collective destiny. For this reason, confessional divisions, like other historical tensions between classes or regions, appeared to the Nazis as a tragic source of racial weakness. By distracting "Aryans" from their joint fate, the confessional conflict had enabled the penetration of "foreign" races and ideas. In Hitler's telling, this was what made movements such as Away from Rome so dangerous. By directing their wrath at Catholics, instead of socialists and Jews, these activists left the German race "completely divided."[21] For Nazi leaders, it was crucial that Christians reimagined their beliefs in ways that emphasized solidarity with all members of the racial community. As Hitler announced in a major 1928 speech, "We are a people of different faiths, but we are one, [and] which faith conquers the other is not the question; rather, the question is whether Christianity stands or falls . . . we are filled with a desire for Catholics and Protestants to discover one another in the deep distress of our own people."[22]

While conflating religious and racial concepts was nothing new in European thought and politics, the notion of "positive Christianity" broke new ground. By defining the two denominations as equal members in forging broader national unity, the Nazis rejected any notion of confessional superiority, which for so long permeated both Catholic and Protestant thinking. This conceptual innovation, which was part of the Nazis' broader claim that racial unity should eclipse all regional and social divisions, was reinforced by the Nazi movement's demographics, especially the prominence of nominal Catholics—most notably, Hitler—among its leaders. For these figures in particular, racial ecumenism provided a path for national integration, overcoming earlier equations of German nationalism with Protestantism. Most importantly, "positive Christianity" demarcated the stark fault lines between Germany's Christian majority and its Jewish minority, which the Nazis always believed stood behind the Bolshevik menace. In many ways, this understanding of Christianity was the foil to the concept of "Judeo-Bolshevism," which the Nazis endlessly utilized to define their enemies at home and abroad. Both fused religion, race, and political ideology into a unified whole.[23] Even though the Nazis, after a few years in power, relinquished their hopes of creating a unified German church, this early desire to transcend confessional divisions was real, endlessly declared in speeches and publications. It was part of the Nazi mission to replace diversity with racial conformity and unity.

Theologies and Politics of Unity: With and against Fascism

During the Nazi movement's early years, when it struggled to gain traction with voters, most Catholics and Protestants ignored Nazi musings on religion. But once the Depression and war propelled the Nazis to power in Germany and later much of Europe, Christian elites felt compelled to respond. Unlike communist militancy, which was met with universal condemnation, the Third Reich had a polarizing impact on Christian thought. On one side stood those sympathetic to the Nazi experiment, believing that it would realize Christian social visions or provide a tactical shield against communism. While perhaps grumbling about certain policies imposed by the Nazis and their client states, such as restrictions on Christian autonomy in education or the liberalization of divorce, they did not question the Reich's legitimacy. In their eyes, this was the best Christians could realistically hope for. This was the case with Pope Pius XI, for example, who initiated cooperation with the Nazis in 1933. Hitler, as Pius put it to the ambassador from France, was far from perfect, but he was "an ally against Bolshevism."[24] In the other camp was the minority that viewed the Nazis' racism as a pagan heresy. For its members, reducing human life to its biological components, which precluded the possibility of conversion, was as materialist as communism. Catholics and Protestants who took this view often insisted that fascism and communism were twin versions of the same "totalitarian" menace. They launched anti-Nazi publications, founded anti-Nazi associations, and at times joined the armed resistance. But what theologians and political theorists in both camps shared was a growing tendency to emphasize the need for Catholic-Protestant reconciliation. Revising old ideas about confessional distinctions, they claimed that the new body politic included all Christians as equals. Both projects were also radically bigger and more ambitious than previous calls for reconciliation. Unlike the short-lived meetings between theologians that took place in Germany in the 1920s, the competing drives for ecumenism were sustained, included large initiatives, and unfolded in multiple countries.

Supporters of Nazism were the first to articulate a vision of ecumenism. Among Catholics, an emblematic figure was the young theologian Robert Grosche, who in a series of influential writings in the 1930s sought to explain why the movement and the Church were in full alignment. According to Grosche's work, which he named the "theology of the Reich," the Nazis' vision of a dictatorial state and nationalist unity realized the Church's belief in "natural" order and hierarchy. Both Nazis and Catholics, he wrote, recognized that parliamentarism fostered endless strife and pitted social groups against each other; both confessions were thus allies in the quest to dismantle it. In Grosche's telling, Nazis and Catholics also shared a desire to organize Germany as a "sacred space," where all associations and institutions, from schools to youth movements, served a unified spiritual purpose. Both groups recognized that salvation was not restricted to the individual; instead, divine grace was a collective endeavor, toward which the entire race worked. One's relationship to divinity, in other words, was mediated through one's "community of blood." To capture the purported overlap between Nazism and Catholicism, Grosche claimed that the Church should be understood as the "Mystical Body of Christ," a concept that gained popularity with some writers in the 1920s to describe the laity's centrality to Christian communities. Just like the "Aryan" body that the Nazis vowed to protect, the term signified some Catholics' understanding that they were cells in a community, both spiritual and biological.[25]

For Grosche, however, this corporal and spiritual unity required more of Catholics than embracing the Nazi project. It also demanded a new approach to Protestants. In his telling, Catholics had to recognize they were not alone in the quest to achieve collective salvation. Their success hinged on engagement with Protestants, who shared the same claim to spirituality. Indeed, Protestants were not heretics in need of conversion, as Catholic dogma had long claimed. Rather, they were brethren who possessed the Church's most important values. They, too, were guided by divine grace and viewed authoritarian unity as the basis for political order. They were as committed as Catholics to the "sacred space" where spirit and politics merged. As Grosche put it in his *The Pilgrim Church* (1938), "We must remember that we all stand in the same place: the world of the Christian believers." Grosche struggled to explain why this similarity evaded thinkers and believers for centuries, but he nevertheless broke with previous Catholic theology to claim that the "Mystical Body of Christ," which earlier writers invoked to describe Catholicism, also included Protestants. Because they shared a similar racial destiny, the two confessions constituted one unified entity.[26]

Grosche's theological phrasing may have been abstract, but his ideas were not obscure. Similar efforts soon caught fire among Catholics who sought reconciliation with both Nazis and Protestants. The theologian Damasus Winzen, for example, at a 1933 conference of Catholic thinkers and politicians in the Maria Laach Abbey, declared that Nazism's rise demanded "a new and tighter cooperation between the churches." The "awakened longing of both German Protestants and Catholics for the Reich," he mused, "should compel all the nation's spiritual leaders toward mutual effort." These sentiments led Winzen to join Grosche in launching the journal *Catholica,* the first Catholic publication dedicated to ecumenism. In its pages some of Germany's leading Nazi-sympathizers explored Protestant texts and highlighted their similarities to Catholic thinking.[27] The Austrian bishop Alois Hudal, who published some of the most prominent efforts to square Catholic teachings with Nazi dogma, also envisioned an ecumenical future. In his book *The German Volk and the Christian West* (1935), he lamented the "wounds" of confessional divide and announced that "he who ... eliminates the religious division, would render the greatest service ... to the German race and Europe's entire cultural leadership." National and racial unity, he explained, could only be achieved "if the division of Christendom in Europe is overcome."[28] The influential theologian Karl Adam, who came out in support of Nazi racism and claimed that divine grace worked differently for each racial group, similarly embraced ecumenism. While his 1920s publications had decried Protestants as agents of anarchy, his 1930s works proclaimed that they in fact lived "a true, devout and Christian life," since they "believe in Jesus and [are] baptized in his name."[29]

Similar talk of confessional unity began to take off among German Protestants. While some pro-Nazi figures continued to view Catholics with reservations, others echoed Grosche's message of spiritual-corporal unity. This was the case with the young Lutheran thinker and educator Alfred Dedo Müller, whose writings enjoyed brief but considerable popularity in the Protestant press in the 1930s. In a series of weekly editorials in the journal *Christianity and Life,* appearing throughout 1933 and 1934, Müller praised the Nazi revolution for its "restoration" of "natural" focus on racist principles. In his booklet *The Struggle for the Reich* (1935), which republished his most popular columns, he argued that "in contrast to earlier revolutions, which were powered by the spirit of the Enlightenment," Hitler's revolution "started from the rediscovery of ancient truths, such as blood and soil."[30] As was the case with Grosche, Müller's enthusiasm also inspired a new approach to Catholicism. A reconciliation between the confessions, he argued, was a necessary condition for establishing a stable and strong post-secular order. To make his case, Müller published the tome *Ethics* (1937), where he aimed to chart similarities between Protestant and Nazi political theory, but also included lengthy explorations of Catholic writings. Both churches and the Reich, Müller explained, shared the belief that social harmony could only be achieved in strong authoritarian states, and the precondition for such states was national unity and racial purity. Like Grosche, Müller invoked the image of Christ's body to describe the two confessions' unity, whereby both relinquished their claim to spiritual monopoly. "No church is the Gospel by itself," he explained at his book's conclusion; the time had come "for a radical overcoming of confessionalism."[31]

Like previous efforts to update Christian teachings, these writings were defined by tension between novelty and claims to having uncovered timeless truths. Protestant writers who echoed Müller's ideas simultaneously praised the Nazis for revolutionizing confessional relations and recognizing doctrinal similarities that long preceded them. The Lutheran theologian Johannes Lortzing, for example, whose early writings celebrated the triumph of the Protestant "spirit of modernity" over "medieval Catholicism," declared after the Nazi victory that doctrinal divisions between the churches, such as the language of the Christian mass, were in fact superficial. What truly mattered, he wrote in *The Unity of Belief* (1934), was the two confessions' overlapping, centuries-old quest for national renewal, which made them complementary parts in Christ's body.[32] The Berlin pastor Hermann Sauer, in his much-discussed *Western Decision* (1938), similarly claimed that the two confessions' old adherence to order was united through a joint commitment to the Third Reich. They were called to realize their solidarity through a war against international communism, which Sauer believed imminent, and which he, like many writers, compared to the historical fight against Islam.[33] These works were not isolated cases, but reflected a growing sentiment among Protestant theoreticians. In 1936 a group of prominent liberal and evangelical theologians called in an open letter for replacing the country's Catholic and Protestant theological faculties with "confession-less" ones (though this plan did not materialize).[34]

One difficulty of this intellectual endeavor was to explain how it squared with four centuries of deep animosities. If doctrinal differences were so marginal, why did it take so long to overcome them? The most prominent Catholic figure to begin revising historical narratives was the historian Joseph Lortz. As late as 1929 Lortz still published fiery anti-Protestant texts, but his enthusiasm for the Nazis led him to rethink his stance.[35] In a series of widely read and translated books, especially the monumental *History of the Church* (1936) and *The History of the Reformation in Germany* (1938), Lortz offered a sympathetic view of Luther and the movement he helped inspire. According to Lortz, early Protestants were not the perverse heretics Catholics had long decried. They were devout and well-meaning Christians whose critique of the Vatican's corruption was in many ways justified. The medieval Church, Lortz lamented, had in fact lost its authority long before Luther arrived. Torn by internal rivalries and competition with emerging nation states, it no longer provided comprehensive spiritual guidance for European life. To Lortz, the Reformation was not a break with Catholic belief in authority but an effort to rejuvenate it. Catholics and Protestants were therefore allies in a historical quest to achieve political stability. The two churches and communities had to engage with each other, a cause Lortz sought to support into the 1940s with ecumenical pamphlets and guides for mutual discussion.[36] Protestants, not far behind, produced their equivalent narratives. The politician and author August Winnig, for example, claimed that Europe's superiority in the modern era, from its technological innovations to colonial might, was the product of cooperation between Christian confessions. The divisions between them, he wrote in *Europe* (1938), which sold almost 100,000 copies, paled in comparison to their similarities; even during the wars of religion they all lived "under the sign of the cross." While Winnig quibbled with the Nazis' insistence on the distinct nature of "Aryans," which he feared could undermine cooperation with other Europeans, the geopolitical implications he drew from history were closely aligned with the Reich's diplomacy. Germany's mission, he explained, was to realize Catholic-Protestant cooperation by establishing a pancontinental empire that would defeat Judaism, the United States, and the Soviet Union.[37]

Though Germany was the site of the most intense interconfessional discourse, it was not the only place where such sentiments emerged. The speed and ferocity of the Nazi revolution, its brutal crushing of both socialists and communists, and its capacity to quickly transform Germany into a superpower, made its interconfessional message resonate across Europe. In Austria, for example, several thinkers began to imagine a new political order in which the two confessions would come together under a strong authoritarian state. The influential editor and thinker Joseph Eberle, who in the 1920s had routinely lambasted Protestants and mused on the reestablishment of Catholicism as state religion, warmed to Protestants as allies in the 1930s. In the pages of his magazine *Beautiful Future,* the leading periodical of the radical right, Catholics such as journalist Friedrich Muckermann and Protestants such as theologian Johannes Lortzing called for confessional unity in the struggle against communism.[38] Vienna's former politician and archbishop, Theodor Innitzer, an advisor to and supporter of Austrian chancellor Engelbert Dollfuss, similarly became interested in anti-socialist interconfessionalism. In 1933 he joined Lutheran charity specialist Ewald Ammende in creating the Interconfessional and International Relief Committee for the Russian Famine Areas. Under Ammende's directorship, the committee organized exhibits and publications on Soviet horrors, including Ammende's popular *Must Russia Starve?* (1933), a lurid account of hunger and violence.[39] The group's most vocal member was the Catholic philosopher Hans Eible, a professor at the University of Vienna and a major figure in Austrian conservatism, who explained in his best-selling *The Meaning of the Present* (1933) that the Nazis' triumph spelled the coming of a pan-continental Christian dictatorship across Europe. Under the Nazi flag, he mused, "members of both confessions, resolutely and enthusiastically, will together fight against Bolshevik atheism."[40]

While the racial tone of German-speaking ecumenists held little appeal in the French-speaking world (Nazi racial theory had little respect for "Latin" people), the message of interconfessional alliance began to circulate among French-speaking Christians. As France experienced growing communist militancy in the 1930s, military defeat in 1940, and participation in the Nazi-led alliance against the Soviet Union after 1941, many replaced their hopes for confessional dominance with visions of cooperation. In 1934 the nationalist Catholic theologian Paul Couturier published an essay in the journal *Apologetic Review* about the shared values of the two confessions. The divisions between them, he claimed, were not spiritual but "psychological," based on outdated stereotypes that should be discarded in favor of dialogue. This message was warmly welcomed by Protestant pastors Berthold Zwicky and Richard Bäumlin, who joined Couturier in founding a forum for interconfessional discussion in the monastery La Trappe des Dombes, outside Lyon. Together they also helped popularize a week of joint prayers for unity, to which Catholics and Protestants soon flocked.[41] Protestant pastor and ultranationalist writer Noël Vesper proclaimed in works such as *The Invention of Europe* (1932) that the two confessions had to join hands in the destruction of the republic and its replacement with authoritarian structures. In the pages of the magazine *Sully,* which Vesper helped edit, writers of both confessions mused about their shared commitment to order.[42]

Such sentiments were not confined to the world of letters. They had a corollary in politics, where radical nationalists began to abandon their adherence to confessionalism. In Belgium, for example, the semi-fascist Rexist party, which began as a Catholic organization, abandoned its close ties to the Catholic establishment. In an effort to overthrow the country's parliamentary system, its leader, Léon Degrelle, forged an alliance with Protestants.[43] The Rexist movement remained small, but a more successful experiment took place in France, where the semi-fascist Cross of Fire party declared its intention to replace the secular republic with Christian authoritarianism. It, too, departed from the radical right's earlier conflations of nationalism with Catholicism; its publications routinely trumpeted the party's openness to Protestants, and in the manifesto *Public Service* (1934) its leader, François de la Rocque, mused about the need for a broad, nonconfessional "spiritual tradition."[44] This reframing of the nation's spiritual essence proved politically auspicious. After it was reorganized as the French Social Party to avoid the state's ban on armed militias, membership swelled to more than one million, by far the country's largest party.[45]

The link between authoritarianism and ecumenism became even more pronounced under the Vichy regime, which sought collaboration with "Protestant" Germany. Few represented this more clearly than the Catholic essayist Henri Massis, one of the radical right's most prominent thinkers. His landmark *Defense of the West* (1927), translated and reviewed by Catholics across Europe, condemned Luther for breaking Catholicism's notions of stability and hierarchy, and claimed that only by returning to Catholicism could Europe overcome the chaos of German Protestantism and Soviet Marxism. Yet once Vichy—where he served as a senior functionary—joined the Nazi-led alliance, Massis rethought this genealogy. In lectures he delivered in occupied France, which were published as *The Discovery of Russia* (1944), he claimed that Catholicism and Protestantism were united in their fight against Bolshevik barbarity.[46] This spirit led Massis and other Catholic thinkers to collaborate with Protestant nationalists, including René Gillouin, in the founding of a pan-Christian academy in Uriage, where they hoped to train France's next elite with authoritarian, hierarchical, and anti-secularist curricula.[47] Vichy's leadership echoed these ideas when it insisted that Christianity be restored to public education and that cultural life was interconfessional. Vichy's leader, Philippe Pétain, appointed Protestants to important positions (the head of the Protestant association was a member of the Vichy national council), ordered youth movements to admit both Catholics and Protestants, and replaced narrow Catholic curricula with broader programs on Christian civilization.[48] Even though anti-Protestant sentiments remained strong among some of the regime's Catholic supporters, Pétain was determined to demonstrate the confessional capaciousness of his authoritarian nationalism, which he extended (rhetorically) to the empire's Muslim subjects. As he declared in 1940, "I do not differentiate among the French; Catholics, Protestants, and Muslims are all my children."[49]

There was a glaring omission in Pétain's declaration: he did not mention France's Jews. This was a trademark of authoritarian ecumenism: its pluralism was limited to Christians (Pétain's inclusion of Muslims was an outlier), and it smoothly coexisted with anti-Semitism. Many advocates of Catholic-Protestant reconciliation conflated Jews with materialist capitalism and socialism. The Catholic historian and ecumenist Albert Mirgeler, for example, peppered his writings with anti-Semitic tirades. In the pages of *Catholica,* he asserted that Christianity's divide opened the dangerous path to Jewish emancipation, and thus to Europe's "decomposition" into materialism and nihilism.[50] Less crass but no less toxic was ecumenical theologian Karl Adam, who insisted that God's grace could not touch Jews. As he explained in 1933, Jews were "racially foreign and will remain racially foreign. It will never be possible to integrate the Jew into the Aryan race."[51] Protestants were equally prone to represent Jews as the adversaries of their new spiritual community. Müller's ecumenical *Ethics,* for example, decried the Jews' lack of "connection to the soil," which he claimed fostered a lack of productivity and spirituality.[52] And Vesper dedicated entire issues of *Sully* to anti-Semitic invectives.[53] As far as authoritarian ecumenism was concerned, reconciliation was not a step toward broader pluralism. Its goal was to solidify and deepen exclusion.

But racism, authoritarianism, and anti-Semitism were not the only sources of ecumenism. In the 1930s the notion of bringing together the confessions also resonated in small circles that bristled at the conduct of the Nazis and their allies, and that sought to adapt Christian social teachings in a more pluralist direction. Even though thinkers in this camp usually did not find fault in the Nazis' virulent anti-socialism (which their writings rarely mentioned), they worried that efforts to bring synergy between Christianity and fascism deformed the churches. Members of these circles were especially distressed at the Nazis' disregard for Christian autonomy in education and their meddling in internal church affairs, both of which became glaringly obvious in the late 1930s when the regime lost patience with Christian organizations. Despite these differences, however, this anti-fascist camp was equally committed to interconfessional language. Mirroring its opponents, many of these thinkers began to claim that a true Christian order against fascism could only be achieved through Catholic-Protestant reconciliation. There was considerable irony in this formulation. It reproduced the intellectual innovation of the very movement it sought to counter. Yet for anti-fascist writers, this seemed like the most effective path to capture the era's theological innovation. They sought to appropriate the corporal concepts used by Grosche and other Nazi sympathizers and turn them against fascism.

The most intellectually comprehensive version of anti-authoritarian ecumenism emerged in France. It was heavily influenced by the philosopher Jacques Maritain, whose magisterial *Integral Humanism* (1936) called on Catholics to engage with other groups as equals to build a pluralist and anti-statist order.[54] While Maritain himself was not particularly focused on engagement with Protestantism, some of his allies were. The key to resisting Nazi-inspired talk of a unified body, they believed, was to counter it with an alternative form of ecumenism. This was the case with Yves Congar, one of the twentieth century's most innovative theologians, whose *Divided Christendom* (1937) was widely translated and reviewed in Europe. Like Maritain (with whom he associated), Congar opposed the calls of authoritarian Christians to mobilize the state against Christianity's enemies. Instead he envisioned Christian life as based on voluntary interactions between social communities. Jesus, he reasoned, could have easily forced humanity to embrace him, but instead he left it to believers to come to him on their own initiative. Congar also condemned any conflation between Christ's body and nationalist political projects. In his eyes, Christ's body included all nations and races, and those who sought to appropriate Christianity for narrow political projects were seeking to "divide Christ [himself]."[55]

Even though this pluralist vision of Christ was aimed at countering the works of authoritarians such as Grosche, Congar emulated their focus on Protestants. The fact that Protestants resided beyond the Church's visible borders, he claimed, did not mean that they were heretics; they were baptized believers who shared God's grace. As he rhetorically asked, was a Protestant not "believing, truly consecrated to God and living a holy life, more a member of the Church than a baptized Catholic who is slack and sinful?"[56] For Congar, the differences between the churches, which manifested in different rituals, laws, and traditions, were an expression of Christ's act of sacrifice in the crucifixion. "The Church," he explained, "is the Body of Christ *crucified*," a broken corpus, which meant it had to accept its inner diversity as divine.[57] Congar warned that it was gravely urgent to accept this denominational friendship in order to resist the rise of Nazi "totalitarianism" and its many Christian epigones. "It is becoming no longer a question of confessional differences within Christendom itself," he ominously wrote, "but a radical choice between the Kingdom of God and the reign of anti-Christ."[58]

Growing worries about the strength of authoritarian ecumenism helped popularize these ideas. In the late 1930s Congar began to organize a series of meetings between Catholic and Protestant figures. Maritain, the philosopher Gabriel Marcel, and other anti-authoritarian writers and thinkers discussed how to form "a Christian front" against modern dictatorships.[59] The coming of Vichy expanded this vision. Protestant pastor Roger Schutz, for example, one of Congar's associates, sought to create a new interconfessional community. In 1940 he established a monastery in the town of Taizé, France, where members (half Catholic and half Protestant) developed shared prayers and liturgy.[60] The following year a group of Catholic theologians led by Pierre Chaillet and Henri de Lubac launched the clandestine anti-Vichy journal *Christian Witness*, publishing anti-Nazi texts by Catholic and Protestant figures side by side.[61] Perhaps more politically consequential, such ideas helped legitimize cooperation between Catholics and Protestants in the French Resistance, especially in the Free France movement in exile. Catholics such as the journalist Maurice Schumann and the Protestant ethnologist Jacques Soustelle worked together to write anti-Vichy propaganda, analyze intelligence, and correspond with British government officials. Charles de Gaulle, who was raised in an ardently anti-Protestant Catholic milieu (in his youth, he sympathized with calls to ban Protestants from public service), followed this path by equating anti-fascism with interconfessionalism. In a 1942 speech, de Gaulle called on the people of France to "gather together either in your [Catholic] churches or [Protestant] temples" to offer up "your prayers and your thoughts to France."[62]

Even though Nazi brutality made it dangerous to express dissent, similar ideas emerged in Germany. Alarmed by what they saw as the Christian surrender to racism, several thinkers, like Congar, sought to respond with an alternative form of ecumenism. Among Catholics, its earliest prominent expression came from Arnold Rademacher, a professor of apologetics (and briefly university rector) from Bonn. Alarmed by the Third Reich's increasing encroachment on organized Christianity, Rademacher warned about the incompatibility of the "total state" and Christian life. The Catholic Church, he wrote in 1937, could flourish only when its members could freely engage with each other in autonomous organizations, which they could not do under the Reich's watchful eye. What is more, Rademacher claimed that Christian solidarity could not be confined to the borders of the nation. Alongside their local loyalties, Catholics belonged to an international community spanning nations and continents. "The greatest calamity," he wrote, would be for ecumenisms' "new forms of belief" to become a vehicle for "political or racist ideas."[63] Yet for

The Birth of Ecumenism from the Crucible of Nazism

Rademacher, Christian resistance to authoritarianism could not come from Catholics alone. In a series of four short books, the most important of which was *The Reunification of the Christian Churches* (1937), he called for a new peace with Protestants, who shared Catholics' "positive principle of life." This conception, Rademacher explained, went beyond mutual anti-socialism. Even more important, both communities believed in voluntary charity, advocated for human dignity, and understood that small communities (such as families and towns) should be protected from state supervision. They were, in short, equally resistant to the Nazi fixation with racial purity and political control.[64]

Although Rademacher died unexpectedly in 1939, his ideas continued to resonate with other Catholic Germans who disliked the regime's growing incursion into Christian autonomy. Their most important leader was Max Metzger, a prominent social activist and writer who in the 1920s led a campaign by Catholic charities against worker poverty and alcoholism. An ardent nationalist, Metzger initially expressed sympathies for the Reich, praising its 1933 "winter campaign" to provide food and clothing to the poor. Soon, however, he came to view as blasphemous their biological fixations and violence. As Metzger sought to mobilize believers against the regime, he followed Rademacher, maintaining that a spiritual anti-Nazi front would have to be interconfessional. Writing in essays and booklets such as *The Sky in Us* (1938), Metzger argued that Catholics and Protestants shared a belief in spiritual autonomy, which required limits on state authority and its management of social relations. These ideas inspired the Una Sancta Brotherhood, an organization founded by Metzger in 1938 to foster discussions between laypeople and charity workers of both confessions. Spreading to Marburg, Frankfurt, Heidelberg, Stuttgart, Munich, and Leipzig, its goal was to show, as Metzger put it, that the "one side's thinking on fundamentals is not essentially different from the other side's." Such activities proved subversive enough in the regime's eyes. In 1943, after the government intercepted an anti-Nazi letter he sent to Protestant clergy, Metzger was arrested by the Gestapo and eventually executed.[65]

Ecumenism soon also became important for Protestant opponents of the Nazis. Through cooperation with Catholics, they hoped to offer an alternative model to religion's racialization. The most forceful spokesperson for this effort was Wilhelm Stählin, a Lutheran and the former director of the country's Protestant youth movement and future bishop of Oldenburg. While Stählin shared much of the Nazis' nationalism and anti-socialism (some of his 1920s writings also occasionally trafficked in anti-Semitism), their crude biologism struck him as profoundly un-Christian, especially because it precluded the possibility of conversion. In a speech on the eve of Hitler's appointment as chancellor, Stählin declared that a racist "secular conception of the state" reduced humans to their biological aspects and was thus as materialist as socialism, an opinion that led him to openly oppose the regime's effort to take over Protestant institutions.[66] The Nazis' triumph led Stählin to raise his skepticism about the regime to an interconfessional register. In works such as *The Church and God's Word* (1937), he sought to capture the language of Nazi sympathizers to declare both Catholics and Protestants equal participants in the "Mystical Body of Christ." This body, he claimed, was not realized through submission to political dictatorship. It was instead a decisively spiritual unity, premised on the autonomy of believers and their communities against the state. For Stählin, the protection of this autonomy bound the confessions, and required Protestants to abandon their earlier hostility to Catholics. The time had come, he proclaimed, for Protestants to treat Luther's anti-Catholic tirades as temporary political statements that were not inherent to his dogma, and to view all Christian brothers as "appointed for the service and help of one another."[67] In fact, Protestants were advised to return to their Catholic roots and adopt the celebration of the saints (long a source of anti-Catholic disdain) or parts of the Catholic liturgy. To further such understanding, Stählin helped organize several large conferences for Catholic and Protestant thinkers and church leaders to discuss similarities between their understandings of grace and prayer. He also helped a group of Protestant writers, headed by Karl Bernhard Ritter, to design *The Order of the German Mass* (1936), a blueprint for interconfessional mass (which incorporated Catholic and Protestant liturgy), as well as a joint calendar and Bible-reading plan.[68]

Despite the anti-Nazi bent of this ecumenism, it was rarely extended to Jews. To be sure, the Nazis' biological determinism, with its rejection of conversion, led some thinkers to question extreme anti-Semitism. The Catholic Austrian Johannes Österreicher gathered a group of anti-Nazi writers who published a manifesto against the depiction of Jews as an unredeemed race. The Swiss anti-Nazi theologian Emil Brunner similarly responded to the Nazis' anti-miscegenation laws by dismissing their racial logic as "nonsense." These works, however, remained rooted in supersessionist and even anti-Semitic logic, in which Jewish suffering was divinely ordained until their conversion. Brunner, for example, blamed

Jewish persecution on their "stubborn" nationalist pride, which he contrasted with Christian supranational solidarity. Alongside others, Brunner continued to assert that there were profound differences between Jews and Christians, and he never talked about a shared, "Judeo-Christian" heritage.[69] More importantly, these efforts to question racist anti-Semitism did not overlap with the formation of Catholic-Protestant anti-Nazism. Led by different figures, the two projects were explored in different publications. Indeed, neither the Catholics Rademacher and Congar nor the Protestant Stählin said much about anti-Semitism. Anti-fascist ecumenism, in short, was not a product of a broad "opening" of Christian horizons. It was a concrete project, confined to engagement between Christians.

The Nazi revolution, then, sparked intellectual innovation in confessional thinking, albeit indirectly. Among its supporters and opponents, a new language emerged that described Catholics and Protestants as brethren. Unlike in previous decades, these calls for cooperation reflected more than strategic and temporary measures against mutual enemies. Theologians and politicians also talked about equal membership in the same community, epitomized by Christ's very body. Ecumenism, however, did not remain confined to the sphere of theology and politics. As the Protestant August Winnig explained in his reflections on European affairs, interconfessional unity "under the cross" could be realized only "when the modern economy granted workers their natural dignity."[70] Indeed, as was the case since the nineteenth century, Catholics and Protestants' thinking about each other was deeply shaped by the "social question." And there, too, the 1930s and 1940s were a period of intense divisions, intellectual innovations, and new, interconfessional alliances.

Economic Theory and Interconfessional Thinking

Since the movement's inception, Nazi plans for the economy echoed Christian social visions. Like Catholic and Protestant theorists since the nineteenth century, the Nazis mused about a "third way" between capitalism and socialism, promising to create a new social order in which both workers and employers prospered and solidarity reigned between the classes. As they did in other areas, the Nazis moved swiftly to deliver on these promises, smashing labor unions and leftist parties. They followed this by establishing "corporatism," a system developed in fascist Italy, where decisions once left to the markets, such as production and wages, were now decided by state-run bodies that included both employers and workers. The Nazi regime also promised to transcend class divisions through the expansion of racialized welfare programs (a feature that at first distinguished it from the Italian model). Nazi leaders initiated bold public works programs, payments to young families, and charity for the destitute. To be sure, for all the fanfare that surrounded these experiments, they did little to foster interclass harmony and mostly functioned as tools to suppress labor activism and control industrial production. Economic inequality remained largely unchanged: whatever gains workers made in the early years of the regime, World War II erased them as war production and shortages led to austerity and poverty. Nevertheless, corporatism became the model for the radical right across Europe, which promised to bring about new solidarity. Collaborationist regimes in Belgium and France, for example, both established "social committees" of workers and employers.[71]

Although the principles of corporatism might have sounded familiar to Christian ears, they sparked intense disagreements among Catholic and Protestant social thinkers. This economic policy entailed the unprecedented expansion of state power, often at the expense of Christian charities, labor unions, and youth groups, which were weakened or disbanded. For many Christian theorists who sympathized with the radical right, the price was well worth paying to achieve social harmony and "natural" inequality. As the German Catholic philosopher Josef Pieper wrote in 1934, "the National Socialist state's social-political drives" realized "the core of the Christian social ethic."[72] Anti-fascist Christians, on the other hand, warned that corporatism destroyed workers' and employers' ability to voluntarily reach the desired inter-class harmony. In their eyes, state overreach was bound to diminish labor's dignity, undermine the sanctity of private property, and ultimately morph into socialism. While thinkers in this camp did not deny that the state played an important role in economic relations—the devastation of the Great Depression made this conviction a near consensus in Europe—they claimed it had to be restricted. The state's main function was to secure labor autonomy, such as the right to unionize, and economic competition. And yet both sides shared an openness to interconfessional discourse. Drawing on the era's theological innovation, some thinkers in both camps claimed that a just and stable economy would realize both Catholic and Protestant principles, and could be realized only through their cooperation. In depth and scope, such framing went far beyond the calls for cooperation against socialism in the nineteenth century. For the first time, a considerable body of texts invoked a joint, pan-Christian social order.

In some ways, corporatism required especially far-reaching changes for Catholics. Since the nineteenth century, Catholics were hesitant about state involvement in economic affairs, and most key proclamations, such as the encyclical *Rerum novarum* (1891), warned that the state's economic meddling might lead to tyranny. In the 1930s, however, worries about an imminent communist revolution overran these concerns, and commentators across Europe claimed that corporatism was a necessary measure on a depression-stricken continent. An important reference for this claim was Pius XI's encyclical *Quadragesimo anno* (1931), the Vatican's main commentary on economic matters, which claimed that state authorities had an obligation to impose social harmony. The defeat of capitalism and socialism, Pius claimed, should follow the model set by fascist Italy (the only country explicitly mentioned in the text), where "the State brings private ownership into harmony with the needs of the common good."[73] Many Catholic economists and social leaders followed the Pope's lead, celebrating efforts to establish state-led solutions. In Germany, the editor and labor leader Theodor Brauer argued that autonomous social organizations, such as Catholic labor unions, had to give way to a vocational system such as state-founded syndicates. As he explained in *The Catholic in the New Reich* (1933), in which he defended the Third Reich, these syndicates would allow workers and employers to create "an organic structure," a term that echoed Nazi discourse on racial solidarity and that led him to join the Nazi Labor Front, the national workers' organization that replaced labor unions.[74] French Catholics updated their economic theory along these lines. In his *Capitalism and the Community of Labor* (1938), the Catholic economist François Perroux called on the state to impose economic peace through syndicates, an ideal he later sought to implement when he helped draft Vichy's labor laws.[75] The Belgian Jean Denis followed a similar path, declaring the Third Reich the only available model for Christians. In 1936 he wrote corporatism into the formal platform of the semi-fascist Rexist party.[76]

Corporatism was also popular with some Protestants. Whether their background lay in liberal or evangelical affiliations, many theorists were pushed by the specter of communist revolution to view state control as a necessary tool for social harmony. The economist Alfred Müller-Armack, for example, in 1932 praised Italian fascism for erecting an economic system based on "discipline and method." Once the Nazis came to power, he gushed in his *State Conception and Economic Order in the New Reich* (1933) that their plans to form syndicates under state control realized a "third way" between individualism and collectivism.[77] The German welfare expert Hans Scherpner concurred, drawing on the authoritarian theories of jurist Carl Schmitt to claim that squabbling by interest groups was unfit for addressing the unprecedented crisis of the 1930s. Only a strong and centralized state such as the Third Reich, he explained in his *Welfare and Politics* (1933), could defend workers' dignity while protecting employers' private property.[78] The Evangelical Social Congress, the country's main Protestant forum on social matters, dedicated several of its annual meetings to Nazi economic policies. One speaker after another explained that the regime's welfare policies and employment program realized the Gospel call for charity.[79] In France, the Protestant and nationalist René Gillouin, who served as Pétain's close advisor and was considered one of the Vichy regime's chief ideologues, similarly envisioned the state as the source of social harmony between workers and employers. As he claimed in the essay collection *France 41: The Constructive National Revolution* (1941), Vichy, as a truly Christian regime, sought to be "national, authoritarian, hierarchical, and social."[80]

While corporatism ultimately did not fulfill the high hopes that many Christians invested in it and failed to convince workers of the significance of social harmony, it had important consequences for inter-Christian relations. This was in part because it convinced many theoreticians of the need for state intervention, a major source of disagreement in earlier decades, as Catholic and Protestant supporters of corporatism began to view each other as allies. Some even went so far as to speak of an ecumenical social theory. This was the case with the theologian Otto Schilling, one of Germany's most famous Catholic thinkers and a cofounder of the Cross and Eagle Association, which sought to reconcile Catholicism and the Third Reich. In the 1920s Schilling insisted on the profound dissimilarities between Catholic and Protestant social teachings. Catholics sought social harmony between classes, he wrote in *The Christian Social Teachings* (1926), whereas Protestants possessed an individualist focus on material prosperity.[81] By the 1930s, however, when Schilling accepted the logic of state intervention, he also described a homology between the two confessions' social visions. The two confessions, he explained in his book *In Defense of Catholic Morality* (1936), shared the conviction that engaging in one's line of work and supporting one's children were a divine calling. They understood that in the modern economy, only the state could guarantee fulfillment of this teaching.[82] Other commentators expressed similar sentiments. In *The Hour of Christianity: A German Reflection* (1936), a popular essay collection that brought together writers of both confessions to reflect on current events, several Catholic contributors agreed that the two confessions shared similar social ethics, and thus had to work together for the success of corporatism.[83]

Protestants also noticed and celebrated this convergence. Going beyond long-held anti-socialist impulses, they claimed that the two confessions shared a positive vision of a harmonious, inter-class peace under the state's protection. Few figures represented this shift more clearly than Georg Wünsch, an influential economic and social theoretician. Typical for thinkers of his liberal milieu, Wünsch had spent the 1920s warning against state involvement in the economy. This led him to criticize not only Marxists, whose materialist worldview he predictably rejected, but also Catholics, who he worried would support the socialists. Long passages from his lengthy *Evangelical Economic Ethics* (1927) warned that the Vatican's proclamations on social matters were too state-friendly (a claim that required a highly selective reading of the Pope's words) and were unfit to face the dynamic competition of the modern economy, which he, like many others, traced to Protestantism.[84] Yet by the time Wünsch published his pro-Nazi tome *Evangelical Political Ethics* (1936), which reflected his reactions to the events of the 1930s, it was not only his anti-statist ideas that fell by the wayside. His anti-Catholicism had also disappeared, replaced by an extensive exploration of similarities between the two confessions' love of work, private property, and communal solidarity. In fact, the book concluded with a rousing call to join the Nazi quest to build interconfessional solidarity through bold economic distribution, especially public works, and expansive welfare for workers. "The fusion of the confessions into the community of Christ may still be a long way off," Wünsch wrote, but its coming could be accelerated by recognizing shared economic visions and working together to realize them under the Nazi flag.[85] The pro-Nazi theologian Müller similarly pointed to the Vatican's statements on social affairs to celebrate the alliance of the two confessions in forging social harmony.[86] And Johannes Beckmann, a welfare leader in the large charity Inner Mission, explained that the fault line in the "intense struggle" over social work no longer passed between the confessions but "between the Christian confessions and [the] irreligious, antiecclesiastical worldviews" of Marxists.[87]

There were considerable intellectual gymnastics involved in explaining why right-wing economic policies were less dangerous than the dreadful statism of Marxists. State officials regulating relations between workers and employers, welfarist state programs, the squeezing of confessional charities: Was that not the socialist hell that Christian polemics had warned about for decades? Indeed, for all their promises to protect private property and "natural" inequalities, the similarities between corporatism under Hitler or Pétain and the planned economy under Stalin seemed meaningful enough that several writers felt compelled to address them. Wünsch, for example, conceded that the differences between Nazi economic policies and the Soviets' five-year plan could seem marginal at first glance. But the two programs were premised on profoundly different ideological intentions: whereas the communists sought to distribute wealth because they viewed materialist considerations as the only important aspect of human life, the Nazis aimed to establish new spiritual solidarities among the community's Christian members. For the Nazis, money and benefits were merely tools to achieve the larger goal of infusing social life with new spiritual meaning. Others, like the Protestant historian and Nazi enthusiast Rudolf Craemer, employed the same tortured reasoning. In works such as *Evangelical Reformation as Political Power* (1933) and *The Struggle for National Order* (1933), Craemer mused that the economic experiment in Germany might seem like socialism but should receive the churches' support because it was based on a "spiritual" rather than materialist ideology.[88] From these commentators' perspective, corporatism was first and foremost a psychological project. Through the state, the people would finally adopt the mental dispositions that Christian social teachings had long expounded.

Yet not all Christians were taken by corporatism. Among those who opposed the Nazis and their collaborators, a competing economic vision emerged that envisioned interconfessional cooperation *against* the radical expansion of state authority. Hostility to corporatist experiments was especially common among reform-oriented Catholics and veterans of Christian labor unions, who had long believed that social harmony was best served by autonomous workers' organizations. In their minds, Hitler's dismantling of Catholic unions and subsuming them into state-led organizations was akin to communism, where all social and economic communities were relegated to state control. This was the opinion of anti-Nazi German writer and politician Nikolaus Gross. The Third Reich's promise of social harmony, he wrote in the journal of the Catholic labor movement, was a façade for total control.[89] Similar ideas were expressed by Austrian politician and writer Ernst Karl Winter, who between 1934 and 1936 published several calls for the empowerment of workers (such as protecting their right to unionize) and even opposition to the persecution of socialists.[90] In France, too, the journals of the Catholic youth movement and the Catholic labor unions spent the 1930s criticizing corporatism as dangerous overreach that did not align with Catholicism's insistence on autonomy (the Vatican's open support for Mussolini's corporations was either glossed over or explained as a tactical necessity). When in 1941 Pétain announced his intention to implement corporatism in France, figures such as labor leader Georges Torcq protested that corporatism was incompatible with the right of workers to choose their social organizations.[91]

Protestant anti-fascists were usually not as focused on organized labor, but they, too, developed a less statist response to the economic crisis. Its main articulators were a group of economists who later became known as the ordo-liberals, named after the journal they launched in Freiburg in 1936, at first titled *Order of the Economy* and later renamed *Ordo*. Drawing heavily on Protestant social theory, writers from this group claimed that a harmonious society required autonomous and self-sufficient communities in which hierarchies between workers and employers were accepted by all. Because such harmony could be sustained only by Christianity, Europe's secularization had led to social disintegration, the manifestations of which included the rise of heartless capitalism and oppressive communism. As Walter Eucken, one of the school's leaders, put it in 1932, both capitalism and socialism were ersatz religions that sought to replace the moral vacuum left by Christianity's decline.[92] Unlike more statist Protestant thinkers, however, ordo-liberals claimed that it was not capitalism as such that threatened interclass solidarity, but its deformation into massive cartels and oligopolies, which in turn fostered the exploitation of workers and the spread of socialist ideas. If those large entities could be broken up, and the principle of economic competition was preserved, workers could support themselves and engage with others in dignity, and a Christian society could once again flourish. Economist Wilhelm Röpke, ordo-liberalism's most influential figure, claimed that overcoming socialism would not be achieved by way of authoritarian corporatism or large-scale welfare programs, which he condemned as eerily close to its left-wing enemy. In his *The Doctrine of Economics* (1937) and his best-selling and widely translated *The Social Crisis of Our Time* (1941), Röpke claimed that state power should be limited to securing the conditions of competition, such as anti-monopoly laws and temporary worker-retraining programs.[93] These ideas did not necessarily entail support for democracy, but they did put ordo-liberals on a collision course with the Nazis. Eucken joined a resistance group in Freiburg, and Röpke went into exile (in Turkey and later in Switzerland), from which he harshly criticized the Third Reich and its allies.[94]

Like their authoritarian-minded counterparts, anti-Nazis recognized their similarities. As the 1930s progressed, and especially after the beginning of World War II, Catholics and Protestants in these circles began to cite each other's work to engage with ecumenical pluralism that was both anti-socialist and anti-corporatist. The young Catholic economist Joseph Höffner, for example, who after the war would become an influential theorist and the archbishop of Cologne, wrote a dissertation on ethics and monopolies under Walter Eucken's supervision. In it, he claimed that the Catholic moral law was in line with market competition, as well as with the Protestant focus on private property (a claim that would help him become a crucial figure in shaping postwar Germany's welfare policies).[95] Protestants in the ordo-liberal school replaced their traditional references to Luther and Calvin as the originators of free and modern economics with broader talk of "Christian" economic teachings. Röpke increasingly cited Catholic writers in support of his ideas in the 1930s, and in *Civitas Humana* (1944) he went so far as to proclaim that his anti-monopolist and anti-corporatist vision was in line with the Vatican's *Quadraesimo anno*. In his own essays, the ordo-liberal economist Eucken also abandoned his conflation of liberalism, socialism, and "Jesuitism," by which he had meant the premodern guild system. In the 1930s and 1940s, Eucken juxtaposed "Christian" support for competition and limited welfare with communist statism and Nazi corporatism.[96]

The Nazis' experiment in corporatist economics, in short, created both new divisions and new alliances in Christian thought. Social theorists and economists could not agree on how to update their anti-socialism to the realities of the 1930s and debated the state's role in taming workers. At the same time, many now envisioned their response to materialism in an interconfessional key: only the overcoming of confessional animosities could position Christians to achieve the long-term goal of constructing a harmonious social order premised on economic peace and class inequality. Yet as in previous decades, the replacement of materialism with hierarchical social harmony was not merely an economic matter. Christian commentators never tired of noting that it was also a gendered and sexual issue: stability and prosperity required men and women to follow the "proper" rules endowed to them by God. This was why the economist Röpke repeatedly beat the drum that the economy's collapse into tragic chaos was partly the product of society's "sexualization." The rise of feminism and sex reforms, he reasoned, radically accelerated Christianity's decline, which was responsible for modernity's political and economic evils.[97] Historians of Christian economic thought have often overlooked these statements, assuming they were offhand tangential remarks. But sexuality remained as central as ever for Christian social theory and a crucial space for shaping emerging ecumenist sensibilities.

Fascist Sexuality and the Christian Divide

At first it seemed as though the Nazis and their allies would fulfill every task that Christians had set out since the nineteenth century. The dictatorships of the 1930s and early 1940s, like confessional writers and politicians before them, inverted feminist discourse by claiming that women's "true" emancipation lay in their mission as mothers. As Hitler put it in a 1936 speech to the National Socialist Women's League, "I am often told: you want to drive women out of the professions. Not at all. I wish only to create the broadest measure of possibility for her to cofound her own family and to be able to have children."[98] Such statements were followed by anti-feminist measures more radical than anything Christian politicians had been able to deliver. In the Third Reich, Vichy France, and elsewhere, the regime offered funds to women who withdrew from the workforce, curtailed women's work in public service, and restricted access to abortion.[99] Similarly in line with the morality campaigns of earlier decades, Hitler, Pétain, and others utilized state power to combat sexual conduct that they deemed unconducive to heterosexual reproduction. Aggressively expanding on the precedent set by Catholic and Protestant organizations, they launched campaigns against homosexuals, prostitutes, and contraceptives, which they blamed on Judaism and socialism. As time passed, however, the Nazis' fixation on racial reproduction occasionally conflicted with long-held Christian convictions. They increasingly showed disregard for marriage by encouraging premarital sex. This was especially true during the war, when even the pretense of protecting chastity was subordinated to military efforts. Across Europe, the Third Reich and its allies reversed course on prostitution and established a vast system of state-managed brothels.[100]

Confronting these radical measures, Christian thinkers updated their thinking about gender and sexuality, sometimes in surprising ways. As with theology and social theory, Christians were deeply divided regarding how to rethink gender and sexuality, and they developed two conflicting visions. The first group, anxious about feminism and sex reformers, praised the radical right's actions as the salvation of the family. Influenced by the rising tide of racism, proponents of this vision also described their celebration of family and reproduction in the language of eugenics, collective health, and heredity. Thinkers in the second group, however, were alarmed by what they viewed as Nazi-led debasement of the family. While they remained committed to heteronormativity and marriage, they claimed that treating reproduction as a collective enterprise reduced both women and men to their biological functions, and thus emptied marriage of its sacred nature; it was no different from Bolshevik materialism (which allegedly replaced families with promiscuity). Anti-fascist Christians therefore began to argue that the family was measured not only by its capacity to reproduce, but also by its ability to provide self-realization and even sexual pleasure to both men and women, a claim that radically broke with previous warnings about carnal desires. While these debates were largely confined within the confessions, they provided new spaces for engagement between them. Echoing developments in theology and social theory, theorists of gender and sexuality began to abandon their insistence on the profound differences between Catholic and Protestant family ethics. At this stage, explicit talk of ecumenism was not yet as prevalent among family writers as it was among economists and social theorists. But the new sensibility could be detected by the disappearance of old tropes about Catholic or Protestant deviancy, which in magazines and marriage guides were now replaced by notions of joint "Christian" teachings.

The person who best represented both the continuities and the shifts among Catholic sympathizers of the radical right was Jacques Leclercq, an influential Belgian sociologist from Louvain and the editor of the journal *The Christian City*. Like Christian writers in earlier generations, Leclercq lambasted feminists' focus on work and legal equality as an "unnatural" distraction from women's mission as mothers. Only giving birth and raising children, he explained in *The Family* (1933), which appeared in several languages and editions, could endow a woman's life with meaning. A childless life "lacks something essential, at once an element of balance and stimulus."[101] Parenthood was in fact so important that its maintenance had to overshadow material considerations. Parents had the duty to have as many children as possible, which Leclercq assumed would require women to stay at home to focus on child-rearing while men remained the main breadwinners. In a similar recycling of earlier tropes, Leclercq endowed families with social significance, claiming that only parents had the natural drive to transfer their own culture and values to their children. This was why the family was the key to "social stability, the stability of ideas and of civilization."[102] For Leclercq, it was therefore obvious that society had a duty to repress the temptations that could incite desires beyond the family unit. Pornography, prostitution, and homosexuality were all expressions of decadence, which inevitably led "to sex anarchy and to the destruction of the family."[103]

These formulations regurgitated well-worn Christian tropes, but Leclercq also adjusted them to the landscape of the 1930s. He argued that for the Christian family to survive, Catholics had to facilitate a further expansion of state power: not only to repress "decadent" sexuality but also to actively increase procreation. In Leclercq's telling, the Great Depression forced many Christians to limit their family size, whereas socialist workers, because of their materialist atheism, continued to procreate (a fact he noted with a potent mix of fear and envy). There was therefore no time to wait for confessional charities to fix the problem: only large-scale intervention could reverse Europe's bleak fortunes. One way to do so was for Catholics to support the establishment and expansion of "family allowances," whereby states provided to married couples with children fixed sums to alleviate financial distress. "Among the causes of a decline in births [is] the material weight of family burdens," Leclercq reasoned, and it was incumbent on the state to alleviate this pressure.[104] Even more important, Catholics had to overcome any hesitancy about eugenics and recognize its positive potential for Europe's birth rates. Parents were to emphasize physical activity, nutrition, and outdoor play for their children to improve the future generation's capacity for work and a chaste life. As Leclercq noted in admiration, all these measures had reached their full potential in Nazi Germany. The Third Reich implemented generous family allowances, compensated women who left the workforce, and promised to regulate the masses' racial health. While Leclercq had qualms with the regime's campaign of forced sterilization, which he considered too aggressive, he still found most of its other measures inspiring.

Nazi Germany, he concluded, was the "most interesting attempt of its kind to raise the birth rate. It is also the only experiment that has yielded tangible results."[105]

This adaptation of Catholic family teachings was common in the mid-1930s. As they cheered the Nazis and their allies' campaigns against feminism and sex reforms, Catholic writers increasingly claimed that their family ethics benefited collective health. An important reference was *Casti connubii* (1930), Pope Pius XI's encyclical on marriage, which reminded believers that women's "true emancipation" required staying at home and raising as many children as possible. Mostly remembered today for its opposition to forced sterilization, the encyclical in fact called for expanding state intervention in procreation. It encouraged state financial support for working parents and considered it permissible for states to restrict unions between "undesirable" people.[106] Writers in Central and Western Europe seamlessly invoked it for their purposes. The German Catholic scientist and family expert Hermann Muckermann, for example, praised Nazi racial policies as the realization of Catholic sexual ethics. In his popular *Eugenics and Catholicism* (1934), which quickly sold thousands of copies, he explained that "it would be surprising" if Catholics "did not progressively assimilate the scientific results of eugenic research" into their ethics, such as avoiding marriages with converts from Judaism.[107] In France, too, Catholic scientist Alexis Carrel claimed in his best-selling *Man, the Unknown* (1935) that the family and the social order it enabled required aggressive racial regulation, including the killing of criminals and the "criminally insane" (the book's German translation included praise for the Third Reich's policies).[108] Lay Catholic organizations, which mobilized in support of anti-feminist and natalist policies, also emphasized their support for eugenics. The Catholic German Women's Association, for example, explained in its publications the need for physical and racial hygiene. And in Vichy France, Carrel and other prominent Catholics joined the influential French Foundation for the Study of Human Problems, the think tank that helped craft the regime's decrees on health and hygiene requirements for marriage.[109]

The effort to update their teachings was also noticeable among Protestants. Some warmed to the belief that the state should complement anti-feminist and anti-sex reform measures with financial and eugenicist policies to encourage "healthy" procreation. A representative figure in this effort was Wilhelm Stapel, one of Germany's most prominent Protestant writers and the editor of the conservative magazine *German Nation-*

hood. Like many in his political universe, Stapel had long insisted that monogamous patriarchal marriage was the center of "civilized" society. Throughout the 1920s he complained about its alleged decline, which he blamed on materialist feminism, sex reformers, and socialists. Like Leclercq, the Great Depression convinced Stapel that the family required new forms of protection. In 1932 he argued that the state had to shore up fathers' authority by launching public works for men and providing financial assistance for mothers so that they could stay home. In parallel with Catholics, Stapel's rhetoric progressively acquired more racist undertones. The family, he wrote, undergirded "superior nations' way of life" and distinguished "life's biological aristocracy" from inferior races, which in this telling, diluted their strength with polygamy and prostitution.[110] Not surprisingly, these concerns led Stapel to become one of Germany's most vocal supporters of Protestant cooperation with the Nazis. Both Hitler and Luther's followers, he gushed, shared a vision of paternal authority presiding over a racially healthy family. In his popular pro-Nazi *Christ's Church and Hitler's State* (1933), which ran through multiple editions, Stapel even claimed that the Reich's political theory was premised on Christian family ethics. Jesus's crucifixion, in this telling, in which God's own son submitted to the father's extreme demands, was meant to instill in children a similar capacity for self-denial and obedience. The Nazis extended this logic to political relations: they invested in the Führer total parental authority, so he could guide his subjects/children slowly into maturity. For Stapel, then, the family provided both spiritual and racial health. It was the key to the church's contribution to the "biological-political community."[111]

Stapel may have been extreme in his conflation of Christian and Nazi family politics, but his enthusiasm for state support and eugenics was not unusual. Though some Protestant thinkers, especially of evangelical background, had been interested in eugenics in earlier decades, the Great Depression substantially popularized these ideas: for many thinkers, politicians, and charity officials, it seemed like the state had no choice but to limit the reproduction of workers, whom they considered atheistic and less worthy, while saving Christian families. Hans Harmsen, for example, a senior leader of the charity Inner Mission, began warning in 1930 that "the procreation of asocial, inferior elements" such as alcoholics (whom he assumed were not Christian) was beginning to surpass those of "socially valuable, productive families." The only cure, he reasoned, was for the state to regulate procreation. Under his guidance, Inner Mission established a eugenics section, which explored how Protestant communities could support racial health. Its marriage clinics, established in the late 1920s to compete with the socialists, began advising young couples to test their chances of transferring hereditary "deformities" before marriage.[112] The same trend could be found in Vichy France, where Protestants who supported the regime equated its hierarchical structures with the healthy family. René Gillouin, for example, claimed that during the Third Republic, the French nation was "ravaged by alcoholism, rotted by eroticism, eroded by a declining birth rate," but that the new authoritarian regime, with its emphasis on hygiene and public health, restored the "traditional family, founded on love and mutual respect and on moral discipline."[113]

To be sure, the overlap between the Christian and the radical right's visions of marriage and sexuality did not mean they were identical, and efforts to reconcile them were at times fraught. As the Third Reich accelerated its efforts to increase "racially healthy" procreation and began encouraging premarital sex, Christians worried about the fate of chastity. For all his vocal embrace of the Third Reich, for example, Stapel complained in 1935 that the regime went too far in its celebration of young bodies. By deemphasizing the significance of marriage for reproduction, it showed a "tendency toward nudism" (a claim that Nazi publications openly mocked as prudish).[114] Observers from other countries shared those mixed feelings. The Belgian Leclercq, even as he praised the Nazis, also wondered if their lack of interest in marriage might foster promiscuity.[115] The same was true in other collaborationist regimes, including Vichy France, where Christians grumbled about certain policies. Christian leaders were scandalized when the regime allowed children of unmarried fathers to claim some financial rights (a policy Pétain approved as a personal favor to his gardener), complained about its refusal to outlaw prostitution, and lambasted a wartime law that subjected French women to labor requirements as "a grave threat to family life."[116] But these worries remained secondary compared to the overarching panic over feminism and sex reformers. For most, the sexual policies of the new dictatorships were close enough, or at least preferable to the alternative. Most Christians adopted a strategy that some scholars dubbed "antagonistic cooperation:" complaining about certain policies while praising the radical right's natalist focus.[117]

Regardless of where they stood on particular population policies, similar intellectual and political developments in the confessions led some commentators to view each other as close allies. Building off and going beyond earlier instances of cooperation against feminists and sex reformers, some Christian writers claimed that Catholic and Protestant family ethics shared a positive vision where women and men happily accepted their different social roles and came together to produce clean, racially healthy children. A case in point was cooperation between Hermann Muckermann, the most prominent Catholic proponent of eugenics, and Protestant scientist and philosopher Bernhard Bavink, who in the 1930s published some of the most widely read efforts to reconcile Protestantism with eugenics.[118] Early in their careers, both Muckermann and Bavink assumed that the two confessions subscribed to different teachings on family, health, and procreation. The Great Depression, however, and especially the parallel turn to eugenics, changed their minds, leading them to co-organize a conference on racial hygiene and co-publish *Heredity and Hereditary Care* (1933). In their respective contributions, both Muckermann and Bavink drew on recent theological innovations in both confessions to claim that one's access to God's grace was mediated through one's nation and race. To live a Christian life therefore required care for hereditary qualities: to ensure that one's own body and offspring were nourished, healthy, and clean. Even more important, it required believers to go beyond their limited circles and protect their broad racial communities. Believers therefore had to support large-scale interventions, such as state subsidies for parents, the issuing of health certificates before marriage, and bans on sexual relations between "inferior" beings. As Bavink asked rhetorically, "Can someone who does not love his race ... love God," who divided humans into biologically dissimilar groups? Both Muckermann and Bavink clarified that their understanding of "Christian" was not confessional but included both Catholics and Protestants. The two churches, they explained, shared a quest to unify the spiritual and the material, to realize God's design in healthy families and nations.[119]

While Muckermann and Bavink were especially devoted to eugenics and confessional cooperation, they represented a new sensitive strain among some Christian experts on gender and sexuality. Accusations of sexual deviancy, which Catholic and Protestant writers directed at one another well into the 1920s, faded, and were supplanted by commentary on joint "Christian" sexual teachings that were premised on patriarchy and racial health. In *The Married Person* (1938), for example, a guide for young couples, the German Catholic Josef Becking talked about a joint Christian commitment to children's physical and spiritual health. Both confessions, he noted, recognized that healthy families were the basis for a strong collective nation.[120] Francophone writers occasionally spoke in this tone. The Belgian Leclercq, for example, noted in *The Family* that both Catholics and Protestants subscribed to the ideal of the patriarchal family. Whatever damage the original Reformers inflicted on marriage centuries ago, he reasoned, it was now clear that Protestants were participating in efforts to drive up birth rates (a claim that Leclercq supported by citing German statistics).[121] Protestant writers similarly began to praise Catholics, claiming that their divergence on clerical celibacy was marginal compared to their unity in patriarchal and healthy families. The prolific German family expert Theodor Haug, for example, used parts of his popular *In the Struggle for Purity and Maturity* (1930) to guide Protestant readers through papal texts on family and marriage. It is "clear," he noted with satisfaction, that such texts shared the Protestants' love for large and healthy families.[122] Even more emphatic was the theologian Alfred Dedo Müller, whose essays and booklets sought to illuminate similarities between Protestantism and Nazi eugenics (especially sterilization). In his *Ethics* (1937), Müller complemented this effort with an excavation of Catholic and Protestant commonalities when it came to family ethics. Both Catholics and Protestants, Müller reasoned, recognized that families were not independent units but cells in the social fabric. Both understood that "marriage is the form of life in which sex and eros become . . . the temple of God's spirit, and [in which] sexual and erotic community of life become the vessel of divine love." Indeed, Müller was so convinced of these shared teachings that he expected the Catholic Church to reverse its opposition to forced sterilization. Through racial science, he explained, God has shown that procreation was the greatest social responsibility, a value long shared by both confessions.[123]

And yet the patriarchal, racially healthy family was not the only principle around which Catholic and Protestant sexual ethics converged. Working in parallel, a group of thinkers in both confessions sought to formulate a conception of gender that envisioned women as able to realize themselves beyond motherhood. They also considerably revised early teachings on male and female sexuality, and began to claim that marriage and sex had legitimacy beyond procreation; rather than being the training grounds for self-control, they were sites of love and sensual pleasure. For writers in this camp, the overriding concern with collective health and birth rates risked reducing the Christian family to secular biologism. It subjected the family to the needs of non-Christian theories, and thus opened the door for promiscuity in a way that resembled socialist materialism. Christians therefore had to view marriage and sex as valuable in their own right, as an expression of divine grace. This anti-Nazi intellectual campaign was at first conducted in a confessional key, with Catholics and Protestants mostly speaking in their respective circles. But soon, like the proponents of eugenics, they began recognizing their similarities and embraced an interconfessional approach.

For some anti-fascist thinkers, the alliance between Christians and the radical right required a rethinking of the churches' intense anti-feminism. Against the image of patriarchal family and society, in which women were relegated to motherhood, they offered a different model, in which partners helped each other realize their individual potential. The influential French Catholic editor Emmanuel Mounier, for example, mocked those who reduced the family to its biological and social functions. They have "never understood anything about its miraculous but fragile fabric," he explained in his *Manifesto of Personalism* (1936), in which love, not race, was "the greatest educator." Mounier did subscribe to notions of chastity and traditional marriage, but he also conceded that they should be released from their patriarchal heritage. "Our social world is one that man has made for men," he explained, and to allow women to fulfill their potential "without imprisoning" them in motherhood was the task of the future.[124] Even more forceful was the anti-fascist Swiss Protestant theologian Emil Brunner, who in a series of writings in the 1930s sought to craft a new and more egalitarian conception of gender relations. "Christian marriage has been confused with the patriarchal attitude," he lamented in *The Command and the Orders* (1932), but this was the product of shifting historical conditions and had "no connection to Christian principles."[125] Brunner agreed with feminist writers that the division between the genders was not merely a natural expression of their innate qualities, but the product of oppression. Because men controlled public institutions and positions and power, he scoffed, they have "artificially riveted woman to her natural destiny, and [have] hindered the free development of her mind and spirit, to which she ... as one who has been made in the image of God, has been called."[126] While Brunner's ideas remained squarely in the confines of heteronormativity, describing same-sex relations and masturbation as perversions, his writings sought to transform the family into a site of *equal* self-realization. The "monogamous marriage," he exclaimed, was designed to allow partners to do "justice to the claims of personality."[127]

Such conceptual innovations, which broke with older support for the patriarchy, also lent themselves to a rethinking of human sexuality. Across the confessional divide, anti-fascist writers responded to the popularity of eugenics and racism by claiming that the purpose of the family, and of sex in particular, was not just procreation but also love and pleasure. The German priest Herbert Doms, for example, drew on earlier ideas developed by theologian Friedrich von Hildebrand to claim that reducing the sexual act to the purpose of procreation was to miss God's intentions.[128] If sexual desire was so much stronger and recurring than hunger or thirst, he reasoned in *The Meaning of Marriage* (1935), this was because its purpose was more than physical; in sexual desire, men and women recognized their unique spiritual essences and, through love, their divinity. Indeed, marriage was a spiritual union in which the couple recognized God's image in each other. Limiting sexual desire to an earthly purpose, such as national and racial health, tainted it with materialist considerations. Doms even provocatively claimed that God intended the ties between man and wife to be stronger than the ties to their offspring. "The bond which joins husband and wife and gives them the right to sexual intercourse," he mused, was "stronger, more lasting, and less easily dissolved than the bond between parents and children."[129] Other opponents of fascist eugenics took the same approach and insisted that the family's purpose was love and affection. *Marriage as Consecrated Life* (1936), Norbert Rocholl's popular layman's memoir about his own marriage, and Franz Zimmermann's *The Two Sexes and God's Intention* (1936) insisted on the supremacy of love and pleasure to procreation.[130]

Anti-fascist Protestants also updated their family ethics to deemphasize the significance of procreation. The purpose of marriage, they claimed, was not to practice self-control, as previous generations of Christian writers claimed, but to experience reciprocal love and pleasure. The Swiss Brunner, for example, condemned what he saw as widespread Christian contempt for erotic feelings and a perverse preoccupation with virginity. In his mind, suspicion of sexuality was the heritage of paganism, and its persistence in Christian circles was "a sign of a terrible anti-Christian inheritance" that "has wrought infinite harm and disaster." Indeed, the Bible demonstrated that the longing for sexual union was in itself pure. After all, Adam and Eve's becoming "one flesh" predated the fall; sexual desire was therefore not more sinful than any other human impulse.[131] The German writer Otto Piper followed suit, claiming that the meaning of sexual love was revealed not in procreation but in the emotional bond it signaled for the two partners. "The sexual impulse is not by itself a temptation of the Devil," he wrote in *The Meaning and Mystery of Sex* (1935), "but rather God uses it to arouse me to a sense of my vocation as a male or female. This call demands a response." Piper added that Christian couples should resist the pressure to become a reproductive factory in the service of "external" forces such as nations and races. The goal of "true marriage" was the creation of "genuine fellowship and complete mutuality," in which men and women were equal in their drive for self-realization (the veiled critique of Nazism was thin, and Piper soon fled into exile).[132] The most popular version of this claim came from the French-Swiss Protestant essayist Denis de Rougemont, whose blockbuster *Love in the Western World* (1937) enjoyed multiple editions in all major European languages. In Rougemont's telling, Europe was a battleground between the Christian family, on the one hand, and communism and Nazi eugenics, on the other. Like heretics in older times, these two regimes sought to channel their subjects' libidos away from the family and toward themselves. The result of these perverse experiments, Rougemont prophesied, could therefore only be social anarchy and war.[133]

One appeal of this focus on pleasure was that it provided a response to the Nazis' vocal claims that Christian ethics were prudish and "unnatural." It also helped explain why Christians who sought to align their natalism with racist causes were in fact betraying the Gospel. For both these reasons, understanding the family as the expression, rather than the taming, of passion gained considerable traction with lay psychologists and sex experts, who sought to popularize anti-fascist sex ethics. The German-Swiss Protestant marriage counselor Theodor Bovet, for example, disparaged writers such as Haug for contrasting Christian love with the erotic drive. Love and eros, he wrote in *Need and Love in Marriage* (1939), citing Brunner and Piper, were deeply intertwined: "It is not only children that are created by the husband and wife by the act of love. The fellowship of marriage is also created by the husband and wife becoming one flesh." To help readers realize this union, Bovet included detailed instructions for increasing pleasure, such as prolonged foreplay and experimenting with new positions. Striving toward orgasm, he claimed, was a problem only outside of the marriage union, as in masturbation or same-sex intercourse; between husband and wife, it was bliss.[134] Bovet was followed by the French-Swiss physician and psychologist Paul Tournier, whose blend of medical and pastoral advice enjoyed a mass readership in multiple languages. Tournier's *The Healing of Persons* (1940) proclaimed that "when God directs the sex life of a married couple, they can practice it divinely," by which he meant transcending the goal of procreation and achieving a "full mutual communion that is carnal, moral, and spiritual all at once."[135]

The significance of these developments for confessional relations would not fully manifest until after World War II, when many of these figures joined the ecumenical project. Yet even in the 1930s and early 1940s, this new conception of marriage helped some articulate a new sense of respect between Catholics and Protestants. The Catholic German writer Matthias Laros, for example, who called on the Church to rethink its focus on procreation, added that Catholics and Protestants shared a similar understanding of marriage. In *Modern Marriage Questions* (1936), a guidebook for young couples, Laros noted that all Christians believed in the centrality of love between men and women. What is more, both confessions recognized that the sexual drive had a function beyond begetting children. While procreation was certainly important, it was also meant to serve as an expression of affection. Laros, who came to view the Nazis as agents of sexual chaos, drew on this conviction as he elevated ecumenical cooperation as the key to Christianity's future. During the 1930s he began editing and publishing the work of ecumenical writers, emerging as a leading figure in the Una Sancta movement, the anti-Nazi organization that encouraged interconfessional dialogue.[136]

Among Protestant anti-fascists, the most indicative example was the German writer Stählin, whose thinking about religion and confessionalism was deeply intertwined with his conception of family and sexuality. In the 1920s Stählin believed in an unbridgeable divide between Catholics and Protestants' visions of sexuality. As late as 1929, in an essay commissioned by the German Evangelical Church for the collection *The Struggle for Marriage,* he recycled stereotypes about contradictory sexual ethics: Protestants believed in family, but Catholics still subscribed to perverse celibacy and viewed procreation as marginal, rather than central, to family life. Stählin lamented mixed marriages between Catholics and Protestants as a symptom of spiritual decline, which he attributed to young people's growing spiritual indifference and alienation from spiritual communities. Pointing approvingly to racial segregation laws around the world, he wondered whether bonding across one's community lines was an unnatural violation of the divine order.[137] Alarmed by the Nazis' biopolitical stances, however, Stählin changed his mind and adopted a new understanding of marriage. Rather than a factory for "begetting and birth," it was a unique spiritual experience, the purpose of which was to lift individuals away from "the chain of an earthly race-connection" and into a new sphere of existence. Stählin followed anti-fascist family theorists in claiming that conjugality was the ultimate expression of divine love. Its purpose was the empowerment of man and woman through the "mystery of our sexual disposition."[138]

This change of heart had important consequences for Stählin's understanding of confessional relations. Long passages of his pathbreaking ecumenical book *The Mystery of God* were dedicated to outlining the similarities between Catholic and Protestant visions of marriage. Stählin argued that the passions of past hostilities had blinded Protestants from recognizing the greatness of Catholic marriage. In their revolt against papal authority, they overlooked uniquely egalitarian features of Catholic marriage, which brought man and wife together in an equal union of love and thus elevated their souls. This was why marriage was the only sacrament that required no priest for its valid consummation. "Husband and wife dispense this sacrament to one another themselves," he mused, "so here the bodily union is 'the mystery,' the sensuous reality with which the gift and power of divine grace will be mysteriously united."[139] Stählin then insisted that for all its doctrinal revolution, the Reformation kept intact this understanding of marriage. It viewed sexuality as a mutual act of giving, in which the married couple transcended biological existence. Stählin therefore called on members of the two confessions to adopt each other's marriage ceremonies and resist the spread of what he saw as "pagan" fixation with biology. Wasn't it obvious, he rhetorically asked, that "the two belong to each other in their deepest meaning?"[140] For Stählin, the 1930s initiated a sense of convergence that was far deeper than earlier interconfessional cooperation against feminism. Catholics and Protestants now seemed to share the belief that the fundamental aspect of human existence was the sanctity of marital affection.

The 1930s and 1940s, then, brought about new fractures and convergences in Christian thinking about gender and sexuality. On the one hand, the era's upheavals cracked the consensus against feminism and sex reforms, which had animated Christian activism since the nineteenth century. Rather than agreeing on their mutual enemies, Catholics and Protestants now fiercely debated whether the radical right was among them. At the same time, that very debate led some thinkers to seek new allies in the other confession. Venturing beyond the tactical cooperation of earlier years, they argued that the two confessions agreed on God's plans for family life, either in healthy procreation or in affection and pleasure. While elaborate writings like Stählin's remained rare in the 1930s and 1940s, they reflected a new mindset, a sense that the two confessions were part of a mutual, spiritual undertaking.

What Comes after the Civilizing Mission? Missionary Thinkers on Race and Indigenous Cultures

The 1930s were a difficult period for European missions. Alongside shrinking resources due to the Great Depression, they also faced new ideological challenges as the notion of the civilizing mission came under fire in both Europe and overseas. In Europe the Nazis mockingly dismissed the notion of "uplifting" other races, whom they considered biologically and thus permanently inferior. In Asia, anti-colonialists launched an intellectual attack on European claims to represent a universal and rational culture to which all nations should aspire. For missionaries, who for decades had conflated evangelization with the task of civilizing non-Europeans, these critiques were unnerving. Could missions flourish if they continued to insist that the path to Christ required adopting European languages, work habits, or family structures? As they sought to answer this question, writers of both confessions made meaningful modifications to missionary theories. Whether they believed that racial theories should inform their work or rejected such theories as un-Christian, missionary elites increasingly argued that European missions had to accommodate local traditions and habits, even if those clashed with European sensitivities. These parallel and overlapping ideas inspired some cooperation between Catholics and Protestants at the time. Far more than in writings on theology, social theory, or sexuality, confessional hostilities remained dominant. But after the war the new focus on local cultures would become central to confessional cooperation.

Within Europe, the most important challenge to the civilizing mission came from the Nazis, whose theory of biological determinism disallowed any notion of cultural improvement. Was it not obvious, party publications asked, that "uplifting" non-Europeans could only lead to race-mixing and cultural aberrations? The regime's leaders insisted that opposition to the civilizing mission distinguished the Reich from earlier forms of German colonialism. In a characteristic comment, Hitler proclaimed that "the German [of previous decades] made himself detested everywhere in the world, because ... he began to play the teacher. It's not a good method of conquest. Every people has its customs, to which it clings, and nobody wants lessons from us."[141] This conviction led the Nazis to criticize the Christian missions as both a futile undertaking to overcome racial boundaries and a distraction from the task of national reconstruction. As Hitler mockingly asked in *Mein Kampf,* would it not be preferable if Christians, "instead of troubling the Negroes with missions that they neither want nor understand ... teach our European humans [how to preserve racial health]?"[142]

Yet the Nazis were not the only ones whose criticism alarmed European missionaries. Drawing on profoundly different ideological sources, Asian nationalists also launched or intensified attacks on Europe's claim to embody civilization's universal standards. In Japan the influential political theorist Shūmei Ōkawa published popular calls for the formation of a pan-Asian civilization, which would overthrow and supplant European dominance. In South Asia, Mohandas Gandhi and Subhas Chandra Bose railed against Europe's "corrupting" and demeaning cultural norms, which they sought to diminish through mass protest.[143] As missionary magazines and speeches noted, such critiques of European supremacy were often accompanied by harsh criticism of Christian missions. Across Asia, and especially in China, anti-colonial activists published leaflets and brochures that warned that the missions were a cover for cultural subjugation.[144] Gandhi's acid comments on Christian missions exemplified such claims. "Christianity in India," the Mahatma said in 1929, "appears to us as synonymous with materialistic civilization and imperialistic exploitation." "If I had the power and could legislate" he added in 1935, "I should stop all proselytizing."[145]

Christians developed several responses to these critiques. Some claimed that missions were not agents of universalist imposition, but in fact enhanced national or racial distinctiveness. An emblematic representative of this school was the German Protestant Siegfried Knak, the director of the Berlin Mission and one of Germany's delegates to the International Missionary Council, the organ coordinating the works of all major Protestant missions. Like most missionary elites in earlier generations, Knak was a proponent of European colonialism, which he believed was a precondition for evangelization. He also shared his predecessors' conflation of Christianity and civilization, claiming that missionaries were the vanguard of Europe's quest to bring Asians and Africans God's blessings in the form of superior technology and medicine. Knak, however, who in public addresses expressed enthusiasm for the Nazi revolution, also drew on the theologies of fascist sympathizers to argue that divine grace operated differently through distinct collectives. Each nation and race was endowed by God to have its own culture and norms, which it had to protect against "corrupting" foreign influences.[146]

This meant for Knak that missionaries were wrong to assume that their values were universal and had to be instilled in non-Europeans. In his much-discussed *Between the Nile and Table Bay* (1931), a lengthy reflection on his travels throughout sub-Saharan Africa, he argued that the impact of excessive Europeanization was tragic: local congregations replaced their ancient music with "horrible and trashy imitations" of European songs and abandoned their tribes' colorful garments in favor of cheap mass-produced imports. Knak therefore claimed that the missions' true task was to help indigenous communities preserve and strengthen their distinct heritage. To endow their flock with dignity, missions had to accommodate local norms, whether payment for brides or circumcision (which for decades were prohibited by Knak's mission). They also had to encourage communities to conduct rituals in local languages—such as Kiswahili, Zulu, or Sesoth—rather than European tongues. In Knak's telling, European missionaries had a new universal duty: to shield Asians and Africans from the cultural threat posed by other Europeans.[147]

Knak's adjustment to the civilizing mission appealed to many in the universe of Protestant missionary thought, especially in Germany. His depiction of missionaries as unique figures who simultaneously embodied Europe's universal message *and* helped foster different groups' unique genius, provided a helpful response to both Nazi and anti-colonial critics.[148] The influential missionary and Africanist Dietrich Westermann, for example, who worked both as a professor in Berlin and as the director of the International African Institute in London, echoed Knak by claiming that missionaries should strike a balance between training Africans for the modern economy and helping them to preserve their local traditions. In his best-selling *The African Today and Tomorrow* (1934), which was published in several languages, he argued that the difference between Africans and Europeans was divinely ordained, and that missions had to help each group to preserve "its own mode of life."[149] Walter Freytag, a prominent administrator in Europe's missionary world, extended these ideas to Asia. His *Young Christianity in the Upheavals of the East* (1938), which reported on his journeys in New Guinea, Indonesia, China, and India, explained that missionaries should confront their European bias by accommodating local practices like child marriage and dowry payments. In his telling, Christianity had to help build national solidarities across classes and tribes, even if those were directed against Europeans.[150] When delegates from all of Europe's major Protestant missions gathered for a conference in Bremen in 1938, such claims were the center of discussion, with special sessions dedicated to Knak's and Freytag's books. Speaker after speaker agreed that responding to anti-colonial nationalism required accommodating Christianity to local norms and traditions.[151]

As missionary writers themselves recognized, there was a tension between their belief in European superiority and universality and their new enthusiasm for cultural distinction. Its most obvious manifestation was in their writings on race, a topic that drew the attention of missionaries even more than it did for Christian theorists of theology, social theory, or sexuality. Like most missionary elites in previous decades, who largely rejected racial Darwinism, writers like Knak and others had some reservations about the Nazis' extreme racism. They routinely claimed that biological determinism, which excluded the possibility of conversion, conflicted with Christ's promise of universal salvation and with the imperative of international Christian solidarity. But in the same breath, leaders of the Protestant mission also agreed that one's ability to worship Christ was determined by one's biology. Over and over, they claimed that cultural expression, whether in law or art, was an expression of one's hereditary baggage: no Asian or African could ever hope to make meaningful contributions to European culture, and European evangelization thus had to help Asians and Africans express their races' distinct qualities. The goal, in Freytag's words, was to support non-Europeans' quest to develop their "race consciousness."[152] This conviction was why many Protestant writers condoned racial segregation, whether between "Aryans" and Jews in Europe or between white and black populations in the colonies. Westermann wrote in a reflection on Africa that segregated communities would best express their "own forms of life."[153] Even writers like Walter Braun, who dismissed Nazi racial theory as unscientific and mocked the claim that the "Nordic race" lay beyond the limits of original sin, hastened to add that the missions' task aligned with racial nationalism. Christ worked among all races, he claimed, by reminding them of their "purity" and their "distinct" racial characteristics.[154]

A similar ambiguity toward theologies of racism, with parallel consequences for the understanding of missionary approaches to non-Europeans, could be detected in Catholic circles. The most important articulator of this uncertainty was the Austrian scholar Wilhelm Schmidt, who was considered a giant in the fields of missionary theory and anthropology. In his early writings Schmidt opposed racist versions of Darwinism, claiming that all humans stem from similar racial origins and share fundamental mental traits. In each and every culture, he argued, one could find a belief in God's revelations, a claim he sought to substantiate in *The Origins of the Idea of God,* a series of twelve volumes that he began publishing in 1926 and continued to write over three decades. In Schmidt's telling, European Christianity was the most pure and developed expression of revelation, which other cultures had slowly corrupted or forgotten. The task of the missionary was therefore to help Asians and Africans "rediscover" God, and thus uplift them to Europe's level.[155] Schmidt's blend of missionary thought and claims to scientific objectivity were popular; the crown prince of the Habsburg Empire appointed him as his personal confessor, and Pope Pius XI funded a whole museum of ethnology under his directorship in Rome.[156] In the 1930s his ideas also put him on a collision course with the Third Reich, whose denial of the possibility of conversion he decried as "pagan." In *Race and Nation* (1934), which Schmidt rewrote in response to the Nazis' triumph, he insisted that biological determinism was inimical to Christ's message. "The soul," he claimed, "has no race" and is "created anew by God each time, for each individual."[157]

Yet like his Protestant counterparts, Schmidt also adapted his thinking in the 1930s, seeking to refute the missionaries' new critics in both Europe and overseas. He argued that racial differences *were* important, because they created different collective paths to salvation. "The body that contains the new soul" upon its birth, he explained, "brings with it [biological] inheritance from countless generations, and that is certainly not without meaning."[158] In this telling, even if physical differences emerged from external factors like climate, their impact on one's soul was so far-reaching that no human could transcend it. Each race had to worship in its own culture, a task that would be made easier for humans if they adhered to strict racial segregation. In Schmidt's eyes, this also required a new missionary focus. Christ's universal message would be best realized by helping Asians and Africans to combat Europe's corrosive influence on indigenous cultures and traditions. These ideas were popular among other Catholic missionaries, who hoped to reconcile their claim for universalism with criticism of the civilizing mission. Albert Drexel, for example, the rector of the institution for missionary studies in Innsbruck, echoed Schmidt's claims by supporting racial segregation while simultaneously criticizing the Nazis as overly racist. In *The Races of Humanity* (1935), he explained that Christ's love would manifest itself most clearly by allowing each human collective to celebrate its own heritage and traditions.[159] Paul Schebesta, who was Schmidt's student and a long-time missionary in the Congo, similarly claimed that the European mission to Africa was to help indigenous populations realize their unique qualities. In *Full Blooded Negroes and Half Dwarves* (1936), a popular and widely translated report of his time with a tribe in the Ituri Forest, he praised Belgian colonial authorities for striking "a difficult balance between ... [their] efforts to civilize the aborigines and at the same time to preserve what is best of their old culture."[160]

It was not just those who sympathized with racial theologies who felt the need to rethink some aspects of the civilizing mission. Anti-fascist thinkers, many of whom firmly rejected racism, also began to wonder whether European missionaries' true service to Asians and Africans was as shields from Europeanization. Among Protestants, the most prominent figure in this camp was the Dutch Lutheran Hendrik Kraemer, a former missionary to Indonesia and a renowned theologian from Leiden. Kraemer was heavily influenced by Swiss theologian Karl Barth, who maintained that God was completely beyond the grasp of humans, a "total other" whose intentions they could never hope to know. In this telling, Christianity was not a component of Europe's rational modernity, as many Protestants had argued since the nineteenth century, but a spiritual dogma that existed beyond history and could not justify any human political or cultural project.[161] In several articles and short booklets in the 1930s, Kraemer drew on these ideas to claim that Christians had to reject any form of nationalist or racial pride. For all their differences, Nazism, anti-colonial nationalism, and Japanese imperialism were equally foreign to the mission's task of bringing universal salvation to all humans. Kraemer dismissed nationalism in all its forms as an idolatry, an arrogant effort to invest earthly politics with the capacity to endow humans with grace without God. Extending a common trope of Christian social theory to the global stage, he claimed that "secular" nationalism emerged from the French Revolution's atheist politics, whose poisonous ideas were then carried around the world by European empires.[162]

Even though Kraemer's ideas were crafted as a critique of writers like Knak and Schmidt, many of his conclusions were similar. This fact was especially on display in *The Christian Message in a Non-Christian World* (1938), a study commissioned from Kraemer by the International

Missionary Council in preparation for its decennial gathering in 1938. Elaborating claims that were mostly implicit in his earlier writings, Kraemer maintained that it was not only the ideologies of German, Indian, or Japanese nationalism that were incompatible with Christ's message of universal salvation. Other Europeans' belief in their own superiority, especially their commitment to the civilizing mission, were an "idolatry," since they reduced Christianity to the service of earthly politics. To remain true to Christianity's liberating potential, missionaries had to respect and encourage the preservation of non-European traditions in Christian communities. "New incarnations and adaptations of Christianity in the concrete Asiatic and African settings are natural and legitimate," he maintained, and Europeans had to abandon their paternalist view of colonial spaces as "religious colonies."[163] While Kraemer cautioned that Asian and African traditions, like all human inventions, could become the source of excessive pride and ultimately eclipse the Gospel, he insisted that their strengthening would be the antidote to Europe's arrogance and imposition. Local traditions like payment for brides or worship of ancestral spirits "have at least as much right to exist as our European lack of them has," and they could "foster a pure and vigorous Christian life."[164]

Kraemer's formulations proved appealing to those who shared his suspicions about nationalism, whether in its Nazi or anti-colonial form. They seemed to offer a justification for Europeans' continued work in the Global South while freeing them from association with claims of cultural or racial superiority. Kraemer's book therefore became the most hotly discussed text in interwar missionary circles. It appeared in five languages, as well as in abbreviated versions; it was distributed by missionary organizations in dozens of countries; and in 1938 it was the center of special discussions in the European conference of Protestant missions in Bremen and the international conference of missions in Tambaram, India, the largest such gathering in history.[165] Indeed, Kraemer's call for anti-fascists to break with the civilizing mission's universal aspirations was echoed by other missionary elites. The Dutch Lutheran Willem Visser 't Hooft, who headed the World's Student Christian Federation and coordinated youth movements and their missionary activity, drew on Kraemer to claim that even if missionaries in the past were right to link Christianity and European norms, this was no longer the case. In *None Other Gods* (1937) he explained that the popularity of communism and fascism had exposed Europe as a "thoroughly secular" space, and thus denied it the right to be the universal measure of progress.[166] Karl Hartenstein, the director of the Basel Mission (a German organization headquartered in Switzerland), also drew on Barth to claim that the missionaries' universal message was one of faith, and not of certain cultural norms. The early apostles, he noted, did not seek to export Jewish or Hellenic norms, but assumed Christ's message could always appeal to all nations and races.[167]

An effort to update the civilizing mission in an explicitly anti-racist key emerged also among Catholics. Their most prominent spokesperson was the Belgian missiologist Pierre Charles, who ran influential annual pan-European missionary conferences in Louvain and published popular guidebooks for missionaries. Like Kraemer, Charles drew on anti-fascist theologians to decry Nazi racism as a materialist heresy, whose opposition to conversion he believed was especially damaging for missions. Rare among Catholic writers, this led him to reject anti-Semitism, which he mocked as a "confused and incoherent" ideology (among other things, he disputed the authenticity of the anti-Semitic tract *The Protocols of the Elders of Zion*).[168] In parallel, Charles also invoked modern science to condemn European racist animosities against Asians and Africans. In works like *Racism and Catholicism* (1939) he argued that modern anthropology has shown that the "so-called primitives" have long held impressive knowledge of geography and physics, as demonstrated by their capacity to travel in deserts or use the night skies for navigation.[169] Indeed, Charles criticized anthropologists like Lucien Lévy-Bruhl, who contrasted European rationality with the "childlike" mind of the "savages," and insisted that Asians and Africans had the highest intellectual, moral, and physical capabilities. As he put it in one essay, "It is difficult to understand how a circumspect observer could accept a doctrine other than that of substantial equality of different races."[170]

As was the case for Kraemer, this conviction led Charles to argue that Christian missions should develop a new respect for Asian and African cultures. While he never questioned the legitimacy of European colonialism as such, and assumed it was a necessary mechanism for introducing modern technology and hygiene, he claimed that missionaries should not participate in the imposition of European norms on indigenous populations. Instead, they had to recognize and celebrate local traditions, liturgies, and languages. As he put it in *The Records of The Missionary Action* (1938), one of the era's most widely read missionary manuals, only by overcoming their "prejudices" and appreciating Asian and African art, music, and law could European Christians "connect with the richness of the indigenous soul." In doing so, they would help realize the human diversity that "divine Providence" has mandated.[171] During the 1930s, Charles labored to popularize his ideas in Catholic missionary circles. The annual gatherings he ran in Louvain, and the essay collections they produced, became major sites in which missionary leaders and activists shared their experiences in trying to "indigenize" their work. Pascal D'Elia, a French missionary in China and professor of missiology in Rome, for example, explained his efforts to incorporate local rites into Christian weddings, while the Dutch Bernard Zuure, a missionary to Burundi, discussed the utilization of local games and sports in building community.[172]

For all the ingenuity such works brought to missionary thinking, they also had important limits. This was because new interest in local traditions was not extended to Muslims, whom Christian writers on both sides of this debate on nation and race continued to view as Christianity's inverse. In essays, books, and missionary conferences, both Catholics and Protestants continued to bemoan what they considered Islam's paradoxical capacity to foster both apathy and fanaticism, which they contrasted with Christianity's ability to foster self-control and self-improvement. Some even drew on the new interest in indigenous cultures to reformulate their hostility to Islam. Kraemer, for example, claimed that Muslims' strange and "superficial" spirituality stemmed from their inability to distinguish religion from political domination. At its core, he explained, Islam was a "secular" project; like German or Indian nationalism, it was interested not in ethics or salvation but in control and power.[173] Such claims were repeated ad nauseam in both Protestant and Catholic writings. Influential German theoreticians like Gottfried Simon and Johannes Witte, clearly projecting their discomfort with Europe's own colonial dominance, criticized Islam's imperialist quest to subject all cultures to its universal creed, which they believed was bound to unleash "persecution and violence."[174] Indeed, the association between Islam and polygamy was one of the reasons even missionary writers most eager to accommodate non-European traditions remained convinced that Christianity could not tolerate the Muslim practice of having multiple wives. As the French Charles exclaimed in a 1934 speech about mission and family, "Muslim polygamy" was where Christian tolerance for indigenous traditions "reaches its limits."[175]

Despite the meaningful shifts and conversions in missionary theory, therefore, there were also important marks of continuity. Most obviously, despite the conceptual links they claimed to find between events in Europe and in the Global South, missionary writers remained convinced that in colonial spaces Christianity was on the winning side; for all their worries about anti-colonial nationalists or Muslims, missionaries remained so confident in Europe's dominance that few could envision colonialism's imminent collapse. The German Protestant Westermann struck a common tone in 1934 when he said, "Today, and for a long time to come, the fate of Africa is indissolubly linked with that of the white race . . . Under the complicated conditions of modern life, Africans are not in a position to take their future into their own hands, nor is Europe disposed to surrender its control over Africa."[176] Indeed, missionary texts maintained a sense of confidence and even optimism that was not as common in other Christian publications. Rather than as beleaguered minorities, they described Christian and missionary-led communities in Asia and Africa as the building blocks toward a vast expansion.

This difference can help explain why the ecumenical revolution unfolding in Europe left few marks on missionary theory. Throughout the 1930s and early 1940s, Catholic and Protestant missionary texts offered parallel ideas but showed no engagement with the growing calls for unity and continued to radiate confessional hostility. The Nazi-sympathizer Knak, for example, warned that Catholics sought to replace local national traditions with universalist Catholic practices. Their influence was so corrosive, he angrily wrote in a popular booklet on East Africa, that they fostered laziness and unthinking submission to authority, and undermined the difference between the genders by encouraging female labor.[177] For all their disagreements about race and politics, the anti-fascist Kraemer shared this critical approach. Catholics, he wrote in a special appendix to *The Christian Message in a Non-Christian World,* sacrificed Christ's gospel by imposing its European version on communities around the world.[178] Catholics directed the same accusations at Protestants. Charles, in several speeches and essays, described Protestants as the agents of Europeanization, which he contrasted to the Catholic respect for Asian and African cultures.[179] From the missionary point of view, Asia and Africa remained a different space from Europe, with different challenges and anxieties.

Nevertheless, the intellectual shifts of this era would play an important role in the history of confessional relations. After World War II, with the unfolding of decolonization, the new interest in Asian and African cultures would become even more central to missionary thinking. By aligning themselves with indigenous traditions, missionaries hoped to secure Christianity's survival in a world of diminishing European influence.

At that time, these ideas would also become the site for Catholic-Protestant cooperation. Two decades after their inception, they would foster ecumenism's spread from Europe overseas.

SPEAKING TO AN AMERICAN audience in the fall of 1941, as Axis troops nearly reached Moscow and Nazi control over Europe seemed imminent, the influential Swiss Protestant writer Adolf Keller lamented the divisions that marked Christian life in Europe. The Third Reich's polarizing effect on Christian communities, he ruefully noted, had sapped the churches of energy and diminished their ability to influence public affairs. "A divided church," he said, will lack a "prophetic voice. The world would consider [it] as *quantité négligeable.*" While Keller's prognosis, which was quickly published as *Christian Europe Today* (1942), was bleak, he found comfort in the budding rapprochement between Catholics and Protestants. The two confessions, he claimed, were brought together by their mutual persecutions under communism and Nazism, recognizing their joint calling. In the 1920s Keller had published intensely anti-Catholic texts, but now he praised engagement with Catholic writers and activists. Perhaps, he argued, it would offer a blueprint for broader Christian rejuvenation, and would enable the two confessions to "find new ways of living together and defending a common Christian heritage."[180]

Keller's account, which is forgotten by historians, was rife with half-truths and errors. He exaggerated Nazi persecutions of Christians and ignored many Christians' continued support for, and at times influence on, the policies of the Third Reich and its allies. Keller, however, captured the conflicting impulses that shaped Christian thought in the 1930s and 1940s. On the one hand, across all major fields of Christian thinking—from theology and political theory to economics, marriage and family, and missionary thought—writers debated how to adjust Christianity to the era of the Depression and radical social experimentation. While they largely remained committed to the principles set in previous decades and continued to secure an order premised on stability and "natural" hierarchies between classes, sexes, and continents, they were deeply divided on whether this goal could be achieved in cooperation with the radical right and its racism. On the other hand, these divisions gave birth to new efforts at Catholic-Protestant reconciliation. Both sympathizers with and detractors of the fascist experiment increasingly abandoned old confessional hostilities and wondered if the "Mystical Body of Christ" included both Catholics and Protestants. Even though this strategy was born from the crucible of the Great Depression and a world war, it proved popular enough to endure. Indeed, it would become the key approach as Christians emerged from the war's destruction and sought to impose their visions during Europe's reconstruction.

CHAPTER 4

Grand Compromises at the Zenith of Christian Power

THE "LONG 1950S"—the years between the end of World War II and the mid-1960s—were a high point for European Christianity. As new organizations and movements sought to fill the vacuum left by the demise of fascism, the churches emerged as one of the continent's largest and most influential civil institutions. Membership in Catholic and Protestant communities soared across all age groups, as did church attendance and participation in Christian youth movements. While this renewed enthusiasm could be attributed to practical calculations, particularly the many services provided by church charities in the war's immediate aftermath, Christianity's reach was vast. Catholic and Protestant publications proliferated, and Christian thinkers served as prominent commentators on contemporary affairs. Perhaps most striking, organized Christianity emerged as politically victorious. Across Central and Western Europe, new parties promised to implement the Gospel's teachings under the banner of "Christian Democracy." Whether by winning elections or joining coalitions as senior members, these parties became a central force in Europe's postwar reconstruction, shaping everything from economics to the regulation of sexuality and colonial policy. In postwar Europe, as one historian stated, Christianity was "victorious among the ruins."[1]

This period was also good for ecumenism. Rather than abandoning the dialogue of the 1930s and 1940s, Catholics and Protestants expanded it: interconfessional organizations, meetings, and publications multiplied. If anything, ecumenism's proponents became more confident. As the 1950s progressed, their texts and speeches shed the apologetic tones they initially employed, and increasingly described their ideas as obvious. As one best-selling Protestant commentator asserted in 1953, ecumenism's move from controversial innovation to the status of common sense was "one of the most significant developments of our time."[2] Few changes reflected this approach more fully than Christian democratic parties' insistence that they were interconfessional. While demographic realities made Catholicism the dominant force in most of these parties (only in Germany and the Netherlands were self-identified Protestant populations large enough to be a major voting bloc), Christian political leaders mused that they could not return to the pre-fascist years; the Christianity of the new era was open to both denominations. This mainstreaming of ecumenism was further evident in efforts to forge political and economic cooperation between Western European states, which Christian democratic leaders spearheaded in the postwar decades. Though many Protestants at first suspected that European integration was a tool of Catholic domination, they increasingly changed their minds and ultimately joined international Christian democratic organizations.

What explains ecumenism's ascendance? How did ecumenism transcend the Nazi moment, which was a key source of its origins, and enter mainstream Christian thought and politics? In part this success stemmed from the persistence of familiar Christian priorities. Despite their electoral triumphs and newfound influence, many believers were convinced that Christianity remained under threat, beleaguered by old enemies newly empowered after the war. Amid the expansion of Soviet power across much of Eastern and Central Europe, and the reconstitution of socialist and communist parties in Western Europe, many Christian writers saw different variations of the same materialist enemy. Swiss Theologian Emil Brunner spoke for many when he warned in a 1947 speech that socialism was a "soul-destroying monster" that once again sought to eradicate spirituality.[3] Feminists and sex reformers also seemed to recover from fascist suppression. Women's suffrage was extended almost everywhere, and the war's enormously destabilizing impact on sexual norms, particularly the proliferation of extramarital and nonmarital relationships, helped inspire a multitude of reform organizations and publications. Finally, decolonization threatened decades of missionary work. With the collapse of European empires, first in Asia and then in Africa, many worried that missionary efforts would be replaced by "anti-Christian" forces, most menacingly Islam. As they reignited campaigns against these perceived dangers, Christian commentators often invoked a need for cooperation. One

German politician explained that Christianity's survival required "a meeting of both confessions."[4]

Ecumenism also benefited from many Christians' myopic understanding of World War II. As historians have noted, Christian elites were notoriously resistant to critical self-examination in the 1940s and 1950s and issued sweeping denials of Christian complicity in the war's horrors. Describing the Third Reich as a secular and materialist phenomenon, they presented sporadic cases of Christian opposition as a narrative of heroic, consistent, and broad resistance. As the German bishop Clemens von Galen put it in an especially cringe-inducing statement, "We [Christians] suffered more under the Nazis than others."[5] Christian elites also emerged from the war convinced that their internal divisions had been an important reason for Europe's collapse into violence. The German Catholic theologian Karl Adam echoed a widespread view when he argued that the war "showed with terrible clarity how the divisions between Christians prevented them from any effective effort to maintain world peace."[6] As self-serving and untrue as this narrative was, the mutual sense of self-victimization it perpetuated fueled interconfessional engagement. It allowed Catholics and Protestants to view each other as necessary allies in securing a stable and peaceful future. This was partly why this narrative was common not only among those with tainted histories, whose crude motivation was not surprising, but also among anti-fascists. Even figures with impressive anti-Nazi credentials, such as Yves Congar, who was harassed by the Nazis and their allies, affirmed this myopia, and joined recovering Nazi sympathizers in interconfessional projects.

This overwhelming desire to overcome earlier ideological divisions meant that postwar ecumenism also entailed important innovations. Alongside cooperation between confessions, its key thinkers and activists also used it as a vehicle for peace between Christianity's different political factions. Eager to leave behind polarizing debates over fascism, which had dominated Christian life in the 1930s and early 1940s, Christian elites sought to disassociate ecumenism from its earlier links to the pro- and anti-fascist camps, and instead developed a set of compromises between them. This shift in ecumenism's function was first visible in the realms of theology and political theory. In the 1930s and early 1940s, ecumenist theories came in two conflicting versions. On one side were fascist sympathizers, who claimed that Catholic-Protestant cooperation helped realize racial unity in an authoritarian, hierarchical, and anti-communist order. On the other stood anti-fascists, who hoped that an interconfessional "Mystical Body of Christ" would defy racism and lead believers toward pluralism. After the war, writers in both camps labored to develop a shared language. They argued that Catholics and Protestants shared a broad commitment to stability and inequality but also agreed that these goals were best achieved through peaceful participation in a pluralist and democratic system. This compromise, strengthened by shared anti-socialism, helped ecumenism become the mainstream of Christian thought. It also had impact beyond the sphere of ideas: it defined the political agenda of the Christian democratic parties, which blended an obsession with social hierarchies with a commitment to pluralist politics.

The second place where new compromise emerged was in the Christian approach to the economy. Since the nineteenth century, Christians had debated how to secure an anti-socialist order premised on both class distinctions and inter-class harmony. In particular they disagreed on the question of state intervention, which some viewed as the best way to create an anti-materialist order and others decried for opening the door for socialist statism. The crisis of the 1930s altered this debate, convincing both Catholics and Protestants that some state intervention was necessary, but it did not resolve it. While those who sympathized with fascism aligned with the authoritarian "corporatist" model of aggressive state management, anti-fascists claimed the state should foster market competition. With the collapse of corporatism and the beginning of postwar reconstruction, a new consensus materialized. Catholics and Protestants largely agreed that inequality and harmony were best served by a combination of state-run welfare programs and economic competition. Labeled by contemporaries "the social market economy," it became the blueprint for the Christian democrats' far-reaching reforms in welfare policies. Because this economic project coincided with Europe's great economic boom in the 1950s, this vision also proved enormously popular. It helped Christian democrats garner support from many Europeans who were not necessarily interested in the churches or their social teachings.

The third new agreement Christians forged regarded gender and sexuality. In many ways the Christian democrats' well-known obsession with marriage and heteronormativity could be understood as the culmination of earlier morality campaigns. As they had done since the turn of the century, Catholic and Protestant activists mobilized to solidify inequality between the sexes, especially through family and employment laws. They deepened the state's restriction on anything they believed could entice people away from marital commitment, whether pornography, abortion, or homosexuality. Equally important for interconfessional relations, Catholics and Protestants sought to shore up the patriarchy by developing a shared justification for their family ethics. While politicians and marriage experts rejected the flirtation with feminism that some anti-fascists offered in the 1930s, they drew on anti-fascist theories to claim that the purpose of Christian marriage was not just procreation and physical health, but also love and sexual pleasure. This adaptation has been recognized by scholars, but less noted is that it advanced interconfessional engagement. Moving beyond the earlier framework of casting feminism and sex reformers as enemies, thinkers of both confessions claimed they shared a *positive* conception of gender and sexuality, and even developed an explicitly ecumenical theory of family ethics. They claimed that only Catholics and Protestants could experience "true" pleasure, a notion that led to the emergence of the first interconfessional manuals and marriage clinics in European history.

Finally, by the late 1950s and early 1960s, Catholic and Protestant elites developed a shared response to decolonization. The postcolonial states that emerged in Asia and Africa in those years had little patience for European paternalism. Many of their leaders pondered whether to restrict the work of missionaries, who for so long had been the face of the "civilizing mission"; some followed the path of Communist China and expelled them altogether. The shared anxieties sparked by this threat brought Catholics and Protestants much closer together. In journals and at conferences, missionary leaders claimed that the two confessions were locked together in a fight against "anti-Christian" enemies. Even more important, Christian writers agreed on ways to preserve their tutelage of non-Europeans after the end of formal empire. Drawing on ideas developed in the 1930s, while stripping them of their original racist or anti-racist meanings, they called for the "indigenization" of liturgy and ceremonies, which they alleged would enhance European authority. Across the confessional divide, they also agreed that European missionaries had to lead Africans and Asians in economic "development." Revisiting their focus on work, Catholics and Protestants touted Europe's superior technology and knowledge as a source of prosperity for non-Europeans. This framing was appealing because it enabled missionary writers and officials to understand their work as achieving contradictory objectives. It allowed the missions to claim that they were simultaneously overcoming earlier colonialist paternalism (by empowering local traditions) and bestowing on Africans and Asians Europe's productive values. These ideas also led Catholic and Protestant missionary theoreticians, who earlier hesitated to join the ecumenical project, to lay claim to a deeply shared task in the Global South. Long after practical cooperation began in Europe, decolonization fostered new ties among missionary organizations and charities, which founded new ecumenical forums and launched joint campaigns for education and economic development.

To be sure, all these successive convergences, and ecumenism's growing popularity more broadly, did not mean that confessionalism ceased to matter. Even the most enthusiastic ecumenists continued to assume that Catholics and Protestants differed in important ways, and most elements of organized Christianity, whether churches, charities, or youth movements, remained confessional. Nor did confessional tensions or stereotypes completely evaporate in Europe. Even the new interconfessional political parties experienced occasional bickering between the two camps, which sometimes blamed each other for deviating from "true" Christian principles or showing loyalty to the "foreign" Vatican. What is more, the borders of ecumenism remained as strict as before. Almost nowhere did its main advocates extend it to Jews or Muslims. And yet Christian sensitivities were marked by a qualitative shift. More than at any time before, talk of a deep and shared affinity between the confessions became common and uncontroversial. The anti-Catholicism and anti-Protestantism of earlier decades was abandoned, increasingly confined to small circles of desperate reactionaries. Even clerical opposition, which in the 1920s had derailed interconfessional discussions between theologians, was unable to stem the tide. When the Vatican warned in 1949 that interconfessional engagement could lead to religious apathy and had to be restricted, Catholics in Central and Western Europe largely ignored it.[7] Ecumenism, in short, was now too appealing for too many Christians. In it they saw a blueprint for realizing the norms and institutions required for human flourishing.

Theologies and Politics of Unity in the Age of Consensus

For the casual observer, the reappearance of ecumenism after World War II might have looked eerily familiar. As Christian intellectual life resumed after a brief interruption imposed by war, Catholic and Protestant writers recycled their claims from the 1930s, declaring that Europe's stability required engagement between the two confessions. Indeed, Christian writers spent very little time reflecting on the war's traumatizing cruelty, whether its mass forced labor campaigns, starvation, or aerial bombing, and even less so the genocide against European Jewry. When mentioned at all in writings and speeches, wartime atrocities were explained in the same way Christian commentators described the French Revolution: Christianity's decline led humans to hubristically discard all tradition, inevitably resulting in violence. The same was true for the Cold War, and the expansion of Soviet power from Europe's periphery to its center. Christian writers understood communism's rise as part of the momentum that had accelerated during the Great Depression, repeating the claim that only an interconfessional alliance could stop it. Continuities between the 1930s and the postwar period could even be detected in ecumenism's intellectual protagonists. The theologians and political theorists who first crafted interconfessional ideas also initiated Catholic-Protestant engagement after the war.

Yet there were also important innovations. Instead of being a battleground between fascist sympathizers and anti-fascists, ecumenism now facilitated an uneasy compromise between them, premised on a new understanding of Christian politics. On the one hand, ecumenical writers categorically rejected authoritarianism. Even those who had praised dictators as Christianity's defenders now agreed that Christian politics should operate through a pluralist electoral system, a claim that proved easier to make after fascism's humiliating defeat. On the other hand, ecumenical writers adopted a narrow conception of democracy that enabled former detractors to live with it. In speeches and publications, they argued that democracy's purpose was not to empower the masses or translate the majority's will into policy, but to provide the conditions that would allow people to willfully embrace existing inequality. To be free, in this telling, was not simply to practice liberal rights, such as freedom of speech and association, but to develop the spiritual and mental capacity to reject egalitarianism. By centering cooperation between Catholics and Protestants around these principles, Christian elites were able to accommodate a broad array of political sensitivities. This compromise, popularized by new publications and think tanks, became the centerpiece of the new powerful political parties.

Few exemplified the blend of continuity and adaptation better than the Catholic historian Joseph Lortz, who emerged as one of the chief ideologues of ecumenism in the aftermath of the war. In the early 1930s Lortz had been an enthusiastic proponent of engagement with the Third Reich, claiming that Hitler's quest to establish a racially unified and authoritarian order aligned with Catholic theology. This conviction also led him to embrace engagement with Protestants: his *History of the Reformation in Germany* (1938), which offered the first sympathetic Catholic account of Luther and his followers, became an ecumenical classic, endlessly cited and invoked by supporters of interconfessional cooperation. When Christian intellectual life resumed after the war, Lortz continued his efforts to promote engagement between Catholics and Protestants. In a series of lectures across Germany that drew large crowds, he claimed that both confessions shared the understanding that human life was plagued by sin. They understood that hubris—expressed in a disregard for tradition and the limits it imposed on human impulses—could only be curtailed by preserving differences between classes and sexes and through political stability. Publishing these talks as *The Reformation as Religious Issue Today* (1948), Lortz repeated his anti-communist tirades from the 1930s to warn that these shared convictions were under threat from materialist temptations. Catholics and Protestants were to cooperate in a joint quest to instill in Europeans the principles of spirituality and self-control.[8]

Though Lortz's reasoning, and his support for hierarchies and order, conformed to his Nazi-era writings, there were also meaningful shifts in his postwar thinking. Most importantly, he systematically cleansed his new writings of any association with the Third Reich, a move that was motivated both by his disappointment with the regime's disregard for Catholic autonomy and by a blatantly self-serving effort to disassociate himself from its harrowing violence. In his postwar texts, Lortz made no mention of corporal metaphors and did not claim that the "Mystical Body of Christ" was realized in earthly collectives such as races. He also omitted his earlier anti-Semitism, did not celebrate obedience and authoritarianism, and dropped explicit condemnations of democracy. Lortz brought his skills at historical revisionism from the Reformation era to recent events, denying that Catholics or Protestants ever supported the Nazis. Instead he narrated Christian experience in terms of victimization and proclaimed that the two confessions' affinity was made obvious by their mutual persecution by, and even resistance to, Hitler. Lortz spent the following decade publishing multiple iterations of this narrative, reminding his readers that Protestants were always allies in Catholicism's quest for salvation. He also sought to popularize them in his booklet *The Reformation: A Handbook of Claims for Ecumenical Conversations*

(1947), which provided Catholics quick advice on how to engage with their Protestant neighbors.[9]

Lortz's updated ecumenism resonated with many former Nazi sympathizers. It allowed them to maintain the alliance they had forged in the 1930s in support of hierarchical order while denying their association with violence. This was the case with the influential theologian Karl Adam, who earlier had sought to reconcile Catholic thought to the Third Reich by embracing both racism and engagement with Protestants. After the war Adam reissued his call for ecumenical engagement, claiming that it would realize their mutual belief in divine grace and tradition. In *Confessional Unity from a Catholic Perspective* (1948), which was translated into all major European languages, he claimed that only such cooperation could curtail humans' hubristic urge to remake society from scratch. Adam, however, also made sure to remove from his writings any references to blood, race, and obedience. Instead he insisted that Christian unity was premised on spiritual affinity, a mutual openness to God's orders. The same strategy was adopted by Protestants such as Alfred Dedo Müller, who in the 1930s claimed that the two confessions were united in the quest to realize salvation through racial unity and eugenics. In lectures he gave just after the Reich's defeat and published as *Prometheus or Christ* (1948), Müller reiterated his belief in Catholics' and Protestants' shared commitment to hierarchy and order but described Nazism as pagan heresy. In a move endlessly repeated in Christian publications, Adam, Müller, and other ecumenists now attributed their ecumenical turn to their alleged disgust with Nazism. As Adam put it in a flagrant rewriting of his own trajectory, it was "when National Socialism began to display itself openly as anti-Christian" that believers in the two confessions understood "that the time had come to bear a *unanimous* witness to Christ."[10]

It would be wrong, however, to view postwar ecumenism as merely a sanitized repeat of Nazi ideas. Veterans of anti-fascist Christianity also relaunched their campaign to bring together the confessions to help believers embrace life in a pluralist environment. This was the case, for example, with the French Dominican theologian Yves Congar, who in the 1930s had envisioned a unified Christian community as the antidote to the Nazis' racial body. After the war, Congar sought to empower believers to question clerical authority, a cause that seemed especially urgent in light of church leaders' silence over Nazi violence. In works such as *True and False Reform in the Church* (1950), he claimed that Christ's teachings required not docile obedience but responsibility through active participation in communal life.[11] Congar linked these ideas to ecumenism and repeated his prewar claim that engagement with Protestants would help believers recognize the presence of grace beyond the Church's borders. Dismissing anti-Protestantism as anachronistic, he insisted in *Luther in Catholics' Eyes* (1950) that Protestants "must be viewed as *religious people*."[12] In Germany, too, the Catholic anti-fascist philosopher Johannes Hessen claimed that ecumenism could help believers take charge of Christian life. If they could forge solidarity with other Christians, he wrote in *Germany's Spiritual Reconstruction* (1946), they would remember that Christianity's essence lay not in mindless deference to authority but in brotherly love.[13]

While this focus on pluralism differed from the emphasis on hierarchy and order by Lortz and others, the anti-fascists shared important objectives with their former opponents. Above all, most of them believed that an interconfessional alliance was needed to combat socialism, the materialist ideology that consumed their attention with the collapse of fascism. This was the case, for example, with Wilhelm Stählin, the German Lutheran youth movement leader and writer, who in the 1930s had offered the most comprehensive ecumenical theory in Protestant circles. A vocal anti-Nazi, Stählin condemned racism as heresy and warned that Nazism's crude focus on blood and bodies at the expense of spirituality was as materialist as socialism's obsession with economics. As an antidote, he had offered ecumenical engagement, which he had hoped would enrich both confessions and empower them to resist the Nazi temptation. For Stählin, however, the collapse of the third Reich did not obviate such cooperation. The reconstitution of socialist and communist parties, and the march of the Red Army across Eastern Europe, meant that reconciliation remained vital to the survival of Christianity. In a series of postwar lectures and publications, such as *Catholic Tendencies in the Evangelical Churches* (1947), Stählin repeated his calls for Christians to embrace each other. As he put it in a 1952 booklet, many ideas that some consider "Protestant" were "exactly those that Luther condemned as the 'mistakes' of Rome!"[14]

As ecumenists themselves were quick to recognize, the perceived challenges of the postwar era made these different versions of ecumenism remarkably consonant. No longer divided by their approach to fascism, writers on all sides agreed that Catholics and Protestants had to cooperate to rebuild Europe and defend it from materialist socialism. The 1940s and 1950s therefore witnessed a new collaboration between factions. In 1946, for example, Lortz and Stählin joined hands to launch the first postwar interconfessional discussion group, dedicated to exploring theological similarities between the confessions. It quickly became an annual affair, bringing together church leaders and theologians in the 1940s and 1950s with its own publications.[15] There was similar cooperation in France, where Congar organized large conferences on ecumenism in Paris in 1949 and 1950. At these events, clergy and church leaders who in the past had conflicting political convictions gathered to discuss mutual interests, such as the translation and republication of Lortz's historical texts, and ways to make their liturgies more similar.[16]

As ecumenism became a site of cooperation between different confessions and political inclinations, it expanded into new circles. Whether motivated by anti-communism or by a desire to open Christianity to pluralism, ecumenism offered Christian thinkers across Europe a way to cast aside divisions in favor of a broad-tent alliance. Indeed, as ecumenism ceased to be strictly associated with either fascist sympathizers or their opponents, it drew new figures into its ranks. The Swiss Protestant essayist Walter Nigg, for example, who during the war showed little interest in ecumenism, now claimed in a series of popular reflections that Catholics and Protestants had to discard their mutual suspicions and recognize their joint commitment to tradition and spirituality. In *Great Saints* (1946) and the follow-up *The Secret of the Monastery* (1953), both of which were widely translated and ran through multiple editions, Nigg warned that failure would surrender Europe to a new "barbarian invasion," a bleak reference to communism.[17] Less commercially successful but no less enthusiastic was the Catholic Swiss theologian Otto Karr, who similarly had no history of ecumenical work but now launched a series of ecumenical seminars to discuss cooperation. Bringing together Catholic theologians such as Oscar Cullmann and Protestant thinkers like Emil Brunner, they emphasized the need to leave behind fantasies of confessional hegemony in favor of engagement.[18] In France a group of Catholic and Protestant theologians launched the ecumenical journal *Verbum Caro* in 1947. Interconfessional cooperation, its essays claimed, could help Christians overcome divisions and find a common language.[19] In the Netherlands and Belgium, too, Catholic and Protestant theologians, who until then had remained on the sidelines of ecumenical efforts, founded new forums for interconfessional discussions. Dutch Catholic bishops even gave these endeavors their formal blessing. They authorized the theologian Jan Willebrands to create the Catholic Conference on Ecumenical Questions, which was tasked with studying theological similarities between the confessions.[20]

Theology mattered, but ecumenism's evolution into a site of compromise was even more consequential in political theory. In many ways, interconfessional cooperation was enabled by the emergence of a new Christian approach to politics. In the 1930s, Catholic and Protestant elites in Germany, France, and elsewhere agreed that their quest to build a stable society required cooperation with new allies, but they intensely debated what political form this should take. While some insisted on a centralized dictatorship, others envisioned a more pluralist arrangement where associations and communities preserved their autonomy. After the war, with the option of right-wing dictatorship seemingly no longer on the table, this debate was replaced with political consensus. Whether begrudgingly or with conviction, Christian elites came to accept democracy's pluralist and electoral realities, so long as they could work through them to resist emancipatory ideologies like socialism, which they considered the first step toward tyranny and the annihilation of people's distinct identities. Few articulated this vision more clearly than the influential German Catholic editor Franz Josef Schöningh, who in a widely read 1949 essay explained that Catholicism should make its peace with democratic pluralism. In a rare display of self-criticism, Schoeningh claimed that Catholic support for dictators was a mistake because it implicated believers in violence. It was better to operate in a pluralist world, where citizens expressed their disagreements through political parties and elections. Christians had to recognize the legitimacy of non-Christians' claims, even if those rejected the notion of original sin. Yet Schoeningh qualified his claims by insisting that democracy was only legitimate if it defended and perpetuated existing inequalities, especially between classes. The democratic idea of "social justice," he explained, "fundamentally excludes the idea of class struggle," which sought to replace reciprocity between citizens with conflict. Such arguments, with their narrow and explicitly non-egalitarian vision of democracy, were repeated in countless books and speeches. They became the new consensus of Christian thought.[21]

What made this understanding of politics appealing was that it could easily accommodate those who once rejected democracy. It allowed them to redefine key democratic terms, such as "freedom," and claim them as their own. This was the case, for example, with the German Protestant social theorist Georg Wünsch. Before the war Wünsch was a vocal supporter of authoritarianism as the only way to maintain stability and defeat socialism. While championing the Third Reich, he also became an enthusiastic proponent of ecumenism.[22] After the war, Wünsch considerably recalibrated his arguments, and claimed that Christianity best prospered in the condition of "freedom." In *Man in Modern Materialism* (1952) he maintained that only through voluntary associations, free speech, and "freedom of action" could believers practice their conscience and follow God's orders. Wünsch took this argument even further, adding that Christianity was the only force that could furnish human freedom. Its conception of human sin forced individuals to recognize their limitations and thus resist hubristic temptation to impose their will on others. This was why those who subscribed to materialist ideologies, whether Nazism or socialism, were inherently opposed to freedom. Believing that all human relations were an expression of one principle, such as race or class, they were driven by inevitable "fanaticism" that submitted all aspects of human life to the state. That Wünsch's logic was circular, describing Christianity as both the precondition for and the result of liberal rights, did not seem to matter. It offered a powerful way to reconcile an authoritarian theory of power to the age of democracy.[23]

Such an understanding of politics was a driving force in the consolidation of postwar ecumenism. The most important organs of Catholic-Protestant cooperation also became sites for articulating and popularizing this framework of hierarchical democracy. A case in point is the Western Academy, a large Christian think tank that was launched in the late 1940s and quickly became one of West Germany's most important intellectual centers. Its conferences brought together hundreds of senior politicians, church leaders, and thinkers in an interconfessional experiment. Its director, the politician and academic Friedrich August Freiherr von der Heydte, was Catholic, and his deputy, Protestant ecumenist Wilhelm Stählin, was Protestant. Its statement of intent, drafted by politician Gerhard Kroll and published as *The Foundations of Western Action* (1951), proclaimed that the two confessions were unified in a quest to "overcome the secularized world through the power of faith and Christ's lordship over all."[24] Its publications, most prominently the influential journal *New West*, helped outline the agenda of postwar Christian politics. In the 1950s these writings, spanning everything from policy recommendations on tax rates to philosophical reflections, maintained that only Christianity breathed meaning and stability into European life.[25]

Less noted by historians, the Academy also crafted a new political language that appealed to different Christian sensibilities. On the one hand, the Academy's publications insisted that Christians should operate in a system that accepted individual freedom and democratic structures. It emphasized concepts such as "freedom" and "choice," terms previously missing from its members' vocabulary.[26] At the same time, it obsessed over the state's responsibility to defend order and stability. Its proposals routinely claimed that differences in income, education, and property were divinely ordained, and that any effort to question them was bound to breed chaos. Indeed, *The Foundations of Western Action* stated that the purpose of democratic institutions was not to empower the masses or directly express their will, but to enable "peoples' orientation towards God."[27] In its telling, "freedom" was the ability to willfully accept one's lot in life without questioning its legitimacy. Both of these convictions found common cause in the Academy's virulent anti-socialism. At events and conferences, speaker after speaker decried Marxist desires to mentally enslave humans, break them emotionally, and bring about what Protestant jurist Hans Dombois called "the extermination of freedom."[28] This political capaciousness meant that the Academy was able to draw figures with conflicting histories. Some members of the Academy, such as Catholic journalist Emil Franzel, had been vocal supporters of the Third Reich, while others, such as Stählin, were committed anti-Nazis.

It is not easy to measure how deeply these ideas resonated within Christian communities. But the campaign to bring together Christians of different confessions and political orientations helped inspire one of the era's most revolutionary experiments in electoral politics. Across Central and Western Europe, Christians founded new parties, which resurrected the older project of anti-socialist mobilization but updated it into an interconfessional and politically flexible key. The most explicitly ecumenical was West Germany's Christian Democratic Union (CDU), which was founded in 1945 in the British occupation zone and soon became a national organization. Under the leadership of Catholic politician and former mayor of Cologne Konrad Adenauer, the CDU brought together clergy, former politicians, and veterans of Christian labor unions who deemed confessional politics ill-equipped for the task of postwar reconstruction. Its manifestos and speeches relentlessly invoked Christian anti-socialism—Adenauer lambasted socialism as a "moral disease" that was "the root of all disorder"—but drew on the breakthroughs of the 1930s to explain that its defeat could only be achieved through an interconfessional alliance.[29] As Gerhard Kroll, one of the party's founders, argued in *Christian Union!* (1946), Europe's reconstruction and the defeat of materialism required "a united political front of all Christians."[30] Many of the CDU's election posters displayed images of Catholic and Protestant churches next to each other. To be sure, the CDU was never free of internal tensions between Catholics and Protestants, especially over funding for confessional schools. Those tensions, however, faded as the 1950s progressed and interconfessionalism became the new norm.[31]

Equally important for the success of the CDU was its broad-tent approach, which blended a considerable range of Christian political convictions. Among its founders were longtime supporters of democracy, such as Adenauer, and even resistance icons such as labor leader Jacob Kaiser, but also authoritarians and Nazi enthusiasts, including politician Hans Schlange-Schöningen and theologian Alfred Dedo Müller (who wrote Nazi ecumenical texts in the 1930s and after the war was a CDU parliamentary delegate). CDU leaders openly acknowledged that their roof was wide enough to shelter recovering Nazis. As one politician rhetorically asked in 1946, "If our ranks include members who earlier stood elsewhere and to the right, why not?"[32] The party's approach to democracy was intentionally narrow. Though fully committed to participation in pluralist electoral politics, its tolerance had harsh limits: in 1953 it criminalized the country's Communist Party and crushed all affiliate organizations, a radical move that echoed authoritarian measures.[33] Combined with the party's interconfessionalism, its accommodation of multiple political factions proved electorally effective. It became the first party in history to harness the majority of the German right into one organization, won a series of national elections, and became the country's ruling party well into the 1960s.

While Germany's mixed religious demographics made the CDU's focus on interconfessionalism especially pronounced, it was not an outlier. Other Christian democratic parties, which were overwhelmingly Catholic in leadership and support, expanded the interconfessional mindset forged in the 1930s and 1940s, making it crucial to their postwar anti-socialist campaigns. In France, when Catholic politicians founded the Popular Republican Movement (MRP) in 1944, they did not restrict membership to Catholics, as Action Française had in the 1920s. Instead they retained the spirit of nonconfessional experiments such as Cross of Fire and even the Vichy regime, and trumpeted their inclusion of the tiny Protestant minority.[34] The Catholic Party of the Netherlands followed a similar path, shedding its predecessor's prohibition of non-Catholic members. Its leaders appointed several Protestant figures to leadership positions, most notably Wim Beyen as minister of foreign affairs, and in 1952 formed a joint coalition with the country's two Protestant parties, the Christian-Historical Union (CHU) and Anti-Revolutionary Party (ARP). This was also the formal ethos of the Belgian Christian Social Party, founded in 1945 to replace the Catholic Party. As its president August Edmond de Schryver declared, one of its key innovations was that it "appealed to all those who embrace the fundamental principles of a Christian culture" and was thus "nonsectarian."[35]

In all these cases, ecumenism's main innovation compared to its 1930s origins was its political flexibility. With local variations, the Christian parties brought together resistance fighters and former collaborators in broad-tent electoral frameworks. Indeed, even though opponents liked to dismiss Christian democratic parties as cover for wartime authoritarianism—French communists famously mocked the MRP and its initials as standing for the "Machine for Reuniting the Pétainists" (Machine à ramasser les pétainistes)—this did not fully capture their political agenda.[36] Their goal was more capacious: to reconcile the belief in the necessity of order and social distinction with democracy. In fact, Christian democratic publications claimed that they alone protected democratic politics. The socialist understanding of democracy, they claimed, rested on the notion of unrestricted popular sovereignty, whereby the masses had the right to impose their will on everyone; guided by hubris, they were bound to dismantle democratic protections and establish dictatorships. As French Christian democratic leader Robert Schuman put it, because "modern democracy" required autonomy and freedom from state imposition, it owed "its existence to Christianity."[37] Such claims were flagrantly false, and ignored many Christians' earlier hostility to democracy, but they provided Christian democrats with a way to accommodate their broad coalition. The German Catholic theologian Romano Guardini captured this meaning when he claimed that Christians believed in a "fortunate unity of order and freedom."[38]

If many politicians felt compelled to forge ecumenism, this was in part due to international considerations. Echoing the Nazis' earlier quest to lead a pan-European crusade against the Soviet Union, Christian democrats viewed the emerging Cold War as a continent-wide struggle that required mobilizing both Catholic-majority and Protestant-majority countries. Few undertakings better illustrate this than early efforts to promote European integration, particularly the push for a European Convention for Human Rights. Historians have noted that Christian politicians were at the forefront of this project, and that Christian language permeated its publications and statements. Winston Churchill, who in the postwar years was integration's most famous proponent, explained in 1948 that the goal was to defend "the health of . . . Christendom."[39] Scholars have also highlighted the anti-Marxist motivations behind this project. Many advocates openly hoped that a supranational court could restrict communist policies in Eastern Europe and curtail socialist ambitions elsewhere. Less noted, however, is that for many participants, integration entailed an interconfessional mindset. In conferences and speeches, its leaders clarified their goal of transcending narrow confessionalism. Churchill, who like many Protestants once viewed Catholicism as a bastion of authoritarianism, helped skeptics overcome their suspicions. As he told a gathering of Dutch parliamentarians in 1946, Catholicism's willingness to join Protestants in a struggle for "the cause of personal freedom throughout the world" was one of the most "profound and beneficent new fact[s]" of the postwar world.[40] Such statements not only encouraged cooperation, but also legitimized the inclusion of figures with questionable political pasts. Alongside Churchill and other icons of anti-authoritarianism, such as French Protestant economist and resistance leader André Philip, conferences and organizations advocating for early integration included figures such as French Catholic Louis Salleron, who was a senior Vichy official and raving anti-Semite.[41]

The ecumenism of the 1950s therefore expanded considerably beyond the experiments of the 1930s. No longer confined to circles of fascist sympathizers and staunch anti-fascists, it produced a new consensus: both between confessions *and* between Christianity's warring political factions, which agreed to operate in a democratic and hierarchical system. This cooperation required heavy-handed revisionism. Repressing ecumenism's earlier associations with fascism, writers now claimed that ecumenists had always agreed on Christianity's emancipatory possibilities. As distant as this story was from the historical record, it proved enormously appealing to Christian elites. For writers and politicians exhausted by earlier divisions and anxious to find new alliances against socialism, ecumenism promised broad-tent cooperation. This cooperation also provided Catholics and Protestants with unprecedented access to state power. It was a power they were soon to wield to establish a new economic and social order.

Christian Economics in the Age of the "Economic Miracle"

Since the nineteenth century, social theory had been a source of both agreement and division between Catholics and Protestants. Almost all Christian economists and social theorists agreed on the need to combat the socialists' materialism, whose blend of egalitarianism and militant atheism they understandably viewed as an existential threat (akin to the French Revolution), and claimed that social order must be premised on harmonious inequality. Yet what this meant in practice was far from decided. In particular, Christians were divided on the state's role in mediating between workers and employers: while some claimed it was inequality's best defense, others maintained that economic relations should be left to free associations and charities. This debate shifted in the 1930s, when most thinkers concluded that some form of state intervention was necessary. It was not, however, resolved: while some advocated for the fascist model of "corporatism," where the state aggressively controlled labor and production, others claimed that it should only provide the conditions for market competition, with minimal welfare. What writers on both sides shared was a new claim to ecumenism. As they fiercely debated each other, several economists and social theorists claimed to represent a synthesis between Catholic and Protestant social visions.

Efforts to forge a joint social and economic theory intensified in the 1950s. The chaos of World War II and the beginning of the Cold War made this task more urgent than ever: with the Red Army occupying much of Europe's eastern parts, and communist parties surging in France and Italy, the materialist threat seemed to be preying on the disorder and despair caused by capitalism's failures and the devastating war. Yet ecumenism of the 1950s was more than a regurgitation of anti-communism, as important as it was. As happened in theology and politics, it also relied on a surprising new compromise. With the collapse of the corporatist model, Catholic and Protestant elites agreed on some version of the anti-fascist model, which contemporaries called "the social market economy." Even those who once called for radical state management now claimed that market competition instilled in individuals the self-discipline and humility that Christian life required, and that welfare would protect the most unfortunate from capitalism's most extreme consequences. Unlike what some historians have argued, this economic theory was not merely a product of compromise between free-market Protestants and welfare-focused Catholics.⁴² Rather, it was the product of a broader intellectual convergence that brought together different ideological factions across confessions. This compromise helped make the economy one of the most important sites for interconfessional cooperation. Once Christian democrats secured power, it also became the centerpiece of their economic policy.

The dominance of anti-socialism was not a foregone conclusion in the postwar era. For a brief moment the prestige that the Soviets acquired in military victory, and the abysmal failure of authoritarian corporatism, led many prominent Christians to wonder if the long-sought goal of social harmony could in fact be achieved through socialist redistribution. The Catholic Austrian social theoretician and politician Josef Dobretsberger, for example, who during the 1930s briefly served as minister of social affairs under Dollfuss's Austrian dictatorship, claimed that Catholic social justice required nationalizing industries and wealth redistribution. Capitalism, he wrote in his *Catholic Social Politics at the Crossroads* (1947), had become so inhumane that efforts to soften its rough edges with limited reforms were no longer viable; Catholics should instead seek a "synthesis" with socialism.⁴³ Similar sentiments were expressed by the Catholic German journalist and editor Walter Dirks, whose magazine *Frankfurt Journal* became a mouthpiece of the Catholic left. In multiple articles he claimed that earlier Catholic models, such as worker-employer associations and state-led corporations, were irrelevant in the era of late capitalism. "The Occident has a new task," he exclaimed, and that is "socialism."⁴⁴ In France the movement that epitomized these efforts was led by "worker-priests," a group of Catholic activists who sought to evangelize workers by joining them in factories and participating in strikes. Their best-selling reports and novels, describing workers' grim and difficult lives, claimed that only radical alterations could sustain the Church's commitment to its social teachings.⁴⁵ These ideas also inspired political innovations; several Catholic leaders advocated for policies long associated with the left. Politicians such as Jakob Kaiser in Germany and Claude Gérard in France called for nationalizing entire sectors (such as energy or steel) and for equal workers' representation in the management of industrial firms.

Similar experiments were briefly in vogue among Protestants. The German pastor and writer Hans Lutz, for example, a prominent politician in the Rhineland, claimed that the casualties of mass industrialization could not rely on voluntary charity. In *Protestantism and Socialism*

Today (1949), he wrote that a church committed to social justice would seek to recognize the legitimacy of Marxism and "realize the works of socialists." It was a goal he sought to achieve in 1946 by launching the forum Workers Community for Christianity and Socialism, where employers, politicians, and workers could discuss plans for the nationalization of industries and workers' participation in management.[46] Even more radical was the pastor Horst Symanowski, who claimed that workers' needs had to be at the center of the church's work, a mission he undertook by working at a cement factory and including workers in crafting his sermons. After his speech to the 1949 national Protestant congress in Germany impressed church officials, they helped him create a large training center in Mainz, where pastors and activists from around the world could learn about the labor conditions and economic struggles of workers.[47] Similar sentiments were apparent in France, where Protestant leaders Jacques Martin and Élie Gounelle relaunched the Social Christians movement, which focused church activism on the poor. In 1946 they founded the *Journal of Social Christianity,* and the following year they held a large congress in Lyon, where speaker after speaker called for radical redistribution.[48] Growing interest in economic reform even spread to unlikely figures, such as Otto Dibelius, a deeply conservative church leader from Berlin who before the war was one of Germany's most vocal antisocialists. In 1947 he helped draft a statement on economic policy, *Nation, State, and Economy with Christian Responsibility,* to express support for land redistribution and large-scale nationalization.[49]

Yet these experiments, which worked against a longer history, proved unable to dislodge anti-socialism from Christian social theory. The flaring of the Cold War had an especially suffocating effect; new communist regimes, anxious to establish themselves in the midst of hostile populations, emulated Soviet Stalinism and persecuted church authorities, confirming Christians' worst fears. The 1948 arrests of Hungary's Lutheran bishop Lajos Ordass and Catholic primate József Mindszenty for alleged conspiracy against the regime were particularly significant. After Mindszenty was put through a show trial and drugged into a forced confession, Catholics and Protestants erupted in rage, mobilizing in anti-communist petitions and demonstrations.[50] Local efforts to promote Christian-Marxist dialogue also came under fire, as Christian politicians and writers warned that they were a Trojan horse for communist infiltration and subversion. In Germany, Protestant churches resumed the publication of anti-communist studies, while in France, Catholic journals ran lurid reports on communist concentration camps.[51] This resurrection of anti-Marxism received the Vatican's stamp of approval in 1949, when Pope Pius XII formally prohibited engagement with "the materialist and antichristian doctrine of the communists" and threatened violators with ex-communication. A few years later Pius and the French hierarchy moved to formally suppress the worker-priest experiment by defrocking many of its members.[52] This ideological continuity was even more obvious in Protestant circles, which often reproduced the hyperbolic images of the 1930s to describe the geopolitical realities of the postwar moment. The German pastor Wilhelm Angel, for example, published a popular booklet that copied almost word for word his 1931 work in which he called for an apocalyptic war between "the West" and "godless Bolshevism."[53] Even advocates of Christian socialism conceded that their project was decisively marginalized. Walter Dirks bemoaned in 1950 that "the restoration of the old world is so complete that one must . . . accept it as a fact."[54]

Christian elites were able to quickly rebuild anti-socialist politics in part because they forged a new consensus around the postwar economic order. Across the confessional divide, Christian social theorists and economists embraced the theory developed by Christian anti-fascists, which claimed that the unequal and harmonious order was best served by states that allowed free competition and supplemented it with minimal welfare. The figure who best captured Catholics' path to this postwar version of anti-socialism was German social theorist Joseph Höffner, who began his career during the war and emerged in the late 1940s and 1950s as one of his country's most prominent economic writers. Like almost all Catholic theoreticians before him, Höffner decried both capitalism and socialism as soulless ideologies. Christians, he claimed in *Social Security and Individual Responsibility* (1953), had to forge an alternative economic system that revolved around not individuals or class but "natural" communities such as families, neighborhoods, or professions.[55] Yet Höffner broke new ground in Catholic social theory by claiming that the competitive market provided the best path to secure this order. In free exchange and competition, people learned responsibility and humility, allowing them to develop voluntary solidarity that contrasted with the "artificial" version imposed by socialist policies. For Höffner, this meant that the state's responsibility in the social realm was not to distribute wealth or provide expansive welfare, which were "incompatible with the Christian image of man." Instead, public authorities had to guarantee the workings of the market, mostly through anti-monopoly laws and by providing citizens with the tools to succeed on their own, such as specialized training. As he put it in *Social Policy in German Mining* (1954), "The state serves social security best by recognizing, promoting, and allowing the development of its citizens' personal responsibility."[56] Höffner went so far as to claim that entrepreneurs best reflected Christian social theory. In works such as *The Ethos of the Entrepreneur* (1956), he argued that this figure broke down the dichotomy between the individual and class that dominated liberalism and socialism, and embodied dynamism, optimism, and creativity.[57] Höffner conceded that some forms of state welfare were necessary, at least when families and local communities could not prevent abject poverty. But the goal of economic policy was to create the conditions for widespread participation in competitive markets. As he put it, what was needed was "social investment, not social redistribution."[58]

In expressing such ideas, Höffner was hardly alone, and not only because the Institute for Christian Social Sciences, which he founded in Cologne, popularized them in many publications.[59] His insistence on competition and limited welfare promised to realize inter-class harmony, defend private property, and preserve social hierarchies. Instead of charities (which were clearly ill-equipped to handle the dislocations of the Depression and the war) or state-led corporatism (which collapsed with fascism), regulated markets would secure social priorities. Multiple scholars therefore echoed Höffner's claims as an alternative to the failed corporatist experiment. The economist Johannes Messner, who had been a leading advocate for corporatism in the 1930s, now argued that only lightly regulated markets could bring about prosperity and peace between the classes. In his *Social Ethics* (1949), he explained that excessive welfare and planning would lead to inflation, whereas market-based payments would increase workers' wealth and improve their conditions. As he argued, "In the free society in accordance with natural law, economic cooperation can ... have only the form of competition."[60] Social theorist Guido Fischer, who began his career as a Nazi economic operative, similarly concluded after the war that the state's main priority was to increase workers' private earnings and possessions through market competition. In a major address to the Western Academy conference on labor, he mused that "a worker's best and most efficient form of ownership was his own private property."[61] When a group of theoreticians and politicians gathered in Munich in 1953 for a Catholic Social Week to discuss economic policy, their final statement proclaimed that "an economy and society organized in freedom" required not only adherence to God but also an embrace of competition. A Christian person, the statement concluded, "feels comfortable in freedom and in the market economy."[62]

The same logic moved from the periphery to the center of Protestant social theory. Its most representative figure was Hans Achinger, who began his career in the 1920s as an official for church charities and emerged after the war as an expert on welfare. In several publications, culminating in his influential *Social Security* (1953), Achinger claimed that the demand for state-led economic support was a symptom of secularization. As Europeans invested human reason with ever-expanding hopes for improvement, they also expected a life free of threats and risks. Achinger also recycled old tropes of Christian social thought to claim that the Enlightenment's focus on individual freedom led to social atomization, whereby community-based welfare such as poorhouses and charities disintegrated. Rather than relying on their neighbors and colleagues, workers had to resort to social insurance schemes to save for retirement. For Achinger, the tragic result of this process was the slow abandonment of personal responsibility, now replaced by the collective management of a faceless state bureaucracy. Workers transferred decisions about economic conduct and the spiritual questions it entailed (How much money does one need to live a good life?) to government officials, forming a dystopian "total state security system."[63] Most alarmingly, this entrusting of one's well-being to the state meant that government officials could decide the individual's economic priorities based on their own preferences. The "politics of security," for which the socialists advocated, sought to "protect the individual for the sake of the whole," a denial of individuality that mirrored the logic of Nazism and communism.[64] Like Höffner, however, Achinger conceded that despite the markets' liberating capacity to foster responsibility and self-reliance, it also required *some* sort of state intervention. Left to its own devices, capitalism was incapable of sustaining communal solidarity and required some supervision if everyone was to receive compensation that reflected their skills. Achinger therefore claimed that the state should establish a limited system of social security, whereby workers' contributions were tied as closely as possible to their income, profession, and family status. This, he concluded with a characteristic anti-socialist gesture, would protect an economic system rooted in "Christian-Occidental thought."[65]

The popularity of Achinger's writings reflected the growing prominence of such ideas. In particular, it echoed the ascendance of ordoliberalism, the intellectual movement developed by anti-Nazi thinkers during the Third Reich that had gained a foothold in postwar German life. The economist Alexander Rüstow, one of ordo-liberalism's most important thinkers, who returned to Germany after spending the war in exile, reiterated his wartime claims that Christian solidarity was best achieved in a society based on free competition. The state's main task was to protect free exchange by breaking business monopolies (which undermined competition), limiting collective bargaining (which limited free labor), and providing basic welfare (to ensure workers' health).[66] The same was true for economist Alfred Müller-Armack, who coined the term "social market economy," chaired the Protestant church commission on social affairs, and became a senior advisor to the German finance ministry. In works such as *Economic Governance and Market Economy* (1947) and *A Century without God* (1948), he claimed that Christian ethics required free exchange as well as protection from the most extreme misfortunes (such as disability). As these thinkers, along with their political patron, finance minister Ludwig Erhard, never tired of asserting, their vision was not one of uncritical support for unregulated capitalism. In *The Failure of Economic Liberalism as a Problem in the History of Religion* (1945), Rüstow argued that classic liberalism had emerged from pagan heresies and flourished only in the aftermath of the French Revolution's assault on Christianity. It was a "quasi-theological perversion" that Christians had to resist by insisting on state regulations and some welfare payments.[67] By the 1950s these ideas also received theological support. Friedrich Karrenberg, one of Germany's most prominent social writers and chief editor of the Protestant Church's *Evangelical Social Lexicon* (1954), explained that all Protestants "who want to be taken seriously" understood the need for free markets and effective regulations.[68]

Building on arguments they had begun crafting in the 1930s and early 1940s, both camps celebrated this convergence as an interconfessional achievement. Embracing each other as allies, they cast their ideas as part of a broadly "Christian" social and economic vision that transcended confessional boundaries. This was especially apparent among the ordo-liberals, who dedicated considerable attention to these issues. Rüstow, for example, wrote long essays explaining that the common association between capitalism and Protestantism was misguided. The ideology of free markets and private property, he claimed, predated the Reformation and was common to both confessions long after, meaning they could both secure its vibrancy.[69] Müller-Armack similarly argued that the two confessions shared a commitment to social harmony and a healthy suspicion of state authority. In his mind, their cooperation was not mere compromise but a deep intellectual overlap, which could pave the way to prosperity and stability.[70] The Catholic Höffner, who during the Third Reich studied with the Protestant ordo-liberal Walter Eucken, highlighted this similarity. In a speech titled "Neoliberalism and Christian Social Teachings," he mused that Rüstow's ideas were in perfect unison with Pius XII's pathbreaking encyclical on economic matters, *Quadragesimo anno* (1931), which called on states to forge harmony between the classes. (Conveniently Höffner did not mention that the encyclical also praised fascism.) Indeed, Catholic and Protestant economists who subscribed to ordo-liberal ideas promoted ecumenical engagement on economic policy. In conferences and seminars, many of which were funded by Christian business owners, they gathered to discuss their intellectual consensus and the most effective way to spread their message.[71] The distance Christian social theorists had traveled since their days of mutual suspicion was made clear as they came to see such efforts as uncontroversial. In 1959 the Protestant theologian Cord Cordes commented that the real task was not to highlight the similarities between Catholics and Protestants, which he considered obvious, but instead to focus on the differences.[72]

Only a few years after ecumenism triumphed in politics, it also began to leave its mark on economic policy. As Europe entered a period of exponential growth in the 1950s, and workers' militancy waned, the belief that free markets and supplemental government payments would secure social stability resonated with policymakers. This was most apparent when Höffner and Achinger cooperated in the crafting of Germany's social security system, the CDU's most ambitious economic policy. Beginning in 1953 and continuing into the following year, chancellor Adenauer began to advocate for an expansion of the country's welfare system, which he hoped would provide an electoral edge over the socialists. After his cabinet was unresponsive due to worries about inflation, in 1955 he appointed Höffner and Achinger to lead a special team of economic experts, which was divided equally between Catholics and Protestants. The report that this team produced, *Reordering Social Benefits* (1955), synthesized Höffner's and Achinger's writings. It celebrated the "dynamic" nature of the market and hailed "competition" and "market intensification" as the best tools for social stability. In the same spirit, it warned against a centralized welfare system, which had been implemented in Britain and was advocated for by socialists. This was unnecessary, the authors claimed, because many elderly people owned their homes, lived with their children, and/or had independent income, meaning they did not require robust public assistance. What is more, the report warned that an overly generous system would undermine social solidarity. Rather than relying on their families and local communities, individuals would turn to state institutions, a distant and anonymous authority. The purpose of the economic system was to resist this trend, and to strengthen small communities, which were the "natural" locations for economic security.[73]

At the same time, *Reordering Social Benefits* conceded that social cohesion required some expansion of state support for the elderly. As Höffner and Achinger explained, "The conditions of modern society mean that social security can no longer be guaranteed by individuals, families, communities, companies, and cooperatives alone without the state's assistance." The state had to mitigate disasters, and more importantly, provide the minimal safety net required for the population to participate in the market economy. The report especially praised the writings of Catholic social theorist Wilfried Schreiber, who claimed that public pensions were an expression of an intergenerational social contract, a principle that Christians had long relied on to legitimize private property. As the authors put it, "the solidarity between the paying workers and the pensioners must be considered as a solidarity between the generations." The report therefore recommended establishing a national, but not universal, pension system. Retirees' pensions were pegged to their lifelong income, with higher earners receiving higher payments, in order to preserve the "natural" inequalities between different capabilities; the system covered only workers and the self-employed; and it was established as a scheme whereby current workers subsidized current retirees, instead of a large state investment.[74] Despite opposition from both free-market advocates and socialists, the CDU adopted the recommendations. With some small modifications, they were passed as a pension bill in 1957. In many ways the system this bill created embodied the broader principles of the CDU's economic policy, including in child support payments, unemployment insurance, and health care. In all those spheres, the interconfessional alliance expanded the safety net, but only to ensure that recipients could sustain the lifestyle of their class and thus remain in their "natural" social position.[75]

The consolidation of ecumenical anti-socialism around the social market economy was not unique to Germany. With some variations, these alliances took place across Europe, where Christian democrats implemented a similar blend of policies. In Austria, the Catholic social theorist

Karl Kummer sought to reconcile Catholicism and the market economy by creating the Institute for Social Policy and Reform, which soon became an important think tank. "Social politics in Austria has reached a turning point," he proclaimed in a 1954 speech to the Western Academy, as Christians recognized that their old hostility to markets "could no longer provide guidance in the modern industrial operations." To achieve this task, he and other sympathetic Catholics initiated cooperation with Protestant ordo-liberals. The Institute launched a book series and a journal on capitalism and Christianity, which was coedited by Alfred Armack-Müller and the pro-market thinker August Maria Knoll, and where writers of both confessions explained the logic of regulated competition. This ideological tack appealed to leaders of the Austrian Christian democratic party, who, like its German counterparts, abandoned their postwar flirtation with socialism in favor of low taxes and competition. The party's manifesto, simply titled "What We Want" (1958), proclaimed that "only the capital of companies and private households will secure competitiveness," enable higher incomes, and thus increase cross-class harmony.[76] In the Netherlands, Catholics and Protestants joined hands to defeat socialist proposals to centralize and expand welfare programs under state authority. Instead, many welfare provisions, from family support to relief for the poor, were funded by the state but were administered through private organizations and charities.[77] In France, too, similar cooperation took place between the Catholic MRP politician François de Menthon and the Protestant economist René Courtin, a senior member of the country's Protestant council. Drawing on their joint work during the war at resistance think tanks, the two advocated for market-based models, where the state was to focus on fostering competition and basic welfare.[78]

The electoral success of this cooperation, of course, relied on much more than ideological innovation and coordination. It benefited from the Christian democrats presiding over meteoric economic growth, particularly the expansion of consumer possibilities for Europe's working classes. As a result, both Catholic and Protestant tirades against consumerism slowly faded in the 1950s. Instead, Christian writers praised rising workers' salaries and their ability to purchase goods as the antidote to socialist collectivism. Christian social theorists came to believe that the solution to class conflict was not mediation between workers and employers. Instead, the goal was to increase economic resources, so that even those at the bottom would benefit from economic growth and become more willing to tolerate continued inequality. For example, the Catholic Höffner argued that the cure for the "social question" was increasing workers' access to private property. In *Christian Social Teachings* (1962), which became his most popular book and went through multiple editions, he claimed that the long-sought harmony between classes would be achieved when workers could afford their own homes and cars. "Personal responsibility will be strengthened," he mused, "and the trend toward the welfare state will be checked."[79] The Dutch Protestant theologian Hendrik van Oyen was even more enthusiastic, gushing in *Affluence and the Christian* (1962) that "the market overflows with goods, wages go on rising, and eventually everyone will be able to afford everything." Thanks to this development, he proclaimed, the very reason for class conflict had evaporated, since "in practice there are no longer any class boundaries." In Van Oyen's eyes, this reality was the key for sustaining Christian charity and friendship. "Because of its greater social equality," he wrote, consumer culture "gives increasing opportunities to create neighborly standards of behavior."[80] The ecumenism of the postwar era, then, preserved earlier anti-socialist ideas but updated them to new conditions, in particular the postwar expansion of consumer capitalism. In the process, it forged a broad conceptual agreement on the nature of "Christian" economics, premised on market competition, limited welfare, and acceptance of inequality.

To be sure, even at its height, this economic cooperation was never without friction, and confessional tensions did not vanish in the postwar era. Thinkers and politicians relentlessly debated whether certain policies were too generous, and thus too close to socialism, or not generous enough, thus risking the triumph of individualist liberalism. These dynamics were especially visible in Germany, where the advisory board of the Ministry of Economics (which helped draft its policies) often split along confessional lines. Oswald Nell-Breuning, the board's most prominent Catholic figure (and one of the country's leading social commentators), often clashed with the Protestant Müller-Armack, whose market-focused outlook he found too far removed from questions of social justice.[81] In the era of Christian democracy, however, such internal tensions were reduced to secondary considerations. After decades of debate, Catholics and Protestants largely agreed on the broad contours of "Christian" economics, premised on securing "natural" inequalities through restricted state-run welfare and capitalist competition.

Repression, Pleasure, and Ecumenical Family Ethics

The war and its aftermath sent shockwaves through Europe's approach to gender and sexuality. The combination of government policies, mass dislocation, and scarcity led millions to experience arrangements beyond the patriarchal family. This change was noticeable during the war, which the Nazis and their allies hoped would solidify male dominance and female dependence. In a dark irony, the mobilization and deaths of countless men led many women to become primary providers and heads of households. Feminism seemed especially vibrant in the immediate postwar moment, when it scored important advances. Women's suffrage arrived in France, Belgium, and Italy, while newly created communist regimes in Poland, Hungary, and other Eastern European countries made women's labor and emancipation a centerpiece. The wartime years also dramatically expanded sexual encounters beyond heterosexual marriage as many people engaged (whether voluntarily or out of desperation) in extramarital or premarital relationships, a trend that continued after the war. Sex reformers sought to seize what they believed was a potential moment of transformation. They relaunched campaigns that were suppressed by fascism, such as expanding access to contraception or decriminalizing same-sex relations.

Catholic and Protestant elites were as adamant as ever that the patriarchal heterosexual family was the foundation of society, and once in power, they mobilized in force to suppress alternatives. But as happened in the fields of theology, politics, and social theory, their cooperation was premised on a new synthesis of different traditions and intellectual emphases. On the one hand, Christian elites continued campaigns from the turn of the century and the interwar years against feminism and sexual reform movements. Especially during the early years of postwar reconstruction, they sought to enshrine inequality between men and women (and between married and unmarried women) and to use state power to restrict perceived threats to heterosexual and procreative families, particularly pornography, homosexuality, and abortion. On the other hand, they updated their intellectual justification for this gender and sexual order. Drawing on ideas coined by anti-fascists in the 1930s, Christian writers claimed that the family was the site of love and sexual gratification. Indeed, if writers in the nineteenth century and the interwar era claimed that the family was a site for learning self-denial and self-control, they now argued the opposite: they depicted it as the *only* space where men and women could experience "true" pleasure. It was the combination of both these trends—harsh patriarchy with a focus on intimate pleasure—that led many commentators to extend ecumenism to the sphere of family ethics. The two confessions, they claimed, shared mutual enemies *and* a positive vision of conjugality.

The belief that the family was the center of the social order had long been a point of agreement between Catholics and Protestants, and this was the case also in the postwar years. Catholics such as the French sociologist Jean Lacroix and Protestants like the German marriage expert Paul Plattner agreed that the family was the training ground for the self-denial and respect on which social solidarity rested.[82] Adapting to the postwar period, Christian writers also argued that the family was the bulwark against the totalitarian state, whether in its fascist or communist manifestations. In countless essays and books, they claimed that the family alone could nourish children with sustained parental (and especially maternal) love, and thus provide an autonomous social sphere where humans could practice spiritual independence and self-sufficiency, in contrast to totalitarian demands to erase the autonomous self by surrendering to the state's demands. These convictions were the reason Christian democratic parties quickly defined themselves as the protectors of the family. In Germany, one of the CDU's earliest publications proclaimed that "the family is the foundation of the social order." The state, another pamphlet explained, "through its wage and tax legislation and its housing policies, is to create the room that [the] family needs to be able to come into being and develop itself fully."[83] In France, the MPR distinguished itself with similar rhetoric. Its first manifesto announced in 1945 that "true education and freedom can flourish only within families. The legislator therefore has a duty to do all that is necessary for the family."[84] Family was just as central to the Belgian Social Christian Party. "The party wants first of all to protect the family," explained its leader in 1946, because "this is the fundamental social group in which the human personality blossoms."[85]

Echoing their initial responses to the feminist movement half a century earlier, Catholics and Protestants agreed that the family was premised on a hierarchical relationship between men and women. As the German Catholic booklet *One Mind, One Way, One God* bluntly asserted, "Each family needs paternal power, a master who carries the burden of all the all-encompassing worry."[86] The influential German Protestant theologian Helmut Thielicke, whose voluminous *Theological Ethics* (1951) was a key reference for Protestant family experts, explained that as the family's representatives in the public sphere, men had the final word in marriage disagreements over property and children's education. "A theological ethics," he wrote, "cannot abstain from declaring ... that the father holds the final decision."[87] This hierarchy also assumed a strict distinction between men and women's social functions. Men's destiny was to be breadwinners and represent the family in the public sphere, while the women's task was to oversee the home and the children. The Catholic family expert Ernst Michel explained in *Marriage: An Anthropology of Sexual Community* (1948) that only a clear division would prevent married couples from trespassing onto each other's autonomy. The Swiss Protestant theologian Charlotte von Kirschbaum similarly complained in *The Real Woman* (1949) that feminists failed to grasp that "humanity exists only in the dissimilar duality of man and woman," and that only by respecting this duality could both enjoy "real dignity."[88] The belief in such divisions persisted even after women entered the workforce in increasing numbers in the 1950s, as Christians continued to insist that women's labor was unnatural and thus should be restricted to the unmarried and to certain professions. The influential Protestant family expert Guido Groeger explained in *Anxiety and Happiness in Sexual Development* (1954) that "We can behave as modern as we want, [but] the life of the girl" can only be fully realized when she becomes "a married woman and mother."[89]

As quickly as they did in the sphere of economic policy, Catholic and Protestant politicians moved to enshrine this agreement in Europe's social order. Building on the foundations they set in the nineteenth century, they resumed their paradoxical quest to create the inequalities they considered natural. The first and main step for this effort was to secure inequality between married men and women. Even as postwar constitutions granted political rights to women in the form of suffrage, this status did not extend to the sphere of family law, where men's authority remained supreme. Wives could not have access to their husbands' business funds (even if they ran the businesses), could not claim joint properties, and lacked the authority to decide which schools their children would attend. Throughout the 1950s, Christian leaders and politicians routinely rebuffed efforts to extend equality into family affairs. In Germany, CDU politicians, with the support of Catholic and Evangelical church leaders, spent years defending family inequality until it was struck down by the German Supreme Court in 1959.[90] Similar opinions continued to undergird Christian politics in France, where family law empowered men over their families, and where feminist efforts to revise inequalities in family law were summarily defeated. Unequal family law was also grounds for interconfessional cooperation in the Netherlands. Even when they did not share power in mutual coalitions, the Catholic and Protestant parties could rely on each other to defeat proposals to end restrictions on the initiation of divorce or to allow women to make claims on family property, which survived until the 1970s.[91]

Christian democrats also went out of their way to diminish women's labor. Here they drew especially on the authoritarian experiments launched in Germany and France in the 1930s and 1940s, and harnessed the emerging postwar welfare systems, of which they were key architects, to aggressively encourage a focus on motherhood.[92] In Germany, the key figure in this effort was the Catholic politician Franz-Josef Wuermeling, who became the minister for family affairs in 1953. Under his leadership, the CDU established a family allowance, which was administered to workers by employers (and not by state institutions, as socialists had wanted) and which was restricted to married couples (most single mothers were denied support).[93] Wuermeling, who was also one of Germany's most vocal natalists, routinely explained that the purpose of such policies was not to lift all working people from poverty—an idea that he condemned as materialist—but to allow women to devote themselves to motherhood, which by extension also would make them dependent on their husbands. The goal, he mused, was to "save our mothers for our families and our children!"[94] In France, too, Christian politicians followed the model established by the Vichy regime and utilized welfare to encourage motherhood and female dependence on male labor. When the Catholic politician Robert Prigent became minister of population and public health, he instituted family allowances, which he, like Wuermeling, conceptualized as an anti-socialist measure.[95] In the Netherlands, an aversion to women's labor brought together Catholics and Protestants, first in joint campaigns by youth organizations and then in legislation. The two confessions helped institute allowances to married families, hoping to deter women from seeking work outside the home.[96]

Alongside anti-feminism, Catholics and Protestants also revived and deepened their joint quest to cleanse the public sphere of visual enticements. Building on the rhetoric and experiences of earlier morality campaigns, they agreed that families must be protected from erotic and pornographic publications, which, alongside violent and trashy novels, threatened to inflame inappropriate passions and encourage premarital sex. The Catholic German theologian Bernhard Häring was especially concerned with youth, whose lack of experience and self-control made them extra vulnerable to temptation. In his influential *The Law of Christ* (1955), which was widely read across Europe, he explained that the state had to restrict such publications, even if that meant curtailing freedom of speech. If it failed to do so, other "ways and means must be found to shut off the ceaseless flow of sewage from so many hidden fountains of defilement," such as boycotts against "immoral" bookstores.[97] A different logic was presented by Paul Althaus, one of Germany's most influential theologians. Althaus believed that God instilled in humans an instinctual link between sex and shame. This, he claimed, was designed not to devalue sexuality as such but to keep it a private matter; it was God's will that the sexual act happen in secret. Instead of repressively controlling people's free speech, censorship of erotic ads, movies, and books was the means to establish a healthy approach to sexuality. "The Christian ethic does not demand of youth principles that destroy life," he explained in *Outline of Ethics* (1953), "but, on the contrary, guidelines that lead to a full and wholesome life in love."[98]

As happened with anti-feminism, this mutual hostility to "trash and filth" fueled interconfessional mobilization. In 1949 the leaders of Germany's Protestant churches relaunched their decades-old campaign, which was paused because of the war, to ban the display of pornographic products and their sale to youth. They were soon joined by Catholic activists (some of whom publicly burned piles of racy magazines); replicating their successful legislative push from the 1920s, they led the CDU to pass the Law about the Distribution of Youth-Endangering Publications in 1953. The legislation established a federal board that included church representatives to regulate and limit the sale of pornographic material and violent texts. Joint mobilization helped pass similar legislation in France, such as the 1949 law that banned the sale of erotic publications to youth. A 1958 decree extended this ban, prohibiting the sale or display of any publication that was licentious, pornographic, or violent. Similar laws also passed in Austria, the Netherlands, and Belgium. Across the continent, Catholics and Protestants built legal bulwarks to defend the family from the alleged threat of sexual agitation.[99]

If censorship proved so popular among both Catholics and Protestants, it was in part because they used it against abortion and same-sex relations. Indeed, in most Christians' eyes those remained the most dangerous temptations, since they allegedly encouraged sexual activity beyond the family and thus led to sexual materialism. As the German Catholic politician Maria Probst explained using standard hyperbole, legalizing abortion would lead to "naked materialism, uninhibited sexuality, [and] dying eros."[100] This masochistic logic, in which freedom to enjoy sex without fear would in fact empty it of meaning, led Christian democrats to aggressively prosecute abortion. In France, Germany, and the Netherlands, the number of legal cases against abortion increased after the war.[101] Equally harsh was the treatment of same-sex relations, especially among men, which Christian commentators viewed as especially prone to targeting children. France preserved the Vichy-era criminalization of same-sex encounters between adults and minors; in the Netherlands, the government reinstated the 1911 anti-homosexuality law passed by a Catholic and Protestant coalition. In Germany and Austria, all male same-sex relations were banned. Imprisonment under these laws, which were at times accompanied by forced castration, surged everywhere. It reached especially monstrous proportions in the Netherlands, where almost 1 percent of the male population over the age of sixteen was registered as an offender by the police.[102]

These repressive campaigns generated considerable cooperation between Catholics and Protestants, but they were not new; after all, opposition to feminism and sex reforms had been central to Christian thought and politics since the nineteenth century, and had led many to support fascism in the 1930s and 1940s. In the postwar era, however, Catholics and Protestants paired this older focus with a new vision of the family that sought to strengthen and legitimatize it as the site of love and pleasure. The reason for this new shift lay in the despondence that many Christian elites felt about the family's future. Despite their aggressive efforts, women in the 1950s continued to enter the workforce, and popular demand for racy publications only increased. As they sought new ways to shore up the family, Catholic and Protestant writers therefore increasingly drew on the family ethics that anti-fascist writers such as Emil Brunner developed in the 1930s. These ideas originally emerged as a critique of Nazi biologism and its Christian supporters, which conflated the family with the racial collective's destiny. Brunner and others, in contrast, insisted that the family's task was to provide autonomy and to foster love and pleasure beyond the state's intrusion. In the postwar era, Christian writers seized on these ideas for new purposes. Ignoring Brunner's flirtation with feminism, they insisted that the family was the counter to women's liberation because it provided partnership and sexual pleasure between parents. This new justification for anti-feminism in fact became the central feature of Christian family thinking. The ascetic vision of self-sacrificing parents eventually gave way to talk of improved sexual techniques, emotional fulfillment, and especially female orgasms; men were encouraged to focus on their partner, and women were instructed that the family, rather than feminism or sexual reform, could be a site of gratification and even a form of sexual liberation. As this vision made its way to the mainstream of Christian thought, its proponents celebrated an exciting area of Catholic-Protestant reconciliation. Radically expanding on the sporadic efforts of the 1930s, writers and sex experts described pleasure as the foundation of a truly interconfessional sexual ethic.

An emblematic example for this new conception of the family was German theologian August Adam's *Primacy of Love,* which was originally published during the war but reappeared in a revised version in 1948 that was widely cited by writers in multiple languages. Building off the work of anti-fascists from the 1930s, Adam chastised some of his fellow Catholics' obsession with censorship and repression, which he described as a failure to develop a positive approach to sexuality. "We have been handing out warnings about the movies and the theater, about fashions and about dancing," he complained, "but we have not succeeded in winning over modern culture as a means of expression to the positive service of Christian betterment."[103] Adam instead maintained that aversion to sex and erotic feelings had no roots in scripture or Christian traditions. Sexual pleasure was a legitimate goal, as long as it was confined to heterosexual marriage. In fact, achieving pleasure was necessary to realize and solidify the emotional ties that made marriage unique. As he explained, "It is not the man who ignores sex, as if it were beneath him, who is virtuous," but instead the "man who recognizes his body for what it is, and can look at it with eyes that are pure."[104]

These ideas were tremendously popular in the 1950s. As they struggled to explain why marriage was so much better than "aberrant" temptations, Catholic writers emphasized the centrality of intimacy and pleasure. The Austrian Catholic marriage expert Friedrich von Gagern, for example, whose writings on sex were international blockbusters, declared in *Marriage Partnership* (1955) that sexual pleasure was the foundation of healthy unions. In his telling, while nonmarital sex was bound to foster fear and shame, the married couple, united by long-term love and trust, could reach unparalleled joy.[105] The French Catholic author Marc Oraison was most explicit, guiding men to help their wives experience orgasm, a goal he viewed as being as important as procreation. As he wrote in *Union in Marital Love* (1956), "Man must strive to make the rhythm of his own reflexes pick up and follow the beat of the woman's rhythm" so they could "synchronize the climax."[106] This focus on sex received a medical stamp of approval when the Dutch Catholic gynecologist J. G. H. Holt published his *The Tide: The Relationship between Fertility and Temperature in Women* (1958). Soon translated into all European languages and celebrated by Catholic doctors and commentators, Holt claimed to have discovered a cyclical change in women's body temperature that correlated to their period of fertility. For Holt, the study's most important implication was that it allowed married couples to engage in sexual activity during most of the month without fearing pregnancy (what contemporaries called the rhythm method).[107]

This focus on pleasure was so innovative because it invested the family with a whole new meaning. Alongside helping men and women to successfully take on their assigned social roles, it also promised emancipation through mutual pleasure. This logic was therefore also popular among Protestants. A pivotal example was the French-Swiss psychologist and doctor Paul Tournier, whose efforts to craft a new approach to sexuality began during World War II but reached a mass audience in in the 1950s and early 1960s. Drawing on anti-fascist writers from the 1930s, Tournier claimed that Protestants were right to warn of the dangers of premarital and extramarital sex, which were little more than the selfish fulfillment of animalistic impulses. Yet they had taken this vigilance too far, condemning sexuality due to shame and frustration with their own desires. In popular works such as *The Bible and Medicine* (1953), Tournier claimed that sexual pleasure was a Christian principle, an expression of marital love. When "God directs the sex life of a married couple," he explained, then husband and wife "can practice it divinely," even if it did not lead to children, "in full mutual communion that is carnal, moral, and spiritual all at once." To make his case, Tournier pointed to the New Testament and noted that Jesus showed few inhibitions about erotic feelings. After all, he associated with prostitutes and accepted kisses from harlots, demonstrating that "his attitude was very far removed from the puritanical contempt of sex which is only too often thought to be Biblical."[108] Tournier's writings instructed couples to explore their sexuality and warned that men's lack of attention to their wives' pleasure was equivalent to rape. He provided detailed anatomical instructions and drawings, which were meant to enable men and women to understand each other's physiology.[109]

These ideas circulated widely among Protestants in Europe, in part thanks to Tournier's own organizational skills; as a senior member of the Christian Medical Association of Europe, he helped establish a multitude of international publications and conferences. The Austrian physician and marriage counselor Bernhard Harnik, who chaired the Christian Medical Association, published two marriage manuals, *The Meaning of Life* (1953) and *The Purpose of Relationships* (1955). These texts, which were also popular in Germany and Switzerland, equated the relationship between men and women to the one between humans and God, which they described as a process of mutual giving. Procreation was important, Harnik claimed, but was only one purpose of this union; it was also to foster spiritual and physical satisfaction.[110] The Dutch theologian Hendrik van Oyen encouraged parents to discuss the nature of eros and desire with their children. In his *Love and Marriage* (1956) he explained that physical attraction was a sign of love, which, if practiced in marriage, could be the source of happiness.[111] In Switzerland, Karl Barth, perhaps the continent's most famous theologian, dedicated long passages in part 3 of his monumental *Church Dogmatics* (1953) to chastising the "Christian discrimination against eros" as "a very old mistake." In his eyes, "the completion of the sexual relation should be integrated into the total encounter of man and woman," even if it did not lead to children.[112]

It was this new focus on pleasure that also fostered the most explicit discussions of a shared, ecumenical family ethics. Reading each other's essays and manuals, writers believed they found allies not only against mutual enemies, but also in a positive vision of an unequal but loving family. The Catholic Adam, for example, claimed in his *Primacy of Love* that Catholic hostility to sexual pleasure was an unfortunate consequence of the Reformation. As part of their competition, Catholics and Protestants had imposed ever-increasing prohibitions, seeking to demonstrate to believers that they alone were true to Christ's message of chastity. This claim allowed Adam to question sex's association with sin and to claim that the two confessions were doctrinally close to each other. Surveying the works of anti-fascist Protestant theologians such as Emil Brunner, who in the 1930s claimed that the family's main function was to provide intimate love, he concluded that Catholics and Protestants could cooperate in fostering tolerance for marital pleasure.[113] While Adam's historical claims were idiosyncratic, the lessons he drew from them were not. In guidebooks and manuals, Catholic proponents of pleasure praised Protestant experts and insisted on broad interconfessional teachings. The Belgian Pierre de Locht, a major authority in family matters, praised Tournier for recognizing Christianity's emancipatory potential. In *Love in the Marriage: Christian Perspectives* (1956), he claimed that Catholics and Protestants alike understood the family's ability to offer satisfaction to parents.[114] The French Catholic journal *Esprit,* which had advocated for a focus on pleasure since the 1930s, similarly indicated that there were no major differences between the confessions. When in 1960 it published a 300-page special issue on sexuality, involving interviews with philosophers, sex experts, and psychologists, it included both Catholics (like Oraison) and Protestants (the young theologian André Dumas) as representatives of the Christian approach.[115]

Even more so than their Catholic counterparts, Protestants were eager to emphasize that this approach did not derive from Luther's or Calvin's teachings but represented a broader and ecumenical vision. They referred to Catholic writings, particularly papal proclamations, to argue that the alternative to feminism and sex reform was sexually satisfying marriage. The Swiss Tournier, for example, referenced writers such as Adam at length, and observed that the sexual act between Adam and Eve predated the fall, and thus was not sinful. Such openness to pleasure, he reasoned, showed that the two confessions were close to each other and could cooperate in normalizing it inside the family. The Austrian Harnik similarly claimed that Catholics and Protestants shared a commitment to pleasure in the family, which in his view made interconfessional marriages likely to succeed. "Many psychologists are inclined to regard religious or denominational problems in marriage only as a point of reference for more deeply based psychological problems," he wrote, but "this attempt is incorrect," because the two confessions subscribed to similar family ethics.[116] The ideas circulated in enough magazines and books that they became common. When the international conference of Protestant doctors gathered in Amsterdam in 1963, speaker after speaker highlighted what they saw as shared Catholic and Protestant devotion to procreation and pleasure in marriage. As one Dutch physician explained, both were engaged in a struggle to treat human sexuality not as a biological or medical affair (which was what proponents of free sex allegedly did), but as an expression of emotional and spiritual well-being.[117]

The person who best embodied the efforts to craft this explicitly ecumenical vision of marriage and the family was the Swiss marriage expert

Theodor Bovet. Combining substantial practical experience—he ran Evangelical marriage counseling centers in Zurich—and literary flair, Bovet emerged as a giant in Christian thinking about marriage and sex. In works such as *The Secret Is Great* (1956), which appeared in all major European languages and ran through multiple editions, Bovet offered a comprehensive response to feminism. On the one hand, his writings emphasized the two sexes' different social missions, which he bemoaned were undermined by feminists. In a healthy society, he maintained, the man "represents the association in the outside world, decides where to live, provides the bread and butter," whereas the wife "experiences God's creative power in her own body as her child grows."[118] Bovet warned readers that the success of marriage depended on women's acceptance of their husbands' sense of authority and their own focus on children. "Most divorces can be traced back to the fact that the husband felt himself to be inferior to his wife, and she accentuated this feeling, until another woman came along who knew how to make a 'head' out of him ... When the wife is stronger, more sensible, more experienced and spirited than the husband and takes care to let him know it, this usually leads to unhappiness and quarreling."[119] At the same time, Bovet claimed that the purpose of true Christianity was not just parenthood, but a deeper spiritual bond, of which sex was the fullest manifestation. "It is not only children that are created by the husband and wife by the act of love," he explained; "the fellowship of marriage is also created by the husband and wife becoming one flesh."[120] Bovet encouraged readers to experiment with creative foreplay and multiple positions, which he emphasized was especially important to empower women. He challenged notions of female sexual passivity to claim that they should take command of the conjugal act, explaining to husbands that they should let their wives initiate it, determine its length, and decide on specific positions.[121] Bovet, then, sought to offer a new justification for the patriarchal family, claiming it did not require masochistic self-denial but empowered women sexually.

Early in his career, Bovet conceived his ideas in strictly confessional terms, contrasting Protestants' openness to pleasure with the Catholics' alleged fixation on procreation, but the developments of the postwar era radically transformed his assumptions. If Catholics embraced more affirmative views of sex, he reasoned, this made them crucial allies in the battle against feminism, sexual materialism, and the disintegration of the family. In *The Secret Is Great* he stated that "the differences between the Protestant and Roman Catholic view on marriage" may have once been considerable, but that this was no longer the case. "On the contrary, discussion and a deepening awareness have led both sides closer to the mystery of marriage."[122] Bovet repeatedly highlighted what he saw as crucial similarities between the two confessions' visions. Citing Catholic writers such as Adam alongside Tournier and other Protestant sources, he exulted that they all recognized the significance of premarital virginity, the centrality of sexual differences, and an affirmation of conjugal pleasure. Bovet systematically surveyed the issues on which the two confessions were at least nominally divided, such as the possibility of divorce, to explain that even there, they shared a mutual worldview. Just like Catholics, he claimed, Protestants assumed that marriage was a lifelong bond and agreed to divorce only when this spiritual possibility ceased to exist. "The Catholic and Protestant attitudes to divorce therefore do not differ fundamentally," he concluded, since "both deny the existence of any legal right to divorce and recognize at most the annulment of a proceeding that has only been a marriage in appearance."[123]

To realize this ecumenical vision, Bovet founded the Interconfessional Christian Institute for Marriage and Family Treatment in Zürich in 1956. Employing therapists of both confessions in joint sessions, it ran evening classes for couples as well as seminars for professional marriage counselors. In 1964, after this work had drawn attention across Europe, landing Bovet numerous invitations to speak at conferences on Christian sex and marriage, the Center launched the ecumenical *Marriage: Magazine for Marriage and Family Counseling,* which was published in three languages (English, German, and French), seeking to synthesize Catholic and Protestant family ethics. Its contributors included some of Europe's most popular Christian writers, such as Austrian-German Catholic author Ida Friederike Görres, alongside a who's who of Christian sexual experts, including Friedrich von Gagern, Pierre de Locht, and Guido Groeger. In its reviews, reports on medical experiments, and advice for couples, the magazine celebrated its ecumenical mission. As its opening statement (likely written by Bovet) put it, "The publishers of this journal are Christian, Catholics and Protestants," who share an understanding of "marriage as an expression and an image of divine love." By the mid-1960s it happily reported the adoption of its model elsewhere; similar interconfessional initiatives were launched in Germany, the Netherlands, and France.[124]

Perhaps the most far-reaching consequences of this unified Christian vision, with its blend of older patriarchalism and a more recent affirmation of pleasure, were shifting sensibilities when it came to interfaith marriages, often called "mixed marriages." If Catholics and Protestants shared such similar views, could they not sustain loving ecumenical families? This was the position of Bovet, who in a keynote address to a German conference claimed that when interconfessional marriages collapsed, it was usually because one of the partners became agnostic, not because of unbridgeable values or disagreements over children's education. Even if man and wife belonged to different churches, if they remained committed to the "natural" social division and to the ethics of partnership and pleasure, they could "lead [a] rich and spiritually fruitful marriage."[125] Others, such as Protestant pastor Joachim Lell, similarly maintained that doctrinal opposition to mixed marriages was too sweeping. Some of these marriages were a sign of waning commitment to one's religious community, but others were the product of shared values, which the churches should not rebuke. A decade later this conviction would spur Lell to lead negotiations between Catholics and Protestants on the possibility of joint marriages.[126] Theologian Heinrich Bornkamm, a prominent figure in Germany's Protestant establishment, similarly asserted that marriage was the key site of interconfessional cooperation. Commenting on the weakening of confessional boundaries, he noted that "all of Germany lives today in one, large mixed marriage."[127] Such opinions remained the minority, and most church hierarchies continued to warn that interconfessional families would lead to indifference, failed marriages, and declining birth rates.[128] But growing support for "mixed marriages" among prominent commentators reflected new sensibilities, at least among laity.

Catholic and Protestant cooperation around gender and sexual ethics in the postwar decades, therefore, relied on both repetition and innovation. On the one hand, it represented the culmination of prolonged Catholic-Protestant cooperation against materialist feminism and sex reform. Further deepening the state's reach into the intimate sphere, it enshrined inequality between the sexes, discouraged female work outside the home, and continued the morality campaigns' quest to "cleanse" the public sphere of temptation. At the same time, it also updated and changed its justification; it paired these restrictions with an emphasis on fulfillment within the family. Drawing on theories developed by anti-fascists in the 1930s, Christian sex experts claimed that the family was a site of sexual satisfaction, the only place where men and women could enjoy true pleasure. Like their consensus on social and economic theory, this reasoning allowed Christians to insist on maintaining old hierarchies while making them more palatable, particularly for those assigned a lower position. This focus on strengthening hierarchy by finding new rationales for subordination proved so successful that it extended beyond Europe. Catholics and Protestants sought to use it in response to dramatic changes in global politics, including the collapse of European colonialism.

The Final Ecumenical Breakthrough: Missions and Decolonization

Decolonization was a cataclysmic shock to the world order. That independence could come so quickly to vast Asian colonial possessions such as India, Pakistan, and Ceylon (1947), Syria and Lebanon (1948), and Indonesia (1949) raised doubts about the long-held notion that Europe's supremacy would last into the foreseeable future. Events were even more dramatic in Africa, which Europeans had long considered the world's most primitive region and thus most in need of tutelage. Despite Europe's brutal efforts to suppress liberation movements, British rule collapsed in Ghana (1957), French control disintegrated in Guinea (1958), and Belgian rule fell in the Congo (1960), followed by the independence of other states and culminating in the chaotic and violent French withdrawal from Algeria (1962). As the French scholar Henri Labouret ruefully observed, decolonization seemed to mark a "new phase" in world history, where European grandeur was swept away by the "awakening" of other continents.[129] To be sure, some commentators adapted to new conditions, paternalistically claiming that Asian and African liberation movements were realizing European ideals, and thus represented the successful outcome of Europe's civilizing mission. Certain forms of empire remained resilient, as many European corporations and governments imposed new economic arrangements on postcolonial states that reconstituted unequal political and economic relationships. Still, during the late 1950s and early 1960s, most observers agreed that Europe's position in the world was both diminishing and becoming more contested than ever. "The veil was torn," remarked French civil servant Jean Vacher-Desvernais in 1962, "reduced to its essentials, decolonization represents above all a series of humiliating ordeals."[130]

Christian missionaries and their European supervisors were especially shaken by the tide of anti-colonial revolts. Across confessional and national lines, they worried that the rise of anti-European sentiments and the collapse of imperial states rendered Western missionaries and their work newly vulnerable. Whether they were led by socialists, nationalists, or Muslims, worried one popular Italian Protestant writer in 1957, "there seems to be a totalitarian strain . . . in the newly independent states in Asia and Africa" that made them hostile to Christianity.[131] It was this sense of disorientation that led to ecumenism's final breakthrough in the missionary sphere in the late 1950s and early 1960s, a few years after it triumphed in Europe. As Catholic and Protestant missionary leaders scrambled to adapt to the decolonizing world, they converged around the same impulses that guided their thinking about economics and gender, simultaneously softening and reinforcing hierarchies. Theoreticians in both confessions drew on innovations from the 1930s to claim that the missions must open themselves to non-European traditions and abandon their quest to "civilize" non-Europeans. At the same time, they also insisted that Europeans played a distinct role as leaders and supervisors, especially in modernizing non-Europeans economically. This task, they claimed, was different from the civilizing mission; it was meant to demonstrate Christianity's capacity to improve life even after colonialism's collapse. This thinking, with its many internal tensions, proved so popular that it inspired ecumenism's pathbreaking institutional manifestations. In ways unseen in the eras of high imperialism or the 1930s, Europe's largest missionary organizations and charities launched interconfessional work, especially in organizing economic development and combating polygamy, two efforts they claimed were the epitome of ecumenical action.

When decolonization began to unfold in Asia, it did not register as a tectonic shift for most Christian commentators. Despite the long associations between Christianity and European dominance, the regimes that emerged in India and Indonesia largely agreed to tolerate missionaries, even if at times they imposed restrictive conditions.[132] The communist revolution in China, however, injected new meanings into anti-colonial uprisings. As part of its campaign to uproot "Western cultural imperialism," the new regime ordered the expulsion of all Christian missions, Catholic or Protestant, and in 1951 shut down all schools, universities, and hospitals run by missionaries. Other newly independent countries followed suit. When in 1958 Guinea became the first sub-Saharan country to declare independence from French domination, its leader, Sékou Touré, ordered a takeover of all missionary institutions in the country—which Touré decried as stooges of European control—and later proceeded to expel all European missionaries. Perhaps most disconcerting from the missionary perspective, such expulsions were paralleled by new avenues for Islam. When Nigeria gained its independence in 1960, for example, Muslim prime minister Abubakar Balewa emerged as its first postcolonial head of state. The cumulative effect of these events, which missionaries viewed as variations of the same threat, was exacerbated by fears of violence. Throughout the 1950s and early 1960s, Christian publications largely ignored colonial violence against local populations but reported in lurid tones on the torture of Chinese Christians or the massacres of missionaries in the Congo.[133]

A sense of missionary competition with communism, nationalism, and Islam was nothing new, but the stakes felt much higher owing to shifts in the missions' relations to state power. Even though most postcolonial movements did not undertake mass expulsions of European missionaries, many leaders proclaimed their intention to end missionary privileges, most importantly by taking over missionary schools, whether Catholic or Protestant. The Central African Republic, for example, upon achieving independence, nationalized the entire missionary school system. Where such measures proved too difficult due to lack of resources or teacher shortages, as happened in the Congo, Ghana, and Uganda, governments allowed missionaries to keep running schools but nationalized their administration, subjecting curriculums, salaries, and building permits to government supervision. Such moves often disappointed local socialists, who hoped for immediate and full nationalization, but they convinced missionary and church leaders that they would soon be replaced by hostile state officials. "The time will soon arrive," one missionary official in Ghana ruefully prophesied in 1963, "when the government will be called upon to assume total control of the entire educational fabric of the country ... the strong grip which the church had on education is giving way."[134] The end of European administration similarly threatened to diminish funding for medical work, publishing, and other endeavors. The entire missionary apparatus seemed on very shaky ground.[135]

All these developments precipitated a pervasive sense of pessimism in both Catholic and Protestant missionary thinking. Even though conversion rates in the former colonies did not change during those years—in some places they even increased—missionaries came together around a mutual sense of a perilous future, as upbeat talk of "uplifting" and expansion gave way to mournful depictions of missions on the defensive. For the first time in at least a century, missionaries of both confessions concluded that Christianity was likely to remain a permanent minority religion in Asia and Africa. The Austrian Johannes Hofinger, for example, one of the era's most influential Catholic missionary theoreticians, predicted throughout the 1950s that events in China—from where he was expelled to the Philippines—were a likely template for Asia and Africa. "The missionary apostolate has entered a new stage with the overthrow of colonialism and the emancipation of the non-white peoples," he wrote in *Worship: The Life of the Mission* (1958). "We all grieve to see ... our opportunities of exercising a formative Christian influence among these people so cut down ... [but] we do not feel that we are in control of this critical condition."[136] Lesslie Newbigin, the general secretary of the Protestant International Missionary Council, similarly argued in a 1958 lecture that the revolt against European dominance altered the fate of Christianity even more than socialism's rise in Europe. "It means," he explained, "that Christian missions now have to work not with the tide but against it."[137] Despite calls by African Christians, such as Senegalese writer Alioune Diop or Nigerian pastor Bolaji Idowu, to celebrate decolonization as the realization of Christian solidarity with the oppressed, European missionaries described the new era with a tragic sense of closing horizons. As one European Protestant operative in the Congo said at a 1963 international conference, in the postcolonial world "Christianity feels itself menaced more and more by non-Christian ideologies."[138]

As they sought to devise a response to these developments, missionary elites forged a new conceptual synthesis. They drew on the conceptual innovations of the 1930s to claim that their new mission was to "indigenize" the churches by embracing non-European languages and rituals. In their origins, these ideas were part of an intense clash between racist and anti-racist writers, who sought to align the missions with or against the Nazis. In the 1950s, however, they were mobilized in new ways, in hope that they could secure their adaptation to the postcolonial world. Hofinger, for example, asserted that to survive their potential expulsion, missionaries had to transfer some pastoral authority to laypeople, such as training them to run marriage ceremonies. In the process, he claimed in *The Communal Worship without a Priest in the Mission* (1956), locals would develop a sense of ownership over their new religion. Employing the same logic, the Catholic Swiss writer Walbert Bühlmann claimed that incorporating native rituals and music to Christian liturgy was an indirect way to enhance European authority. In *Africa between Yesterday and Today* (1959), which enjoyed multiple editions and translations, he explained that this approach would disassociate Christianity from European control, making Africans more inclined to support Europe in case of wars against Muslims and communists.[139] That these ideas were presented as a tragic necessity *and* as a way to counter declining European influence was one reason they proved popular. When in 1959 dozens of bishops and general secretaries of missionary societies gathered at a conference in the Dutch missionary institute in Ninjmegen, host Alphons Mulder lamented that without "indigenization," Christian life in Asia and Africa "would hardly be possible." The Vatican was supportive, approving the use of local languages in some rituals in India, Indonesia, the Congo, and other countries, and Protestant churches similarly revised their liturgy to include local traditions.[140]

Those ideas may have been old, but what was new was their ecumenical framing. More than a decade after reconciliation triumphed in Europe, missionary writers and operatives began to wonder whether decolonization did not require a similar cooperation in the Global South; perhaps, they claimed, it would help missions adjust to the new world and find common language with non-Europeans. Among Catholics, the key figure linking decolonization with interconfessionalism was Joseph Blomjous, a Dutch Catholic bishop in Tanzania who in 1959 helped launch the influential ecumenical journal *African Ecclesiastical Review*. Drawing on earlier anti-racist theories, Blomjous claimed that the rise of new "nations and races" spelled the end of Christianity's deep association with Western civilization. To appeal to Africans or Asians, the Church should support local practices and cultures, vocally oppose racial prejudice, and "embrace ... the rich diversity of mankind." Most importantly, Blomjous called on Christians to abandon their unrealistic dreams of becoming the dominant force in postcolonial spaces. As a permanent minority, they had to understand themselves as an "indirect apostolate," inspiring others not through conversion but through charity.[141]

For Blomjous, the first step toward this goal was engagement with Protestant missionaries. By making peace with their historical enemy, Catholics would demonstrate their humility and openness to a more pluralist society. In fact, Protestants could inspire Catholics to engage in the postcolonial mindset. "They," Blomjous asserted without much evidence, "more than ourselves, seem to be aware of the extent of the non-Christian world, of its diversity, and of the challenge that it represents." Cooperation with Protestants could sustain the Catholic mission's operation in the postcolonial world. As he put it, "It is precisely on the ground of mission work that the question of ecumenism becomes more vital, more obvious and urgent."[142] Other Catholic clergy and writers stationed in Africa, such as German Hans Burgman (in Uganda) or British John Jordan (in Nigeria), employed the same logic, and called for interconfessional engagement as the key to indigenization. As one British Catholic missionary put it, the "vast and revolutionary changes" of African independence made it imperative for the church to show that "it is not a fossil transplanted from the Jordan Valley" but instead a flexible institution that could make peace with former adversaries.[143]

The high hopes that this framing invested in ecumenism made it appealing also to many Protestants. Their most prominent spokesperson was Lesslie Newbigin, a Scottish missionary theoretician whose writings were widely translated and discussed in Europe. Like Blomjous, decolonization led Newbigin to claim that Christianity's European heritage was a toxic burden. In his view, Christians had no choice but to "make it clear that the Church is a colony of heaven and not a colony of one of the western people."[144] For Newbigin, it seemed clear that the path for such transformation went through interconfessional peace, a topic to which he had paid no attention before decolonization's unfolding in Africa. This was because Christianity's division into different churches was itself a legacy of "Western cultural history," a theological squabble that made little sense to those outside Christendom's traditional borders. According to Newbigin, any Christian "who goes into the midst of the great reawakened cultures of Asia and Africa" is confronted with the same bewilderment over Christianity's internal division. "If it is true that Jesus is the Savior of all men," they are asked by non-Christians, "how is it that you who speak in his name are unable to live as one family?" For Newbigin, it was evident that ecumenical unity was necessary both for separating Christianity from European cultural residue and for engaging non-Christians. As he explained in *Is Christ Divided?* (1961), unity would demonstrate Christianity's ability to change over time and adapt to the needs of new nations and cultures.[145] This reasoning appealed to other commentators and soon circulated in missionary writing. Works such as *Human Diversity and Christian Unity* (1958), by the Dutch Reformed theologian Ben Marais, and *Christ in the Global Horizon* (1962), by the German missionary writer Jan Hermelink, claimed that only Christian unity could appeal to non-Europeans.[146]

As was the case with earlier ecumenical theories in Europe, this talk of pluralism was in tension with its narrow Christian focus. If the missions' main challenge in the postcolonial world was to finally recognize other religions and cultures as equals, why would Catholics and Protestants be the key communities for engagement, and not other faiths? The two confessions were strange allies in an effort to adapt the churches to the era that came after European supremacy. After all, weren't their historical roots tied to imperial control and the civilizing mission? In a telling omission, ecumenical writers avoided such questions. For all their insistence that ecumenism would one day lead to engagement with "human diversity," they never specified how or when this would happen, and their statements about other cultures remained vague. The pages of the *African Ecclesiastical Review,* for example, the most important ecumenical publication in the missionary world, never mentioned Christian scholars such as Louis Massignon, who believed in Christian-Muslim cooperation, nor did it publish works by or on Muslims.[147] In many ways ecumenism was less the realization of diversity and more its appropriation toward narrow ends. It conveniently depicted peace with other Europeans and Christians as the best adjustment to the postcolonial era. It thus allowed commentators to claim they were overcoming the missions' historical ties to colonialism while also preserving the notion of European Christian distinctiveness.

Indeed, despite Blomjous's or Newbigin's insistence on diversity and humility, the defining characteristic of ecumenical rhetoric was its obsession with adversity. Just like their counterparts in Europe framed their engagement against socialism and feminism, ecumenical writers often recycled tropes from the imperial era and the interwar period to describe their work as a desperate effort to hold back communists, Asian and African nationalists, and Muslims from taking over postcolonial states. The influential French Dominican writer Marie-Joseph Le Guillou, who published several works on global interconfessionalism, claimed it was a matter of self-defense. In 1959 he argued that ecumenism was a spiritual bulwark against "the expansion of . . . Islam in Africa" and other religions in Asia, which were emboldened by the retreat of European empires.[148] Vincent Donovan, a Catholic bishop in Tanzania (and Blomjous's close collaborator), similarly lamented in 1959 that Africa's impending independence was bound to bolster Islam's "totalitarian" quest to control all state institutions. If Catholics and Protestants had to end the "scandal" of their division, it was because neither were "separately strong enough to offset Islam."[149] Even as they sought to celebrate Christian pluralism and diversity, many writers insisted that Islam was a monolith. Almost no one mentioned internal theological or regional differences. This was in part why ecumenist writings were saturated with the military rhetoric of struggle and confrontation. Fridtjov Birkeli, the former director of the Norwegian missions and bishop of Stavanger, described communism, nationalism, and Islam as a unified threat to Christian survival overseas. All those forces, he thundered in a highly publicized 1959 speech, were hell-bent on isolating and "exterminating" European religion. To avoid this potentially tragic fate, Birkeli explained, Protestants and Catholics had to move past their previous bickering and forge broad cooperation. "Only when 'ecumenical mission' ... become[s] the slogan of the era," he said, "could the churches of Africa and Asia come together and defend themselves from their enemies."[150]

Missionary ecumenism was therefore marked by an unresolved tension between the desire to discard the missions' European baggage and the belief that Europeans had to band together against threatening enemies. And both impulses helped inspire the first practical efforts to institutionalize large-scale cooperation between the confessions in the missionary field. After informal conversations at the first interconfessional missionary meeting in Brussels in 1958, the Catholic Blomjous, the Protestant Newbigin, and sympathetic European mission leaders in 1961 created a unified database of missionary activity. With the support of clerical authorities, the Protestant-led Institute for Social Studies in The Hague and the Catholic-run Center for Social and Socio-Religious Studies in Brussels coordinated a joint study by Catholics and Protestants, recording all European mission work in Africa and Asia. This massive undertaking—with cautious estimates of a missionary workforce of 20,000 Europeans and 500,000 Asians and Africans—was to provide the raw material for further ecumenical action. Staffed by personnel from Protestant and Catholic missions, the project's members drafted plans for resource sharing and joint missionary training, especially for teachers and nurses.[151]

Once this experiment was successfully completed, Blomjous and Newbigin radically expanded it by establishing the Society, Development, and Peace Committee (SODEPAX) in 1965, which brought together major European Christian charities and missionary organizations, from the Vatican's Caritas Internationalis and Belgian Catholic Emergency Relief Committee to the Protestant Swiss Basel Mission and Swedish Lutheran Missionary Union. Headquartered in Geneva, its officials coordinated a wide variety of joint actions in twenty Asian and African countries. These spanned joint building and funding medical centers in Uganda, translating the Bible into Kituba and Lingala (in Congo) and Toruba (in Nigeria), organizing anti-alcohol seminars in South Korea, and hosting theological discussion groups in Taiwan.[152] Of special interest to SODEPAX were experiments with radio and television, which held the promise of spreading the message of interfaith development in areas where literacy was not universal. The German Catholic priest and media specialist Franz-Josef Eilers traveled from the Philippines to Hong Kong and Kenya, running interconfessional classes for local clergy and laymen on how to harness the airwaves by producing short skits and films with scenes from the Bible.[153] All these undertakings were explained as part of the European-led quest to disentangle the missions from their ties to European colonialism. As one SODEPAX operative in Kenya explained, such public display of confessional unity would show "that Christianity is not labeled as a western import."[154] Yet just like the ideas that inspired it, the work of missionary ecumenism harbored a restrictive vision of pluralism. At no point did SODEPAX initiate engagement with non-Christian communities or consider inviting Asian and African nationalists to their discussions. In fact, when one operative floated the idea of organizing a meeting with Muslims in Southeast Africa, it was summarily rejected on the grounds that it was futile.

Nothing embodied ecumenism's function in missionary circles—to reconcile Christianity to a postcolonial world while preserving Europeans' role as guides and models—more than SODEPAX's obsessive focus on economic and social matters. In particular, its members centered Catholic-Protestant cooperation on "development," which in the 1950s and 1960s became a dominant framework for European thinking about international relations. Drawing on ideas that were popular among social scientists on both sides of the Atlantic, advocates of development claimed that the "advanced" nations of Western Europe and North America should help Asians and Africans grow their economies. Whether through private or public investment, the logic went, they had to export modern agricultural techniques, train locals in new industrial technology, and invest in infrastructure. For theoreticians of development, whose logic relied on the racialized distinction between "modern" and "traditional" peoples, these schemes were designed for much more than bringing prosperity to the unfortunate. Like the civilizing mission of earlier decades, training for modern economic techniques was meant to "uplift" the Global South into the rational, industrious habits that Europeans purportedly possessed. After World War II, with their hold on colonial possessions increasingly shaky, European governments rushed to embrace development and established a panoply of agencies to fund foreign investment. Accompanied by a barrage of propaganda, they hoped such programs would increase Asians' and Africans' loyalty to Europe and prevent their drift toward "irrational" anti-colonial desires such as nationalism, communism, or pan-Islamism. While economists, social scientists, and diplomats intensely debated how development should be implemented in practice, many believed it was the key to global stability. The French politician and development official Jacques Ferrandi argued that only economic development would foster the "competence, modesty, and courage" that was necessary for life in the modern world.[155]

Both Catholic and Protestant theoreticians seized on development as the solution to their anxieties in a postcolonial world. If missions participated in development schemes, they hoped, they could help dissociate Christianity from its historical links to colonialism and reframe it as a force eager to help Africans and Asians help themselves. This was the conviction that animated Louis Joseph Lebret, a French social scientist and development's most famous Catholic theoretician. In his influential *Suicide or Survival of the Occident?* (1958), he claimed that development would help the masses recognize both Europe's and Christianity's superiority to communism, African and Asian nationalism, and Islam.[156] What is more, development's focus on seemingly technical and nonpolitical issues such as machines, fertilizers, and irrigation could offer missions legitimacy in postcolonial societies. Dutch Protestant economist Egbert de Vries argued in *Man in Rapid Social Change* (1961) that development could and would take place even after Asians and Africans took control of their own states; Europe's mission, after all, was universal.[157] There was some awkwardness in this embrace of development, since some of its theoreticians claimed that this movement from a "traditional" to a "modern" and technologically advanced world would also encourage secularization. Christian writers dismissed such concerns, however, claiming that Christian involvement in development was necessary. Only Christian charity, the logic went, could inspire people to use new technology in the service of the public good. Christian elites embraced the hope that development would preserve their quest to "uplift" the Global South beyond the collapse of empire. In 1958 the World Council of Churches (WCC) launched a study group chaired by de Vries to promote Christian development, while in 1960 the Nouvelles équipes internationales (NEI), the international forum of Christian democratic parties, organized its first international conference on development.[158]

Grand Compromises at the Zenith of Christian Power

Because the goals of development rhymed so neatly with their agenda, in which Europeans were to foster goodwill among postcolonial societies by bestowing on them superior techniques, missionary ecumenists seized on it with enthusiasm. In its first years of operation, SODEPAX launched a multifront effort to expand Christian development work. It organized numerous conferences and seminars, in Europe (Switzerland, Austria, and the Netherlands), Africa (Kenya, Lesotho, Malawi), and Asia (Indonesia and Japan). At these events, missionary operatives, laypeople, and economists of both confessions discussed how their communities could either contribute to or benefit from missionary investment in development efforts. The Belgian Catholic charity official August Vanistendael argued at a meeting of European aid organizations that "strengthening the economy" of poor nations "through agriculture, industry, commerce, and natural resources" was Christians' most effective way "to show deep respect for the conscience and freedom of ... developing countries."[159] SODEPAX's publishing arm also issued a stream of pamphlets and booklets, which were distributed to missionaries, churchgoers, and scholars. With titles such as *World Development: Challenge to the Churches* and *The Development Challenge,* they called on Christian organizations to launch their own investment schemes and published manuals for those in English, French, Dutch, Spanish, Italian, and German. SODEPAX also established local interconfessional committees in dozens of countries, helped support local events on development, and cooperated with UN initiatives, such as funding for development education in Indonesia.[160]

Within a year of its founding, SODEPAX began funding its own development initiatives. Without coordination or consultation with postcolonial officials, who often sought to control economic initiatives, missionary operatives launched multiple interconfessional projects, all designed to expand economic activity. An indicative example is the Rulenge diocese in northwest Tanzania, where Catholic and Protestant missionaries jointly sponsored eleven credit unions (which then funded irrigation systems); one hospital with a full-time doctor; a dispensary and maternity center; a preschool program that supervised the distribution of food; a class on women's education in health care and home crafts; the joint installation of electric fences (to prevent animals from damaging crops); the introduction of mechanized maize mills, rice mills, and a tractor; and the establishment of a local library of publications on development. Similar endeavors were reported from other countries that had recently become independent. In Kenya, interconfessional teams ran seminars on economic development; in the Ivory Coast they established shared hospitals. In Malawi they built bridges and schools; in Indonesia they helped build new irrigation systems and mills. Development and its comforting promise to recharge the Christian mission to a new world, and especially to disassociate it from whiteness, proved so central to ecumenical work that some commentators saw them as identical. As one SODEPAX official mused in a letter from Cameroon, through development "we demonstrate that we are not Catholics or Protestants, but Africans."[161]

Finally, missionary ecumenism coalesced around the perennial struggle against polygamy, a practice that had long been condemned by both confessions but that never before inspired mutual action. As was the case with its embrace of development, missionary thinking in the field echoed ideals circulating in Europe, arguing that heterosexual unions were not only divinely ordained but also a site of pleasure and women's liberation. The Anglican missionary (and later archbishop) of Uganda Leslie Brown, a forceful advocate for interconfessional missionary cooperation, explained that Catholics and Protestants shared the unique vision of "true equality between husband and wife." In *The Christian Family* (1959), coauthored with his wife, Winifred, he explained that polygamy disparaged women and prevented them from experiencing true marital love. On the Catholic side, the editors of the *African Ecclesiastical Review* focused on the battle between monogamous and polygamous families. In the journal's quarterly consultation section, which usually focused on ways to update marriage and family life to African settings, author after author reminded readers of the need to combat and uproot the practice of marrying multiple wives. When missionary delegates from across Africa gathered in 1963 in Mindolo, North Rhodesia, for a pan-continental conference titled The Christian Home and Family Life, they issued a lengthy statement (likely drafted by the ecumenist Lesslie Newbigin) on the stark opposition between the Catholic-Protestant idea of monogamy and polygamy's evils. Polygamy, they explained, "is not compatible with the spirit of Christ" and was "a consequence of original sin."[162]

This rhetoric had practical consequences. In the aftermath of independence, many new states also sought to reform laws on marriage, inheritance, and other family matters. Instead of the patchwork systems inherited from colonial authorities, which largely left family law to local religious officials, governments in Guinea, Central African Republic, Malawi, and elsewhere sought to create a standardized system.[163] For many missionaries, this seemed like a unique opportunity to inscribe their own views on state laws and thus on the entire population (a possibility that colonial authorities had always rejected out of hand). Wherever possible, they encouraged banning, or at very least restricting, polygamy by allowing courts the right to dissolve marriages deemed "unequal," even if those were sanctified by religious leaders, or limiting the registration of marriages. Catholic-Protestant advocacy campaigns therefore sprung up in postcolonial states, seeking to mobilize local populations around the Christian vision of marriage. The largest took place in Uganda, where dozens of Catholic and Protestant writers, missionaries, and church leaders (almost all Europeans) in 1963 founded the Uganda Joint Christian Council to coordinate mutual action. In response to the government's announcement that it would reform family law, the Council organized letter-writing campaigns, publication blitzes, and demonstrations that called for the criminalization of polygamy. The virtue of monogamy was not only that it was "the law of God," but also that it promoted society's economic development. Polygamy, explained one of its statements, "delays the progress of a people, destroys law and order, and the high degree of culture that a nation has attained . . . History is witness to this fact: Polygamy is practiced in undeveloped countries; monogamy in developed countries."[164]

Compared to developments in Europe, the missionary ecumenical project had only modest results. For all the self-important rhetoric that surrounded it, missionary work did not dramatically change the world: its joint educational projects did not diminish Islam's appeal, development initiatives did not eradicate poverty, and campaigns over family laws were mostly unsuccessful. Missionary elites' adherence to European paternalism mostly persisted, but the confessional divide in the missionary sphere did not. Just as quickly as it smashed formal imperialism, decolonization helped end the perennial sense of intra-Christian competition.

IN ITS ORIGINS, ecumenism was controversial. It was part of the internal Christian debate over fascism: whether the Third Reich and its allies should be embraced, begrudgingly accommodated, or fiercely rejected. In the long 1950s, however, ecumenism became a project of reconciliation between those camps, which enabled it to vastly extend its reach. No longer an effort on the margins of Christian Europe, it became, to borrow the words of Arthur Schlesinger, the "vital center." This meant that ecumenism displayed many continuities, especially in Christian elites' anxieties about socialism, feminism, and anti-colonial movements. But it also was marked by considerable intellectual innovations, which merged theories of different Christian camps into new strategies. In politics, Christians agreed to accept democracy and pluralistic politics, with the goal of arresting the left's advances. In economics, they agreed that unequal and harmonious class relations would be secured through market competition and limited welfare. They also agreed that marriage and the family would be protected by harshly repressing non-heteronormative arrangements and encouraging sexual pleasure. And in the Global South, they hoped that adaptation to the postcolonial world would take place through liturgical reforms and economic development. This association between ecumenism and inter-Christian compromise also helped the interconfessional alliance to increase its reach. By the early 1960s, ecumenism had become a central feature of Christian political and organizational life, which allowed Christian parties to reach power and shape key public policies across Central and Western Europe.

Ecumenism's popularity also helped it gain unprecedented support from the highest church authorities. With the death of Pius XII in 1959, even the Vatican abandoned its long opposition to cooperation with Protestants. In 1960 the newly appointed Pope John XXII created the Secretariat for Promoting Christian Unity as part of preparations for the coming Second Vatican Council (1961–1965). Led by two well-known ecumenists, the German Augustin Bea and the Dutch Johannes Willebrands, it drafted the Catholic Church's statement on Protestants, declaring them "brethren in faith." In 1964 the bishops who gathered in Rome approved the text as the decree *Unitatis redintegratio,* making it the Church's official doctrine. "For men who believe in Christ and have been truly baptized," they declared, "are in communion with the Catholic Church even though this communion is imperfect."[165] Protestant church leaders similarly embraced ecumenism as a formal principle. In 1961, at a world congress in New Delhi, Protestant churches and missions declared their enthusiasm for cooperation with Catholics. Figures such as Marc Boegner, the president of France's Federation of Protestant Churches, and the Dutch Lutheran Willem Visser 't Hooft, president of the World Council of Churches, traveled to Rome to advise in drafting *Unitatis redintegratio.*[166] In the following years, the Vatican and the WCC initiated several projects together, such as joint discussion groups in Europe and cooperation on biblical translation in Africa.[167]

As it turned out, however, this consensus was short-lived. Thinkers of different factions and inclinations were so focused on reconciling with one another that they did not anticipate a new challenge: the emergence of a new critical generation. Indeed, the placid ecumenism of the 1950s was soon to meet surprising and very different alternatives. In the 1960s and 1970s a new cohort of Catholics and Protestants called for an interconfessional alliance to destroy Christianity's century-old focus on order and stability.

CHAPTER 5

Radical Ecumenism in the 1960s and 1970s

FOR HERBERT MARCUSE, the sociologist and New Left icon, the late 1960s and early 1970s seemed like a period of unprecedented possibilities. In the proliferation of protests that rocked much of the industrial world, he believed that he was witnessing "the emergence of a new Subject," one that was ready to take on all the globe's injustices. Unlike the working class, which had largely abandoned its revolutionary aspirations, these protestors still talked about overthrowing capitalist oppression. As Marcuse asserted in *An Essay on Liberation* (1969), they recognized that they lived in an "obscene society" that was "stuffing itself and its garbage cans" while letting the poor languish in hunger. Even more promising in Marcuse's eyes, many protestors in this period went beyond economic demands to attack sexism, racism, and imperialism—particularly the Vietnam War—recognizing their mutual constitution. They thus engaged in a multifront "anti-authoritarian rebellion," a psychological campaign against the very legitimacy of stifling social hierarchies. Perhaps most opportune, Marcuse believed that the protestors, while minorities in their own countries, were bolstered by the political turmoil in the Global South. The wars in Cuba and Vietnam, he mused, and the efforts of Latin American, Asian, and African states to form a "nonaligned" bloc, shook "the capitalist metropoles" and undermined their capacity to manufacture consent. While Marcuse acknowledged the vast differences between the demonstrations in Europe and the guerilla fighting in Asia, he claimed they were united in a joint project. They were all part of the

"Great Refusal," the resistance of the oppressed against "the great game that is rigged against them."[1]

As was the case for most figures of the New Left, Marcuse had little room for the Christian churches in his vision of liberation. In his mind, Christianity was an intellectual tool of capitalism, patriarchy, and imperialism, part of the postwar order that needed to be demolished.[2] Historians have often repeated this judgment and assumed that Christians were hostile to the era's protests.[3] But a large contingent of Catholics and Protestants in fact viewed the New Left as an exhilarating opportunity: a chance to align Christianity with Marcuse's "anti-authoritarian rebellion." For many theologians and lay activists, Christianity's historic focus on social harmony, the patriarchal heterosexual family, and a "civilizing mission" was a betrayal of Jesus's emancipatory message. In their eyes, the gospel's "true" teaching, which church authorities had neglected and even falsified, required supporting the "wretched of the earth": those who suffered for their poverty, gender, sexual orientation, and race. Christians therefore had to abandon their fixation with social order and restrictions on people's behavior, whether through state regulation or moral condemnation. Instead, their task was to expand the political imagination and eliminate existing hierarchies.

This campaign to transform European Christianity entailed a radical break with precedent. Catholic and Protestant anti-authoritarians drew on Marcuse to question not only the norms of the postwar order, but also the preoccupations that had governed Christian life since the nineteenth century. In the sphere of politics and economics, reformers lambasted the quest to achieve cross-class "cooperation," which they condemned as a cover for capitalist exploitation. Christians, they argued, had to not only accept class conflict but intensify it, and bring about the end of private property. In fact, they should permanently mobilize against all social hierarchies, whether in education or politics, a task that anti-authoritarians sought to achieve by creating new associations and lay organizations. In matters of gender, Christians witnessed for the first time the rise of radical feminist theology. Its main proponents questioned men and women's assigned social roles, and launched campaigns against patriarchal authority. This project also entailed a new approach to sexuality. Feminist thinkers questioned not only the Catholic prohibition on contraception, which had been reaffirmed by Pope Paul VI in 1968, but also both confessions' long opposition to abortion and same-sex relationships. Finally, and least recognized by historians, the spirit of anti-authoritarianism also fostered a new conception of the relationship between Europe and the Global South. Inspired by theologians from Latin America, Asia, and Africa, Catholic and Protestant anti-authoritarians in Europe attacked the missions and their focus on development as a form of neocolonialism, and called instead for a radical and global redistribution of wealth. In all those spheres, these Christians sought to end the churches' long quest of disciplining and pacifying "unruly" subjects. Instead, the goal was to empower and radicalize them.

These ideas occasionally echoed the works of earlier generations, whether 1930s anti-fascists like Emil Brunner or 1950s postcolonial theologians like Joseph Blomjous, but their implications were far more radical. The thinkers who articulated them broke taboos—ranging from heteronormativity to the belief that Europe's was the "advanced" civilization—that their predecessors took for granted. Most profoundly, anti-authoritarian Christians refused to ground their political visions in notions of God-given "natural" order. In their eyes, all social relations were subject to criticism in a never-ending process of contestation. This conviction occasionally borrowed from "liberation theology," the radical socialist theories that emerged at the same time in Latin American churches. But it was mostly the product of European conditions, and most of these thinkers developed their ideas before encountering liberation theology.

Alongside the explosion of New Left activism, the new school of Christian thought was shaped by Christianity's shrinking fortunes in Europe. Throughout the 1960s and 1970s, participation in church life entered a period of accelerated decline. A host of sociological trends, particularly the mass migration to cities and the increase in women's labor outside the home, drastically reduced European church attendance, participation in Christian organizations, and interest in Christian publications. Statistics varied across region and denomination, but commentators recognized that organized Christianity no longer enjoyed the widespread appeal it once had. Some journalists even announced Christianity's "death."[4] While many church authorities viewed this trend as confirmation of the corrosive impact of secularism, anti-authoritarian Christians contested that view. In their minds, believers had to overcome their historical suspicion of atheists, and recognize their brotherhood in an unjust world. In fact, some of this school's leading figures claimed that Christians should emulate nonbelievers. Instead of fearing an all-knowing God who supervised and judged humans like an intimidating father, they had to imagine divinity as an equal, residing in all humans. In this telling, the purpose of worship was to forge political solidarities with strangers, with the goal of radical equality. As the German theologian Dorothee Sölle, one of this school's leaders, wrote, a prayer geared toward social justice transforms the feudal "relationship of domination between God and humans" into one "based on mutuality."[5] The era of protest, in short, was more than a period of contestation between the churches and a rapidly de-Christianized society. New Left theories and activism also helped inspire an effort to develop a new relationship between Christians and God, a new religious subject.[6]

Yet for all its ingenuity, this effort to revolutionize Catholicism and Protestantism did preserve something from previous generations. In an ironic twist of history, most of its proponents remained deeply committed to ecumenism. Even though Catholic-Protestant cooperation originally solidified around the principle of order and hierarchy, anti-authoritarian Christians viewed ecumenism as essential to their project of protest. In countless essays and books, they echoed their predecessors' claim that the two confessions shared similar approaches to salvation and therefore had to work together. They also duplicated the earlier generation's habit of creating interconfessional organizations, such as advocacy groups, think tanks, and publications. Their ecumenism, however, also had new ideological content. Rather than being a joint fight against non-Christian religions and political movements, anti-authoritarians' ecumenism was to be the first step toward a new embrace of the non-Christian world. Through engagement with each other, Christians were to begin the process of psychological self-examination and ultimately break their dependence on stifling social norms. In many ways, the fact that anti-authoritarian Christians did not discard ecumenism, but instead took it for granted as the vehicle for their radically new agenda, signaled its ultimate triumph. Even those who rejected its original goals now viewed Catholic-Protestant cooperation as a necessary step to expand Christianity's impact on public life.

Despite its intensity, revolutionary ecumenism was ultimately defeated. By the early 1980s even its most optimistic members recognized their marginalization: church authorities dismissed their demands as erroneous, and most Christian communities preferred to focus on other issues, such as sex education. Even at the height of their activism, anti-authoritarian Christians never enjoyed the influence of their Christian democratic predecessors. They did not create large political parties, and certainly did not control state institutions. Because of this fate, it is tempting to focus on the weaknesses of their project. Like Marcuse's call for a "Great Refusal," its vision of a decentralized and permanent mobilization against all authority proved too difficult to sustain. Its commitment to the "marginalized and the oppressed," terms that at the time began to dominate progressive social thought, did not appeal to most Europeans. Yet this anti-authoritarian project was also the product of immense intellectual imagination. Its key figures coined new terms, language, and images, and employed creative ways to reread ancient texts. In many ways this movement was the last effort to substantially rethink the meaning of Christianity in Europe. For a brief moment, it seemed as if it could forge new realities.

The Emergence of Anti-Authoritarian Ecumenism from the New Left

One of the New Left's main tenets was its focus on psychology. Its main theoreticians claimed that oppression was most effective when internalized, when society's least fortunate members came to view their oppression as natural. This was especially true in modern industrial society, which required endless work and extreme repression of one's natural desires. Under a relentless barrage of propaganda, workers were induced to accept their own exploitation. This was in part why both capitalist and communist societies, which New Left thinkers disdained as equally oppressive, were so violent. As people's frustration over work and self-denial inevitably accumulated, they were provided outlets through brutality against minorities and wars of aggression. For Marcuse and others, who drew on the earlier work of Sigmund Freud, Theodor Adorno, and Wilhelm Reich, this meant that liberation entailed much more than redistributing wealth and power. The "Great Refusal" required the mental capacity to question authority in its many forms, whether that of teachers, politicians, or employers. According to such thinkers, this mental liberation would be the reward for abolishing capitalism and replacing it with a socialist society. Alongside regained autonomy and freedom from excessive work, people would be freed from the psychological terror of supervision.[7]

Marcuse had already articulated some of those ideas in the 1950s, but it was only in the following decade that they enjoyed widespread resonance. For a sizable cohort of readers across Europe, especially young students, the link between economics, politics, and psychology helped explain why the growing comfort in which they lived felt suffocating: rather than offering new possibilities, so the logic went, it necessitated conformity and alienation. The Vietnam War seemed especially to confirm Marcuse's analysis. If so many people in capitalist societies, including West European governments, supported such senseless destruction, was it not an obvious expression of capitalism's inhumane capacity to manufacture obedience? As student activism began to pick up steam in the mid-1960s, and then exploded in a spectacular series of violent protests in 1968, many of its leaders therefore envisioned their movement as a mental project. Building barricades, clashing with police forces, forcing curricular changes in universities: such actions were partly designed to break the barrier of fear they saw as undergirding capitalism. Many of those who gathered in conventions and demonstrations, from Paris to Amsterdam to West Berlin, believed that this focus was the main feature that distinguished their movement from earlier socialists' failed challenges to capitalism. As one West German activist explained, the generation inspired by the New Left for the first time sought "psychological liberation."[8]

At first glance the Christian vision for industrial society seemed like the ultimate antithesis of these New Left ideas. The European churches had spent almost a century insisting that inequality between employers and workers was natural, and that a "healthy" psychology meant accepting one's assigned social position. But in the 1960s and 1970s a growing chorus of Christian thinkers began to question these assumptions. They claimed that Christianity's "true" teachings, which were shared by both Catholics and Protestants, required the psychological approach espoused by Marcuse. In this interpretation, Jesus's main call was for believers to challenge their adherence to authority. This teaching had been stifled by church authorities, who for two millennia had aligned with the powerful, but the upheavals of the 1960s, especially regarding the Vietnam War, allowed both Catholics and Protestants to rediscover it. Christians were therefore tasked with applying these rediscovered lessons both inside and outside the churches. They had to facilitate a broader project of psychological liberation, which was to lead to social revolution. Like many before them, thinkers in this camp struggled to explain why the Gospel's main message was obscured for so long. They also never quite explained why its meaning was suddenly revealed in this particular moment. Sidestepping such questions, anti-authoritarian Christians sought to radically rethink both Europe's social order and the churches' role in it. In the process, they also developed a new basis for ecumenical action.

The most important Catholic voice to articulate this new vision was the German theologian Johann Baptist Metz, who in a series of provocative publications offered a new understanding of humans' relationship with God. According to Metz, Christians had mistakenly imagined God as an all-knowing father who provided stability and comfort in a chaotic world. Because God's affirmation was never explicitly evident, they projected it onto society, viewing its conventions and traditions as an expression of God's will. In Metz's eyes, however, this was a betrayal of Christianity's nonconformist core. As he explained in *Poverty of Spirit* (1962), the lesson of Jesus's suffering and social humiliation was that humans should embrace discomfort, recognize the emptiness of social norms, and disrupt compliance. Metz thus called on Catholics to question tradition as a source of social legitimacy. Most of the time, he argued, invocations of the past fostered "self-aggrandizement" and complacency. In an additional series of articles in 1966 and 1967, Metz claimed that Christianity's most valuable contribution to social life was eschatology, its reflections on humanity's fate in the end of times. In this promise of radical rapture, one that would destroy all hierarchies and norms, humans could find the inspiration for critical self-questioning and new possibilities.[9] For Metz, this was Christians' role in the world: to make all that society has normalized seem foreign, strange, and open to transformation.[10]

As abstract as this vision may have been, its social implications were concrete and far-reaching. For Metz, adherence to God's message required a revolutionary anti-capitalism. Borrowing from philosopher Marc Bloch, who claimed that Marxism and Christianity shared a messianic vision, Metz claimed that Christians' long-standing defense of the "natural" hierarchies between classes betrayed Jesus's critical message. Not only did it tolerate capitalist exploitation, but it also privatized ethics: it led Christians to judge actions as purely individual, instead of recognizing them as expressions of communal and social relations. For Metz, the task was therefore to resurrect Jesus's revolutionary spirit by recognizing its collective dimensions. "The salvation on which the Christian faith is based," he argued in a 1967 address, is "not a private salvation . . . the scandal and promise of Christian salvation are public."[11] Metz therefore claimed that to achieve the social conditions required for grace, Christians had to join the Marxist struggle, even if that potentially entailed violence. "Where the social status quo contains as much injustice as in capitalist society," he explained, "then a revolution ... may not be prohibited even in the name of Christian love."[12] This approach also entailed skepticism about the Cold War, whose logic of perpetual anti-Communist mobilization was already losing popularity in Europe during the 1960s. From 1966 to 1968 Metz was a member of a group of Christian social theorists, led by Austrian writer Ernst Kellner, who initiated dialogue with communists in a series of conferences in Vienna and Prague.[13]

Although much of this political message echoed the earlier Christian interest in Marxism, which briefly bloomed in the 1940s, Metz's ideas quickly took on very different characteristics. In *Theology of the World* (1968) and subsequent publications, he envisioned anti-capitalism as the basis for a broad and permanent critique of authority. Unlike his predecessors, Metz invested little hope in communist parties or even the working class. Like New Left thinkers, he considered them prone to conformism and authoritarianism, a sentiment that only strengthened after the Soviets invaded Czechoslovakia in 1968 and crushed efforts to democratize the Eastern bloc. Metz instead hoped to inspire a different revolutionary subject, one who was driven by a desire to expose and dismantle all forms of oppression. This included not only capitalism, which Metz considered injustice's most extreme manifestation, but also oppression in family relations and educational institutions. Christianity's purpose was "to actualize the critical potential of faith in regard to society."[14] Perhaps most innovative, Metz borrowed from the critical theory of the Frankfurt School to claim that capitalism's exploitation and brutality were normalized primarily through intellectual and informal norms. Christian eschatology was therefore meant to disrupt the complacency and apathy of everyday life with discomforting images, to help inspire the courage for anti-authoritarianism. As he explained in his short book *Christ's Liberating Memory* (1970), the purpose was to make social suffering (which the capitalist system so aggressively concealed) present and felt.[15] Metz named this kind of theory "political theology," a term he sought to wrestle away from its association with the authoritarian jurist Carl Schmitt. Rather than serving state authorities, its purpose was to rattle them with "Christ's eschatological message."[16]

Metz's anti-authoritarian message appealed to many. Its vision of a nonconformist and disruptive struggle circulated among a cohort of Catholic thinkers who in the late 1960s and early 1970s sought to replace the old talk of inter-class harmony with militant anti-capitalist confrontation. The influential Dutch theologian Robert Adolfs, for example, claimed in his widely translated book *The Grave of God* (1966) that the Church's commitment to anti-socialism had produced obedient and apathetic subjects. Catholic social teachings since the encyclical *Rerum novarum* (1891), he scoffed in an unusual critique of this canonical text, were merely a meek accommodation of capitalism; the time had come to overthrow it. A year later some Catholic students in Germany established the group Critical Catholicism, which dedicated several publications (including a journal carrying its name) to rethinking Catholic social theory in a New Left key. Two of its editors, Ben van Onna and Erik Rupp, lambasted the church as an indoctrination arm of "late capitalist society," and invoked Metz's ideas to demand ecclesiastical democratization and support for the large-scale nationalization of industries.[17] In France, too, several Catholics drew on the works of Herbert Marcuse to criticize what they described as "one-dimensional Christianity." Like capitalism, so the logic went, the church taught workers to suppress their legitimate frustrations, a process that led to increasing aggression and irrationality.[18] In the late 1960s and early 1970s, these and other writers gathered around the journal *Concilium,* which appeared simultaneously in all major European languages and included contributions from scholars, theologians, and theoreticians across the continent. Under the editorship of German theologian Franz Böckle, it echoed Metz's ideas by dedicating issues to Christianity and secularism, eschatology, revolutionary Marxism, and anti-war activism.[19]

This vision of a multidirectional resistance, and especially its focus on perpetually self-critical revolutionary subjects, was in part why Catholic radicalism appealed so much to students. Whether they studied in Catholic institutions or were members of Catholic associations elsewhere, many found in this vision of "political theology" the language that captured their self-appointed role as the vanguard of a radically democratic society. In Germany, for example, the students who gathered around the Critical Catholicism group sought to disrupt the 1968 national Catholic congress that gathered in Essen. Against scheduled discussions on social teachings and the need for cross-class harmony, they ran sit-ins protesting the Church's "unholy alliance" with capitalism, conformism, and Cold War militarism.[20] The effort to take this agitation beyond the ecclesiastical border continued in the ranks of the German Catholic student association, which further radicalized as mass protest failed to bring down capitalism or end American brutality in Vietnam. Its members joined demonstrations and sit-ins against capitalism and European support for the war, and in its 1971 general meeting in Würzburg, it adopted a Marxist platform, written by Metz's students, calling for "human liberation ... [and] change of social-economic conditions."[21] In the Netherlands, students at the Catholic Institute at the University of Tilburg and Catholic University Nijmegen helped initiate the wave of riots that took over the country's universities in the spring of 1969. Occupying administrative buildings, they demanded radical democratization, and temporarily renamed the Catholic Institute for Economic, Social, and Juridical Studies as Karl Marx University.[22] The French Catholic student organization, Mission Étudiante, similarly took a left turn, lambasting the episcopacy for its refusal to endorse the riots of 1968. It launched "base communities," in which members lived communally and met for prayers and joint political discussions (without clerical involvement); these continued into the 1970s. Unlike previous efforts to merge Catholicism and Marxism, these initiatives spent relatively little energy on outreach to the working class, let alone on working in factories. They instead sought to form small communities of anti-authoritarian agitation. As Mission Étudiante declared in 1970, it was "an association of believers ... situating itself within the revolutionary current."[23]

Efforts to reconcile Christianity with the New Left were also underway among Protestants, whose thinkers also began to break centuries-old conventions by questioning the legitimacy of hierarchies and stability. The most influential figure in this effort was German theologian Jürgen Moltmann, whose *Theology of Hope* (1965) was an immediate sensation, running through seven editions in two years and appearing in seven European languages. Like Metz, Moltmann argued that Christianity's core message was its eschatology. The promise of a future radical rupture, he explained, was meant to repeatedly shake believers from complacency and inspire hope in their ability to change existing orders. As he forcefully put it, "From first to last, and not merely in the epilogue, Christianity is eschatology, is hope ... and therefore also revolutionizing and transforming the present."[24] In Moltmann's thinly veiled criticism of Christian democracy, state institutions since the Roman Empire had persistently sought to co-opt and domesticate Christianity, using it to legitimize unjust social hierarchies. But this was a distortion of Christ's message of perpetual discontent; as Moltmann put it, "the Christian church's service to mankind in not to keep this world as it is ... but to transform it and help it become what it is promised to be."[25] For Moltmann, this implied an openness to Marxism's revolutionary tradition. Like Metz, he had spent the mid-1960s participating in discussion groups and conferences that brought together communist thinkers and Christians to discuss mutual interests.[26]

Mirroring Metz's trajectory, Moltmann's ideas radicalized in the face of students' militant activism. In a series of articles, culminating in *The Crucified God* (1972), he offered a new vision of God that was both communal and revolutionary. According to Moltmann, God's image as an omnipotent and judging father was a grotesque invention of oppressive powers. By projecting authority onto heaven, they amplified people's doubts and fears and dismantled their critical capacity. As an alternative, Moltmann invoked the trinity to claim that God himself contained multiple entities, including believers. "One does not pray to God as a heavenly Thou, but prays *in* God," an act in of discovering one's self-worth and solidarity with others.[27] Moltmann drew on this anti-authoritarian notion to claim that Jesus's crucifixion and resurrection should be read as a critique of all social hierarchies. His humiliating death among criminals was a reminder that "what public opinion holds to be lowliest, what the state has determined to be disgraceful, is changed into what is supreme." It showed that "the authority of God is no longer represented by those in high positions, the powerful and the rich, but by the outcast Son of Man."[28] Moltmann therefore concluded that fulfilling Jesus's message called for radical overcoming from all forms of inequality. He argued that this "theology of the cross" emphasized resisting society's cruelty and called for liberation "from the prisons of capitalism," racism, and ecological degradation. Indeed, Moltmann came to see capitalism as the most powerful incarnation of humanity's broader tendency to internalize submission. Overcoming it therefore required constant agitation and confrontation.[29]

Moltmann's blistering attack on Christian social theory resonated with growing sentiments in the Protestant universe, where his work became the subject of intense commentary.[30] It gave voice to a cohort of thinkers who sought to replace the churches' old quest for social order and harmony with militant anti-authoritarianism. The influential German theologian Helmut Gollwitzer, whose leading role in opposition to nuclear armament and remilitarization in the 1950s made him a visible public figure, radicalized this social critique. In support of the student riots—their leader in Germany, Rudi Dutschke, was Gollwitzer's student and an active participant in Protestant life—he called in *The Rich Christians and Poor Lazarus* (1968) for the overthrow of capitalism and the establishment of radical democracy.[31] That same year the Protestant publishing house Kaiser launched a new book series titled "Protestantism and Revolution," in which young journalists and writers like Georg Eichholz and Gerhard Steck advocated for similar ideas.[32] Similar trends appeared in the Netherlands, where scholars who earlier did not show revolutionary zeal now talked of eschatology's radical command. Both Arend van Leeuwen, in *Critique of Heaven and Earth* (1970), and G. H. ter Schegget, in *Class Struggle and Strike: A Theologian Motivation* (1972) (both authors were prominent Protestant theoreticians), envisioned a global uprising against capitalism as the path for anti-authoritarian love.[33] In France, Georges Casalis, editor of the journal *Social Christianity*, began musing in 1967 about the "theology of revolution" and ran special issues on New Left ideas and supported student activism.[34] Perhaps the most sophisticated theoretician was the German theologian Dorothee Sölle, who drew on the Frankfurt School to offer a psychological critique of Christian social teachings. According to Sölle, the churches' social teachings led believers to internalize suffering as normal. As a result, they produced aggressions through projections. Sölle therefore claimed that Christianity had a dual task, both to destroy capitalist "brutalization" and to foster a critical self-assessment of one's internalization of capitalist values such as achievement and consumerism. Only then could Christians understand a "political interpretation of the gospel."[35]

As happened among Catholics, this support of student protest and emphasis on critical self-assessment had a galvanizing effect on activists. It inspired Protestant students in seminaries and universities, who saw their generation as the vanguard of a revolution against established order, one that would finally eclipse the disappointedly tame working class. In 1967, for example, the Protestant student association of West Berlin held special seminars on Marxist psychology. One speaker argued, citing Herbert Marcuse, that Luther's promise of liberation could be achieved in the modern world only by abolishing capitalism's excessive repression and legitimizing pleasure.[36] A year later, as German universities were rocked by protests, their Protestant counterparts in Tübingen, Frankfurt, and other cities formed a series of "critical synods" that demanded that local churches join an anti-capitalist front (especially by advocating for large-scale nationalization of industry and withdrawal from Cold War alliances). Alongside ecclesiastical activism and publications on the Frankfurt School, they also launched lay organizations such as the Red Council and the Thomas Müntzer Collective (named after the leader of a violent peasants' uprising), which organized strikes and teach-ins about Marxist theory.[37] Similar initiatives also took place in the Netherlands, where students from Amsterdam's Protestant Free University joined sit-ins and study groups of Frankfurt School texts. Education, explained one of their leaders in 1971, had to be democratized, so that "science, society, and the military-industrial complex [could] be dismantled."[38] And in France, leaders of the Protestant scouts and student federations joined New Left agitation. In the highly publicized manifesto *Church and Power* (1971), drafted by Casalis, they declared that capitalism was beyond reform and called for its violent replacement with egalitarian order.[39]

The similarity between these Catholic and Protestant projects went beyond the embrace of anti-authoritarian Marxism. On a more profound level, it entailed a parallel rethinking of Christianity's relationship to secularism. Ever since the nineteenth century, Christian social theorists had deplored what they saw as Europeans' increasing apathy toward God's grace. Whatever economic system they advocated for, from limited welfare to corporatism to market competition, was meant to halt this indifference. The new generation of thinkers, however, broke with this tradition. They not only claimed that secular ideologies like socialism were legitimate, but went so far as to argue that fulfilling God's command paradoxically required Christians to live as if he did not exist. The Protestant Sölle, for example, maintained in her theological tract *Christ the Representative* (1965) that Jesus's last words on the cross—"My God, why have you forsaken me?"—were meant to wean humans from the infantile desire for an interventionist divinity. If God's own son died so "powerless, homeless, alienated," was it not clear that God was absent from human life? For Sölle, this meant that Christianity's task was to forge solidarity between all humans—believers and nonbelievers alike—to overcome this tragic fate. As she put it, "We, too, can play God for one another," providing comfort and justice.[40] The Protestant Moltmann similarly insisted that God's absence from the world was repeatedly confirmed in the atrocities of "Auschwitz, Hiroshima, and Vietnam," an equation between Nazism and American aggression that was popular among protestors. Theology's goal after "the death of God," in this telling, was to help Christians recognize their alliance with all those who suffer, and to work together for a more just world.[41] To add the aura of martyrdom to their claims, both Catholics and Protestants in this camp increasingly invoked Lutheran theologian Dietrich Bonhoeffer, who two decades earlier was arrested and executed by the Nazis. His prison notes, in which he enigmatically predicted God's evacuation from the world and Christianity's mutation into a secular dispensation, suddenly enjoyed tremendous attention, and were cited and translated across Europe.[42]

Paradoxically, it was this insistence on Christianity's openness to secularism that also opened new possibilities for Catholic-Protestant relations. Even as they sought to bury the previous generations' social theory, revolutionary Christians maintained their ecumenism and hoped it could be used for new political purposes. This was the case for Metz, for example, who wrote extensively on interconfessional relations. In his telling, Catholicism's embrace of the secular world entailed the demolition of its own borders. Rather than narcissistically reaffirming their own traditions, believers had to find the "eschatological conscience" wherever it existed so that they could fulfill Christ's promise to redeem all of humanity. As Metz put it in *Reformation and Counter-Reformation Today* (1969), "Self-transcendence is not a subsequent addition to the Church but the basis of its establishment." In Protestants, Metz claimed to find the most significant and immediate community that shared a revolutionary potential. By celebrating their mutual commitment to disruption, the two confessions would forge a "faith that has comprehended the sign of the times."[43] Moltmann similarly claimed that engagement with Catholics went far beyond practical cooperation over a mutual political agenda. Instead, it was a necessary step in the church's "liberation" from capitalism's "Babylonian captivity." In Moltmann's telling, recognizing each other's revolutionary aspirations was bound to have an awakening effect on both confessions. It would confirm the "universality of the eschatological hope," and thus Christians' imperative to participate in resistance. Neither Metz nor Moltmann ever assumed that confessional difference would dissolve completely, but they both nevertheless predicted that confessional divides would be eclipsed by a joint revolutionary future. As Moltmann mused in 1975, Catholics and Protestants would form a unified "council," speaking in one voice and acting together on political questions.[44]

There was, to be sure, considerable irony in invoking ecumenism in the service of an anti-authoritarian socialism. After all, the entire history of Catholic-Protestant cooperation, from its practical beginnings in the 1880s to its full blossoming in later decades, revolved in part around efforts to defeat socialism with harmonious inequality. Indeed, both Metz and Moltmann echoed some of the ideas they sought to dislodge. Like their anti-materialist predecessors, they claimed that transcending historical divides would enrich both confessions and would better position them to realize their social visions. Despite this irony, the two initiated an intense intellectual cooperation. For almost a decade ecumenism was the main avenue through which they sought to participate in Christian intellectual life. After taking part in several joint events and publications, they jointly published *The Church in the Process of Enlightenment: Aspects of a New "Political Theology"* (1970), a mutual meditation on their political agenda.[45] This text became the opening volume in the influential book series Society and Theology, coedited by Metz and Moltmann and produced through the cooperation of the Catholic publishing house Grünewald and its Protestant equivalent, Kaiser. They also coauthored *History of Suffering* (1974), an exploration of the two confessions' approach to progress and social disruption.[46] Along with these works the two theologians also sought to build a new ecumenical canon by publishing a series of radical works, again through cooperation with the Grünewald and Kaiser publishing houses. The most notable titles included works by an American missionary and revolutionary in Latin America, Richard Shaull, the Black theology writer James Cone (with introduction by the American liberation theologian Frederick Herzog), the socialist Dutch theologian Frans van den Oudenrijn, and the Peruvian liberation theology icon Gustavo Gutiérrez.[47] This collaboration also had some institutional manifestations. In 1969 Metz was invited to found theological studies in the newly established university at Bielefeld, which itself was an effort to create a progressive form of higher education. In a departure from other universities, the theological institution was interconfessional, which Metz declared was a necessary step in the ecumenical struggle against oppression and racism.[48]

The intellectual cooperation between Metz and Moltmann may have been unusually deep and prolonged, but it was not exceptional. Either ignoring or seeking to overcome ecumenism's historical origins, many proponents of Christianity's fusion with anti-authoritarian politics assumed that their agenda entailed interconfessional cooperation. In France, for example, a group of Catholic and Protestant lay thinkers responded to the 1968 riots by calling for an ecumenical celebration of Pentecost. Led by the Protestant editor Georges Casalis and philosopher Paul Ricoeur, it envisioned lay-led cooperation in support of radical activism. As Ricoeur said, the students on the streets had "built a bridge" between the confessions "that our theologies and our ecclesiology had not yet constructed."[49] Even though such engagement was not endorsed by church authorities, it continued and grew in the following years. Together with Catholic theologian Bernhard Häring, Casalis helped organize an annual gathering of anti-authoritarian ecumenists from across Europe. Running throughout the 1970s in Strasbourg and publishing its own book series, the standing group was meant, in the words of one participant, to "replace the old and disappointing ecumenism" of the 1950s with a new and "revolutionary" cooperation.[50] The journal *Concilium*, the main intellectual publication of Catholic New Left sympathizers, similarly made ecumenism one of its main preoccupations. It published multiple Protestant contributions and regularly held forums on interconfessional cooperation. Crucially, such publications emphasized that the purpose of this unity was not to defeat secular materialism, as their predecessors had claimed, but to embrace its socialist version. A case in point is French Catholic theologian Yves Congar, who in the late 1930s called for a Christian front against the secular menace, but who now understood ecumenism as a welcome breaking of the churches' borders. In the lead article to the interconfessional collection *Post-Ecumenical Christianity* (1970), he wrote that Christian unity "is to be found in the common service" of non-Christians, "in joining together . . . [to fight] towards justice, for the poor, against all forms of oppression."[51]

It was in this context Catholic-Protestant engagement was also systematically extended to Jews, who in earlier ecumenical texts had been either vilified or ignored. In the early 1960s a new generation of activists and writers initiated a critical assessment of Christian anti-Semitism. Inspired in part by high-profile trials of Nazi criminals, they labored to expose clerical silence over the Holocaust (Pope Pius's wartime complicity drew particular attention) and initiated dialogue with Jewish communities.[52] While these efforts hardly registered with the ecumenists of the earlier generation, who never mentioned them in their meetings and writings, they became central to the anti-authoritarian ecumenism of the 1960s and 1970s. Sölle, for example, described her struggle against conformism and violence as repentance for anti-Semitism. If Christian hatred of Jews had clearly enabled the Nazi genocide, she wrote, "the least we can do for its victims is to rethink our Christian faith, for their sakes and in the light of their fate."[53] Moltmann saw in the Jewish tradition the seed of a revolutionary messianism whose persistence through history was meant to disrupt Christian complacency. As he wrote in a contribution to the interconfessional volume *Christians and Jews* (1974), "The presence of the Jews constantly forces Christians to see that they are not yet at their goal, and that their Church too is not their goal ... Instead ... in brotherly openness, they are still on the way."[54] The most far-reaching was Metz, who increasingly made confronting anti-Semitic violence central to revolutionary theology. In his formulation, the horror of Auschwitz should become a "dangerous" memory, repeatedly reflected upon, so that it would perpetually shock believers out of complacent self-love and a bourgeois mentality.[55] For all these thinkers, who joined Christian-Jewish dialogues, this confrontation with anti-Semitism was meant to have a cleansing effect on the churches. By breaking with supersessionist hopes for Jewish conversion, which persisted among many theologians well into the 1960s, and recognizing Jews as autonomous and equal communities, Christians would take a key step toward a truly universal solidarity.[56]

Like its predecessors from the 1940s and 1950s, this ecumenism also had a political corollary. Its first manifestation was in the Netherlands, where in 1968 a group of Catholic priests from Rotterdam and Haarlem formed the political association Septuagint. This name, which invoked an apocryphal story about the miraculous parallel translation of the Old Testament into Greek by seventy writers, reflected its conception of divine grace's communal nature. Under the leadership of Jos Vrijburg, Septuagint called for a new social vision that entailed both ecclesiastical democratization, such as the election of clerics, and the empowerment of the "poor and oppressed."[57] Dutch bishops ignored Septuagint, but its message resonated with Protestants. Led by Pastor Bert ter Schegget, dozens of Lutheran activists joined, making it an interconfessional association. In the following years, as thousands of lay activists and clerics joined its ranks, Septuagint emerged as a prominent engine of Dutch agitation. Its members participated in demonstrations against the war in Vietnam, capitalist inequality, and Dutch membership in NATO.[58] Its statements, too, progressively became more militant, describing Christianity as the source of permanent resistance to hierarchies. Its 1972 manifesto, drafted by ter Schegget, envisioned the formation of "critical communities," in which members of both confessions functioned as "a countermilieu" until capitalism was replaced by a "classless" society; at least a hundred such communities were founded across the country.[59] This radicalization was paralleled by continent-wide ambitions, as Septuagint forged ties with activists across Europe. In 1970 it convened the World Congress of Radical Priests in Amsterdam, where thousands of activists (both lay and clerical) from Belgium, Germany, and France joined to discuss their mutual aspirations. Under the moto "To liberate the church in order to liberate the world," it sought to push the church toward a new social vision.⁶⁰

German activists followed a similar path to fuse anti-authoritarianism and ecumenism. Echoing New Left insistence on "the unity of theory and praxis," they took it for granted that operating beyond confessional borders was integral to demolishing ecclesiastical and political hierarchies. In January 1968 a group of theology students in Bochum founded a group they called the Democratic-Ecumenical Action Alliance. Its purpose, according to its first statement, was to combine "inner liberation" with "political agitation," a task it sought to fulfill through multiple interconfessional gatherings.⁶¹

Such student activism lost some of its intensity in the 1970s, but ecumenism remained central to radical Christians. Its most famous expression was the Ecumenical Working Group, founded in 1968 to bring together theologians, scholars, and lay activists of both confessions in political advocacy. The group, whose highest-profile members included the Protestant theologian Sölle and the influential Catholic novelist Heinrich Böll, sought to embody the principles of critical and democratic political engagement. Its meetings, which took place monthly at the Gothic Antoniter Cathedral in Cologne, transformed worship into political teach-ins: along with prayers written by participants, they held collective debates about political controversies, usually based on pre-circulated statements (a format borrowed from student activism). Its pamphlets, which were soon published by a cooperative of Catholic and Protestant presses, repeated the blending of revolutionary theology and Marxism. As one of its members, Mechtild Höflich, explained, "A group that calls itself Christian must find ways to stop social inhumanity," and this meant advocating for "socialism in the broadest sense."⁶² Perhaps because its members included not only students but also older and established theologians like Sölle, these political night prayers, as they soon came to be known, became a media sensation. Drawing thousands of participants, they were reported widely in the press and were emulated by groups in Switzerland and the Netherlands.⁶³

More than any other group in the universe of radical Christianity, the night prayers took confessional differences to be expressions of a rigid and submissive mindset. While they never claimed to dissolve the difference between Catholics and Protestants, they equated confessional divisions with consumerist narcissism. As their first prayer admonished, distinguishing "between Catholic and Protestant school prayers" was akin to "carefully differentiating between Persil and other dish soaps." Believers' energy instead should be directed at the need to "socialize property" and resist bureaucratic authoritarianism in both capitalist and Stalinist form.[64] The group maintained this conception of interconfessionalism, as a vehicle for expanding political horizons, as it took on an ever-growing list of political issues. After mobilizing against the war in Vietnam (its first public poster declared "Vietnam is Golgotha!"), it launched campaigns protesting discrimination against foreign workers, the death penalty, and militarization. Echoing Metz's critical approach to tradition, its publications almost never referred to works of previous generations or invoked the authority of papal proclamations. Those, as one prayer put it, were the intellectual tools of "administrative bodies, state institutions, and military barracks," and were thus destined to be eclipsed by the revolutionary future.[65]

New Left ideas, in short, reverberated well beyond university campuses. They also inspired a new, socialist, and anti-authoritarian Christian social theory, which in turn helped solidify a new Catholic-Protestant ecumenism. In some ways, even in the landscape of far-reaching revolutionary aspirations, the task that anti-authoritarian Christians took upon themselves was uniquely ambitious. Many New Left activists framed their struggle in generational terms, as a revolt against their parents, whereas the effort to merge Christianity with anti-authoritarian socialism broke taboos that had dominated Christian social theory since the nineteenth century. Yet one of the few things that Metz, Moltmann, and others did preserve from their predecessors was the belief that Catholic-Protestant cooperation could play a role in realizing their social vision. As German theologian Bernhard Häring put it in a 1971 conference of ecumenical radicals, it was the basis for "the web of contestations" that Christians were destined to cast on the world.[66]

Farewell to the Family: Radical Christian Sexuality

For many protestors in the 1960s and 1970s, oppression was not just the product of capitalism. Internal submission to authority, they claimed, also defined the intimate sphere; taboos and prohibitions regulated people's behavior as partners, parents, and lovers. Liberation therefore required a new politics of gender and sexuality. In order to emancipate themselves, Europeans had to experiment with arrangements that did not assign strict gender roles and that embraced sexuality beyond the heterosexual family.

Radical Ecumenism in the 1960s and 1970s

To be sure, proponents of reform were often ambivalent about women's entry into the workforce or society's increasing celebration of carnal pleasure. As feminist Germaine Greer put it in her best-selling book *The Female Eunuch* (1970), those were often superficial concessions that served to oil capitalism's oppressive machine.[67] Protestors also disagreed on crucial issues like the desirability of monogamy. Yet despite those internal tensions, the proliferation of activism around feminist and queer causes in those decades helped bring about substantial changes to Europe's regulation of gender and sexuality. Bolstered by fading fears of depopulation thanks to the postwar "baby boom," reformers helped to weaken or eliminate unequal family laws and restrictions on abortion and same-sex relationships. In many ways Europe witnessed the partial disintegration of the gender and sexual regulatory system that Christians had worked to create since the late nineteenth century and had solidified under Christian democracy.

Feminist and sexual reform movements were hardly a new phenomenon in modern Europe, but the responses they inspired among Christians in the 1960s and 1970s were unprecedented. For the first time, their advocates faced not only Christian condemnation, but also a sympathetic Christian embrace. A group of Catholic and Protestant writers launched a blistering attack on the churches' obsessive insistence on men's and women's differing social functions. Jesus's emancipatory message, they claimed, was exactly the opposite: it was a call to shatter social rules and allow autonomous choice, though whether women and men were the same or inherently distinctive remained an open question. This campaign was followed by an equally radical effort to rethink Christian sexuality. Inspired by New Left theories, Catholics and Protestants dismissed the confinement of sex to the family as despotic and sadistic, and vocally supported abortion and queer rights. As was the case with their antiauthoritarian counterparts, proponents of this new Christian intimacy took it for granted that liberation could only be achieved through ecumenical frameworks. They believed that Catholics and Protestants shared the same sexist heritage, from which both had to be liberated. The claims of 1950s ecumenists, then, about the two confessions' similar sexual ethics, were ironically turned against the very norms they had sought to bolster.

One could detect a shift in the Christian conception of gender even before feminism's explosion in the late 1960s. As female labor outside the home ceased to be a predominantly working-class phenomenon, and became more common among the middle-classes, Christian writers of both confessions agreed that motherhood could potentially coincide with work and financial independence. Theological manuals on work and marriage increasingly shifted their attention away from conflicts that stemmed from men's and women's allegedly different "natural" desires for work and family, which had dominated such publications earlier in the twentieth century. Instead, they discussed the realities of families with two parents working outside the home, and encouraged men to join their wives in parental tasks. The French Catholic specialists Jean-G. Lemaire and Evelyne Lemaire-Arnaud, for example, whose book *Resolution of Marital Conflicts* (1966) was widely translated, dedicated a long section to ameliorating men's discomfort at their wives' employment. "What do we have to fear," they rhetorically asked, "if men and women's roles begin to assimilate and even overlap?"[68] Similar sentiments were expressed by Karl Horst Wrage, one of Germany's most influential experts on family and sexuality who would later author the Protestant formal guidelines on sexual matters. His book *Responsibility in Marriage* (1965), which went through multiple editions, reminded men that women's self-fulfillment might entail an independent career.[69] But even though such publications often also advocated for women to have equal say in decisions about children's education or family finances, they nevertheless remained committed to the logic of gender essentialism. They repeated ad nauseam the claim that mothers were more emotionally invested in parenthood, and thus were naturally constituted to be the main caregiver.

Alongside this moderate shift, however, both confessions also witnessed a much more radical challenge to their dominant family ethics. Across Europe a new cohort of theologians and family experts emerged who sought not only to appropriate feminism's language, but also to embrace and implement its insights. Among Catholics, the pioneering figure in this effort was Catharina (Tine) Halkes, a longtime activist in Catholic lay organizations turned theologian, whose book *The Storm after the Calm: Women's Place in the Church* (1964) appeared in several languages and was widely reviewed in the Christian press. According to Halkes, the church's entire clerical structure was premised on misogyny. This was why all positions of authority in the church were not only male but also celibate: this tradition reflected a pathological fear that social and sexual interactions with women diminished men's intellectual and spiritual faculties. Halkes further argued that this gendered segregation, and the inequality it prescribed between men and women, stood on theologically shaky foundations. The New Testament may have included some sexist passages, most famously Paul's proclamation in 1 Corinthians that "women should remain silent," but those hardly were timeless rules integral to its message. Like the apostles' tolerance of slavery, they were expressions of the period's dominant norms, which could and should be abandoned in new realities. Drawing on the theological innovations of Metz and others, Halkes claimed that female subordination was the product of the churches' misguided embrace of Thomas Aquinas and his medieval belief in each individual's "assigned" role in hierarchical society. Clerical prejudice thus obscured and distorted the emancipatory message of Jesus, whose early followers, Halkes noted, included many women.[70] To translate her claims into practical work, in 1965 Halkes worked with the support of a Dutch bishop to establish a new program in Amsterdam to train laypeople for pastoral work. Halkes was its director, and most of its participants were women.[71]

The implications of Halkes's readings stretched far beyond ecclesiastical matters. Most of *The Storm after the Calm* was dedicated to the status of women in family and social relations, which for decades was deeply impacted by Christian insistence on the two sexes' different "callings." In Halkes's telling, the sexist anxieties that undergirded clerical celibacy also infected Christian marriages. Rather than viewing conjugal relations as partnerships of equals, men relegated women to the private sphere, denied them authority over property and education, and demeaned their labor by separating it from income. Childcare, Halkes noted, is not just a selfless act of love, but a form of uncompensated work. Combing through both the Old and the New Testaments, Halkes invoked passages about marriage that offered a different model, one based on equality and love. As she put it, the capacity to bear children is not the only measure of a "fruitful" marriage, nor was it even marriage's main function. Both partners' ability to achieve autonomy and engage with the world as they saw fit, including a choice of career paths for both partners, were love's other "fruits." Catholics, therefore, had to support women's equality to men in marriage, in family law, and in the public sphere. They also, Halkes implied, must accept women's right to control their own reproduction, including the right to use contraception.[72]

This emphasis on love over procreation may have resembled what some reformers had claimed since the 1930s, but Halkes's approach was far more iconoclastic. She not only dismissed papal pronouncements about motherhood and procreation as outdated and misguided, but also rejected the very focus on family and motherhood as the telos of female life. Christian anti-feminism, Halkes scoffed, had long utilized family responsibilities—and men's freedom from that burden—to restrict women's options and autonomy. It particularly diminished the lives of unwed women, who instead of being celebrated as valuable community members, were persistently described in Christian texts as damaged and "colorless" creatures filled with paralyzing "fears and doubts." Halkes drew on recent sociological research to bemoan how the Christian obsession with motherhood curtailed solidarity between married and unmarried women. Rather than jointly campaigning against sexism, their interactions were marred by judgments and resentment. Perhaps most radical, Halkes echoed left-leaning psychology by linking her feminist message to political anti-authoritarianism. The struggle against the patriarchy, she explained, was a campaign "not only in the family, but everywhere in society, which is shaped by family institutions." It was thus a "revolt against all forms of paternalism," including in the workplace, school, and politics. Dispensing with decades of Catholic theorizing, Halkes rejected the notion that the family was the cornerstone of social stability. Instead her writings described the family as a training ground for "democratization" and self-determination for both children and parents.[73]

Halkes may have been unusually visible—curious journalists covered her from across Europe, making her a celebrity of sorts—but she was hardly an isolated case in her efforts to merge Christian ethics with feminism. Across Europe, a group of Catholic writers, almost all of them women, echoed her critique of the church's family ethics. The Swiss journalist Gertrud Heinzelmann, for example, published the collection *We Won't Keep Silence Any Longer!* (1965), in which young Catholic women from across the continent confronted their subordination. In her own contribution, Heinzelmann argued that the church had to declare its support for women's work and self-determination beyond marriage, home, and family, because "the time is forever past when a woman must accept the authority of some man or other from cradle to grave."[74] The Norwegian writer Kari Elisabeth Børresen, whose book *Subordination and Equivalence* (1968) was quickly translated in multiple languages, offered a scorching critique of Catholic history. In her telling, the early church was open to female authority, but Augustine and Thomas Aquinas relied on the Middle Age's faulty understanding of the female body to develop a sexist theology. Ever since, she claimed, their ideas plagued Christian thinking and undergirded its opposition to feminism. The most radical voice was the young German theologian Elisabeth Schüssler, whose book *The Forgotten Partner* (1964) and subsequent articles dismissed the claim that women's "true" calling was motherhood. Christianity's task, she claimed, was to demolish sexual hierarchies and to build a new society free of paternalism.[75]

What distinguished these texts from their predecessors, and what their titles' focus on oppression and defiance so powerfully reflected, was their desire to go beyond moderate feminists' calls for equality. While they celebrated female labor inside and outside the home, demanded legal equality in family matters, and advocated for women's ordination in the church, these writers both foreshadowed and drew inspiration from radical feminism, which exploded in the late 1960s and the 1970s. Radical feminists argued that female liberation required the demolition of social norms and traditions. Catholic feminists echoed theoreticians like Germaine Greer to describe feminism as a broad revolt against oppressive authority. Schüssler, for example, warned that the struggle for female employment was only relocating the church's masochistic ethos from the home to the workplace. "The 'angel in the house' has become the 'angel at the conveyor belt or at the typewriter,'" she said in 1971 in an address to the Catholic women's organization St. Joan's International Alliance; liberation could arrive only if women helped overthrow "the masculine authoritarian structures of our economy and society."[76] Børresen sought to develop a theological justification for such thinking by questioning the churches' gendered understanding of authority. God, she claimed in 1975, was not male but a combination of both sexes, a "male-female" entity whose true message for humanity was the need to transcend rigid dichotomies. For Børresen, this fact had clear implications for social relations. Women's liberation was to arrive not by entering masculine spaces, but by questioning their legitimacy as "natural."[77]

By the early 1970s the assault on long-held gender norms was also underway among Protestants. The most prominent figure here was the German Elisabeth Moltmann-Wendel, who began her career as a teacher and as an assistant to her husband, Jürgen Moltmann, but quickly became an influential theologian in her own right (and whose feminist choice to hyphenate her family name was still unusual at that time). Like Halkes, whom she read and often cited, Moltmann-Wendel lambasted the churches' long-standing appropriation of feminist rhetoric and their equating motherhood with "true" freedom. Giving birth and taking care of children, she noted, were brief and transitory periods, and even in their most taxing stretches they did not preclude other options and choices.

More importantly, the very notion that women had an "essence" or fixed nature, which Christian writers about sex took for granted, erased women's diverse experiences and desires. "An ontological determination of woman's nature," she wrote in her polemical book *Human Rights for Women: Christian Initiatives for Women's Liberation* (1974), keeps women "captive in ... biological chains." Like her Catholic counterparts, Moltmann-Wendel invoked the metaphor of slavery to claim that the Christian fixation with motherhood was mostly meant to legitimize female self-denial and subjugation. The family, by demonstrating to the child different modes of behaviors between the parents, was society's earliest and most intimate effort to socialize children into sexually segregated professions, earnings, and opportunities.[78]

Perhaps more than any other Christian writer, Moltmann-Wendel expanded on the link between her feminism and radical social critique. Like the participants in the political night prayers in Germany, Moltmann-Wendel described the churches' social teachings as the legitimizing arm of oppressive state politics. In *Liberty, Equality, Sisterhood* (1977), a collection of lectures she gave to Protestant women's organizations in the early 1970s, she wrote that the churches' focus on "natural" inequality and self-denial disciplined children and adults into believing that "self-surrender and self-sacrifice" were "the undisputed and highest ethical norms." Such meek obedience, in this telling, was especially pronounced in capitalist society, with its fetishization of hard work and reliance on exploitation. It was particularly harmful to women, who through socialization around motherhood internalized the alleged value of suffering and thus thought it natural to seek the most difficult and lowest-earning jobs. The churches' ideal of family life, that is, had a "stabilizing" function for a society rife with injustice. This oppressive function, however, had little to do with Jesus's original message. The sacrifice of living creatures to satisfy deities, Moltmann-Wendel claimed, was a pagan ideal, attached to the Gospel by those who failed to recognize that Jesus's ultimate sacrifice of the self was meant to free humanity from repeating it. While Moltmann-Wendel, like many New Left thinkers, was skeptical that sexual pleasure alone could emancipate people from oppression, she nevertheless believed it was necessary to legitimize it. Christians, she claimed, had to shed their suspicion of bodily pleasure so they could challenge capitalism's ethics of masochistic self-denial.[79]

Like Halke's impact on Catholics, Moltmann-Wendel's ideas gave voice to an emerging cohort of feminists. Gathering in study groups and conferences, Protestant journalists, social scientists, and theologians began to offer a new, anti-patriarchal model for emancipation. The Swiss psychologist Josef Duss-von Werdt, for example, who replaced Theodor Bovet as head of the influential Institute for Marriage and Family in Zurich, in 1972 convened the first pan-European Protestant conference on radical feminism. In the subsequent volume of papers from the conference, *Man and Woman: Partners Yet?* (1973), French sociologist Evelyne Sullerot attacked women's socialization into lower-income professions and employers' hostility to parental leave, and Belgian journalist Angelika Boese lambasted the media and fashion industries' objectification of the female body.[80] German Protestant organizations quickly followed with similar initiatives. The German Evangelical Women's League sponsored the studies of Magdalena Hartlich, a therapist who worked in Protestant family counseling services and turned her focus to sexism's debilitating psychological impact on families.[81] In 1974 the League also organized a German-Austrian gathering, where Moltmann-Wendel delivered papers alongside icons of radical feminism, including psychologist Jutta Menschik, journalist Hannelore Mabry, and abortion rights activist Alice Schweitzer. Participants in those undertakings, like radical feminists more broadly, differed in their opinions on men's role in the feminist struggle, but they all agreed that even fathers were deformed by the patriarchy. As Hartlich declared in her paper, society's insistence that parenting was the mother's task denied the father his "natural inclination" to cuddle the child and care for it, which then damaged his capacity for solidarity and emotional connection in work and politics.[82]

Like the anti-feminism that it sought to dislodge, this undertaking was not free of tensions. If Christianity's "true" message was emancipatory and egalitarian, how did this go unrecognized by Christians for so long? Indeed, unlike most radical feminists, who often described their project as being without precedent in Europe's patriarchal history, Christian feminists felt compelled to root their legitimacy in tradition. But the churches' record constituted difficult raw material: both scripture and centuries of interpretation overflowed with sexism, subordination of women, and (especially in the Old Testament) sexual violence. Despite this challenge, the leaders of Christian feminism took on the task of "recovering" feminist models, which they believed were suppressed by later male theologians. Only by doing so could Christians overcome their grim record and, by extension, contribute to the feminist struggle more broadly. In Moltmann-Wendel's words, "Imagination is necessary in a church and a theology which has lost touch with women."[83] Halkes, expanding on her earlier work, described Jesus's mother as a symbol of feminist autonomy. Creatively reading the New Testament, she insisted that Mary's motherhood was marginal to her self-conception as an autonomous woman.[84] Moltmann-Wendel provided similarly sympathetic and creative portraits of Jesus's early followers, such as Mary Magdalene. As she explained in her book *Becoming Their Own Person: Women around Jesus* (1979), which ran through nine editions, women were just as important for Christianity's history as Peter or Paul, exemplifying as they did the spirit of charity.[85] These writers were aware that this effort was not free of anachronism, projecting as it did their preoccupations onto the past. They also knew that selectively invoking those isolated cases as legitimizing precedents was at odds with claiming that the rest of the churches' history was irrelevant to the present. But as Halkes later argued, retrieval of the past was a necessary "clearing away" of sexist "rubbish," an intellectual "dynamite" designed "to destroy the rigid structures of traditional Christian thinking."[86]

Even though this rethinking of family and gender ethics was revolutionary—and despite its proponents' claims, very much unprecedented—it remained committed to the ecumenical logic that preceded it. In fact, the one thing Christian feminists shared with their predecessors was a sense that Catholics and Protestants were partners in a mutual project. As early as 1967, at the initiative of several lay organizations across Europe, the first interconfessional conference on women's shifting status in society gathered in Taizé, France. Its participants—scholars, charity workers, and activists from across Europe—discussed how to improve women's ability to fulfill themselves beyond the family. The French Protestant pastor André Dumas argued that if women were "overtaxed" by the dual responsibilities of parenting and work, it was men's and society's responsibility to alleviate their load.[87] As feminist activism both gathered steam and radicalized, interconfessional cooperation increased. Church authorities kept their distance, but Catholic-Protestant gatherings became regular events, dedicated to topics such as early education and women's ordination (the latter gathering, which met in Geneva in 1970, included a keynote address by Halkes).[88] In 1974 thousands of activists and writers from across Europe gathered in West Berlin for an ecumenical convention on "sexism," a term that was itself still relatively new in Europe. After a series of addresses on topics ranging from family law reforms and childcare to pornography, the delegates crafted a joint text that described feminist demands, such as payment for mothers' work in the home, as realizing the Gospel. In the published volume of addresses presented at the conference, *Sexism in the 1970s: Discrimination against Women* (1975), one paper declared that a woman "is a complete human being" regardless of her family status, and that society should be structured to accommodate "all her potentials."[89]

Nothing demonstrates ecumenism's established position more than the minimal verbiage it seemed to require as time passed. Earlier in the twentieth century, Catholics and Protestants insisted that their joint antifeminism relied on diverging views on gender, and the ecumenists of the 1950s went at great length to explain why they shared mutual views. In contrast, the feminists who sought to overcome their legacies treated interconfessionalism almost intuitively, as a reality that required little justification. This fact was on full display in the first efforts to institutionalize European Christian feminism, which took off in 1978. That year, dozens of European theologians, pastors, journalists, and students of both confessions gathered in Brussels to discuss their project of female emancipation. After keynote addresses by Halkes and Moltmann-Wendel, they discussed how churches' fears of the female body fueled countless forms of gendered oppression; the list stretched from unequal pay to rape, the first time Christian writings tied forced sex to the churches' sexism. They also agreed that feminist liberation required the overthrow of other systemic oppressions, including racial discrimination, militarism, economic inequality, and torture.[90] Without much commentary on their confessional distinctions, participants suggested the establishment of a standing organization that would encourage feminist approaches to Christian matters. By the time those plans materialized a few years later, with the creation of the Ecumenical Forum of European Christian Women, the cooperation of Catholics and Protestants was considered obvious. Its multilingual gatherings and publications, most importantly its international essay collection *Handbook of Feminist Theology* and its running journal, took it for granted that confessional differences paled in comparison to the joint task of liberation.[91]

The focus of such reformatory efforts did not remain limited to women's social status. As in the past, they both inspired and drew on shifts in Christian thinking about sexuality, and especially the rise of a radical ecumenical campaign to legitimize sexuality beyond the family and to reject heteronormativity. Across the confessional divide, writers in the late 1960s and 1970s drew on New Left theories to offer a new understanding of the relationship of sex to politics. Christians' historic focus on restricting pleasure, they claimed, was part of the workings of authoritarianism. By fostering guilt, shame, and self-denial, it produced docile subjects who craved paternalist approval. To fulfill Jesus's promise of liberation, it was therefore necessary to combat restrictions on sexuality and sexual expression. Even though writers in this group sometimes justified their causes in practical terms, claiming that a refusal to revise sexual teachings would push many believers out of the churches, their agenda was ultimately ideological. They sought to rethink the meaning and nature of "proper" sexuality: rather than the basis for social stability (as morality campaigners had claimed since the 1890s) or heterosexual pleasure (as Christian marriage experts maintained in the 1950s), sexuality had to be a training ground for self-emancipation and political resistance. Like the feminists, proponents of this campaign envisioned the process of redefining sexuality as a new site for Catholic-Protestant cooperation. Together, they were to eliminate the churches' fixation on chastity and restrictions on sexual expression.

To be sure, these radical campaigns built upon earlier efforts at liberalization. In the mid-1960s, as Europeans were noticeably becoming less rigid in their approach to sexuality, some Christian thinkers responded by questioning earlier restrictions. Among Catholics, the main focus was the long ban on contraception, which received renewed urgency with the arrival of birth control pills in Europe, even though their circulation was initially restricted by age or marital status. The Belgian family expert Louise Janssens and the Dutch Willem van der March, for example, claimed in 1963 that it was legitimate for married couples to express their love without it leading to pregnancy.[92] They were followed a few years later by the prominent German theologians Franz Böckle and Bernhard Häring, who argued that economic and social shifts (especially rising costs) made caring for children much more difficult than before; couples should therefore be able to limit their procreation.[93] Prominent Protestant writers, for their part, argued that premarital cohabitation and even sex could be permissible if they ultimately led to marriage. In his book *Sexuality: Insights and Standards* (1966), Siegfried Keil, the director of the Protestant church's family counseling services, explained that young couples often had legitimate reasons to delay formal marriage, and that it was understandable if they expressed their love physically before then.[94] Even masturbation was rehabilitated. Karl Horst Wrage's popular *Man and Woman* (1966) went beyond the efforts of previous decades to claim that the practice was not only harmless but actually useful in preparing boys and girls for marriage. "What is harmful," he argued, was "parental disapproval or condemnation as sinful . . . of the pleasant sensation."[95]

As meaningful as these changes were, they were relatively subtle and retained most of the presuppositions of earlier decades. They still assumed that sexuality was legitimate only within the family unit, and only if it included the promise of marriage or potential procreation. This was true even for much of the backlash sparked by Pope Paul VI's encyclical *Humanae vitae* (1968), which famously restated the Vatican's opposition to contraception, and which consumed much of the scholarship on Christianity and sexuality in this period. Defying some reformers' hopes, the encyclical continued the tradition of appropriating feminist rhetoric against women's emancipation. The encyclical insisted that denying women bodily autonomy in fact empowered them, since sex without procreative potential reduced their value in men's eyes to sexual pleasure, thus "disregarding their physical and emotional equilibrium."[96] Even though the statement angered many prominent thinkers and clergy—the bishops of Germany, Belgium, and Austria formally protested it—most of the opposition did not question the centrality of the procreative family. Much of the anger revolved around ecclesiastical authority, and especially the pope's unusual decision to ignore a Vatican-appointed committee's recommendation to loosen restrictions on contraception. Even vocal opponents of the encyclical, like Häring, insisted that sexual activity without marriage and potential procreation was a "selfish" perversion. As he admonished, "The conjugal act," even inside marriage, "must not be viewed as a mere pleasure seeking."[97]

For a radical group of thinkers, however, the problems with the churches' approach to sexuality extended far beyond clerical authority or contraception. In their eyes, both Catholics and Protestants adhered to sexual ethics that ultimately served capitalism and authoritarianism. Writing for the German group Critical Catholics in 1968, for example, Hermann Böckenförde and Bernhard Wilhelmer lambasted Christian prohibitions against nonmarital sex as a form of "domination." The purpose of those admonitions, they claimed, was to force people into a life of constant fear, so they would be obedient workers and submissive subjects. Böckenförde and Wilhelmer therefore rejected not only *Humanae vitae,* which they described as a symptom of an "inhumane" worldview, but also the association of sexual desire with sin, and the Christian celebration of the family. Citing recent psychological research, they claimed that "true" Christian education would instead expose children to nudity and sex, so they could grow up free of guilt and become anti-authoritarian citizens.[98] Similar ideas also began to circulate among radical Protestants, who claimed that the churches' sexual ethics was a psychological prop for capitalism. German pastor and activist Werner Simpfendörfer, for example, maintained in his book *Open Church—Critical Church* (1970) that admonitions against temptation were meant to normalize suffering, and thus to diffuse revolutionary impulses. If Christians were to form the "community of alternative" life, which aspired to equality and freedom, they had to discard their historic obsession with the family.[99]

The distance between this new approach and earlier reforms was especially apparent in its unprecedented assault on taboos. One vivid example was the campaign surrounding abortion, a topic on which Catholics and Protestants had cooperated for decades but that now galvanized interconfessional calls for decriminalization. Few better represented the effort to rethink this topic among Catholics than the French Dominican writer Jacques-Marie Pohier, who was vice-rector of the prestigious Saulchoir seminary and an influential editor. Beginning in 1969, and especially after the French parliament began discussing reforms to its abortion laws in 1972, Pohier expressed support for women's right to willfully terminate pregnancies. Doing so, he wrote in the Catholic magazine *Light and Life,* was not an interference with "nature," at least not more so than any other medical procedure, and as such it did not violate divine imperatives. Perhaps more important, Christian talk of life's "sanctity" could not be reduced to mere biological existence. God's grace was also measured by a child's well-being, its ability to grow up without abuse, poverty, or illness. Pohier therefore turned the talk of life's value against abortion's opponents, claiming that it was *they* who devalued human life. As he put it in a 1973 interview, "I do not see what sin there would be against respect for life by eliminating a fetus that . . . one knows cannot have a minimum level of human life. On the contrary, it is out of respect for life that it must be eliminated."[100]

Pohier's ideas enjoyed considerable resonance. In 1973 the French Jesuit journal *Études* ran a special forum that challenged the long-standing opposition to abortion. Repeating Pohier's words, its editor, Bruno Ribes, claimed that termination was permissible if it protected parents and child from "dehumanization."[101] In Belgium, family expert Pierre de Locht, who for years headed the country's influential Catholic network of family and marriage counseling, argued that a fetus should not necessarily be considered a person if it was not desired by its parents. In 1973 he provocatively appeared in a demonstration supporting Willy Peers, a doctor whose arrest after admitting to managing abortions sparked the nation's first large-scale (though ultimately failed) movement for decriminalization.[102] In Germany, the theologian and doctor Stephan Pfürtner used abortion to criticize the churches' long campaign to institutionalize their sexual morality through state institutions. Not only was it absurd to treat the fetus as an autonomous human, he explained in his polemical book *Church and Sexuality* (1972), and a violation of women's bodily autonomy; most importantly, it was not the churches' business to impose their will through laws. Pfürtner reminded his readers that throughout the Middle Ages, Christian writers deplored the existence of prostitution but never advocated that it should be made illegal. An "authentic" Christian approach would therefore liberate states from managing sexuality or reproduction.[103]

Even more radical critiques emerged among Protestants, who often linked abortion access to the feminist cause. Here the most eloquent was theologian Dorothee Sölle, who along with her political writing and activism in the political night prayers, published a most blistering critique of the churches' stance. Drawing on New Left theories, Sölle lambasted both Catholic and Protestant talk of the sanctity of life as hypocritical. Both confessions' interest in the child's life, in her acidic words, "ended at birth": after that moment, Christians accepted as a given their "hostile society," in which "children are a nuisance to their parents, property owners, car drivers, homeowners, and public authorities." Both churches showed little agitation against Cold War militarization, wars, and the death these caused. Opposition to abortion, Sölle therefore claimed, was instead intended to control and subjugate women by making the sexual act dangerous. It also was designed to criminalize women's quest for self-realization beyond motherhood, especially for working-class women, for whom an unwanted child often created forced dependency and economic ruin. For Sölle, Jesus's call for solidarity with the weak necessitated support for decriminalization. As she rhetorically asked, when it comes to abortion, "who is the injured, the defenseless, the weak? Is it the fertilized protozoa, or is it the mother who is compelled by law to carry the child . . . regardless of her wants and needs?"[104] Paralleling Catholic trends, Sölle's claims circulated across national lines. In France, the influential Protestant theologian André Dumas, who was a major voice in matters of sexuality, reasoned that abortion was permissible because it fell under God's command to Adam and Eve to subdue nature. Prohibiting abortion, he added, reduced women to their biological function and thus "desacralized" their existence.[105] In Switzerland, too, Protestant theologian Gyula Barczay dismissed forced births as a materialist biologism that was against God's will.[106]

Like the project of feminist theology, these efforts regarding abortion quickly became interconfessional. Because they took it for granted that natalist Christian ethics were broadly "Christian" and not confessional, they viewed their advocacy as necessarily mutual. In France, for example, the Catholic Pohier and the Protestant Dumas joined in 1969 to convene a study group on abortion. The group included Christian doctors, social workers, and theologians, who for several years gathered information and held discussions about women's experiences with illegal abortion. Published as *Abortion and Respect for Human Life* (1972), the group's materials sympathetically described women as victims of a dehumanizing system, and warned against the criminal system's oppressive impact on family life (though not without a few members expressing dissenting opinions). As the psychologist and group member Françoise Jardin put it in one of her comments, forced birth for young women could be "experienced as death."[107] In Germany, the political night prayer group around Sölle similarly launched an interconfessional campaign in 1971 in support of decriminalization. It organized a series of lectures, in which figures like the feminist Protestant lawyer Barbara Just-Dahlmann argued that compulsory birth violated the constitutional right of human dignity. The study group further published a popular booklet on the "old age misery," which combined historical, legal, and theological studies on the links between abortion restrictions, sexism, and subjugation.[108]

This cooperation was not just facilitated by the changing legal status of abortion, though it became increasingly accessible across Europe in the 1970s and 1980s. For Pohier, Sölle, and others, the Catholic and Protestant opposition to abortion epitomized a broader anxiety about pleasure, which served to discipline believers into political obedience. Pohier, for example, claimed that the insistence on the link between sex and childbearing deformed love, because it injected fear into one's most intimate relations. The goal of pastoral care, he argued in his book *The Christian, Pleasure, and Sexuality* (1974), was to release couples from such fears so they could become more assertive and independent humans.[109] Sölle similarly remarked that opposition to abortion was rooted in an "animal conception of sexuality," which both confessions shared. While she was skeptical that sexual pleasure alone had anything emancipatory about it—like Moltmann-Wendel, she claimed it could easily be commodified by capitalism—she insisted that freeing it from pregnancy could ease believers' ambivalence about its legitimacy.[110] This was in part why Christian proponents of abortion often sought to legitimize their case by focusing on disabled children, whose own suffering—and the pain they allegedly inflicted on their parents—they described as inhumane. Their existence symbolized the polar opposite of pleasurable life. Indeed, even as they sought to rethink Christian understanding of the body, Christian radicals unintentionally echoed the claims of Christian eugenicists from the 1930s. Their ethical universe was almost diametrically opposed to that of the eugenicists, but they agreed that forcing hereditary illnesses on children was a violation of Christian love.[111]

Alongside abortion, perhaps the most iconoclastic challenge to the churches' family ethics was the interconfessional campaign for gay liberation. Even though most Catholic and Protestant elites did not resist loosening of legal restrictions on homosexuality in the 1960s and 1970s—most European countries either decriminalized homosexuality or removed some restrictions, such as higher ages of consent—they were hardly enthusiastic. Focused as they were on marriage as the locus of sexuality, most Christian publications and speeches described decriminalization as inconsequential, because they assumed that gay relations would remain private; public disapproval of them was so sweeping that they could not threaten heterosexual family structures.[112] Indeed, even texts that sought to offer some tolerance of homosexuality struggled to describe it as anything but illness. *The New Catechism* (1966), for example, the Dutch Catholic bishops' effort to modernize the church's teaching, called on believers to show charity to gay men and women. In the same breath, however, it also instructed "those who know that they are homosexuals" to seek medical and mental help, and warned against its normalization, lest it corrupt "many who were really quite capable of normal sexual sentiments."[113] The German Protestant churches struck a similar tone in their widely discussed *Memorandum to Questions of Sexual Ethics* (1971), which provided instructions for family and sexual life. Even though it faintly voiced its opposition to "unreflective" homophobia, it also conclusively described homosexuality as "sexual aberration," and recycled homophobic fears about gay predators by warning that "children and youth must be protected from seduction, advertisement, and propaganda for homosexuality."[114]

While advocates for gay rights had criticized church teachings since the late nineteenth century, in the 1970s those voices for the first time now appeared inside the Christian universe. As with feminism and abortion, the efforts to release homosexuality from its stigma of shame and to legitimize its expression in public quickly took on an interconfessional character. In 1970 the Dutch pastor Bernardus Witte and the Catholic psychologist J. L. Grubben published *Homophilia,* a study of Christian treatment of homosexuality. Quickly translated and reviewed across Europe, it claimed that the Old Testament's condemnations of same-sex love were not part of God's timeless message. Like misogynistic statements, they reflected the era's norms and should be discarded. In fact, Witte and Grubben claimed that homophobia was a symptom of a sexually repressed society, in which guilt-ridden people projected onto queer people their anxieties about transgression. Catholics and Protestants therefore had to join the project of gay liberation.[115] Two years later the French Catholic Gérald La Mauvinière left Arcadie, the country's main organization for gay rights, and founded in Paris its Christian equivalent, David and Jonathan. Officially interconfessional, its meetings and its bulletin, *Christianity and Homophilia,* brought Catholics and Protestants together to discuss reforming the churches' norms and combatting discrimination. Within a few years, David and Jonathan opened branches across France and Belgium, providing a home for local activism. Its patron, Catholic priest Jacques Perotti, proclaimed that "the slow emergence of a positive homosexual identity" was a sign of salvation after "long years of rejection, destruction, and intimidation."[116]

The quest to transform ecumenism into a vehicle of sexual liberation reached its clearest manifestation in Germany. In 1977 the hospital pastor Heinz Brink used Germany's congress of Protestant churches in Berlin to launch a new organization for gay advocacy. Though his request to be formally included in the event was denied by the organizers, he was joined by several dozen activists to form the "general homosexual community." The group received heightened attention when it was endorsed by Helmut Kentler, a prominent Protestant sexologist, whose revolutionary approach to sexual education, such as calling on parents to expose children to nudity and sexual desire, made him a well-known media entity. It quickly became a national organization, with branches springing up in Cologne, Munich, and several other cities. As its activities proliferated, several dozen Catholic activists also joined these groups. Without any debate or resistance, the organization changed its name to The Ecumenical

Working Group for Homosexuals in the Church. In the next few years it became a key organization for gay rights activists in Germany. It also expanded beyond the country's borders, opening branches in Austria and Switzerland.[117]

If the group's participants found it so easy to work in an interconfessional setting, it was in part because they shared similar lines of argumentation. Catholics and Protestants agreed that the Bible's brutal hostility to homosexuality was like its sexism or opposition to abortion: a reflection of the text's historical context. Because that hostility so clearly contrasted with Jesus's message of love and communal solidarity, so the logic went, it could be dismissed as irrelevant. But like the gay rights activism that helped inspire it, the ecumenical group's main focus was less institutional prohibitions (such as the prohibition against hiring gay people for church jobs) and more informal norms. As the group's first pamphlet, *There Are Many Christian Homosexuals!* (1978), explained, it was not only church authorities or states who led gay men and women to conceal their sexual identities. It was also community members' hostility, mockery, and bullying. The ecumenical working group therefore appealed to communities to cease treating homosexuality as a shameful illness. Gay desire, it explained, "is part of one's sexuality, which has been granted to all people in God's good creation." A truly Christian community, in this telling, required liberating gay men and women from their forced "ghetto," instilling in them the courage "to integrate" into their social surroundings. Only by breaking the division between their private life and their public life could "homosexuals ... find life" in Christianity.[118]

By the 1970s, in short, ecumenism gave to the field of gender and sexuality a theoretical framework similar to that of social theory. It brought together a cohort of radical thinkers and activists who together sought to rethink the long established Christian aversion to feminism and sexual reform. Perhaps most far-reaching, the thinkers of this new school abandoned Christians' long invocation of "nature" as the basis for interconfessional cooperation. Rather than the churches' traditional and paradoxical use of admonitions and laws to create the order they claimed was natural, these thinkers argued that Christians were called to expand people's ability to embrace and express their desires. For Sölle, such struggles for liberation were the key to building not only a new and just social order, but also a new relationship with God. Instead of fearing "a distant God exacting sacrifice and self-denial," humans were to learn self-realization, "agreement and consent, [to be] at one with what it is to be alive." This was the true purpose of ecumenical action. When Christians join each other, "solidarity will replace obedience as the dominant virtue."[119]

Theologies of the Third World

Forged as it was in the crucible of protests against the Vietnam War and Cold War divisions, the European New Left always had a global outlook. In writings and in speeches, its leaders relentlessly called for participation in the Global South's struggle against the Global North's violence and hegemony. Indeed, many activists conceived of their protest as part of the worldwide mobilization against what Ghana's president and anti-colonialist icon Kwame Nkrumah famously called neocolonialism. By attacking capitalist relations and values, they also claimed to take on the web of finance, trade arrangements, and military power that continued to subjugate Latin America, Asia, and Africa to Northern corporations and states. This was why European protestors often celebrated and claimed to be allies of anti-imperialist leaders like Che Guevara. As German student leader Rudi Dutschke proclaimed in a speech, Europe, Latin America, and Asia were all battlefields in the global confrontation between "anti-authoritarianism, world-wide revolution, and authoritarian imperialistic counter-revolution."[120]

This self-identification with guerilla fighters, of course, sometimes entailed a heavy dose of projection and narcissism, conflating protest with life-threatening violence. It also was at times a sign of desperation: if protest in Europe was unable to bring down the capitalist system, perhaps a revolution would come from elsewhere. Yet the New Left focus on the Global South also inspired new forms of activism and self-understanding. When radical West German feminists traveled to Vietnam and China to learn about education policies in those countries, for example, they sought to rethink Europe's position in the world: rather than seeing Europe as a universal model to be exported, they imagined it as a testing ground for liberation praxis that was created by anti-colonial movements.[121] This interest continued even after the end of the war in Vietnam; in particular, it coalesced around support for the New International Economic Order (NIEO), a series of proposals introduced in 1974 by a group of countries from Latin America, Asia, and Africa. Calling for new trade arrangements, new forms of labor management, and extensive redistribution of resources, it was designed to shift global power from the world's wealthy countries to poor ones, and to demolish colonialism's lasting legacies.[122]

For Christians sympathetic to the New Left, building new ties to the Global South seemed like an especially urgent task, one that required critical self-assessment. Could the missions overcome their long history of paternalism and cooperation with empire, and become part of global liberation? Earlier, in the wake of decolonization, Catholic and Protestant missionary thinkers believed they had solved this conundrum. Seizing on the concept of development, they converged around "uplifting" non-Europeans through economic training. By the 1970s, however, development came under fire. First in Latin America, and then also in Asia and Africa, Catholic and Protestant thinkers attacked it as both paternalist and destructive, a tool to integrate the world's poor into capitalism's inhumanity; in this, it was merely new dressing for an older civilizing mission. The only teaching that realized Christ's message, they decided, was one that inspired redistribution, both domestically and internationally. For a new cohort of Catholic and Protestant thinkers, this critique of development offered a new path forward for Europeans: one that would finally eradicate the logic of the civilizing mission and replace it with a new, global solidarity. This missionary thinking was certainly new, especially in its unprecedented engagement with non-European writings, but it nevertheless preserved the ecumenical framework that preceded it. Like the anti-authoritarian and feminist theories, it took Catholic-Protestant cooperation as a given, and sought to imbue it with new political meanings.

Critiques of development, and the missions' participation in it, began to circulate among anti-authoritarian Christians in the late 1960s. Development's association with European, and especially American, foreign policy, particularly the horrors visited upon Vietnam, severely tarnished its claim to be a postcolonial and benevolent endeavor. Its critics were especially inspired by the emergence of "dependency theory," whose proponents claimed that Western capitalism intentionally kept the Global South in a state of impoverishment in order to exploit its workers and resources indefinitely. In both Catholic and Protestant student meetings in 1968, speakers criticized development as a cover for imperialist violence. What the Global South realty needed, they claimed, was the nationalization of international corporations and a global redistribution of wealth.[123] The German Ecumenical Working Group, the country's main hub for socialist and feminist activism, similarly devoted one of its meetings to "developmental aid's vicious circle," claiming that its purpose was to deepen the exploitation of workers in the Global South. Its leader, Dorothee Sölle, in fact made European responsibility for dispossession central to her ethics, arguing in her *Political Theology* (1971) that "with each banana that I eat, I choose to rob a farmer from their income and to participate in United Fruit Company's plunder of Latin America."[124] Septuagint, the continent's largest organization for anti-authoritarian Christians, similarly extended its anti-capitalist message to criticize development. Its 1970 convention invited advocates of dependency theory from Latin America, and then, as a gesture to its global outlook, changed its name from the Assembly of European Radical Priests to the International Assembly of Christian Solidarity.[125]

It was, however, the rise of liberation theology from the Global South, first from Latin America and then also from Asia and Africa, that propelled the critique of development to the center of Christian missionary thinking. Among Catholics its most influential spokesperson was the Peruvian Gustavo Gutiérrez, a former doctor turned theologian, whose provocative writings quickly gained international circulation. According to Gutiérrez, the missions' participation in development projects was a betrayal of Jesus's emancipatory message. Not only did it help solidify the Global South's perpetual dependency on Western trade, but on a more profound level it also shored up oppression: with empty promises of future prosperity, it helped train the poor to accept their present misfortunes. As Gutiérrez put it, Christianity "sacralized situations of injustice and oppression."[126] The churches' task, however, was to attack social hierarchies, both domestically and internationally. Christians had to see existing inequalities as a collective sin, and to mobilize believers against "poverty and misery beyond all national frontiers." Perhaps most important, Gutiérrez followed the anti-authoritarian logic of Metz and Moltmann (whose works he discussed at length) to claim that development's focus on harmony should be replaced by a focus on confrontation. In his book *A Theology of Liberation* (1971), his most influential work, he argued that the churches had to emphasize "the conflictual aspect of the economic, social, and political process," and empower the poor in Latin America, Asia, and Africa in their fight against "wealthy nations and oppressive classes." Indeed, Gutiérrez envisioned a new kind of Christian social theory, centered on the struggles of the planet's marginalized and dispossessed. In an explicit gesture to Marcuse's *Essay on Liberation,* he claimed that only through "the great refusal" and protests against inequality could Christian theory acquire "human content."[127] Similar ideas were articulated by the Uruguayan Juan Luis Segundo and the Brazilian Hugo Assmann. All of these thinkers espoused a social and economic theory centered on conflict.[128]

Even though historians have sometimes described liberation theology as a Catholic creation, it was also deeply shaped by Protestant writers.[129] In this sphere, the most influential figure was the Brazilian Rubem Alves, whose book *A Theology of Human Hope* (1969) quickly became a foundational text for radicals. Drawing heavily on both Moltmann and Marcuse, Alves lambasted the Christian focus on stability. The true source of solidarity, he claimed, was among "the slaves, the wrenched of the earth, the outcasts, and marginals," who recognized the violence on which society was premised and were thus open for liberation. This was why, like Gutiérrez, Alves rejected development as an intellectual sedative. In his eyes, its purpose was to incorporate the poor into consumerist society, in which the chasing of commodities and entertainment helped distract the oppressed from their masochistic existence. Echoing dependency theory, Alves claimed that the prosperity of capitalist societies was premised on the persistent exploitation of the Global South's resources and labor. European investment in Latin America, Asia, and Africa could never close the gap between North and South, because the North's entire economic system required alliances with brutal dictators, and thus "the creation of death, destruction, and terror."[130] Alves therefore echoed Moltmann in claiming that Christianity's social teaching lay in eschatology. Only in the spirit of a radical break and violent revolutions could Christians claim loyalty to Jesus's words. As happened in Catholic circles, Alves's call for a confrontational social theory signaled the rise of new trends in Latin American thought. He was joined by thinkers such as the Argentinian José Miguez Bonino and the Uruguayan Julio de Santa Ana, who spent the 1970s advocating against development and in support of the NIEO.[131]

Crucially, the project of liberation theology entailed a forceful rejection of Europe's function as the center of Christian life. Even as they drew on Europeans like Marcuse, Metz, and Moltmann, liberation theologians claimed to displace Europe as the universal model for Christian thinking. Gutiérrez, for example, argued that despite the claims of proponents of development, its goal was never to empower believers in the Global South. Its paternalist logic, which set Europe as the benchmark for universal progress, was instead a direct continuation of colonialism, in which converts in the Global South were vehicles for Europeans' megalomaniac ambitions. In Gutiérrez's polemical phrasing, the churches of the Global South were still subjected to an "ecclesiastical colonial treaty." They supplied "the raw materials" in the forms of the faithful and donations, while the churches of the North supplied the "manufactured goods" of social and religious teachings, clerical leadership, and an indoctrination apparatus of schools and training programs. Liberation theology, and especially its focus on conflict, was therefore part of the intellectual struggle against the "civilizing mission."[132] Alves similarly claimed that European theology, as transmitted through the missions, performed for non-Europeans a function analogous to that performed by capitalist media in the metropole. Its purpose was to foster in the nonwhite people "an oppressed consciousness," so they could blame global inequality on themselves rather than rise up against it. This is why liberation theologians frequently invoked the anti-colonialist writer Frantz Fanon, and especially his claim that violence would have a purifying impact on the oppressed subjects. In their minds, the purpose of liberation theology was to destroy Europe's hegemony in global Christianity.[133]

This rejection of earlier missionary theory, and of development in particular, quickly took on ecumenical features. These Latin American writers did not seek to replace the Catholic-Protestant cooperation that came before them. Instead, like the anti-authoritarian and feminist writers in Europe, they sought to invest it with new political meanings. Gutiérrez, for example, claimed that social harmony, "the traditional subject matter of ecumenism," had become "outdated." But in its place a new unity was destined to emerge, premised on joint action against poverty and oppression. Invoking initial cooperation between Catholic and Protestant activists in the organization ISAL (Church and Society for Latin America), which educated and mobilized poor communities to try to achieve better conditions, Gutiérrez claimed that this would be the new horizon of emancipatory Christianity. It would bring "collaboration between Christians of different denominations within the framework of a clear commitment to political liberation."[134] The Protestant Bonino similarly claimed that liberation entailed a Catholic-Protestant alliance around advocacy against injustices. Such practical cooperation would ultimately eclipse doctrinal differences, and would remind Christians that political action is far more significant than abstract reflections.[135] Indeed, liberation theology's first appearance in the missionary universe was at a conference organized by

SODEPAX, the organization created to promote Catholic-Protestant cooperation in development and missionary projects. When its members gathered in 1969 for a conference in Cartigny, Switzerland, the Catholic Gutiérrez and the Protestant Alves appeared together to launch an attack on the organization's agenda. Both Gutiérrez, whose presentation became the outline for *A Theology of Liberation,* and Alves explained that ecumenism required a new orientation, in which the suffering of the weak was channeled into rebellion. As Alves proclaimed, "Our task is to discover where and how the Spirit is groaning today and to help human communities to transform the wordless groaning into articulate and conscious speech."[136]

In both its anti-colonial message and its ecumenical framework, liberation theology soon acquired global dimensions. Inspired by the launch of the NIEO in 1974, Sergio Torres, a Chilean Catholic priest living in exile in Belgium, launched a new international forum for thinkers of the Global South. The Ecumenical Association of Third World Theologians (EATWOT), as it was called, was meant to provide Christians from Latin America, Asia, and Africa with the space to meet beyond the confines of European-dominated missions, and to reorient the churches around revolutionary agendas. After Tanzania's president (and one of the NIEO's architects) Julius Nyerere offered to host, EATWOT held its first congress in Kipalapala in 1976. At the congress the leading voices of Latin American liberation theology, like Gutiérrez and Alves, joined African and Asian thinkers, like the Catholic Ngindu Mushete from the Congo and the Protestant Emerito Nacpil from the Philippines, to map theological support for anti-colonial mobilization. Along with annual gatherings that took place in Dar es Salaam (1976), Accra (1977), and São Paulo (1978), and a journal that published participants' contributions, EATWOT also organized a series of regional meetings, that sought to translate liberation theology to local conflicts.[137] In one of the African gatherings in 1977, for example, anti-apartheid icon Desmond Tutu talked about Christians' role in "the evangelical aim of awakening in blacks a sense of their intrinsic worth as the children of God."[138] As its name indicated, EATWOT was premised on confessional cooperation (its membership was equally divided between Catholics and Protestants), which its participants described as the first step toward broader liberation. Torres declared in his opening address to one of the African meetings that the Third World offered "a new kind of ecumenism," a "unity in praxis as service for the poor."[139]

Because EATWOT's anti-colonial agenda, like that of the NIEO, provided an umbrella for a diverse set of concerns, it went beyond liberation theology's original focus on economic redistribution. The inclusion of Asian and African thinkers in its ranks (and, in 1979, also Black North Americans) meant that it expanded ecumenism to new concerns and topics. The Catholic writer from Sri Lanka Tissa Balasuriya, for example, who became the organization's leading figure from Asia, claimed that Christ's appearance in the world was not limited to his incarnation in Jesus's human form, but was present in all spiritual striving for justice. It was Europeans' colonial fixation on control that led them to claim "a monopoly of Christ," instead of recognizing grace's operation in other religions. As he explained in his opening remarks to the Asian meeting in Sri Lanka, Christians' participation in the struggle against the "World Apartheid" of unequal wealth had to acknowledge "other religions and their contribution to human liberation."[140] The Cameroonian thinker Engelbert Mveng similarly maintained that a narrow focus on economic equality risked reproducing European class preoccupation, and thus would conceal colonialism's many other legacies, especially the persistence of racism. In one address he argued that the people of the Third World had been robbed of "their identity, history, ethnic roots, language," and that they could be liberated only by destroying "the universal derision that has always accompanied the 'civilized' world's discourse upon and encounter with Africa—and still accompanies it today."[141] EATWOT, in short, sought to go beyond the intellectual critique of development and to demolish the paternalist logic on which it was based.

While Christians from the Global South had long criticized European paternalism and racism, the rise of Third World theology had a significant impact on some European theoreticians. The radical nature of its challenge to missionary thought, captured in its militant rhetoric, and its uncompromising commitment to the world's oppressed, resonated with those who sought to claim Christianity for anti-authoritarian visions. To be sure, there was something self-serving in this support for anti-colonialist sentiments more than a decade after most European countries no longer directly controlled colonial possessions. Unlike liberation theologians from Latin America, who often experienced persecution, violence, and exile, European sympathizers did not risk nearly as much in adopting unpopular views. Moreover, like the New Left's celebration of anti-colonialists in Latin America, Asia, and Africa, proclaiming support for EATWOT always risked perpetuating the instrumental approach to non-Europeans it sought to challenge. After their hopes for European revolution in the churches began to fade, some anti-authoritarians transferred their hopes southward, hoping that the Global South could bring about the social transformation they had failed to achieve. As one Catholic mused in a characteristic infatuation, the global "war of the oppressed against their oppressors" could be won because "Vietnamese peasants can virtually overthrow an American president, and a group of Guatemalan *guerrilleros* can shake the West German government."[142] Yet even with these limitations, the turn of several Europeans to Third World theology marked a considerable shift in missionary theory. It forged a new kind of missionary ecumenism, in which Europe was no longer the center of world Christianity, and missions' main task was to encourage anti-colonialist consciousness.

An emblematic Catholic figure for the shift from development to revolution was the French economist and missionary thinker Vincent Cosmao. A student of the development theorist Louis-Joseph Lebret, Cosmao at first subscribed to the belief in Europe's mission to "uplift" non-Europeans through economic training. In the 1960s he founded a center for the study of development (which trained African agronomists and economists), published popular tracts on the churches' role in development, and joined SODEPAX as an advisor.[143] The Vietnam War, however, and an encounter with liberation theology, radicalized Cosmao. After meeting Gutiérrez and Alves in 1969 (in the SODEPAX consultation), he came to view global inequality as the product of European exploitation. It was, as he put it in his book *Development and Faith* (1972), part of Europe's—and the churches'—collective "sin," which began with imperialism and racism. Like the anti-authoritarian and feminist writers with whom he aligned, Cosmao began to understand Jesus's words as a message of subversion. Rather than a life of comfort and stability, Jesus's life was meant to expose normalized brutality and delegitimize existing hierarchies.[144] Applied to the missionary world, liberation theology appeared to Cosmao to be a necessary trigger for intellectual recalibration. It was a call to replace Europe's persistent paternalism, and the structural inequality it entailed, with a global community of equals. In an effort to popularize this new thinking in Europe, Cosmao initiated the translation of Guttiérez's work into French, along with published interpretations of Guttiérez for French Catholic readers.[145]

Cosmao was equally enchanted by the launch of NIEO in 1974 and the founding of EATWOT a year later. Both organizations, he claimed, presented Europeans with an opportunity to overcome the long equation between themselves and heights of modernity; by doing so, they could open themselves to new forms of solidarity. In a series of articles throughout the 1970s, culminating in his book *Changing the World* (1979), Cosmao harshly criticized the missions' focus on development projects, which he described as ineffectual or tools intended to integrate the Global South into international capitalism. If Europeans were to play any role in world politics, they should mobilize to force their own countries' acceptance of the NIEO's new taxation and trade schemes. As he put it, "We must construct an economy and a set of social relationships effectively designed to transform the resources of our planet and to place them at the disposal of all who need them."[146] Europe's history of brutal exploitation in the colonies, along with electoral realities, made such goals utopian, but Cosmao insisted that the churches were uniquely positioned to support them. They could lend their intellectual apparatus to education campaigns, which would help dislodge Europeans' ideological paternalism. This was in part why Christian imagery and language were important, and especially Third World theology: its new description of salvation as a collective act of resistance could help believers imagine new realities in familiar terms. Cosmao, in short, sought to turn on its head the link that European missionary thinkers had long established between Christian belief, mentality, and economics. Instead of claiming that European Christians would transform non-Europeans into productive subjects, non-European theology was to liberate *Europeans* through universal solidarity.[147]

Cosmao was not alone in seeking to expunge European paternalism from Catholic missionary thought. Figures across the continent seized on Third World theology in an effort to offer a new role for Christian missions. The Belgian sociologist François Houtart, for example, who also directed an influential think tank on global economics, spent the 1970s publishing devastating attacks on development. Building factories and infrastructure not only was ineffectual in eliminating poverty (a reality Houtart demonstrated in a series of sociological studies on India), but in fact made economic dispossession worse by breaking workers' ties to family businesses. Citing Fanon, Houtart claimed that missionary participation in development was an active contribution to global oppression, part of the church's historic alliance with hierarchies. As he explained in his widely translated book *The Church and Revolutionary Movements* (1971), the time had come to discard this baggage and embrace "the aspirations of the oppressed" who "accept conflict as a fact of life."[148] In Germany, missionary thinker Ludwig Rütti similarly claimed that the entire missionary project was tainted by a colonialist mindset. In works like *Missionary Theology* (1972), he argued that the missions' task was to demonstrate, through political action, their commitment to the exploited.[149] In the Netherlands, influential writer (and former missionary to Burundi) Jacques Van Nieuwenhove published studies on liberation theology and its implications for European missions.[150] For these and other figures, who also helped organize conferences and special forums on liberation theology for European readers, Third World liberation was as urgent as socialism or feminism. In Houtart's words, the Global South had launched a "planetary class struggle" against Northern supremacy, and the churches had to join it.[151]

Third World theology also garnered sympathy among Protestants. In those circles, the key figure was the French writer Georges Casalis. Well known as an anti-authoritarian writer and a key figure in Protestant organizations' support for student activism, Casalis was also an influential missionary theoretician. In 1963 he helped draft the World Council of Churches' plans for missionary action after decolonization, which focused on reforming liturgy and engaging in economic development.[152] In the early 1970s, however, the Vietnam War pushed Casalis to follow Cosmao's trajectory. He concluded that Europe's missionary project had been an epic exercise in oppression, designed to instill lethargic obedience in non-Europeans. The only path out of global inequalities was to embrace the NIEO and Third World theology, which Casalis helped introduce to European audiences by organizing the first international conference on it in Europe.[153] In the same way that Metz sought to invoke the memory of anti-Semitism to encourage critical self-reflection, Casalis claimed that EATWOT was an opportunity for Europeans to confront their long participation in colonial oppression. As he put it in *Correct Ideas Don't Fall from the Skies* (1977), his most comprehensive reflections on social theory, Third World theology "provided us with a mirror reflecting the pillage and murder committed by the 'developed' countries," which should shake Christians into supporting international liberation.[154]

Unlike Cosmao, Casalis envisioned Europeans taking a role in this struggle less as advocates for economic policies like the NIEO and more as supporters of new education. In particular, he was inspired by Brazilian educator Paulo Freire, who in works like *Pedagogy of the Oppressed* (1968) called for revolutionary and anti-authoritarian teaching. Based on literacy campaigns he led among the poor, Freire argued that the teacher's task was not to impart knowledge to students, but to foster critical assessment of authority, a process he named "conscientization." By focusing on communal learning and action, students would feel empowered to question and ultimately bring down social hierarchies. In a range of writings, Casalis claimed this had to become the new ethos of European missions. Instead of evangelization and development programs, they had to support conscientization, encouraging the poor in the Global South to rise up against their subjugation. In Casalis's eyes, the most promising aspect of Freire's theory was its requirement that teachers renounce their authority and engage with students as equals. Through joint participation in collective actions, they would develop horizontal relationships, in which the teacher would change as much as the students. Applied to the mission fields, Casalis believed that this kind of education could train Europeans out of their paternalism and into new solidarities.[155]

Casalis's approach, and especially his focus on anti-authoritarian education, resonated in some missionary circles. Protestant theoreticians hoped it would provide the solution to the tension between their emancipatory aspirations and their positionality as Europeans. The Swiss Walter Hollenweger, who was a prominent missionary functionary at the World Council of Churches, implemented Freire's ideas by developing a new theory of communal outreach, in which the missionary joined local communities by staging local plays, drawing on local cultures and traditions to develop anti-authoritarian sentiments.[156] The influential missionary writer Hans-Jochen Margull similarly sought to popularize a missionary outlook that aligned with liberation theology. In collections such as *No One-Way Street: From Western Mission to World Mission* (1973), which ran through multiple editions, he published harsh critiques of development and racist paternalism.[157] Those ideas gained enough traction that in the international meeting of Protestant missions in Thailand in 1973, delegates called for a moratorium on European support for charity and development in the Global South. Instead, they agreed to fund conscientization education projects, which would mobilize poor farmers against international corporations.[158] Those ideas became reality when the World Council of Churches hired Freire as a consultant and sponsored his educational campaigns in both Africa and Latin America throughout the 1970s. The WCC also translated his writings and made them required readings for its training programs for missionary activities.[159]

Some found this focus on education to be too tame and argued that missionary support for Third World liberation had to include support for violent resistance. They therefore mobilized Christian organizations to combat the last vestiges of European imperialism. In 1973, after vocal advocacy, European missionary officials helped fund the WCC's large financial support for guerilla forces in Mozambique, Angola, and Guinea-Bissau, who were still fighting to topple Portugal's empire. As their reports trumpeted, their donations were used to purchase guns, hand grenades, and bullets. For all the paradoxes entailed in Europeans' patronage of anti-colonial liberation, such actions offered a sort of repentance for the missions' historical cooperation in colonialism. As the missionary delegates who authorized them explained in a statement, their purpose was to "support those struggling for freedom from unjust and dehumanizing systems perpetuated by dominant nations and bodies."[160]

Like the anti-authoritarian and feminist theories developing at the same time, and like the Third World theology they sought to bolster, these new missionary approaches remained committed to ecumenism. Even though missionary cooperation first solidified around development, those who sympathized with Third World theology sought to turn it on its head. This was certainly the spirit in which Casalis articulated his advocacy for liberation theology and EATWOT, which he declared to be the most important advance in Christian thought. Echoing Gutiérrez's reflections, as well as his own writings on socialism, Casalis claimed that Christian resistance to colonialism and racism required transcending confessional boundaries. "In an era when the world is being exploited by imperialist powers and their multinational companies," he explained in 1977, "only a revolutionary ecumenism . . . can confront and resist exploitation and deal them blow by blow, clearing the way to a democratic future." In fact, Casalis claimed that the models for "true" ecumenism were the liberation struggles in Algeria, Vietnam, and Angola, which he claimed demonstrated the capacity of the oppressed to overcome their oppressors. "A new definition of ecumenism is being worked out," he mused. "It is the practical multinational solidarity of persons of all ideologies and faiths united for the liberation of their brothers and sisters who are still enslaved everywhere in the world."[161] This understanding, in which Catholic-Protestant peace was the first step toward broader solidarity, was common among European proponents of liberation theology, who throughout the 1970s published multiple interconfessional collections and convened an array of ecumenical conferences on liberation theology's relevance to European life.[162] As the Dutch Protestant missionary thinker Theo Witvliet put it, Third World theology offered "a new kind of unity."[163]

Those efforts culminated in 1976 with the launching of the European EATWOT Support Committee, an international ecumenical organization to promote Third World theology in the former metropole. Led by the Catholic Cosmao and the Protestant Casalis, it brought together sympathetic thinkers and missionary leaders of both confessions to provide funding for EATWOT's meetings; indeed, European organizations, especially from France, Germany, the Netherlands, and Belgium, financed most of its activities. The Support Committee further sought to popularize its message by funding the translation of its publications into all major European languages.[164] Cosmao, Casalis, and other sympathizers organized conferences and publications in Europe, where thinkers and lay activists gathered to discuss liberation theology's meaning for themselves. These quickly became prime gathering spaces for anti-authoritarians and feminists, who by the late 1970s repeatedly mourned their failure to revolutionize the European churches, but now hoped that pressures from the Global South would succeed in this task.[165] An emblematic expression of this view came from the Catholic Johann Baptist Metz, who in the late 1960s described the students' revolt as Christianity's "second reformation," an epochal shift that would revolutionize its values. Later, speaking in 1983 at an EATWOT congress in Geneva, he instead mused that it was the rise of Third World theology, and the transition from a "Eurocentric" church to a "polycentric world church," that marked this "second reformation." For Metz, whose blend of disappointment with Europe and high hopes for the Global South was characteristic of those who sympathized with Third World theology, this shift also entailed a redefinition of ecumenism. Instead of being "primarily oriented toward unity among the Christian denominations (as in Europe)," he explained, it would focus on "unity among the churches of the First World and the Third World."[166]

Just like the emergence of anti-authoritarian Christianity entailed a sustained reflection on Judaism, this reorientation of missionary ecumenism also entailed a new approach to Islam. European proponents of Third World theology sought to follow EATOWT's lead and extend ecumenism to new frontiers by confronting their long history of Islamophobia. The Dutch Catholic missiologist Peter Antes, an enthusiastic supporter of liberation theology, claimed, for example, that fears of Muslim aggression were a projection of Europe's own colonial aspirations. In effect, Christians and Muslims shared a belief in tolerance and pluralism.[167] The German Protestant Olaf Schumann, who worked in Egypt and Indonesia before becoming the director of the Germany's missionary academy, also sought to provide a conceptual language for cooperation. In his book *The Muslims' Christ* (1975), a study of Muslim reflections on Christianity, he claimed that the two religions shared a conception of divine grace. An especially critical approach was offered by the Dutch Catholic writer Arnulf Camps, who was also a central figure in the EATWOT Support Committee. In a lengthy study on Christianity's engagement with other religions, *Christianity and the World's Religions* (1976), he praised Islam as a religion of pluralism, and called for dialogue and coexistence. These texts, to be sure, still sweepingly described Islam as a unified and even essentialist entity. And they occasionally still trafficked in Orientalist stereotypes (Camps, for example, still wondered whether Islam had a "fatalist" streak to it). Still, they marked a considerable departure in the European missionary imagination. For the first time, proponents of Catholic-Protestant cooperation envisioned their project as extending beyond the churches' borders.[168]

Finally, and as was the case since the late nineteenth century and well into the era of decolonization, missionary thinking about politics and non-Christians had a sexual dimension. For the first time in decades, ecumenism sought to offer a new treatment of the ultimate taboo, polygamy. Here, the most important voice was the American Catholic missionary Eugene Hillman, a prolific ecumenist whose writings quickly became the reference point for reformatory thinkers of both confessions in Europe. First in a 1968 article in the journal *Concilium,* and then in his book *Polygamy Reconsidered* (1975), Hillman condemned the long-standing prohibition against non-monogamous arrangements as a remnant of "Western ethnocentrism." Was it not obvious, he argued, that it was yet another expression of Europeans' individualism and their perverse inability to imagine sharing property with others? What is more, the absolute rejection of polygamy, and especially missionaries' insistence that monogamy liberated women, was premised on arrogance. As he rhetorically asked, "Do the mass of African women accept polygamy ... simply because they do not know any better? Are they so dull that they do not know what is good for them?" Perhaps most important, Hillman recovered multiple forgotten theologians who over the centuries had claimed that marriage's main purposes—procreation, the expression of love, and membership in the Christian community—could align with multi-parent families. Allowing polygamy, he therefore claimed, would both liberate missions from a colonial mindset and realize the task of forging new and global solidarities.[169]

The 1970s, then, were the high-water mark of revolutionary ecumenism not only on the domestic front, but also in European thinking about missions and the Global South. In interconfessional cooperation, many believed that they had found new purpose for Europeans: bringing about an era free of European dominance. For all the awkwardness this vision implied, it was nevertheless a major departure. It broke not only with the recent infatuation with development, which was the missions' initial response to decolonization, but also the much longer history of European tutelage: it sought to discard Europe's status as the benchmark of religious, economic, and social progress. Indeed, European proponents of Third World theology for the first time assumed that the main subject of their teachings did not reside overseas. Rather, those who most needed education were Europeans, so that they could imagine a world beyond European dominance.

LIKE THE NEW LEFT that helped inspire it, the project of revolutionary ecumenism was ultimately defeated. Similar to the majority of Europeans, most church authorities and communities did not embrace the call for radical liberation and largely marginalized its advocates. In the sphere of social theory, both Catholic and Protestant doctrinal statements dismissed the talk of anti-capitalist revolution. Exasperated by the apathy of their communities, the major organizations of anti-authoritarian Christianity ceased their operation: the German night prayers group disbanded in 1972; Septuagint followed in 1975. Many of the Christian youth and student organizations either disaffiliated themselves from the churches or dissolved. Similar dynamics defined the struggle of feminists and sex reformers, whose success was confined to creating autonomous forums. Church authorities, especially Catholic ones, mostly doubled down on the two sexes' complementary natures and on heterosexual family ethics. Indeed, for the rest of the twentieth century, the most visible mobilizations of Christian organizations were their opposition to abortion, sexual education, and same-sex relationships.[170] Liberation theology, too, did not become hegemonic in European churches and missions. In 1974 many leaders of Europe's Protestant missions, alarmed by the WCC's support for armed struggled, joined the Lausanne Covenant, a statement that dismissed liberation theology as a cover for Marxism, a sentiment that was later duplicated in a formal Vatican condemnation.[171] As a result, EATWOT lost much of its steam. Its meetings continued (and still take place today), but its European Support Committee dissolved, and without its resources EATWOT stopped publishing its proceedings and journal. By the mid-1980s most advocates of radical reforms were despondent. As Pohier bemoaned in 1985, their quest to transform European Christianity amounted to "nothing."[172]

The revolutionary ecumenical project, however, did more than create small spaces of dissent in European Christianity. Ironically, it also extended the logic of Catholic-Protestant cooperation into new spheres. Indeed, even though Metz, Moltmann, and their allies harshly rejected earlier models of Christian politics, they also echoed them. Like their predecessors, they envisioned Catholics and Protestants as engaged together in mutual struggles on which humanity's fate rested. This was in part why, despite their very real break with the social, sexual, and missionary teachings of earlier decades, they sometimes shared a rhetoric of conflict and struggle. Their targets were new—corporations, the patriarchy, and development—but their invocation of apocalyptic imagery was not. They still depicted Christians as engaging in a heroic fight against a chaotic and sin-filled world. In this regard, the upheavals of the 1960s and 1970s marked both a broad revolt against the principles of earlier generations and their triumph. Ecumenism was now the language of both order and protest.

Conclusion

WHEN THE FRENCH novelist Annie Ernaux reflected on her life in 2007, she was struck by how much Christianity's role in European life had changed. In the 1950s, when Ernaux was a child in the small town of Yvetot, churches seemed to be everywhere. Religious teachings "provided the official framework of life," and church rituals and holidays "governed time"; repeating the claims that one read in Christian publications "was, for everyone, an outward sign of morality and the promise of a destiny ... It bestowed human dignity, without which our lives would resemble those of dogs." What Christian writers and clerics preached carried so much weight that their commands outweighed all others. Their words alone "gave legitimacy to the great moments of existence."[1] By the late twentieth century, however, the world was very different. While rites and holidays remained, organized Christianity no longer provided the all-encompassing social structure and ethical guidance it once did. Parents and teachers stopped repeating Christian lessons to their children, and young adults no longer sought advice in Christian magazines, marriage guides, or missionary reports. All of this happened without much intention. Christianity simply lost its appeal, until it "unceremoniously vanished from our lives." For Ernaux, it was especially noteworthy that the central terms of Christian discourse, such as sin and grace, so quickly became irrelevant. They had become part of "an unintelligible vocabulary, an obsolete mind-set."[2]

Ernaux's experience was shared by countless Europeans, which can leave the mistaken impression that the ecumenical project was ultimately unsuccessful. After all, the indifference she described was exactly what the leading advocates of Catholic-Protestant reconciliation sought to prevent;

Conclusion

their hope was to secure Christian ethics, as they understood it, as the center of European life. By this measure, the achievements of ecumenism were indeed short-lived. The postwar surge in church attendance, lay activism, and intellectual production quickly faded, and by the 1970s, organized Christianity entered a period of free fall. Europeans increasingly left the churches and their affiliated organizations, showed decreasing interest in Christian holidays and ceremonies, and ceased reading Christian publications. Instead of the militant atheism and anti-clericalism they had so long feared, the churches' decline came at the hands of widespread apathy. By the twenty-first century, once-formidable youth movements and think tanks had folded, and many churches in Central and Western Europe have been converted into social clubs or gyms.

But these later developments should not distract us from ecumenism's astonishing successes. Even if it did not fulfill all its advocates' hopes, it dramatically altered fundamental features of European thought and politics. For four centuries, most Europeans had taken it for granted that Catholics and Protestants were profoundly different from, and hostile to, each other. Those animosities only intensified in the nineteenth century and were central to how many Christians understood themselves and their world. Catholic and Protestant elites attributed an endless list of negative qualities to each other, from political subversion and economic backwardness to criminality and sexual perversity. These sentiments mattered beyond the sphere of ideas, because the churches and their affiliated lay organizations remained crucial forces for Europeans' socialization. While the churches' formal authority was not as dominant as it was in the early modern period, millions continued to view confession as central to their place in the world. The conflicts between different confessional milieus therefore had far-reaching consequences. They often led to mass campaigns of discrimination and political oppression.

The end of these animosities was therefore a dramatic and revolutionary process. They did not slowly recede until they organically evaporated, and their decline was not a side effect of Christianity's shrinking fortunes after the 1970s. Instead, reconciliation between Catholics and Protestants in Central and Western Europe was an intentional and bold intellectual project. Its foundation lay in the late nineteenth century, when Catholics and Protestants developed a set of overlapping concerns about socialism, feminism, and imperial civilizing missions. It grew into a coherent program in the 1930s, as both sympathizers and opponents of the Third Reich came to believe that Christianity was facing unprecedented threats that necessitated mutual engagement. Ecumenism consolidated in the following decades, when it became the mainstream of Christian thought and interconfessional "Christian Democratic" parties emerged as potent political forces. And it reached its conclusion when it was embraced by radical activists. The unique nature of this effort becomes clear when contrasted to the persistence of confessional hostilities elsewhere in Europe. In Spain, legal discrimination against Protestants was only removed in the late 1960s; in Ireland, animosities lasted well into the end of the twentieth century.

Alongside its intentional nature, ecumenism was also a popular and wide-ranging project. Rather than an imposition by clerical authorities, it emerged from the work of lay figures, who crafted it over diverse fields of knowledge. It unfolded among theologians, political theorists, economists, family experts, and missionaries, and in each sphere it introduced conceptual innovations. The reception of these works was always complex, but there is enough evidence to know that they resonated with many believers. Millions purchased ecumenical books and magazines, joined interconfessional organizations, and voted for parties that claimed to promote the agendas that Catholics and Protestants jointly crafted. The broad appeal of these ideas was in part why confessional reconciliation had consequences far beyond the intellectual sphere. It encouraged and legitimized Christians' efforts to implement new welfare legislation, institute novel regulations of gender and sexuality, and create new missionary organizations. In this regard, ecumenism was a crucial process in the history of twentieth-century Europe. The policies it engendered influenced the lives of millions, including those who cared little for the churches in their everyday lives.

Perhaps most important, ecumenism's lasting appeal, in both its exclusionary and its inclusive versions, lay in its creativity. As this book shows, a capacity for intellectual innovation was perhaps the most important feature of Christian life in the modern era. The decades between the 1880s and the 1970s were a period of rapid change. Almost every single social institution was altered by new forms of mass politics, the expansion of industrial capitalism, the rise and fall of empires, apocalyptic world wars, and traumatic dislocations. The Christian churches were some of the most important institutions to give meaning to these upheavals. They produced narratives that explained unfamiliar realities, and they offered plausible strategies to address them: visions of how to organize social relations, family ethics, and Europe's relationship to the rest of the world.

Even though Christian writers routinely presented themselves as mere conveyers of eternal truth, they constantly updated their reasoning and thinking. At every moment they articulated new solutions to new problems. They offered, in short, comprehensive and flexible visions of human flourishing. This was in part why those who prophesied their imminent death were repeatedly proven wrong. The Catholic and Protestant universes survived political and social upheavals that other movements and intellectual projects did not.

The alliances and divergences that this creativity produced were so strong that they had long afterlives. Even after the steep membership decline in organized Christianity, ecumenical cooperation remains a powerful framework for activism on matters of economics, sexuality, and Europe's relationship with the world. In 2014, for example, as the continent was in the midst of a debilitating economic crisis, a group of Catholic and Protestant leaders in Germany issued a call to return to the "social market economy" of the postwar era. Formally endorsed by the heads of the country's Catholic and Protestant churches, they insisted on the need for solidarity and reciprocity between workers and employers, which would be sustained through both economic and mental changes. Alongside minimal financial regulation and decent welfare benefits, the statement called for a new "culture of responsibility," in which members of different classes engaged each other without excessive demands.[3] These ideas, however, continue to be countered by alternative alliances, which view interconfessional cooperation as the basis for a radical assault on capitalism. In its booklet *Against the Neoliberal European Mainstream!* (2019), the German organization League for Religious Socialists drew on 1970s ideas of the anti-authoritarians to call for massive debt forgiveness, investment in public works, a focus on green initiatives, and the breaking of employers' power.[4] These and other organizations have also sought to mobilize believers on an international level. Through the International League of Religious Socialists, activists from across Europe and the world have sought to infuse their communities with enthusiasm for redistribution.

The same convergences and divisions that emerged during the twentieth century continue to shape Christian thought and action around matters of sexuality. Catholic and Protestant opponents of feminism, marriage equality, and especially trans rights continue to cooperate in joint campaigns and writings. In 2014, for example, a group of Christian writers and church leaders from across Europe issued the manifesto *Resist Gender*

Ideology! Drafted by the German Lutheran theologian Peter Beyerhaus, it warned that the "apocalyptic" progressive assault on marriage and gender difference had "Satanic origins" and that countering it required pan-Christian cooperation.[5] It was a call that many conservatives heeded through organizations like the World Congress of Families, and that brought millions of believers to the streets in demonstrations against gay rights (such as in France in 2015).[6] Yet ecumenism is also central to reformers, who still campaign to expand the horizons of Christian dogma. Organizations such as The Ecumenical Working Group for Homosexuals in the Church, founded in the 1970s, continue to challenge church authorities by endorsing same-sex marriage, bisexuality, and more recently gender-affirming medical procedures. In contrast to their opponents, these reformers view interconfessional work as geared toward further inclusion. As participants in a 2022 European gathering in Switzerland explained in a statement, "We have to overcome hierarchical power and pretended service and instead become a church of equals: equal in rights and dignity."[7]

These interconfessional groupings also continue to clash over Europe's relationship to the Global South. While the number of European missionaries has declined dramatically and their writings no longer fascinate European readers, the question of how to engage with Asians and Africans remains central to Christian thinking. For right-wing organizations like The Observatory on Intolerance and Discrimination against Christians, founded in 2013 by Catholic and Protestant politicians and thinkers, Europe has a defensive mission beyond its borders. Asia and Africa, in their telling, were oceans of anti-Christian hostility, and it was Europeans' responsibility to save Christian minorities from persecution. The Austrian Catholic politician Gudrun Kugler said in a 2015 keynote address to a conference of activists in Vienna that European governments had to fight the "torture ... regular mass killing ... and genocide" that befell Christians around the globe.[8] Left-wing activists, on the other hand, envision ecumenism as the basis for a broad set of new solidarities, both economic and religious. Building on the projects of the 1970s, the International League for Religious Socialists began to include organizations from South Africa and the Philippines and made reparations and ecological policies central to its agenda. It also extended membership to Muslim organizations, in what its members called a broad coalition to support "God-given dignity" to "each individual human being."[9]

Conclusion

The result of these internal struggles could matter enormously, and not only for practicing Christians. This is because the cause of Christianity has become central to Europe's most dominant and disruptive political force in recent years: the resurgent radical right. Figures like Marine Le Pen in France and Giorgia Meloni in Italy, who have led far-right parties to the center of European politics, often declare that "European civilization" is deeply rooted in Christian teachings. In their eyes, this remains the case even for those who no longer pray or affiliate with a church: Christianity's "heritage" continues to live in the allegedly European values of hard work, adherence to order, and respect for tradition. Like Catholics and Protestants of previous generations, that is, they understand Christianity not as a matter of private belief or even specific dogma, but as a set of norms and dispositions that distinguish Europeans. Meloni herself epitomizes this approach. Even though she publicly ignores Catholicism's teachings on marriage by being a proud single mother, she has also proclaimed herself to be "a Christian" who "will defend God, the fatherland, and the family."[10] For the radical right, therefore, preserving European life requires not only a harsh campaign against European Muslims and immigrants, who are deemed a "foreign" and menacing threat to Europe. It also requires a mobilization against liberal principles of universal rights (like freedom of worship or speech), which allegedly undermine Europe's ability to promote Christianity in education and public policy. Crucially, the radical right builds on the ecumenical revolution by assuming that Catholicism and Protestantism have equal claims to "Christianity." In most of its publications and proclamations, the two appear as indistinguishable.

It is easy to view such appeals to Christianity as superficial, a euphemistic cover for Islamophobia or racist nativism. But the radical right owes much more to Christian thought; many of its luminaries borrow key concerns and terms that animated Christians from the 1880s to the 1960s. Even though socialism no longer sparks the anxieties it once did, far-right figures often invoke the logic and language that Christians have used against it. As the nationalist Italian editor and commentator Annalisa Terranova claimed, Muslims and liberals share a hostility to spiritual self-realization, and the campaign against them was therefore a "spiritual struggle against materialism."[11] Far-right activism also builds on earlier efforts to strengthen the heterosexual family. While its parties accept female participation in labor and politics—many of its leaders are women—its policy proposals aim to make it easier for women to stay at home. The far-right party Alternative for Germany declared in its 2016 platform, "There is a misconceived view of feminism, which favors women with a career above mothers and housewives . . . [but] the emphasis should once again be placed on the time and care parents give towards their children."[12] Similarly, the far right often proclaims its hostility to alternative sexuality. Even as some parties promise to defend gay rights, radical leaders and thinkers direct venom at trans people or the field of gender studies, which they consider parts of a broad plot to "destroy the natural distinction between men and women."[13]

In the international sphere, far-right activists routinely echo earlier missionary concerns about Europe's need to protect Christian communities from violence in Asia and Africa. Meloni asked with characteristic hyperbole, "Why do we spend our time fighting all types of discrimination, but we pretend not to see the greatest ongoing persecution: the genocide of the world's Christians?"[14] Indeed, even though commentators have often noted links between the far right and interwar fascism, the far right's own leaders describe themselves as resurrecting the midcentury project of "Christian democracy."[15] Hungary's prime minister Viktor Órban, the continent's most prominent far-right politician, has explained that his goal was to recover "old-fashion Christian democracy . . . to bring it out again, dust it off, and modernize it."[16] One can doubt Órban's claims to this lineage, because Christian democrats did not share the far right's hostility to the free press or pluralism more broadly. But what is beyond doubt is the far right's insistence that it represents "true" Christianity.

Despite Ernaux's observations, then, Christianity has hardly faded from European public life. Many still claim to speak on its behalf and seek to mobilize it toward concrete political aims. If the history told in this book is any indication, both Catholics and Protestants will continue to debate the legitimacy of such invocations. Without waiting for clerical permission, they will update their teachings on human life and will forge new strategies for living in the modern world. As before, the choices made by Christians will have important consequences. Across different spheres of life, they will influence the lives of many Europeans, Christian or not.

NOTES

ACKNOWLEDGMENTS

INDEX

NOTES

Introduction

1. Max Weber, *The Protestant Ethic and the Spirit of Capitalism* (Penguin, 2002).
2. Alfred Baudrillart, *L'église catholique, la renaissance, le protestantisme: Conférences données a l'Institut catholique, Janvier–Mars, 1904* (Blud, 1908).
3. Walther von Loewenich, "Europa oder christliches Abendland?," in *Europa und das Christentum*, ed. Joseph Lortz (Steiner, 1959), 15–32, here 30. Unless stated otherwise, all translations are my own.
4. Walter Nigg, *Vom Geheimnis der Mönche* (Artemis, 1953). The quote is from the English translation, *Warriors of God: The Great Religious Orders and Their Founders* (Knopf, 1959), 4.
5. Johannes Hessen, *Der geistige Wiederaufbau Deutschlands* (Schröder, 1946), esp. 93–101, here 94.
6. Viktor Cathrein, *Der Sozialismus* (Herder, 1890). The quote is from the English translation, *Socialism Exposed and Refuted* (Benzieger, 1892), 41.
7. Alois Hudal, *Deutsches Volk und christliches Abendland* (Tyrolia, 1935), 20.
8. Walter Freytag, *Die junge christenheit im umbruch des Ostens: Von Gehorsam des Glaubens under den Völkern* (Furche, 1938), 257.
9. Georg Wünsch, *Der Mensch im modernen Materialismus als Aufgabe christlicher Verkündigung* (Mohr, 1952), 14.
10. Gaston Mercier, *L'esprit protestant: Politique-religion* (Perrin, 1901).
11. John Connelly, *From Enemy to Brother: The Revolution in Catholic Teaching on the Jews* (Harvard University Press, 2012); Darcie Fontaine, *Decolonizing Christianity: Religion and the End of Empire in France and Algeria* (Cambridge University Press, 2016).
12. Hessen, *Der geistige Wiederaufbau Deutschlands*, 94. On different forms of religious pluralism, see Till van Rhaden's pathbreaking *Jews and Other Germans: Civil Society, Religious Diversity, and Urban Politics in Breslau* (University of Wisconsin Press, 2008).
13. I borrow the term "long twentieth century" from Edward Ross Dickinson, *The World in the Long Twentieth Century* (University of California Press, 2018).
14. For similar focus, which has been a central inspiration for my own thinking, see James Chappel, *Catholic Modern: The Challenge of Totalitarianism and the Remaking of the Church* (Harvard University Press, 2018).
15. Sarah Shortall, *Soldiers of God in a Secular World: Catholic Theology and Twentieth-Century French Politics* (Harvard University Press, 2021); Edward Baring, *Converts to the Real: Catholicism and the Making of Continental Philosophy* (Harvard University Press, 2019).

16. See, for example, Dagmar Herzog, *Intimacy and Exclusion: Religious Politics in Pre-Revolutionary Baden* (Princeton University Press, 1996).

17. See, for example, Lucia Pozzi, *The Catholic Church and Modern Sexual Knowledge, 1850–1950* (Palgrave Macmillan, 2021); Sarah Jäger, *Bundesdeutscher Protestantismus und Geschlechterdiskurse, 1949–1971* (Mohr Siebeck, 2019); Dagmar Herzog, *Sex after Fascism: Memory and Morality in Twentieth-Century Germany* (Princeton University Press, 2005).

18. See, for example, Richard Hölzl, *Gläubige Imperialisten: Katholische Mission in Deutschland und Ostafrika, 1830–1960* (Campus, 2021); Jeremy Best, *Heavenly Fatherland: German Missionary Culture and Globalization in the Age of Empire* (University of Toronto Press, 2021); Elizabeth A. Foster, *Faith in Empire: Religion, Politics, and Colonial Rule in French Senegal, 1880–1940* (Stanford University Press, 2013); J. P. Daughton, *An Empire Divided: Religion, Republicanism, and the Making of French Colonialism* (Oxford University Press, 2006).

19. For a rare exploration of this process, see Sebastian Conrad, *Globalisation and the Nation in Imperial Germany* (Cambridge University Press, 2010).

20. A recent example is Gerard V. Bradley and E. Christian Brugger (eds.), *Catholic Social Teaching* (Cambridge University Press, 2019). The scholarship on the Second Vatican Council is too vast to summarize; the best overview, which includes references to most major accounts, is John W. O'Malley, *What Happened at Vatican II* (Harvard University Press, 2010).

21. On this point see, for example, Shortall, *Soldiers of God;* Chappel, *Catholic Modern;* Mark Edward Ruff, *The Battle for the Catholic Past in Germany, 1945–1980* (Cambridge University Press, 2017).

22. See, for example, Brandon Bloch, *Reinventing Protestant Germany: Religious Nationalists and the Contest for Post-Nazi Democracy* (Harvard University Press, 2025); Justin Reynold, "Against the World: International Protestantism and the Ecumenical Movement between Secularization and Politics, 1900–1952" (PhD diss., Columbia University, 2016); Brian Stanley, *The World Missionary Conference, Edinburgh 1910* (Eerdmans, 2009); Matthew D. Hockenos, *A Church Divided: German Protestants Confront the Nazi Past* (Indian University Press, 2004).

23. Alongside the works cited above, these studies include Martin Conway, *Catholic Politics in Europe, 1918–1945* (Routledge, 1997); Giuliana Chamedes, *A Twentieth-Century Crusade: The Vatican's Battle to Remake Christian Europe* (Harvard University Press, 2019); Piotr H. Kosicki, *Catholics on the Barricades: Poland, France, and "Revolution," 1891–1956* (Yale University Press, 2018); Susannah Heschel, *The Aryan Jesus* (Princeton University Press, 2006); Marco Duranti, *The Conservative Human Rights Revolution: European Identity, Transnational Politics, and the Origins of the European Convention* (Oxford University Press, 2017); Wolfram Kaiser, *Christian Democracy and the Origins of the European Union* (Cambridge University Press, 2007).

24. For works that focus on interactions during the era of World War II, see, for example, Thomas Brodie, *German Catholicism at War, 1939–1945* (Oxford University Press, 2018), and Thomas Grossböltig, *Losing Heaven: Religion in Germany since 1945* (Berghahn, 2015). The quote is from Wilhelm Stählin, *Katholisierende Neigungen in der evangelischen Kirche* (Schwabenverlag, 1947).

25. The decline of confessional milieus is the center, for example, of John A. Coleman's influential *The Evolution of Dutch Catholicism, 1958–1974* (University of California Press, 1978). The quote is from the Vatican II statement on engagement with Protestantism, *Unitatis redintegratio* (November 21, 1964), §3, http://www.vatican.va/archive/hist_councils/ii_vatican_council/documents/vat-ii_decree_19641121_unitatis-redintegratio_en.html.

26. On modern states' regulation of religion, see, for example, Saba Mahmood, *Religious Difference in a Secular Age: A Minority Report* (Princeton University Press, 2015);

Emily Greble, *Muslims and the Making of Modern Europe* (Oxford University Press, 2021); Judith Surkis, *Sex, Law, and Sovereignty in French Algeria, 1830–1930* (Cornell University Press, 2019).

27. Kosicki, *Catholics on the Barricades*.

28. For comparative perspective, see Erika Helgen, *Religious Conflict in Brazil: Protestants, Catholics, and the Rise of Religious Pluralism in the Early Twentieth Century* (Yale University Press, 2020).

29. On the birth of these ideas, and the different agendas they helped legitimize, see, for example, Kevin M. Schultz, *Tri-Fate America: How Catholics and Jews Held Postwar America to Its Protestant Promise* (Oxford University Press, 2011); K. Healan Gaston, *Imagining Judeo-Christian America: Religion, Secularism, and the Redefinition of Democracy* (Chicago University Press, 2019).

30. On the anemic reception of "Judeo-Christianity" in postwar Europe, see Noah B. Strote, "Sources of Christian-Jewish Cooperation in Early Cold War Germany," in *Is There a Judeo-Christian Tradition? A European Perspective*, ed. Emmanuel Nathan and Anya Topolski (De Gruyter, 2016), 75–100.

31. Olaf Blaschke, "Das 19 Jahrhundert: Ein Zweites Konfessionelles Zeitalter?," *Geschichte und Gesellschaft* 26 (2000): 38–75.

32. Paul Fechter, "Die Fremdheit," *Deutscher Fundschau* 61 (1935): 18–25.

33. Yves Congar, *Chrétiens désunis: Principes d'un "œcuménisme" catholique* (Cerf, 1937).

34. See, for example, Erik Linstrum, *Age of Emergency: Living with Violence at the End of the British Empire* (Oxford University Press, 2023); Amit Prakash, *Empire on the Seine: The Policing of North Africans in Paris, 1925–1975* (Oxford University Press, 2022); Jordanna Bailkin, *The Afterlife of Empire* (University of California Press, 2012); Amelia Lyons, *The Civilizing Mission in the Metropole: Algerian Families and the French Welfare State during Decolonization* (Stanford University Press, 2015); Todd Shepard, *The Invention of Decolonization: The Algerian War and the Remaking of France* (Cornell University Press, 2006).

35. There are exceptions, most notably Elizabeth A. Foster, *African Catholic: Decolonization and the Transformation of the Church* (Harvard University Press, 2019); Elizabeth A. Foster and Udi Greenberg (eds.), *Decolonization and the Remaking of Christianity* (University of Pennsylvania Press, 2023); and Elizabeth A. Foster and Giuliana Chamedes (eds.), *Decolonization and Religion in the French Empire*, special issue, *French Politics, Culture & Society* 33, no. 2 (2015).

1. Anti-Catholicism and Anti-Protestantism in the Long Nineteenth Century

1. Jaume Balmes, *El Protestantismo comparado con el catolicismo en sus relaciones con la civilización europea* (José Tauló, 1842). Throughout this chapter I use the English translation, *Protestantism and Catholicism Compared in Their Effects on European Civilization* (John Murphey, 1892), 247. There is no comprehensive study of Balmes's reception in Europe; for a few reflections, see Andrea Acke-Kreysing, *Taming the Revolution in Nineteenth-Century Spain: Jaime Balmes and Juan Donoso Cortés* (Campus, 2022), 197–202.

2. Napoleon Roussel, *Les nations catholiques et les nations protestantes: Comparées sous le triple rapport du bien-être, des lumières et de la moralité* (Meyrueis, 1854). The quotes are from the English translation, *Catholic and Protestant Nations Compared in Their Threefold Relations to Wealth, Knowledge, and Morality* (Ward, 1855), 1:111.

3. Most scholarship has focused on national settings. Alongside the many works cited below, see in particular Helmuth Walser Smith's foundational study *German Nationalism*

and *Religious Conflict: Culture, Ideology, Politics, 1870–1914* (Princeton University Press, 1995). For comparative studies of anti-Catholicism, see Manuel Borutta, *Antikatholizismus: Deutschland und Italien in Zeitalter der europäishen Kulturkämpfen* (Vandenhoeck und Ruprecht, 2011), and Timothy Verhoeven, *Transatlantic Anti-Catholicism: France and the United States in the Nineteenth Century* (Springer, 2010).

4. There are exceptions, such as Smith, *German Nationalism,* and Olaf Blaschke's article, "Das 19 Jahrhundert: Ein Zweites Konfessionelles Zeitalter?," *Geschichte und Gesellschaft* 26 (2000): 38–75.

5. Secular anti-Catholicism has dominated scholarship. See, for example, Christopher Clark and Wolfram Kaiser (eds.), *Culture Wars* (Cambridge University Press, 2003). On Jewish anti-Catholicism, see Ari Joskowicz, *The Modernity of Others: Jewish Anti-Catholicism in Germany and France* (Stanford University Press, 2014).

6. Timothy Tackett, *The Coming of the Terror in the French Revolution* (Harvard University Press, 2015), 256–261, 315–316.

7. On earlier precedents, see Peter Lake, *The Antichrist's Lewd Hat: Protestants, Papists, and Players in Post-Reformation England* (Yale University Press, 2002); Owen Stanwood, *The Empire Reformed: English America in the Age of the Glorious Revolution* (University of Pennsylvania Press, 2011).

8. Joseph de Maistre, "Reflections on Protestantism in Its Relations to Sovereignty," in *Critics of the Enlightenment: Readings in the French Counter-Revolutionary Tradition,* ed. Christopher Olaf Blum (ISI Books, 2004), 133–157, here 133, 135. Similar notions appear also in de Maistre's influential *Du Pape* (Rusand, 1819). More broadly on this trope, see Darrin McMahon, *Enemies of the Enlightenment: The French Counter-Enlightenment and the Making of Modernity* (Oxford University Press, 2001), 143–144.

9. Galart De Montjoie, *Histoire de la révolution de France* (Crapart, 1791). On the book's significance, see Burdette C. Poland, *French Protestantism and the French Revolution* (Princeton University Press, 1957), 145. On the popularity of these tropes in anti-revolutionary pamphlets, see Bryan Banks, "The Protestant Origins of the French Revolution: Contextualizing Edgar Quinet in the Historiography of the Revolution, 1789–1865," *Journal of the Western Society for French History* 42 (2014): 65–74.

10. For a helpful overview, see Dale K. Van Kley, *Reform Catholicism and the International Suppression of the Jesuits in Enlightenment Europe* (Yale University Press, 2018); Ulrich L. Lehner, *The Catholic Enlightenment: The Forgotten History of a Global Movement* (Oxford University Press, 2016).

11. Cited in Klaus Schatz, *Papal Primacy from Its Origins to the Present* (Liturgical Press, 1996), 148.

12. For a helpful overview, see John W. O'Malley, *Vatican I* (Harvard University Press, 2018), 55–95.

13. Félicité de Lamennais, *Essai sur l'indifférence en matière de religion* (Tournachon-Molin et Seguin, 1817). Quotes are taken from the English translation, *Essay on Indifference in Matters of Religion* (Hastings House, 1895), 182, 198. For a rare reflection on Lamennais's anti-Protestantism, see Helena Rosenblatt *Liberal Values: Benjamin Constant and the Politics of Religion* (Cambridge University Press, 2008), 176–179.

14. Balmes, *Protestantism and Catholicism Compared,* 365, 367, 364.

15. Tuska Benes, *The Rebirth of Revelation: German Theology in an Age of Reason and History, 1750–1850* (University of Toronto Press, 2022).

16. On the social basis of this milieu and its ideology, though focused on later decades, see Stefan-Ludwig Hoffmann, *The Politics of Sociability: Freemasonry and German Civil Society, 1840–1918* (University of Michigan Press, 2007).

17. Charles de Villers, *Essai sur l'esprit et l'influence de la Réformation de Luther* (Paris, 1804). The quotes are from the English translation, *An Essay on the Spirit and Influence of the Reformation by Luther* (London, 1805), 138, 257, 280. On the evolution of de Villers's thinking and its reception, see, for example, Michael Printy, "Protestantism and Progress in the Year XII: Charles Villers's *Essay on the Spirit and Influence of Luther's Reformation* (1804)," *Modern Intellectual History* 9, no. 2 (2012): 303–329.

18. Benjamin Constant, *Principes de politique* (Eymery, 1815). The quote is taken from the English translation, "The Principles of Politics Applicable to All Governments," in *Constant: Political Writings* (Cambridge University Press, 1993), 171–307, here 285. On Constant and other French liberals' confessional thinking, see Helena Rosenblatt, "On the Need for a Protestant Reformation: Constant, Sismondi, Guizot and Laboulaye," in *French Liberalism from Montesquieu to the Present Day*, ed. Raf Geenes and Helena Rosenblatt (Cambridge University Press, 2012), 115–133.

19. Francois Guizot, *Cours d'histoire moderne* (Pichon et Didier, 1829); the quote is taken from the English translation, *General History of Civilization in Europe* (Appleton, 1847), 358.

20. Heinrich Gottlieb Tzschirner, *Protestantismus und Katholicismus aus dem Standpuncte der Politik* (Baumgarner, 1822); see also Tzschirner, *Das Reactionssystem, dargestellt und geprüft* (Fleischer, 1824), esp. 152–188. For similar claims, see, for example, Arnold Heeren, *Vermischte historische Schrifte* (Röwer, 1821).

21. Heinrich von Sybel, *Die politischen Parteien der Rheinprovinz, in ihrem Verhältniss zur preussischen Verfassung geschildert* (Buddeus, 1847), 35. On Sybel, see Michael B. Gross, *The War against Catholicism: Liberalism and the Anti-Catholic Imagination in Nineteenth-Century Germany* (University of Michigan Press, 2005), 194–195.

22. Merle D'Aubigné, *Histoire de la Réformation* (Guers, 1835–1853). The quote is from the English translation, *History of the Reformation in the Sixteenth Century* (Carter and Bro., 1875), 1:74.

23. On the rise of evangelical thought in post-Napoleonic Germany, see Andrew Kloes, *The German Awakening: Protestant Renewal after the Enlightenment, 1815–1848* (Oxford University Press, 2019). On the Netherlands, see Fred van Lieburg, *Opwekking van de natie: Het protestantse Réveil in Nederland* (Hilversum, 2012).

24. Guillaume Groen van Prinsterer, *Ongeloof en revolutie* (Luchtmans, 1847). The quote is taken from the English translation, *Lectures on Unbelief in Revolution* (Wedge, 1989), 406.

25. Guillaume Groen van Prinsterer, *Le parti anti-revolutionnaire et confessionnel dans l'Église reforméé des Pays-Bas: Étude d'histoire contemporaine* (Höveker, 1860). The quote is from the English translation, *Christian Political Action in the Age of Revolution* (Canon Press, 2022), 59.

26. Marc H. Lerner, *A Laboratory of Liberty: The Transformation of Political Culture in Republican Switzerland* (Brill, 2012), esp. 265–320. The international following of the Swiss conflict is discussed in Joachim Remak, *A Very Civil War: The Swiss Sonderbund of 1847* (Westview Press, 1993), esp. 176.

27. Roussel, *Catholic and Protestant Nations Compared*, 239.

28. Giuseppe Mazzini, "From a Revolutionary Alliance to the United States of Europe," in *A Cosmopolitanism of Nations: Giuseppe Mazzini's Writings on Democracy, Nation Building, and International Relations* (Princeton University Press, 2009 [1850]), 132–136, here 133.

29. For a helpful overview, see Stefan-Ludwig Hoffmann, *Civil Society, 1750–1914* (Palgrave Macmillan, 2006).

30. First Vatican Council, Dogmatic Constitution *Pastor aeternus* (July 18, 1970), https://www.ewtn.com/catholicism/teachings/vatican-is-dogmatic-constitution-pastor-aeternus-on-the-church-of-christ-243. On the council more broadly, see O'Malley, *Vatican I*.

31. Karl von Hase, *Handbuch der protestantischen Polemik gegen die Römisch-Katholische Kirche* (Breitkopf und Härtel, 1865). The quote is taken from the English translation, *Handbook to the Controversy with Rome* (Religious Tract Society, 1862), 2:501.

32. Adolf Zeising, *Religion und Wissenschaft, Staat und Kirche* (Wilhelm Braumüller, 1873), 431, 457.

33. Paul Hinschius, *Die päpstliche Unfehlbarkeit und das vatikanische Koncil* (Universitäts-Buchhandlung, 1871), 27.

34. Émile de Laveleye, *Le Parti clérical en Belgique* (Buschmann, 1872). The quote is taken from the English translation, "The Clerical Party in Belgium," *Fortnightly Review* 18 (1872): 503–518, here 508, 513.

35. William Gladstone, *The Vatican Decrees in Their Bearing on Civil Allegiance* (Murray, 1874), 35, 27. See also Gladstone's subsequent *Vaticanism: An Answer to Reproofs and Replies* (Murray, 1875).

36. Geoffrey Cubitt, *The Jesuit Myth: Conspiracy Theory and Politics in Nineteenth-Century France* (Clarendon, 1993).

37. Jules Michelet, *Des Jésuites* (Hachette et Baulin, 1843), quote taken from the English translation, *Jesuits and Jesuitism* (Whittaker, 1845), 46. On the popularity and influence of this text, see, for example, Verhoeven, *Transatlantic Anti-Catholicism*, 24–40.

38. Heinrich Wiskemann, *Die Lehre und Praxis der Jesuiten in religiöser, moralischer und politischer Beziehung* (Georg Luckhardt, 1858), 43. On the popularity of those tropes among German Protestants, see Gross, *The War against Catholicism*, 89.

39. Sabina Pavone, "The History of Anti-Jesuitism: National and Global Dimensions," in *Jesuits and Globalization*, ed. Thomas Banchoff and José Casanova (Georgetown University Press, 2016), 11–130. On the expulsion of the Jesuits from Germany, see, for example, Matthew P. Fitzpatrick, *Purging the Empire: Mass Expulsions in Germany* (Oxford University Press, 2015), 39–67.

40. The scholarship on the *Kulturkampf* is vast. For some excellent examples, see Rebecca Ayako Bennette, *Fighting for the Soul of Germany: The Catholic Struggle for Inclusion after Unification* (Harvard University Press, 2012); Borutta, *Antikatholizismus*; Gross, *The War against Catholicism*.

41. Peter Jan Margry and Henk de Velde, "Contested Rituals and the Battle for Public Space: The Netherlands," in Clark and Kaiser, *Culture Wars*, 129–151.

42. Els Witte, "The Battle for Monasteries, Cemeteries, and Schools: Belgium," in Clark and Kaiser, *Culture Wars*, 102–128.

43. Philip Nord, *The Republican Moment: Struggles for Democracy in Nineteenth-Century France* (Harvard University Press, 1995), 91–113; Judith Surkis, *Sexing the Citizen: Morality and Masculinity in France, 1870–1920* (Cornell University Press, 2006), 29–32.

44. This description of Los von Rom is based on Smith, *German Nationalism*, 206–232.

45. Ernest Renauld, *La peril protestant* (Tolra, 1899); Julien Fontaine, *Les infiltrations protestantes et le clerge francais* (Retaux, 1901). For similar sentiments, see A. Tollaire, *Les anglais en Égypte: L'ossature de la trahison* (Pierret, 1899).

46. Jean-Baptiste Maraval, *Le protestantisme au XVIe et au XIXe siècle* (Henri Amalric, 1899).

47. Pierre Froment, *La trahison protestante* (Pierret, 1899). For similar ideas, see Gaston Mercier, *L'esprit protestant: Politique-religion* (Paris: Perrin, 1901). On this trope in Catholic thought, see Michèle Sacquin, *L'antiprotestantisme en France de 1814 à 1870: Entre Bossuet et Maurras* (École des Chartes, 1998).

48. Alfred Baudrillart, *L'église catholique, la Renaissance, le protestantisme: Conférences données a l'Institut catholique, Janvier–Mars, 1904* (Bloud, 1905). The quotes are taken from the English translation, *The Catholic Church, the Renaissance, and Protestantism* (Kegan Paul, 1907), 118, 133.

49. Charles Maurras, *Le dilemma de Marc Sangnier: Essai sur la democratie religieuse* (Latines, 1907), 225. On the Dreyfus affair and anti-Protestantism, see Jean Baubérot, "Antisémitisme et antiprotestantisme de la 'République des Républicains' à l'affaire Dreyfus," *Archives Juives* 49, no. 1 (2016): 114–133; Jean Baubérot and Velntine Zuber, *Une haine oubliée* (Albin Michel, 2000).

50. Roussel, *Catholic and Protestant Nations Compared*, 1:70.

51. Armand Audiganne, *Les populations ouvrières et les industries de la France dans le mouvement social du 19ᵉ siècle* (Capelle, 1854).

52. Wilhelm Heinrich Riehl, *Die Deutsche Arbeit* (Cota, 1861), esp. 16–27.

53. Émile de Laveleye, *Le protestantisme et le catholicisme dans leurs rapports avec la liberté et la prospérité des peoples* (Muquardt, 1875); quotes are taken from the English translation, *Protestantism and Catholicism in Their Bearing upon the Liberty and Prosperity of Nations* (William Clowes and Sons, 1875), 24, 52, 63.

54. Max Weber, *The Protestant Ethic and the Spirit of Capitalism* (Penguin, 2014). Scholarship on Weber's thesis is vast. For two illuminating works on its evolution and Weber's social and intellectual background, see Guenther Roth, *Max Webers deutsch-englische Familiengeschichte, 1800–1950* (Mohr Siebeck, 2001); Peter Ghosh, *Max Weber and the Protestant Ethic: Twin Histories* (Oxford University Press, 2014).

55. Louis-Gaston de Ségur, *Causeries familières sur le protestantisme d'aujourd'hui* (Libraires de Notre Saint, 1859). The quote is from the English translation, *Plain Talk about the Protestantism of Today* (Donahoe, 1868), 215–216.

56. Jean-Baptiste Malou, *La fausseté du protestantisme démontré* (Goemaere, 1857). The quote is from the English translation, *The Falsehood of Protestantism Demonstrated* (Dolman, 1858), 31.

57. Joseph Mausbach, *Kernfraen christlicher Welt- und Lebensaunschauung: Gedanken und Vorträge* (Zentralstelle des Volksvereins für das kathol. Deutschland, 1905), 20.

58. Prosper de Haulleville, *L'avenir des peuples catholiques* (Haenen, 1876); quotes taken from the English translation, *Social Aspects of Catholicism and Protestantism in Their Civil Bearing upon Nations* (C. Kegan Paul, 1878), 76.

59. Georges Goyau, *L'Allemagne religieuse: Le protestantisme* (Perin, 1898). For similar claims, see Anatole Flamérion, *De la prosperité comparée des nations catholiques et des nations protestantes: Au point de vue économique, moral, social* (Bloud, 1899).

60. Roussel, *Catholic and Protestant Nations Compared*, 1:13, 2:238.

61. Alexander von Oettingen, *Die moralstatistik und die christliche Sittenlehre: Versuch einer Socialethik auf empirischer Grundlager* (Deichert, 1868). On Oettingen's influence, see, for example, Theodore M. Porter, *The Rise of Statistical Thinking, 1820–1900* (Princeton University Press, 2020 [1986]), 178–189.

62. Martin Offenbacher, *Konfession und soziale Schichtung* (Mohr, 1900).

63. Ségur, *Plain Talk,* 219–220.

64. Hermann Krose, *Der Einfluss der Konfession auf die Sittlichkeit* (Herdersche, 1900).

65. Hans Rost, *Der Selbstmord* (Bachem, 1905). See also Rost, *Beiträge zur Moralstatistik* (Paderborn, 1913). On the evolution of Catholic thinking about statistics, including its anti-Protestant bent, see Benjamin Ziman, *Encounters with Modernity: The Catholic Church in West Germany* (Berghan, 2014), 24–62.

66. Roderick Phillips, *Untying the Knot: A Short History of Divorce* (Cambridge University Press, 1991), 1–46.

67. Scholarship on this transition is vast. For a still helpful overview, see Edward Shorter's classic *The Making of the Modern Family* (Basic Books, 1975).

68. On the construction of this discourse and early challenges to it, see, for example, Joan B. Landes's still-helpful *Women and the Public Sphere in the French Revolution* (Cornell University Press, 1988).

69. Jacques Marie Louis Monsabré, *Conférences de Notre-Dame de Paris* (Année dominicaine, 1888). The quote is from the English translation, *Marriage Conferences Delivered at Notre Dame, Paris* (Benziger, 1890), 43–45.

70. For helpful background, see Timothy Verhoeven, *Sexual Crime, Religion and Masculinity in Fin-de-Siècle France: The Flamidien Affair* (Palgrave Macmillan, 2018).

71. Otto Corvin, *Historische Denkmale des christlichen Fanatismus* (Gebauer, 1845), 231, 253.

72. Roussel, *Catholic and Protestant Nations*, 234.

73. Verhoeven, *Transatlantic Anti-Catholicism*; Borutta, *Antikatholizismus*.

74. Edward Mathieu, "The Christian Love of the German Middle Class," *German Studies Review* 34, no. 2 (2011): 305–324.

75. Hase, *Handbook to the Controversy*, 181.

76. See, for example, the historical work of Gustav Freytag, *Bilder aus der deutschen Vergangenheit* (Schlüter, 1859), vol. 1.

77. Charles Chiniquy, *Le prêtre, la femme et le confessionnal* (Gassart, 1874). The quotes are from the English version, *The Priest, the Woman, and the Confessional* (Gibson, 1874), 76, 103–105.

78. The most popular work in this genre, alongside Chiniquy, was Luigi Desanctis, *The Confessional* (John Kensit, 1887). Written by an Italian convert from Catholicism to Protestantism, the text ran through dozens of editions and was translated across Europe. See also Daniel von Kászony, *Der Teufel im Beichtstuhl* (Röhl, 1872).

79. Roussel, *Catholic and Protestant Nations*, esp. 235–236.

80. Christian Carl Josias Bunsen, *Die Zeichen der Zeit* (Brockhaus, 1855). The quote is taken from the English translation, *Signs of the Times* (Smith, Elder, and Co., 1865), 145.

81. Johann Bluntschli, *Psychologische Studien über Staat und Kirche* (Beyel, 1844), 85. On Bluntschli's gendered political theory and activism, see Borutta, *Antikatholizismus*, 276–283.

82. On the short-lived efforts to reform Catholic teachings on celibacy, see Dagmar Herzog, *Intimacy and Exclusion: Religious Politics in Pre-Revolutionary Baden* (Princeton University Press, 1996), 19–52.

83. Félix Dupanloup, *Le mariage chrétien* (C. Douniol, 1869), 153.

84. Monsabré, *Marriage Conferences*, 32–33.

85. Dupanloup, *Le mariage chrétien*.

86. See, for example, Monsabré, *Marriage Conferences*, esp. 149–150; Ignaz von Döllinger, *Luther: Eine Skizze* (Herder, 1851); Johannes Janssen, *Geschichte des deutschen Volkes seit dem Ausgang des Mittelalters* (Herder, 1876–1892).

87. Franz Xaver Brors, *Moderne A.B.C. fuer Katholiken aller Stände: Kurze Antworten auf die modernen Angriffe gegen die Katholische Kirche* (Kevelaer, 1902); quote taken from the English translation, *The Catholic's Ready Answer* (Benziger Bros., 1915), 158.

88. Haulleville, *Social Aspects*, 218.

89. Conrad von Bolanden, *Die Freidenker* (Pustet, 1872). The quote is from the English translation, *The Progressionists* (Catholic Publication Society, 1873), 91.

90. Alphonse Daudet, *L'Évangéliste, roman parisien* (Dentu, 1883).

91. Ludwig von Hammerstein, *Katholizismus und Protestnatismus* (Paulinus, 1894).

92. François Martin, *De l'avenir du protestantisme et de catholicisme* (Tolra et Haton, 1869), 26.

93. Monsabré, *Marriage Conferences*, 215.

94. Rebekka Habermas and Richard Hölzl (eds.), *Mission Global: Eine Verflechtungsgeschite seit dem 19. Jahrhundert* (Böhlu, 2014); Dana L. Robert (ed.), *Converting Colonialism: Visions and Realities in Mission History* (Eerdmans, 2008).

95. See, for example, Benjamin Schmidt, *Innocence Abroad: The Dutch Imagination and the New World, 1570–1670* (Cambridge University Press, 2001); Owen Stanwood, "Between Eden and Empire: Huguenot Refugees and the Promise of New Worlds," *American Historical Review* 118, no. 5 (December 2013): 1319–1344; Stanwood, *The Empire Reformed: English America in the Age of the Glorious Revolution* (University of Pennsylvania Press, 2011). A helpful comparative framework on Catholics and Protestants in this era is Linda Gregerson and Susan Juster (eds.), *Empires of God: Religious Encounters in the Early Modern Atlantic* (University of Philadelphia Press, 2011).

96. Gustav Warneck, *Abriss einer Geschichte der protestantischen Missionen von der Reformation bis auf die Gegenwart* (Martin Warneck, 1883). The quote is from the English translation, *Outline of a History of Protestant Missions from the Reformation to the Present Time* (Gemmel, 1884), 80.

97. Gustav Warneck, *Protestantische Beleuchtung der römischen Angriffe auf die evangelische Heidentum* (Wertelsmann, 1884), 466.

98. Carl Mirbt, "Die Missionsmethode der römiach-katholischen Kirche," *Allgemeine Missions-Zeitschrift* 28 (1901): 264, 266–267.

99. Alexander Merensky, "Welches Interesse und welche Anteil hat die Mission an der Erziehung der Naturvölker zur Arbeit?," *Allgemeine Missions-Zeitschrift* 14 (1887): 162. On the centrality of anti-Catholicism to German Protestant missionary elites, see Jeremy Best, *Heavenly Fatherland: German Missionary Culture and Globalization in the Age of Empire* (University of Toronto Press, 2021), 123–129.

100. François E. Daubanton, *Prolegomena van protestantsche zendingswetenschap* (Kemnik und Zoon, 1911), 85. On Dutch Protestant missionary thought and anti-Catholicism, see Jan A. B. Jongeneel, "Protestant Missions and Mission Studies in the Netherlands: Encounter with Roman Catholicism," in *Missions and Science: Missiology Revisited*, ed. Carine Dujadin and Claude Prudhomme (Leuven University Press, 2015), 77–86.

101. Julius Richter, "Die evangelischen, besonders deutschen Missionen," *Allgemeine Missions-Zeitschrift* 21 (1894): 435.

102. For some helpful background, see Brian Stanley, *The World Missionary Conference, Edinburgh 1910* (Eerdmans, 2009).

103. See, for example, Ruth Rouse and Stephen Neill, *A History of the Ecumenical Movement* (SPCK, 1970).

104. Gustav Warneck, "The Mutual Relations of Evangelical Missionary Societies to One Another," in *Report of the Centenary Conference on the Protestant Missions of the World, Held in Exeter Hall* (Nisbet, 1888), 2: 431–437, here 437.

105. *Report of the Centenary Conference*, 1:85.

106. On this episode, see Best, *Heavenly Fatherland*, 113–142. On similar events in Cameroon, see Heinrich Berger, *Mission und Kolonialpolitik: Die katholische Mission im Kamerum währen der deutschen Kolonialzeit* (Neue Zeitschrift für Missionswissenschaft, 1978), 336–337.

107. Giancarlo Collet, "German Catholic Mission Science," in Dujadin and Prudhomme, *Missions and Science*, 99–110.

108. The quote is from the English translation of Schwager's most comprehensive anti-Protestant text, *Die brennendste Missionsfrage der Gegenwart* (Missionsdruckerei, 1913),

published in English as *The Most Vital Problem of the Day* (Mission Press, 1915), 95–96. On anti-Protestantism in German Catholic missionary thought, see Albert Wu, "In the Shadow of Empire: Josef Schmidlin and Protestant-Catholic Ecumenism before the Second World War," *Journal of Global History* 13 (2018): 165–187.

109. On Dupont and anti-Protestantism, see, for example, Ian Linden, *Catholics, Peasants, and Chewa Resistance in Nyasaland* (University of California Press, 1974), esp. 148–150.

110. The prevalence of such rhetoric is described in Aylward Shorter, *Cross and Flag in Africa: The "White Fathers" during the Colonial Scramble, 1892–1914* (Orbis, 2006), 205–207, quotation at 206.

111. The quote is from Leo XIII, *Sancta Dei civitas* (December 3, 1880), clauses 8 and 13; English translation available at http://w2.vatican.va/content/leo-xiii/en/encyclicals/documents/hf_l-xiii_enc_03121880_sancta-dei-civitas.html. The same ideas were later repeated in multiple statements, such as *Ad extremas* (June 23, 1893), which is available at https://www.vatican.va/content/leo-xiii/en/encyclicals/documents/hf_l-xiii_enc_24061893_ad-extremas.html.

112. Joseph Brucker, *La liberté religieuse á Madagascar* (Imprimerie Yvert et Tullier, 1897), 15.

113. On this episode, and on the significance of confessional animosities in Madagascar more broadly, see J. P. Daughton, *An Empire Divided* (Oxford University Press, 2006), 167–204, on which this description is based.

114. Oliver Zimmer, "Beneath the 'Culture War': Corpus Christi Processions and Mutual Accommodation in the Second German Empire," *Journal of Modern History* 82 (June 2010): 288–334.

115. Ignaz von Döllinger, *Über die Wiedervereinigung der christlichen Kirchen* (C. H. Beck, 1872). Döllinger's efforts to foster interconfessional understanding are discussed in Thomas Albert Howard, *The Pope and the Professor: Pius IX, Ignaz von Döllinger, and the Quandary of the Modern Age* (Oxford University Press, 2017), esp. 190–211.

116. This episode is explored in James D. Bratt, *Abraham Kuyper: Modern Calvinist, Christian Democrat* (Eerdmans, 2013), esp. 64–86.

2. Mutual Dreams of Order in an Unruly World, 1880s–1920s

1. Henri Massis, *Défense de l'Occident* (Plon, 1927). The quotes are from the English translation, *Defense of the West* (Harcourt, Brace, 1928), 50, 212.

2. See Gerhard Ohlenmüller, *Het protestantisme en katholicisme in den tegenwoordigen tijd* (J. A. v. Ketel, 1923); and the essays collected in *International League for the Defence and Furtherance of Protestantism* (International League for the Defence and Furtherance of Protestantism, 1931).

3. Matteo Liberatore, *Principii di Economia politica* (Befani, 1889). The quotes are from the English translation, *The Principles of Political Economy* (Art and Book, 1891), 153.

4. Joseph Mausbach, *Die Stellung der Frau im Menschheitsleben* (Volksvereins, 1906), 28.

5. On anti-Christian activism, see, for example, Todd Weir, *Red Secularism: Socialism and Secularist Culture in Germany* (Cambridge University Press, 2023); Carl Strikwerda, *A House Divided: Catholics, Socialists, and the Flemish Nationalists in Nineteenth-Century Belgium* (Rowman and Littlefield, 1997), esp. 109–211; Robert S. Stuart, "A 'De Profundis' for Christian Socialism: French Marxists and the Critique of Political Catholicism, 1882–1905," *French Historical Studies* 22, no. 2 (1999): 241–261. On the intellectual efforts to marry scientific atheism and socialism, see, for example, Sebastian Prüfer, *Sozialismus statt Religion: Die deutsche Sozialdemokratie vor der religiösen Frage, 1863–1890* (Vandenhoeck

und Ruprecht, 2002); David Stack, *The First Darwinian Left: Socialism and Darwinism, 1859–1914* (New Clarion, 2003).

6. Carolyn J. Eichner, *The Paris Commune* (Rutgers University Press, 2022), 71–75.

7. Cited in Andrew Lees, *Cities, Sin, and Social Reform in Imperial Germany* (University of Michigan Press, 2002), 86.

8. Leo XIII, *quod apostolici muneris* (December 20, 1878), http://www.vatican.va/content/leo-xiii/en/encyclicals/documents/hf_l-xiii_enc_28121878_quod-apostolici-muneris.html #11. On Leo and his anti-socialism, see Joe Holland, *Modern Catholic Social Teaching* (Paulist Press, 2003), 107–145.

9. Émile de Laveleye, *Le socialisme contemporain* (Uitgever, 1881). The quote is from the English translation, *The Socialism of Today* (Field and Tuer, 1884), 137.

10. Viktor Cathrein, *Der Sozialismus* (Herder, 1890).

11. Antoine Pottier, *La cooperation et les sociétés ouvrières* (Lithographie Demarteau, 1889), 23, as cited in Strikwerda, *A House Divided*, 218.

12. Paul Misner, *Social Catholicism in Europe: From the Onset of Industrialization to the First World War* (Crossroad, 1991); Norbert Friedrich and Traugott Jähnichen (eds.), *Sozialer Protestantismus im Kaiserreich* (LIT, 2005).

13. Wilhelm Emmanuel von Ketteler, *Die Arbeiterfrage und das Christentum* (Kirchheim, 1864), esp. 32–96, quote at 100. The term "materialism" was used in Christian writing in the 1850s and 1860s to describe some scientists' belief that life was governed by material, not spiritual, forces, but Ketteler was one of the first to use it in economic theory. Frederick Gregory, *Nature Lost? Natural Science and the German Theological Traditions of the Nineteenth Century* (Harvard University Press, 1992).

14. Ketteler, *Die Arbeiterfrage*, 147.

15. Ketteler, *Die katholiken im Deutschen reiche. Entwurf zu einem politischen programm* (Kirchheim, 1873). On Ketteler's early work, see Martin O'Malley, *Wilhelm Ketteler and the Birth of Modern Catholic Social Thought* (Utz, 2008). On Ketteler's work for the Center Party, see Johannes Wenzel, *Arbeiterschutz und Centrum* (Germania, 1893), 15–17.

16. Franz Hitze, *Die sociale Frage und die Bestrebungen zu ihrer Lösung* (Bonifacus, 1877); Hitze, *Die Quintessenz der socialen Frage* (Bonifacus, 1880). The quotes are from Hitze, *Kapial und Arbeit und die Reorganisation der Gesellschaft* (Bonifacus, 1881), 33.

17. The quote is from a speech that was originally given in 1871 and was reprinted in Albert de Mun, *Ma vocation social* (Lethielleux, 1877), 67–75, quotation at 70. On Mun's early writings and activism, see Benjamin Martin, *Count Albert de Mun: Paladin of the Third Republic* (University of North Carolina Press, 2011).

18. Joseph Scheicher, *Der Klerus und die soziale Frage* (Rausch, 1884). On Scheicher's journalist work, see John Boyer, *Political Radicalism in Late Imperial Vienna* (University of Chicago Press, 1981), 159.

19. Leo XIII, *Rerum novarum* (May 15, 1891), no. 49, available at http://www.vatican.va/content/leo-xiii/en/encyclicals/documents/hf_l-xiii_enc_15051891_rerum-novarum.html. The scholarship on *Rerum novarum* and its reception is vast. Two helpful examples are Ernest L. Fortin, "'Sacred and Inviolable': Rerum Novarum and Natural Rights," *Theological Studies* 53 (1992): 203–233; Lillian Parker Wallace, *Leo XIII and the Rise of Socialism* (Duke University Press, 1996), 254–277.

20. Albert Schäffle, *Kapitalismus und Socialismus* (Laupp, 1870); Schäffle, *Bau und Leben des socialen Körpers* (Laupp, 1875–1878); Hans Frambach, "The Relationship of Economy and Ethics in the Works of Albert Schäffle," in *Albert Schäffle*, ed. Jürgen Backhaus (Haag + Herchen, 2010), 75–90.

21. Albert Schäffle, *Die Quintessenz des Socialismus* (F. A. Perthes, 1875); Schäffle, *Die Aussichtslosigkeit der Socialdemokratie* (Laupp, 1885).

22. August Pfannkuche, *Was liest der deutsche Arbeiter?* (Mohr, 1900); Reinhold Seeberg, *Die Kirche und die soziale Frage* (Deichert, 1896). More broadly on the Congress, see Friedrich and Jähnichen, *Sozialer Protestantismus im Kaiserreich;* Harry Liebersohn, *Religion and Industrial Society: The Protestant Social Congress in Wilhelmine Germany* (American Philosophical Society, 1986).

23. See, for example, Charles Gide, *Du rôle pratique du pasteur dans les questions sociales* (Paris: Uitgever, 1889); Tommy Fallot, *Notre programme* (Fischbacher, 1892). On Fallot and the association, see, for example, Janet Horne, *The Social Laboratory for Modern France* (Duke University Press, 2002), 115–118; Christopher Chalamet, *Revivalism and Social Christianity* (Lutterworth, 2017), esp. 13–18.

24. Abraham Kuyper, *Ons Program* (Amsterdam: Kruyt, 1879); quotation is from the English translation, *Our Program* (Christian's Library Press, 2013), 253, 255. On Kuyper, see James D. Bratt, *Abraham Kuyper: Modern Calvinist, Christian Democrat* (Eerdmans, 2013).

25. Joan L. Coffey, *Léon Harmel: Enterpreneur as Catholic Social Reformer* (University of Notre Dame Press, 2003); more broadly on paternalist experiments in France at the time, see Susan Pedersen, *Family, Dependence, and the Origins of the Welfare State: Britain and France, 1914–1945* (Cambridge University Press, 1993), 285.

26. On France, see Misner, *Social Catholicism in Europe,* 162–168. On Germany, see Eric Dorn Brose, *Christian Labor and the Politics of Frustration in Imperial Germany* (Catholic University of America Press, 1985), esp. 72–80. On Belgium, see Strikwerda, *A House Divided,* esp. 232–240.

27. Édouard Gruner, "Introduction," in *Congrès international des accidents du travail* (Librairie Polytechnique, 1889), 7. On Gruner, see Horne, *A Social Laboratory,* 127–130.

28. Paul Rabinow, *French Modern: Norms and Forms of the Social Environment* (University of Chicago Press, 2014), 168–210, here 180.

29. Adolf Stoecker, *Die Bibel und die sociale Frage: Vortrag im Evangelische Arbeiterverein zu Nürnberg* (Duits, 1879).

30. Kuyper, *Our Program,* chap. 20, on the social question.

31. The best work on the emergence and development of the Christian Socials remains Boyer, *Political Radicalism.* On the party's economic policies, see John Boyer, *Culture and Political Crisis in Vienna: Christian Socialism in Power* (University of Chicago Press, 1995), 14–20.

32. Heinrich Pesch, *Die sociale Befähigung der Kirche* (Germania, 1890); Pesch, *Liberalismus, Socialismus, und christliche Gesellschaftsordnung* (Herder, 1900).

33. *Bericht über die Verhandlungen des 5. Evangelisch-sozialen Kongresses* (Wiegandt, 1894), 97–120, here 5.

34. On France, see Misner, *Social Catholicism in Europe,* 162–168. On Germany, see Brose, *Christian Labor,* esp. 72–80. On Belgium, see Strikwerda, *A House Divided,* esp. 232–240. For an overview on the growth of Catholic labor organizations, see Michael P. Fogarty's still-useful *Christian Democracy in Western Europe, 1820–1953* (University of Notre Dame Press, 1957), 186–210.

35. Ludwig Weber, *Die sociale Organisation des römischen Katholicismus in Deutschland* (Arein, 1888). On Weber and the Protestant outreach to workers, see Gert Lewek, *Kirche und soziale Frage und die Jahrhundertwende* (Erziehungsverein, 1963); Norbert Friedrich, *Die christlich-soziale Fahne empor! Reinhard Mumm und die christlich-soziale Bewegung* (Kohlhammer, 1997), esp. 60–140.

36. On Patrimonium, see Claudia Hiepel et al., "The Formation of Christian Working-Class Organizations in Belgium, Germany, Italy, and the Netherlands," in *Between Cross and Class: Comparative Histories of Christian Labour in Europe, 1840–2000,* ed. Lex Heerma

van Voss et al. (Peter Lang, 2005), 49–80. On the social question, see Kuyper, *Our Program*, chap. 20. On Switzerland, see Fogarty, *Christian Democracy*, 183–185.

37. Fogarty, *Christian Democracy*.

38. Pesch, *Liberalismus, Socialismus*, 1:135. For earlier anti-Protestantism, see, for example, Pesch, *Die sociale Befähigung*.

39. On Kuyper and Ketteler, see Bratt, *Abraham Kuyper*, 223.

40. Schäffle, *Die Aussichtslosigkeit der Socialdemokratie*, 349.

41. The quote is from William L. Patch, *Christian Trade Unions in the Weimar Republic, 1918–1933* (Yale University Press, 1985), 17; see 1–33 for the formation of interconfessional unions. See also Misner, *Social Catholicism*, 270 onward.

42. Ellen Lovell Evans, *The Cross and the Ballot: Catholic Political Parties in Germany, Switzerland, Austria, Belgium and the Netherlands* (Humanities Press, 1999).

43. Joseph Mausbach, "Christlich-Katholische Ethik," *Kultur der Gegenwart* 1, no. 4 (1906): 521–548; Max Turman, *Le catholicisme social* (Felix Alcan, 1901); Turman, *Activités sociales* (Felix Alcan, 1907).

44. Adolph Wagner, *Allgemeine oder theoretische Volkswirtschaftslehre* (C. F. Winter, 1876). See also Wagner, *Rede über die soziale Frage* (Wiegaant und Grieben, 1872); Wagner, "Finanzwissenschaft und Staatsocialismus," *Zeitschrift für die gesamte Staateswissenschaft* 43 (1887): 37–122.

45. On Monod, see Rachel G. Fuchs, *The Poor and Pregnant in Paris: Strategies for Survival in the Nineteenth Century* (Rutgers University Press, 1992), 72–74; Timothy B. Smith, *Creating the Welfare State in France* (McGill-Queen's University Press, 2003), 28, 33, 43.

46. The quote is taken from Nathan Bates Witham, *German Workers' Insurance* (University of Wisconsin Press, 1974), 127.

47. On the formation of Germany's welfare programs, see, for example, Greg Eghigian, *Making Security Social: Disability, Insurance, and the Birth of the Social Entitlement State in Germany* (Michigan University Press, 2000); E. P. Hennock, *The Origin of the Welfare State in England and Germany* (Cambridge University Press, 2007).

48. Patrick Pasture, "Building the Social Security State: Comparative History of Belgium, the Netherlands, and Germany," in Voss et al., *Between Cross and Class*, 251–284. More broadly, see Tjitske Akkerman, "Political Participation and Social Rights: The Triumph of the Breadwinner in the Netherlands," in *Gender, Participation, and Citizenship in the Netherlands*, ed. Jet Bussemaker and Rian Voet (Routledge, 1998), 38–50.

49. Élie Gounelle, "Man and Property," in *The Stockholm Conference 1925: The Official Report of the Universal Christian Conference on Life and Work Held in Stockholm, 19–30 August, 1925*, ed. George K. A. Bell (Oxford University Press, 1926), 161–171.

50. *XIV Session de la Semaine sociale de France (Strasbourg, 1922)* (Gabalda, 1922).

51. F. Busé, "The Child and the Adolescent in Industry," in Bell, *The Stockholm Conference 1925*, 204–210. For statements in the same spirit, from the same volume, see also Wilhelm Kähler, "Untitled," 129–131; Jakob Schoell, "The Church and Moral and Social Problems," 218–225; and August Springer, "Untitled," 211–217. On the conference's goals in international politics, see for example Justin Reynolds, "Against the World: International Protestantism and the Ecumenical Movement between Secularization and Politics" (PhD diss., Columbia University, 2016), 111–156.

52. This episode is explored in Patch, *Christian Trade Unions*, 63–75, quotation at 66.

53. "Was wir wollen," *Una Sancta* 1 (1925): 1–2, here 1. On this initiative, see Paul Metzlaff, "The Beginnings of Ecumenism in Germany: From the Hochkirche Movement to the Development of the Una Sancta Group," in *A History of the Desire for Christian Unity*, vol. 1, ed. Luca Ferracci (Brill, 2021), 659–678.

54. Cited in Patch, *Christian Trade Unions*, 67.
55. Pius XI, *Mortalium animos* (January 6, 1928), available at https://www.vatican.va/content/pius-xi/en/encyclicals/documents/hf_p-xi_enc_19280106_mortalium-animos.html.
56. Paul Misner, *Catholic Labor Movements in Europe: Social Thought and Action* (Catholic University of America Press, 2015), 88–92.
57. Schoell, "The Church," 220.
58. Augustin Rösler, *Die Frauenfrage vom Standpunkte der Natur, der Geschichte und der Offenbarung* (Josef Roller, 1893), 101.
59. Wilhelm Emmanuel von Ketteler, *Die Arbeitsbewegung und ihr Streben im Verhältnis zu Religion und Sittlichkeit* (Kirchheim, 1869), esp. 20–24.
60. Cited in Mary Lynn Stewart, *Women, Work, and the French State: Labour Protection and Social Patriarchy, 1879–1919* (McGill-Queen's University Press, 1989), 63.
61. The congresses are mentioned in Parker T. Moon, *The Labor Problem and the Social Movement in France* (Macmillan, 1921), 153.
62. On Germany, see Manfred Schick, *Kulturprotestantismus und soziale Frage* (Mohr, 1970), 79; Ursula Baumann, *Protestantismus und Frauenemanzipation in Deutschland* (Campus, 1993), 79–98. On the Netherlands, see Tom-Eric Krijger, *The Eclipse of Liberal Protestantism in the Netherlands* (Leiden, 2019). On France, see Steven Hause, "Social Control in Late Nineteenth-Century France: Protestant Campaigns for Strict Public Morality," in *Confronting Modernity in Fin-de-Siècle France*, ed. Christopher E. Forth and Elinor Accampo (Palgrave Macmillan, 2010), 135–149. On socialism and feminism, see, for example, Anne Lopes and Gary Roth, *Men's Feminism: August Bebel and the German Socialist Movement* (University of Michigan Press, 2000).
63. Cited in Inge Bleijenbergh and Jet Bussemaker, "The Women's Vote in the Netherlands," in *The Struggle for Female Suffrage in Europe*, ed. Blanca Rodriguez-Ruiz and Ruth Rubio-Marin (Brill, 2012), 175–190, here 179.
64. A valuable overview is Karen M. Offen, *European Feminisms, 1700–1950: A Political History* (Stanford University Press, 2000); Stanton is cited at 153.
65. Rösler, *Die Frauenfrage*, 91. On the composition of this book, see Giesela Breuer, *Frauenbewegung im Katholizismus* (Campus, 1998), 47–48.
66. Friedrich Paulsen, *System der Ethik* (Hertz, 1889). The quote is from the English translation, *A System of Ethics* (Scribner's and Sons, 1889), 625.
67. Rösler, *Die Frauenfrage*, 87.
68. Cited in Karen Offen, *European Feminisms*, 197.
69. The address was published as Elisabeth Gnauck-Kühne, *Die soziale Lage der Frau* (Liebmann, 1895), quotation at 31. On Gnauck-Kühne and her activism, see Baumann, *Protestantismus und Frauenemanzipation*.
70. Steven C. Hause and Anne R. Kenney, "The Development of the Catholic Women's Suffrage Movement in France, 1896–1922," *Catholic Historical Review* 67, no. 1 (January 1981): 11–30.
71. On France, see Emily Machen, *Women of Faith and Religious Identity in Fin-de-Siècle France* (Syracuse University Press, 2019); Odile Sarti, *The Ligue patriotique des françaises: A Feminine Response to the Secularization of French Society* (Garland, 1992). On Germany, see Baumann, *Protestantismus und Frauenemanzipation*. On Austria, see Laura S. Gellot, "Mobilizing Conservative Women: The Viennese 'Katholische Frauenorganisation' in the 1920s," *Austrian History Yearbook* 22 (1991): 110–130.
72. Charles Turgeon, *Le féminisme français* (Larose, 1902), 1:343.
73. Mausbach, *Die Stellung der Frau*.
74. Friedrich Mahling, *Probleme der modernen Frauenfrage* (Agentur des Rauhen Hauses, 1907).

75. Iwan Bloch, *Das Sexualleben unserer Zeit* (Marcus, 1907), 59. Quotation is from the English translation, *The Sexual Life of Our Time* (Falstaff Press, 1937).

76. Cited in Selma Sevenhuijsen, "Mothers as Citizens: Feminism, Evolutionary Theory and the Reform of Dutch Family Law, 1870–1910," in *Regulating Motherhood*, ed. Carol Smart (Routledge, 1992), 166–168, here 183.

77. The process of writing and passing the code is described in Christiane Berneike, *Die Frauenfrage ist Rechtsfrage* (Nomos, 1995), and Ann Taylor Allen, *Feminism and Motherhood in Germany* (Rutgers University Press, 1991), 137–148.

78. Marian van der Klein, "Risks of Labour: Maternity Insurance and Economic Citizenship in Pre-1940 Europe," in *Reciprocity and Redistribution: Work and Welfare Reconsidered*, ed. Gro Hagemann (Pisa University Press, 2007), 87–112.

79. Friedrich Wilhelm Foerster, *Marriage and the Sex Problem* (Gardner, 1911), 79.

80. Rösler, *Die Frauenfrage*, 105.

81. Berneike, *Die Frauenfrage ist Rechtsfrage*; Allen, *Feminism and Motherhood*.

82. Ellen Key, *Love and Marriage* (Putnam, 1911), originally published as *Lifslinger* (Bonnier, 1905).

83. Anna Fischer-Dückelmann, *Das Geschlechtsleben des Weibes* (Bermühler, 1900); Madeleine Pelletier, *L'émancipation sexuelle de la femme* (Giard, 1911). The quote is from Edward Ross Dickinson, *Sex, Freedom, and Power in Imperial Germany, 1880–1914* (Cambridge University Press, 2015), 225.

84. Tracie Matysik, *Reforming the Moral Subject* (Cornell University Press, 2008).

85. Gustav von Rohden, *Ehe und freie Liebe: Ein Wort zum Individualismus in der Frauenfrage* (Warneck, 1911), 110.

86. Joseph Mausbach, *Ehe und Volksvermehrung* (Volksvereins-Verlag, 1916), 8.

87. Arthur Vermeersch, *Probléme de la natalité en Belgique* (Action catholique, 1909), xx.

88. Hermann Roeren, *Die öffentliche Unsittlichkeit und ihre Bekämpfung* (Bachem, 1904). On Roeren and his influence, see Andrew Lees, *Cities, Sin, and Social Reform in Imperial Germany* (University of Michigan Press, 2002).

89. Despite their transnational character, there is no comprehensive or comparative study of Catholic anti-vice campaigns. On Germany, see Edward Ross Dickinson, "The Men's Christian Morality Movement in Germany, 1880–1914," *Journal of Modern History* 75, no. 1 (2003): 59–110. On France, see Annie Stora-Lamarre, *L'enfer de la IIIe Republique: Conseurs et pornographes, 1881–1914* (Imago, 1990), esp. 105–125. On the Netherlands, see Michael Wintle, *An Economic and Social History of the Netherlands, 1800–1920* (Cambridge University Press, 2000), 330–331. On Austria, see Marianne Fischer, *Erotische Literatur vor Gericht* (Braumüller, 2003).

90. Herman Bavinck, *Het christelijk huisgezin* (J. H. Kok, 1908); the quote is from the English translation, *The Christian Family* (Christian Library Press, 2012).

91. Ernst Schultze, *Schundliteratur* (Weisenhaus, 1909). Similar argumentation can be found in, for example, Karl Brunner, *Unserer Volk in Gefahr! Ein Kampfruf gegen die Schundliteratur* (Volkstümliche Bücherei, 1911).

92. On Germany, see Dickinson, "Men's Christian Morality Movement"; on France, see Steven C. Hause, "Social Control in Late Nineteenth-Century France: Protestant Campaigns for Strict Public Morality," in Forth and Accampo, *Confronting Modernity*, 136–149. On the Netherlands, see Wintle, *An Economic and Social History*.

93. Florence Rochefort, "The Abolitionist Struggle of Pastor Tommy Fallot: Between Social Christianity, Feminism, and Secularism," *Women's History Review* 17, no. 2 (2008): 179–194.

94. The conceptual link to socialism is discussed in Dickinson, "Men's Christian Morality Movement."

95. Michel Foucault, *The History of Sexuality*, vol. 1 (Vintage, 1990).
96. Joseph Fonssagrives, *Conseils aux parents et aux maitres sur l'éducation de la puerté* (Poussielgue, 1902). On Fonssagrives and Catholic sexology more broadly, see Lucia Pozzi, *The Catholic Church and Modern Sexual Knowledge, 1850–1950* (Palgrave Macmillan, 2021), esp. 89–120.
97. Bloch, *The Sexual Life of Our Time*.
98. Ibid., 1.
99. Friedrich Wilhelm Foerster, *Sexualethik und Sexualpädagogik* (Kempten, 1907); quote is from the English translation, *Marriage and the Sex Problem* (Stokes, 1912), 25, 37.
100. Foerster, *Marriage*, 25, 32. On the evolution and reception of Foerster's work, see Tracie Matysik, *Reforming the Moral Subject*, esp. 95–115.
101. On the cooperation and disagreements between Maugeret and Bérenger (especially over the question of prostitution's legal status), see Stora-Lamarre, *L'enfer de la IIIe République*, 119–125; Carolyn J. Dean, *The Frail Social Body: Pornography, Homosexuality, and Other Fantasies in Interwar France* (University of California Press, 2000), 34–38.
102. Lotte C. van de Pol, "The History of Policing Prostitution in Amsterdam," in *Regulating Morality*, ed. Hans Krabbendam and Hans-Martien Ten Napel (Maklu, 2000), 97–112, esp. 102–103; Joyce Outshoorn, "The Struggle for Bodily Integrity in the Netherlands," in *European Women's Movements and Body Politics*, ed. Joyce Outshoorn (Palgrave Macmillan, 2015), 52–84.
103. Franz Weigl, *Die interkonfessionellen Männervereine* (Breer und Thiemann, 1910), 129.
104. A smaller Christian congress against pornography took place earlier in Bern, in 1896, but contemporaries referred to the gathering in Paris as the first large-scale event of this kind. Annie Stora-Lamare, "Censorship in Republic Times," in *International Exposure: Perspectives on Modern European Pornography*, ed. Lisa Z. Sigel (Rutgers University Press, 2005), 48–67.
105. On the conceptual justification for these laws, see Chelsea Schields, "Combating the Sensuality of the Youth: Youthful Sexuality and the Reformulation of Desire in the 1911 Dutch Vice Laws," *Gender & History* 31, no. 1 (2019): 115–131. See also J. C. J. Boutellier, "Prostitution, Criminal Law, and Morality in the Netherlands," *Crime, Law, and Social Change* 15, no. 3 (1991): 201–211. Brummelkamp is cited in Schields, "Combating the Sensuality of the Youth," 125.
106. Lynn Abrams, "Prostitutes in Imperial Germany, 1870–1918: Working Girls or Social Outcasts?," in *The German Underworld: Deviants and Outcasts in German History*, ed. Richard Evans (Routledge, 1988), 189–209.
107. Steven C. Hause, "Social Control in Late Nineteenth-Century France: Protestant Campaigns for Strict Public Morality," in Forth and Accampo, *Confronting Modernity*, 136–149; Kenneth Garner and Richard Abel, "Regulating a Risky Business: Film, Censorship, and Public Safety in Prewar France," *Yale French Studies* 122 (2012): 160–185.
108. Richard von Krafft-Ebing, *Psychopathia Sexualis*, 12th ed. (Ferdinand Enke, 1903).
109. Kara L. Ritzheimer, *"Trash," Censorship, and National Identity in Early Twentieth-Century Germany* (Cambridge University Press, 2016), esp. 220–273.
110. Cited in Cornelie Usborne, *The Politics of the Body in Weimar Germany* (Macmillan, 2000), 89, 76.
111. Gideon Reuveni, *Reading Germany: Literature and Consumer Culture in Germany before 1933* (Berghahn, 2005), 221–273; Patrick Major, "'Smut and Trash': Germany's Culture Wars against Pulp Fiction," in *Mass Media, Culture, and Society in Twentieth-Century Germany*, ed. Karl Christian Führer and Corey Ross (Palgrave Macmillan, 2006), 234–250.
112. Van de Pol, "Policing Prostitution in Amsterdam," 102.

113. Paul Smith, *Feminism and the Third Republic* (Clarendon, 1996); Laura Levine Frader, *Breadwinners and Citizens: Gender in the Making of the French Social Model* (Duke University Press, 2008).

114. Cited in Lou Roberts, *Civilization without Sexes* (University of Chicago Press, 1994), 71–72.

115. Arthur Berriedale Keith, *The Belgian Congo and the Berlin Act* (Clarendon, 1919), 304.

116. Gustav Warneck, *Die gegenseitigen Beziehungen zwischen der modernen Mission und Cultur* (Gütersloh, 1879). Quotes are from the English translation, *Modern Missions and Culture: Their Mutual Relations* (Edinburgh, 1883), 327, 331.

117. An important exception that explores the interrelated missionary thinking about work in Europe and Africa is Sebastian Conrad, *Globalisation and the Nation in Imperial Germany* (Cambridge University Press, 2010).

118. Cited in François Renault, *Cardinal Lavigerie* (Athlone, 1994), 138. On Lavigerie and his influence, see, for example, Joseph W. Peterson, *Sacred Rivals: Catholic Missions and the Making of Islam in Nineteenth-Century France and Algeria* (Oxford University Press, 2022), 141–174.

119. Amandus Acker, "Aufgabe der katholische Mission in den Kolonien," *Jahrbuch über die deutschen Kolonien* 2 (1910): 119.

120. Cited in Richard Hölzl, *Gläubige Imperialisten* (Campus Verlag, 2021), 83.

121. Quoted in Jules Chomé, *Indépendance congolaise: Pacifique conquête* (Éditions de Remarques Congolaises, 1960), 5.

122. Carl Büttner, *Kolonialpolitik und Christentum* (Winter, 1885). See also Büttner, "Mission und Kolonien: Vortrag auf der sächsischen Missionskonferenz in Halle 1885," *Allgemeine Missions-Zeitschrift* 12 (1885): 97–104.

123. Carl Paul, *Die Mission in unseren Kolonien* (Richter, 1898), 12.

124. Lothar Dahle, "Wie soll die Verkündigung des Evangeliums durch Missionare beschafen sein, damit sie Boden be den Heiden finde?," in *Verhandlungen der elften kontinentalen Missionskonferenz zu Bremen, Juni 1905* (Buchhandlung der Berliner evangelischen Missionsgesellschaft, 1905), 92–106, here 98, 100.

125. Cited in Peterson, *Sacred Rivals*, 149.

126. Albert Réville, *Prolégomènes de l'Histoire des Religions* (Fischbacher, 1881). The quote is from the English translation, *Prolegomena of the History of Religions* (Williams and Norgate, 1884), 221.

127. Alexander Merensky, "Welche Interesse und welchen Anteil hat die Mission an der Erziehung der Naturvölker zur Arbet?," *Allgemeine Missions-Zeitschrift* 14 (1887): 146–167, here 157.

128. Cited in Miel Groten, "Difference between the Self and the Heathen: European Imperial Culture in Dutch Missionary Exhibitions, 1909–1957," *Journal of Imperial and Commonwealth History* 47, no. 3 (2019): 490–513, here 497.

129. Johannes Warneck, *Die Lebenskräfte des Evangeliums: Missionserfahrungen innerhalb des animistischen Heidentums* (Warneck, 1908).

130. See, for example, Gustav Warneck, "Unsere Stellung zu der modernen Weltevangelisationstheorie," in *Verhandlungen der neunten kontinentalken Missionkonferenz zu Bermen, Mai 1897* (Martin Warneck, 1897), 36–56, as well as 56–63 for the minutes of the discussion that followed, in which similar opinions are expressed. The quote is from Conrad, *Globalisation and the Nation*, 91.

131. *Report of Commission II: The Church in the Mission Field* (Edinburgh, 1910), 262.

132. Norbert Weber, "Ziele und Wege der Eingeborenen-Erziehung," in *Verhandlung des deutschen Kolonialkongress* (Berlin 1910), 673–683, here 674.

133. Amandus Acker, "Die Erziehung der Eingeborenen zur Arbeit," *Jahrbuch über die deutschen Kolonien* 1 (1908): 117–124, here 118.

134. Friedrich Schwanger, "Die Bedeutung der Arbeitserziehung für die Hebung der primitive Rassen," *Zeitschrift für Missionswissenschaft und Religionswissenschaft* 4 (1914): 278–298, here 280. German Catholic missionaries' interest in labor is discussed in Hölzl, *Gläubige Imperialisten*, 59–64.

135. *Missions belges de la Compagnie de Jésus* (December 1900), 453. On Belgian missionaries' approach to labor, see Barbara A. Yates, "The Triumph and Failure of Mission Vocational Education in Zaire, 1879–1908," *Comparative Education Review* 20, no. 2 (June 1976): 193–208.

136. Réville, *Prolegomena*, 222.

137. Carl Mirbt, *Mission und Kolonialpolitik in den deutschen Schutzgebieten* (Mohr, 1910), 103.

138. Leopold Diestelkamp, untitled comments, in *Verhandlungen des deutschen Kolonialkongress 1905* (Dietrich Reimer, 1906), 434–436.

139. Mirbt, *Mission und Kolonialpolitik*, 102.

140. Dietrich von Schwartz, untitled comments, in *Verhandlungen des deutschen Kolonialkongress 1905*, 440–441, here 441.

141. Conrad, *Globalisation and the Nation*, 87.

142. Johannes Warneck, *Die Lebenskräfte*.

143. Mirbt, *Mission und Kolonialpolitik*, 106–110.

144. Ivan de Pierpont, *Au Congo et aux Indes: Les jésuites belges aux missions* (Bulens, 1906), 104. Discussed in Yates, "The Triumph," 198.

145. Cited in Mirbt, *Mission und Kolonialpolitik*, 108.

146. Josef Froberger, "Die Polygamie und deren kulturelle Schäden," in *Verhandluingen des deutschen Kolonialkongresses, 1910*, 629–638.

147. Arthur Vermeersch, *La femme congolaise: Ménagère de blanc, femme de polygame, chrétienne* (Dewit, 1913).

148. Theodor Grentrup, "Die Eheschliessungsformern in den nicht-christlichen Völkern," in *Düsseldorfer Missionskursus*, ed. Friedrich Schwanger (Aachen Xaverius, 1919), 71–82.

149. Cited in Conrad, *Globalisation and the Nation*, 97.

150. Franz Michael Zahn, "Eheordnung für die evangelische Mission," in *Verhandlungen der neunten kontinentalken Missionkonferenz zu Bermen, Mai 1897* (Martin Warneck, 1897), 10.

151. See, for example, the discussion of the topic in Gustav Warneck, *Evangelische Missionslehre* (Perthes 1897) 3:301–317; and in *The Ecumenical Missionary Conference in New York, 1900* (American Tract Society, 1900), 277–281.

152. For a similar shift in missionary tolerance of circumcision, which diminished as the act became considered "uncivilized," see Karolin Wetjen, "Der Körper des Täuflings: Konstryktionen von Körpern und die Bschneidungsdebatte der Leipziger Missionsgesellschaft," in *Der Schwarze Körper als Missionsgebiet*, ed. Linda Ratschiller and Siegfried Weichlein (Böhlau, 2016), 73–94.

153. The most comprehensive study of the missionary approach to polygamy is B. J. Esser, *Zending en polygamie, de gedragslijn der christelijke zending* (Hollandia Drukkerij, 1905).

154. Gustav Warneck, *Evangelische Missionslehre*, 3:301–302.

155. Hubert Hansen, "Welche Aufgabe stellt die Ausbreitung des Islam den Missionen und Ansiedlern in den deutschen Kolonien?," in *Verhandlungen des Deutschen Kolonialkongress 1910* (Reimer, 1910), 659.

156. Josef Froberger, "Welche ist der Kulturwert des Islam fuer koloniale Entwickelung?," in *Verhandluingen des deutschen Kolonialkongresses, 1905*, 529. See also Froberger, "Die Polygamie," 629–638.

157. The letter is reproduced in Charles Lavigerie, *Oeuvres choisies* (Librairie Poussielgue frères, 1884), 165–166.

158. Dietrich Westermann, "Die Berbreitung des Islams in Togo und Kamerun," *Die Welt des Islams* 2, no. 4 (1914): 188–276.

159. Karl Meinhoff, "The Moslem Advance in Africa," in *Islam and Missions: Being Papers Read at the Second Missionary Conference on Behalf of the Mohammedan World at Lucknow, January 23–28, 1911*, ed. E. M. Wherry (Fleming Revell, 1911), 76–99. Similar notions appear in Erich Schultze, *Soll Deutsch-Ostafrika christlich oder mohammedanisch werden?* (Berlin evangelische Verlag, 1913).

160. Gottfried Simon, *De Mohammedaansche Propaganda en de Protestantsche Zending* (De Mildt, 1909). More broadly on Dutch missionaries and their views on Islam, see Karel Steenbrink, *Dutch Colonialism and Indonesian Islam* (Rodopi, 2006), 98–123.

161. Julius Richter, "Der Islam eine Gefahr unsere afrikanischen Kolonien," in *Verhandluingen des deutschen Kolonialkongresses, 1905*, 510–527; Rebekka Habermas, "Islam Debates around 1900," in *Migration and Religion*, ed. Barbara Becker-Cantarino (Rodopi, 2012), 123–154.

162. Mirbt, *Mission und Kolonialpolitik*, 28.

163. Schultze, *Soll Deutsch-Ostafrika christlich*, 48.

164. Eustachius Nagel, untitled comments, in *Verhandlungen des deutschen Kolonialkongress 1905*, 441–442.

165. Esser, *Zending en polygamie*.

166. See, for example, the case discussed in Foster, *Faith in Empire*, 141–168.

167. The centrality of claims for temporal difference in colonialism is explored most famously in Anne McClintock, *Imperial Leather: Race, Gender, and Sexuality in the Colonial Context* (Routledge, 1995).

3. The Birth of Ecumenism from the Crucible of Nazism

1. Friedrich Muckermann, "Katholiken und Protestanten," *Essener Volkszeitung* 8, no. 18 (December 18, 1932), unpaginated.

2. Georg Wünsch, *Evangelische Ethik des Politischen* (Mohr, 1936), 653.

3. My typology here and throughout the chapter draws heavily on James Chappel, *Catholic Modern: The Challenge of Totalitarianism and the Remaking of the Church* (Harvard University Press, 2018).

4. Yves Congar, *Chrétiens désunis: Principes d'un "œcuménisme" catholique* (Éditions du Cerf, 1937). Quotes here are taken from the English translation, *Divided Christendom: A Catholic Study of the Problem of Reunion* (G. Bles, 1939), 88.

5. Doris L. Bergen, *Twisted Cross: The German Christian Movement in the Third Reich* (University of North Carolina Press, 1996), 101–118.

6. Victoria Smolkin, *A Sacred Space Is Never Empty: A History of Soviet Atheism* (Princeton University Press, 2018); Stephen A. Smith, "Bones of Contention: Bolsheviks and the Struggle against Relics," *Past & Present* 204, no. 1 (2009): 155–194; Daniel Peris, *Storming the Heavens: The Soviet League of the Militant Godless* (Cornell University Press, 1998).

7. Stewart A. Stehlin, *Weimar and the Vatican* (Princeton University Press, 1983).

8. Julius Ruiz, *The "Red Terror" and the Spanish Civil War* (Cambridge University Press, 2015).

9. Giuliana Chamedes, *A Twentieth-Century Crusade: The Vatican's Battle to Remake Christian Europe* (Harvard University Press, 2019); Pius XI, *Divini redemptoris* (March 19, 1937), available at https://www.vatican.va/content/pius-xi/en/encyclicals/documents/hf_p-xi _enc_19370319_divini-redemptoris.html.

10. The information on the committee is taken from Stadtarchiv Mönchengladbach, Algermissen papers, no. 15/7/5. More broadly, see Heinz Hürten, *Deutsche Katholiken* (Paderborn, 1992); Stefan Ummenhofer, *Wie Feuer und Wasser? Katholizismus und Sozialdemokratie in der Weimarer Republik* (Berlin, 2003); Horstwalter Heitzer, "Deutscher Katholizismus und 'Bolschewismusgefahr' bis 1933," *Historisches Jahrbuch* 113 (1993).

11. Henri Massis and Robert Brasillach, *Les cadets de l'Alcazar* (Plon, 1936). On the text's reception, see Philippe Chenaux, *L'église catholique et le communisme en Europe* (Éditions du Cerf, 2009).

12. From the source collection "Fear of Communism: Anti-Communism in Belgium," University of Leuven, https://kadoc.kuleuven.be/pdf/publicaties/expo/expo28.pdf, p. 26.

13. The information on the German churches' campaign and list of sponsored publications is based on microfiche 1639–1941, EZA 5/124, Ecclesiastical Protestant Archives of Germany, Berlin.

14. E. H. Kossmann, *The Low Countries* (Clarendon, 1978), 603–606.

15. International Social Institute, *The Churches and the World Economic Crisis: Report of the International Study Conference on Unemployment, Basel, April 25–29, 1932* (Life and Work, 1932).

16. Cited in Kurt Böhme, "Das Weltgewissen gegen Russland: Die Stimme der christlichen Kirchen zu den Religionsverglogungen," in *Notbuch der russischen Christenheit*, ed. Karl Cramer (Eckart, 1930), 229–241, here 235.

17. Report, "Der Paritätische Ausgleichsausschuss" (March 16, 1933), EZA 1/721.

18. Hilaire Belloc, *Crisis of Civilization* (Fordham University Press, 1937); Matthes Ziegler, *Der Protestantismus zwischen Rom und Moskau* (Hoheneichen, 1937).

19. Speech in Munich, October 25, 1930, in *Adolf Hitler: Reden, Schriften, Anordnungen*, vol. 4, pt. 1, ed. Constantin Goschler (Munich: Saur, 1996), 33. For a discussion of National Socialist confessional politics, see Todd H. Weir, "Hitler's Worldview and the Interwar Kulturkampf," *Journal of Contemporary History* 53 (2018): 597–621. Scholarship on the Nazi approach to Christianity is vast. For two good summaries, see Doris L. Bergen, "Nazism and Christianity: Partners and Rivals?," and Manfred Gailus, "A Strange Obsession with Nazi Christianity," both *Journal of Contemporary History* 42, no. 1 (2007), 25–33, 35–46.

20. Adolf Hitler, *Hitler: Reden und Proklamationen, 1932–1945* (Löwith, 1974), vol. 1, pt. 1, 82.

21. Adolf Hitler, *Mein Kampf* (Institut für Zeitgeschichte, 2016), 1:213–215.

22. Quotes from the party programs are taken from "The Program of the German Works' Party: The Twenty-Five Points," in *The Third Reich Sourcebook*, ed. Anson Rabinbach and Sander L. Gilman (University of California Press, 2014), 12–14, here 14. Hitler's speech is quoted in Richard Steigmann-Gall, *The Holy Reich: Nazi Conceptions of Christianity* (Cambridge University Press, 2003), 60–61.

23. For interesting reflections on Hitler and Christianity, see Weir, "Hitler's Worldview"; Derek Hastings, *Catholicism and the Roots of Nazism* (Oxford University Press, 2010); Samuel Koehne, "The Racial Yardstick: 'Ethnotheism' and Official Nazi Views on Religion," *German Studies Review* 37 (2014): 575–596.

24. Cited in Ludwig Volk, *Das Reichskonkordat* (Grünewald, 1972), n25.

25. Robert Grosche, "Die dialektische Theologie und der Katholizismus," *Catholica* 1 (1932): 1–18; Grosche, "Der sakrale Raum," *Catholica* 2 (1933): 91–94.

26. Robert Grosche, *Pilgernde Kirche* (Herder, 1938), 116.

27. Damasus Winzen, "Gedanken zu einer Theologie der Reiches," *Catholica* 2 (1933): 97–116, here 100, 108. See also Winzen, "Mythus des Blutes und Mysterium des Blutes," *Liturgisches Leben* 1, no. 1 (1934): 2–10. For *Catholica*'s early efforts at ecumenism, see, for example, Walter Dirks, "Das Gebot und die Ordnung," and Auguste Schorn, "Die Theologie

des Reiches und der deutsche Katholizismus," both *Catholica* 2 (1933): 61–72, 73–81. See also Damasus Winzen, "Die sakramentalehre der Kirche in ihrem Verhältnis zur dialektischen Theologie," *Catholica* 1 (1932): 19–36; Albert Mirgeler, "Der geschichtliche Auftrag der Reformation," *Catholica* 3 (1934): 145–159.

28. Alois Hudal, *Deutsches Volk und christliches Abendland* (Tyrolia, 1935), 20. For Hudal's efforts to reconcile German nationalism and Catholicism, see, for example, Hudal, *Rom, Chrisentum, und deutsches Volk* (Tyrolia, 1935).

29. The quote is from Karl Adam, *The Spirit of Catholicism* (Macmillan, 1937), 177. The book was originally published in 1924 but was revised and republished in several editions in the 1930s. For further examples, see also James Chappel, "The Fascist Origins of German Ecumenism," in *Germany and the Confessional Divide*, ed. Mark Edward Ruff and Thomas Grossbölting (Berghahn, 2022), 125–144.

30. Alfred Dedo Müller, *Der Kampf um das Reich* (Brönner, 1935), 9.

31. Alfred Dedo Müller, *Ethik* (Töppelmann, 1937), 451–452.

32. Johannes Lortzing, *Um die Glaubenseinheit* (Schlusche, 1934). See also Lortzing, "Für die Wiedervereinigung der Protestanten mit Rom 2," *Schönere Zukunft* 8, no. 22 (February 26, 1933): 506–507.

33. Hermann Sauer, *Abendländische Entscheidung: Aryscher Mythus und christliche Wirklichkeit* (Hinrichs, 1938).

34. Matthias Wolfes, *Protestantische Theologie und moderne Welt* (De Gruyter, 1999), 341–366.

35. Joseph Lortz, *Katholischer Zugang zum Nationalsozialismus, kirchengeschichtlich gesehen* (Münster, 1933); Lortz, *Geschichte der Kirche in Ideengeschichtlicher Betrachtung* (Aschendorff, 1936); Lortz, *Die Reformation in Deutschland* (Herder, 1938–1939). The chapters on Nazism were conveniently omitted from the English translation, *The History of the Church* (Bruce, 1938). On Lortz's relationship to the Nazis, see Robert A. Krieg, *Catholic Theologians in Nazi Germany* (Continuum, 2004), 56–82.

36. Joseph Lortz, *Die Reformation: Thesen als Handreichung bei Okumenischen Gesprächen* (Kyrios, 1941).

37. August Winnig, *Europa: Gedanken eines Deutsches* (Eckart, 1938), 88.

38. Muckermann, "Katholiken und Protestanten." Republished in *Schönere Zukunft* 18, no. 8 (January 29, 1933): 412. See also Johannes Lortzing, "Für die Wiedervereinigung der Protestanten mit Rom," *Schönere Zukunft* 8, no. 20 (February 12, 1933): 449–451. On Eberle's shift, see Peter Eppel, *Zwischen Kreuz und Hakenkreuz* (Böhlau, 1980), 193–196.

39. On the committee, see Stéphanie Roulin, "A Martyr Factory? Roman Catholic Crusade, Protestant Missions, and Anti-Communist Propaganda against Soviet Anti-Religious Policies, 1929–1937," *Twentieth Century Communism* 7 (July 2014): 153–173, esp. 162; Ewald Ammende, *Muss Russland hungern?* (Baumüller, 1935).

40. Hans Eibl, *Vom Sinn der Gegenwart: Ein Buch von deutscher Sendung* (Braumüller, 1933). The quote is from Eibl, "Lehren aus dem Aufstief des Nationalsozialismus," *Schönere Zukunft* 7, no. 33 (May 15, 1932): 759–761 and 790–792, here 759. Eibl's influence is discussed in Janek Wasserman, *Black Vienna: The Radical Right in the Red City, 1918–1938* (Cornell University Press, 2014).

41. Paul Couturier, "Pour l'unité des chrétiens: Psychologie de l'octave de prières du 18 au 25 janvier," reprinted in Couturier, *Oecuménisme spirituel* (Casterman, 1963), 46–63, which also includes some of Couturier's other ecumenical essays. On the establishment of the discussion groups, see Geoffrey Curtis, *Paul Couturier and Unity in Christ* (SCM, 1964), esp. 225–237, 251–257.

42. Noël Vesper, *L'invention de l'Europe* (Terrasses, 1932). On the magazine *Sully*, see Robert Zaretsky, *Nimes at War* (University of Pennsylvania Press, 1995), 20–26.

43. Martin Conway, *Collaboration in Belgium: Léon Degrelle and the Rexist Movement* (Yale University Press, 1993).

44. François de la Rocque, *Service public* (Éditions Bernard Grasset, 1934), 98.

45. Sean Kennedy, *Reconciling France against Democracy: The Croix de Feu and the Parti social français, 1927–1945* (McGill-Queen's University Press, 2007); Caroline Campbell, *Political Belief in France, 1927–1945* (LSU Press, 2015).

46. Henri Massis, *Defense of the West* (Harcourt, Brace, 1928); Massis, *Découverte de la Russie* (Lardanchet, 1944). On the genesis of Massis's conception of the West, see Paul Mazgaj, "Defending the West: The Cultural and Generational Politics of Henri Massis," *Historical Reflections/Réflexions historiques* 17, no. 2 (1991): 103–121. On the shift in his writings in the 1940s, see Chappel, *Catholic Modern*, 101.

47. John Hellman, *The Knight-Monks of Vichy France* (McGill-Queen's University Press, 1993).

48. On the youth movements, see W. D. Halls, *Politics, Society, and Christianity in Vichy France* (Berg, 1995), 296–297; Emily Marker, *Black France, White Europe: Youth, Race, and Belonging in Postwar France* (Cornell University Press, 2022), 68–73. On education, see Nicholas Atkin, "Church and Teachers in Vichy France, 1940–1944," *French History* 4 (1990): 1–22, here 13.

49. Cited in Ethan Katz, "Secular French Nationhood and Its Discontents: Jews as Muslims and Religion as Race in Occupied France," in *Secularism in Question,* ed. Ari Joskowicz and Ethan Katz (University of Pennsylvania Press, 2015), 168–188, here 174.

50. Albert Mirgeler, "Der Einbruch des Judentums in die christliche Geschichte," *Catholica* 2 (1933): 117–124.

51. Karl Adam, "Deutsches Volkstum und katholisches Christentum," *Theologische Quartalschrift* 14 (1933): 40–64, here 47. On Adam, see Kevin Spicer, *Hitler's Priests: Catholic Clergy and National Socialism* (University of Illinois Press, 2008).

52. Müller, *Ethik,* 317.

53. *Sully,* July 1938.

54. Jacques Maritain, *Integral Humanism* (University of Notre Dame Press, 1996 [1936]), 143–345.

55. Congar, *Divided Christendom,* 88.

56. Ibid., 222.

57. Ibid., 223.

58. Ibid., 275.

59. Étienne Fouilloux, *Les catholiques et l'unité chrétienne du XIXe au XXe siècle* (Le Centurion, 1982), 238.

60. Nancy Sanders Gower, "Reformed and Ecumenical: The Foundation of the Community of Taizé" (PhD diss., Fuller Theological Seminary, 2010).

61. Sarah Shortall, *Soldiers of God in a Secular World: Catholic Theology and Twentieth-Century French Politics* (Harvard University Press, 2021), esp. 88, 110–112.

62. The formation of the interconfessional alliance is described in Geoffrey Adams, *Political Ecumenism: Catholics, Jews, and Protestants in de Gaulle's Free France* (McGill-Queen's University Press, 2006); Rémi Fabre, "De Gaulle et les protestants," in *Charles de Gaulle: Chrétien, homme d'état* (Foundation Charles de Gaulle, 2011), 351–370. The quote is from Adams, *Political Ecumenism,* 48.

63. Arnold Rademacher, *Wiedervereinigung der christlichen Kirchen* (Peter Hanstein, 1937), 73.

64. Ibid, 18.

65. See, for example, Max Metzger, *Der Himmel in uns* (Kattowitz Katholische Buchdruckerei, 1938); Metzger, "Aufbruch zu Una Sancta," *Theologie und Glaube* 33, no. 1

(1941): 16–22, here 3. Some of Metzger's writings were published later in Metzger, *Was trennt uns Christen?* (Augsburg Christkönigsgesellschaft vom Weissen Kreuz, 1948). On Metzger's shifting attitudes to the Third Reich, see Dagmar Pöpping, *Abendland: Christliche Akademiker und die Utopie der Antimoderne, 1900–1945* (Metropol, 2002), 187–199. On his ecumenism, see Christian Hess, *Ohne Christus, ohne tiefstes Christentum ist Krieg: Die Christkönigsthematik als Leitidee im kirchlich-gesellschaftlichen Engagement Max Josef Metzgers* (Bonifatius, 2016), esp. 297–323.

66. Wilhelm Stählin, *Das Reich als Gleichnis* (Aschendorffsche, 1933), 4–5. See also Stählin, *Kirche und Menschenbildung* (Buchdrückerei des Eckartshauses, 1933).

67. Wilhelm Stählin, *Die Kirche Jesu Christi und das Wort Gottes* (Furche, 1937), 144. See also Stählin, *Mysterium: Vom geheimniss Gottes* (Stauda, 1936), which also appeared in English as *The Mystery of God* (Concordia, 1936).

68. *Die Ordnung der deutschen Messe* (Stauda, 1936).

69. Johannes Österreicher, "Die Kirche Christi und die Judenfrage," *Die Erfüllung* 2, no. 5–6 (1937): 3–32; Emil Brunner, "Zur Judenfrage," *Neue Schweizer Rundschau* 3, no. 7 (1935): 385–397, here 390. On the Catholic project against racist anti-Semitism, see John Connelly, *From Enemy to Brother* (Harvard University Press, 2012), 152–160.

70. Winnig, *Europa*, 55.

71. On the institution of corporatism in Europe in the 1930s, see Antonio Costa Pinto, *Corporatism and Fascism: The Corporatist Wave in Europe* (Routledge, 2019).

72. Josef Pieper, *Das Arbeitsrecht des neuen Reiches und die Enzyklika Quadragesimo anno* (Aschendorff, 1934), 6.

73. Pius XI, *Quadragesimo anno* (May 15, 1931), 15, https://www.vatican.va/content /pius-xi/en/encyclicals/documents/hf_p-xi_enc_19310515_quadragesimo-anno.html.

74. Theodor Brauer, *Der Katholik im neuen Reich* (Kösel und Pustet, 1933), 67.

75. François Perroux, *Capitalisme et communauté de travail* (Librairie du Recueil Sirey, 1938). The Catholic response to Vichy's policies is discussed in Halls, *Politics, Society, and Christianity*, 241–268.

76. Jean Denis, *Bases doctrinales de Rex* (Rex, 1936); Conway, *Collaboration in Belgium*.

77. Alfred Müller-Armack, *Entstehungsgesetze des Kapitalismus* (Junker und Dünnhaupt, 1932); Müller-Armack, *Staatsidee und Wirtschaftsordnung im neuen Reich* (Junker und Dünnhaupt, 1933). For background, see Young-Sun Hong, *Welfare, Modernity, and the Weimar State* (Princeton University Press, 1998), 203–232.

78. Hans Scherpner, *Fürsorge und Politik* (C. Heymann, 1933).

79. Klaus Erich Pollmann, "Der Evangelische-Soziale Kongress in der Zeit des Nationalsozialismus," in *Sozialer Protestantismus im Nationalsozialismus*, ed. Nobert Friedrich and Traugott Jähnichen (Lit, 2003), 11–24. Additional Protestant publications that praised Nazi economic policies are reviewed in Heinz-Dietrich Wendland, "Zur Lage der Sozialethik," *Seelsorge* 10 (1934): 219–229.

80. René Gillouin, "Pétain," in *France 1941: La révolution nationale constructive*, ed. André Bellessort (Éditions Alsatia, 1941), 79–80.

81. Otto Schilling, *Die christlichen Soziallehren* (Oratoriums, 1926).

82. Otto Schilling, *Apologie der katholischen Moral* (Schöningh, 1936), esp. 196–219.

83. Kurt Ihlenfeld (ed.), *Die Stunde des Christentums: Eine deutsche Besinnung* (Eckart, 1936).

84. Georg Wünsch, *Evangelische Wirtschaftsethik* (Mohr, 1927).

85. Georg Wünsch, *Evangelische Ethik des Politischen* (Mohr, 1936), 653.

86. Müller, *Ethik*.

87. Cited in Hong, *Welfare, Modernity*, 188.

88. Wünsch, *Evangelische Ethik des Politischen*, 608–609; Rudolf Craemer, *Evangelische Reformation als politische Macht* (Vandenhoeck und Ruprecht, 1933); Craemer, *Der Kampf um die Volksordnung von der preussischen Sozialpolitik zum deutschen Sozialismus* (Hanseatische, 1933).

89. These publications are discussed in Vera Bücker, *Nikolaus Gross: Politischer Journalist und Katholik im Widersand des Kölner Kreises* (Lit, 2003).

90. See, for example, Ernst Karl Winter, "Christentum oder Sozialismus?," *Wiener Politische Blätter* 4 (1936): 1–11. Winter's trajectory and influence are discussed in Chappel, *Catholic Modern*, 123–128.

91. Halls, *Politics, Society, and Christianity*, 251.

92. Walter Eucken, "Staatliche Strukturwandlungen und die Krisis des Kapitalismus," *Weltwirtschaftliches Archiv* 36 (1932): 297–321; Eucken, *Grundlagen der Nationalökonomie* (Fischer, 1940). See also Franz Böhm, *Die Ordnung der Wirtschaft als geschichtliche Aufgabe und rechtsschöpferische Leistung* (Kohlhammer, 1937).

93. Wilhelm Röpke, *Die Lehre von der Wirtschaft* (Springer, 1937); Röpke, *Die Gesellschaftskrisis der Gegenwart* (Rentsch, 1941).

94. Scholarship on the early years of the ordo-liberals is vast, though the role of Protestant social theory in their writings has not been explored in detail. For initial efforts, see Philip Manow, "Ordoliberalismus als ökonomische Ordnungstheologie," *Leviathan* 29, no. 2 (2001): 179–198; Tim Petersen, "Emil Brunner's Social Ethics and Its Reception in Ordoliberal Circles," in *60 Years of Social Market Economy*, ed. Christian L. Glossner (Konrad-Adenauer-Stiftung, 2010), 43–68.

95. Joseph Höffner, *Wirtschaftsethik und Monopolie im fünfzehnten und sechzehnten Jahrhundert* (Fischer, 1941).

96. Walter Eucken [K. Heinrich, pseud.], "Zur Kritik des Sozialismus," *Die Tatwelt* 1, no. 4 (April 1925): 40–42.

97. Röpke, *Die Gesellschaftskrisis*, 8.

98. Adolf Hitler, "The Task of Women," in *Nazi Culture*, ed. George Mosse (University of Wisconsin Press, 1966), 39–40.

99. Scholarship on the Nazis and their allies' approach to gender is vast. For helpful overviews, see, for example, Jill Stephenson, *Women in Nazi Germany* (Routledge, 2001); Miranda Pollard, *Reign of Virtue: Mobilizing Gender in Vichy France* (University of Chicago Press, 1998); Rachel G. Fuchs, *Contested Paternity: Constructing Families in Modern France* (Johns Hopkins University Press, 2008), 240–257.

100. Dagmar Herzog, *Sex after Fascism* (Princeton University Press, 2005); Julia Roos, "Backlash against Prostitutes' Rights: Origins and Dynamics of Nazi Prostitution Policies," *Journal of the History of Sexuality* 11, no. 2 (2002): 67–94.

101. Jacques Leclercq, *La famille* (Société d'études morales, 1935). Quotes are from the English translation, *Marriage and the Family* (Pustet, 1937), 19.

102. Leclercq, *Marriage and the Family*, 17.

103. Ibid., 159.

104. Ibid., 227

105. Ibid., 246

106. Pius XI, *Casti connubii* (December 31, 1930), https://www.vatican.va/content/pius-xi/en/encyclicals/documents/hf_p-xi_enc_19301231_casti-connubii.html.

107. Hermann Muckermann, *Eugenik und Katholizismus* (Dümmlers, 1934), 4. See Herzog, *Sex after Fascism*, 42–44.

108. Alexis Carrel, *L'homme, cet inconnu* (Plon, 1935).

109. Ingrid Richter, *Katholizismus und Eugenik in der Weimarer Republik und im Dritten Reich* (Schöningh, 2001), 337–349; Andrés Horacio Reggiani, *God's Eugenicist: Alexis Carrel and the Sociobiology of Decline* (Berghahn, 2007).

110. Wilhelm Stapel, "Eigentum und Sozialismus," *Deutsches Volkstum* 34 (1932): 701–709; Stapel, "Die Einehe," *Deutsche Volkstum* 31 (1929): 641–648, here 645.

111. Wilhelm Stapel, *Die Kirche Christi und der Staat Adolf Hitlers* (Hanseatische, 1933), 86. Stapel's ideas on families have not received much scholarly attention. For a brief discussion, see Stefan Breuer, *Ordnungen der Ungleichheit: De deutsche Rechte im Widersreit ihrer Ideen* (Wissenschaftliche, 2001), 249–250.

112. Hans Harmsen, "Grudsätzliches unserer Arbeit: Bevölkerungspolitische Neuorientierung unserer Gesundheitsfürsorge," *Gessundheitsfürsorge* 5 (1931): 3–4; Annette F. Timm, *The Politics of Fertility in Twentieth-Century Berlin* (Cambridge University Press, 2010), 106–107.

113. René Gillouin, "Responsabilité des écrivains et des artistes," *Journal de Genève* 8–9 (February 1942): 3. Gillouin's writings on family and reproduction are discussed in Francine Muel-Dreyfus, *Vichy and the Eternal Feminine* (Duke University Press, 2001), esp. 35–36.

114. Cited in Herzog, *Sex after Fascism*, 48; see 44–50 for Christian complaints about Nazi promiscuity.

115. Leclercq, *Marriage and the Family*, 205.

116. Pollard, *Reign of Virtue*, 170. See also Christophe Capuano, *Vichy et la famille* (Presses Universitaies de Rennes), 149–175.

117. Winfried Süss, "Antagonistische Cooperation: Katholische Kirche und nationalsozialistisches Gesundheitswesen in den Kriegsharen, 1939–1945," in *Kirchen im Krieg: Europa, 1939–1945*, ed. Karl-Joseph Hummel and Christoph Kösters (Schöningh, 2009), 317–341.

118. See, for example, Bernhard Bavink, *Die Naturwissenschaft auf dem Wege zur Religion* (Diesterweg, 1933).

119. Hermann Muckermann, "Eugenik und Volkswohfahrt," and Bernhard Bavink, "Eugenik und Welanschaaung," both in *Erblehre—Erbpflege*, ed. Zentralinstitut für Erziehung und Unterricht (E. S. Mittler, 1933), 24–39, 92–102, quotes at 99.

120. Josef Becking, *Der Eheliche Mensch* (Pustet, 1938).

121. Leclercq, *Family and Marriage*, 227.

122. Theodor Haug, *Im Ringen um Reinheit und Reife* (Steinkopf, 1930).

123. Müller, *Ethik*, 264, 286–287.

124. Emmanuel Mounier, *Manifeste au service du personalisme* (Montaigne, 1936); quote is from the English translation, *A Personalist Manifesto* (Longmans, 1938), 107–109. See also Mounier, "La femme aussi est une personne," *Esprit* 45, no. 4 (June 1936): 291–297; this article was part of a special issue edited by Mounier, dedicated to egalitarian sex relations and featuring essays by feminists such as Marguerite Grépon.

125. Emil Brunner, *Das Wort Gottes und der moderne Mensch* (Zwingli, 1937). The quote is from the English translation, *Man in Revolt* (Westminster, 1938), 379.

126. Brunner, *Man in Revolt*, 355.

127. Emil Brunner, *Justice and the Social Order* (Harper, 1943), 143. Brunner's writings on marriage and sexuality are usually overlooked by scholars, but some brief reflections on them can be found in Don S. Browning and John Witte Jr., "Emil Brunner," in *Christianity and Family Law*, ed. John Witte Jr. and Gary S. Hauk (Cambridge University Press, 2017), 307–322.

128. On Hildebrand and the reception of his work, see Chappel, *Catholic Modern*, 115–123.

129. Herbert Doms, *Vom Sinn und Zweck der Ehe* (Ostdeutsche, 1935); the quote is from the English translation, *The Meaning of Marriage* (Sheed and Ward, 1939), 7.

130. Norbert Rocholl, *Die Ehe als Geweihtes Leben* (Dülmen, 1936); Franz Zimmermann, *Die beiden Geschlechter in der Absicht Gottes* (Grünewald, 1936).

131. Emil Brunner, *Das Gebot und die Ordnungen* (Mohr, 1932). The quote is taken from the English translation, *The Divine Imperative* (Lutterworth, 1937), 364, 367.

132. Otto Piper, *Sinn und Geheimnis der Geschlechter* (Furche, 1935). The quotes are from the English translation, *The Biblical View of Sex and Marriage* (Scribner, 1941), 105, 123.

133. Denis de Rougemont, *L'amour et l'Occident* (Plon, 1939).

134. Theodor Bovet, *Not und Liebe in der Ehe* (Rascher, 1939).

135. Paul Tournier, *Medicine de la personne* (Delachaux et Niestlé, 1940).

136. Matthias Laros's most important writings on marriage and sexuality are "Revolutionierung der Ehe," *Hochland* 27 (1930): 193–207; and *Moderne Ehefrage* (Staufen, 1936). Laros's role in interconfessionalism is discussed briefly in Robert Krieg, *Catholic Theologians*, 79.

137. Wilhelm Stählin, "Die Mischehe," in *Der Kampf um die Ehe*, ed. Gustav Schlipköter and Albert Böhme (Bertelsmann, 1929), 148–163.

138. Stählin, *The Mystery of God*, 192, 195.

139. Ibid., 195.

140. Ibid., 196.

141. *Hitler's Table Talk: 1941–1944* (Enigma Books, 2000), 23–24.

142. Adolf Hitler, *Mein Kampf* (Franz Eher, 1933), 446.

143. There is vast scholarship on the anti-colonial critique of the civilizing mission in the interwar period. For an overview (which also discusses the cases of Japan and South Asia), see Cemil Aydin, *The Politics of Anti-Westernism in Asia: Visions of World Order in Pan-Islamic and Pan-Asian Thought* (Columbia University Press, 2007). The links between some Asian anti-nationalists and the Third Reich are explored in David Motadel, "The Global Authoritarian Moment and the Revolt against Empire," *American Historical Review* 124, no. 3 (2019): 843–877.

144. On anti-Christian agitation in China, see Rebecca Nedostup, *Superstitious Regimes: Religion and the Politics of Chinese Modernity* (Harvard University Press, 2009). The missionary response to it is reconstructed in Albert Wu, *From Christ to Confucius: German Missionaries, Chinese Christianity, and the Globalization of Christianity, 1860–1950* (Yale University Press, 2016), 137–160.

145. The first quote, originally from 1929, is from Clifford Manschardt (ed.), *The Mahatma and the Missionary: Selected Writing of Mohandas Gandhi* (Regenry, 1949), 70. The second quote is from Susan Billington Harper, *In the Shadow of the Mahatma: Bishop V. S. Azariah and the Travails of Christianity in British India* (Taylor and Francis, 2000), 138.

146. Siegfried Knak, *Mission und naionale Bewegung* (Komissionsverlag, 1933).

147. Siegfried Knak, *Zwischen Nil und Tafelbai: Eine Studie über Evangelium, Volkstum und Zivilisation am Beispiel der Missionsproblem unter den Bantu* (Heimatdienstverlag, 1931), esp. 215–243, quote at 115. Some of these claims echoed the works of the German missionary Bruno Gutmann, which received renewed attention in the 1930s. See, for example, Bruno Gutmann, *Das Recht der Dschagga* (Beck, 1936).

148. The sympathies of many Protestant missionary elites for the Nazis are discussed briefly in Werner Ustorf, *Sailing on the Next Tide: Missions, Missiology, and the Third Reich* (Lang, 200).

149. Dietrich Westermann, *Der Afrikaner heute und morgen* (Essener, 1934). The quote is from the English version, *The African Today and Tomorrow* (International Institute of African Languages and Cultures, 1934), 26. See also Westermann, *Africa and Christianity* (Oxford University Press, 1935).

150. Walter Freytag, *Die junge Christenheit im Umbruch des Ostens: Von Gehorsam des Glaubens under den Völkern* (Furche, 1938).

151. *Verhandlungen der 18. Kontinentalen Missionskonferenz zu Bremen vom 19–23 Mai 1938* (Missionsverlag der Norddeutschen Missionsgesellschaft, 1938), esp. 12–17.
152. Freytag, *Die junge christenheit*, 257.
153. Westermann, *The African Today and Tomorrow*, 165, and more broadly, 148–166.
154. Walter Braun, *Heidenmission und Nationalsozialismus* (Heimatdienst, 1932), 15.
155. Wilhelm Schmidt, *Der Ursprung der Gottesidee: Eine historisch-kritische und positivie Studie* (Aschendorffsche, 1926–1955).
156. On Schmidt's early work, and its place in the broader history of cultural anthropology, see Suzanne Marchand, "Priests among the Pygmies: Wilhelm Schmidt and the Counter-Reformation in Austrian Ethnology," in *Worldly Provincialism: German Anthropology in the Age of Empire*, ed. H. Glenn Penny and Matti Bunzl (University of Michigan Press, 2003), 283–315.
157. Wilhelm Schmidt, *Rasse und Volk* (Pustet, 1935), 42. On Schmidt and his students' response to Nazi racial theory, see Reinhard Blumauer, "Wilhelm Schmidt und die Wiener Schule der Ethnologie," in *Völkerkunde zur NS-Zeit aus Wien, 1938–1945*, ed. Andre Gingrich and Peter Rohrbacher (Verlag der Österreichischen Akademie der Wissenschaft, 2017), 37–62.
158. Schmidt, *Rasse und Volk*, 43.
159. Albert Drexel, *Die Rassen der Menschheit: Eine Einführung in das Problem* (Felizian Rauch, 1935). On the Vatican's interest in Schmidt's and Drexel's writings, see Peter Rohrbacher, "Österreichische Missionsexperten und das Ringen um den vatikanischen Standpunkt im 'Rassendiskurs' der Zwischenkriegszeit," *Römische Historische Mitteilungen* 62 (2020): 221–248.
160. Paul Schebesta, *Vollblutneger und Halbzwerge* (Pustet, 1936). The quote is from the English translation, *My Pygmy and Negro Hosts* (Hutchinson, 1938), 277. See also Schebesta, *Die Bambuti-Pygmaen vom Ituri: Ergebnisse zweier Forschungsreisen den zentralafrikanischen Pygmaen* (Capenhout, 1938).
161. The most famous articulation of these ideas appeared in Barth's *Epistle of the Romans*, which appeared originally in 1919 and in revised and expanded version in 1922.
162. See Hendrik Kraemer, "Christianity and Secularism," *International Review of Missions* 19 (1930): 195–208; Kraemer, "Imperialism and Self-Expression," *Student World* 28 (1935): 328–348; Kraemer, *De wirteken van het syncretism* (Boekencentrum, 1938).
163. Hendrik Kraemer, *The Christian Message in a Non-Christian World* (International Missionary Council, 1938), 313, 37.
164. Ibid., 325.
165. The information about the distribution of Kraemer's book and its abbreviated versions are based on the document "List of Distribution of Kraemer's Book" (undated, probably early 1938), folder 5, box 262.007; and the pamphlet, "Shortened Version of Dr. Hendrik Kraemer's *Christian Message in a Non-Christian World*," box 262.001; both in World Council of Churches Archives, Ecumenical Center, Geneva, Switzerland. The International Missionary Council considered the discussion of the book so important that it published a special collection of reflections on it by missionary leaders from around the world, *The Authority of the Faith* (Oxford University Press, 1939). Also see the discussion of Kraemer's book at the European conference in *Verhandlungen der 18. Kontinentalen Missionskonferenz zu Bremen vom 19–23 Mai 1938* (Missionsverlag der Norddeutschen Missionsgesellschaft, 1938), 17–19. The discussion at the international conference in Tambaram is reconstructed in Ludwig Frieder, *Zwischen Kolonialismuskritik und Kirchenkampf: Interaktionen afrikanischer, indischer und europäischer Christen während der Weltmissionskonferenz in Tambaram 1938* (Vandenhoeck und Ruprecht, 2000), esp. 305–319.
166. Willem Visser 't Hooft, *None Other Gods* (Harper, 1937), 85.

167. Karl Hartenstein, *Die Mission als theologisches Problem* (Furche Verlag, 1933). See also Hartenstein's reflections on Kraemer's book in Hartenstein, "The Biblical View of Religion," in International Missionary Council, *The Authority of the Faith*, 126–147.

168. Pierre Charles, *Les protocoles des sages de Sion* (Casterman, 1938). Charles had already expressed skepticism about the document in the 1920s, but the rise of Nazism and the popularity of anti-Semitism among Catholics across Europe led him to expand and update his tract in the 1930s. See Maurice Olender, *Race and Erudition* (Harvard University Press, 2009), 9–30.

169. Pierre Charles, *Racisme et catholicisme* (Casterman, 1939).

170. Cited in Connelly, *From Enemy to Brother*, 54.

171. Pierre Charles, *Le dossier de l'action missionnaire: Manuel de missiologie* (Éditions de l'Aucam, 1938), esp. 77–81, 85–88, 101–109; quotation at 87–88. See also Charles, *Missiologie* (Desclée De Brouwer, 1939).

172. Pascal M. D'Elia, "La doctrine du mariage dans la Chine d'autrefois et dans celle d'aujourd'hui," in *Mariage et famille aux missions: Compte rendu de la douzième semaine de missiologie de Louvain*, ed. Pierre Charles (Museum Lessianum, 1934), 43–57; Bernard Zuure, "Missie en ontspanning: Sport en spel bij de Barundi," in *Expectatio Gentium: Compte rendu de la XIIIe semaine de missiologie de Louvain 1935* (Brouwer, 1936), 224–251. Similar themes were also at the center of the missionary congress of the Belgian organization Aucam; see *Le deuxième congrès de l'Aucam, 13-14-15 avril 1935* (Éditions de l'Aucam, 1835).

173. Kraemer, *The Christian Message*, 215–226. Christianity's difference from Islam was also the topic of Kraemer's presentation to the pan-European missionary conference in Bremen in 1938; see *Verhandlungen der 18. Kontinentalen Missionskonferenz zu Bremen*, 17–18.

174. The quote is from Gottfried Simon, "Der Islam als Missionsgegner," in *Das Buch der deutschen Weltmission*, ed. Julius Richter (Klotz, 1935), 37–41, here 41; Johannes Witte, *Die Christus-Botschaft und die Religionen* (Vanderhoeck und Ruprecht, 1936).

175. Pierre Charles, "Discours d'ouverture," in Charles, *Mariage et famille aux missions*, 11–13, here 12.

176. Westermann, *The African Today and Tomorrow*, 1.

177. Siegfried Knak, *Wiederaufbau in Ostafrika* (Berliner evangelisch. Mission, 1930), 12–15. For similar sentiments, see, for example, Julius Richter, "The Missionary Crisis," *International Review of Missions* 23 (1934): 313–324.

178. Kraemer, *The Christian Message*, 403–405. Similar accusations against the Catholic Church appear throughout the book.

179. See, for example, Pierre Charles, "Théologie de la conversion: Théorie catholique et théorie protestante," in *Les conversions: Compte-rendu de la huitieme semaine de missiologie de Louvain* (Édition de l'Aucam, 1930), 28–38; Henri Dubois, *Le répertoire africain* (Sodalité de S. Pierre Claver, 1932).

180. Adolf Keller, *Christian Europe Today* (Harper, 1942), 207, 255. For Keller's earlier, anti-Catholic sentiments, see, for example, his "Present Conditions in the European Churches," *Federal Council Bulletin* (June–July 1923): 16–18.

4. Grand Compromises at the Zenith of Christian Power

1. Joachim Köhler and Damian van Melis (eds.), *Siegerin in Trümern* (Kohlhammer, 1998).

2. Walter Nigg, *Vom Geheimnis der Mönche* (Artemis, 1953). Quotation is from the English translation, *Warriors of God: The Great Religious Orders and Their Founders* (Knopf, 1959), 4.

3. Emil Brunner, "Our Attitude as a Christian Church to Communism," paper delivered at the informal staff conference "The Churches and the Conflict between Communism and Democracy" at the Ecumenical Institute, Bossey, Switzerland (December 1947), folder Christianity and Communism, box 422.002, World Council of Churches Archives, Ecumenical Center, Geneva, Switzerland (hereafter cited as WCC Archives).

4. Cited in Maria Mitchell, *The Origins of Christian Democracy: Politics and Confession in Modern Germany* (University of Michigan Press, 2012), 84.

5. Cited in Mitchell, *Origins of Christian Democracy*, 80. On the formation of this narrative, see, for example, Mark Ruff, *The Battle for the Catholic Past in Germany, 1945–1980* (Cambridge University Press, 2017), 13–46.

6. Karl Adam, *Una Sancta in katholischer Sicht: Drei Vorträge* (Patmos, 1948), 102.

7. Sacred Congregation of the Holy Office, *On the "Ecumenical Movement"* (December 20, 1949), https://www.ewtn.com/catholicism/library/on-the-ecumenical-movement-2070.

8. Joseph Lortz, *Die Reformation als religiöses Anliegen heute* (Paulinus, 1948); Gabriele Lautenschläger, *Joseph Lortz: Weg, Umwelt, und Werk eines katholischen Kirchenhistoriker* (Echter, 1987).

9. Joseph Lortz, *Der unvergleichliche Heilige* (Patmos, 1952); Lortz, *Die Reformation: These als Handreichung bei Ökumenischen Gesprächen* (Kyrios, 1947).

10. Adam, *Una Sancta*, 102, emphasis in the original.

11. Yves Congar, *Vraie et fausse réforme dans l'église* (Éditions du Cerf, 1950).

12. Yves Congar, *Luther vu par les Catholiques, ou de l'utilité de faire l'histoire de l'histoire* (Revue des Sciences Philosophiques et Théologiques, 1950), 7, emphasis in the original. See also part 3 of Congar, *Vraie et fausse réforme*, which focuses on the Reformation and Protestantism.

13. Johannes Hessen, *Der geistige Wiederaufbau Deutschlands* (Schröder, 1946).

14. Wilhelm Stählin, *Katholisierende Neigungen in der evangelischen Kirche* (Schwabenverlag, 1947); Stählin, *Was ist lutherisch? Zum Selbstverstaendnis der lutherischen Kirche im ökumenischen Gespräch* (Stauda, 1952), reproduced in Wilhelm Stählin and Adolf Köberle, *Symbolon: Vom gleichnischaften Denken* (Evangelisches Verlagswerk, 1958), 248–282, here 256.

15. Tagungen of evangelischen and katholischen Oekumenischen Arbeitskreises, 1949–1960 (May 15, 1962), EZA 6/8303, Ecclesiastical Protestant Archives of Germany, Berlin. For one of its most important publications, see Lortz et al., *Europa und das Christentum* (Steiner, 1959). For (incomplete) background on those meetings, see Barbara Schwahn, *Der ökumenische Arbeitskreis evangelischer und katholischer Theologen von 1946 bis 1975* (Vandenhoeck und Ruprecht, 1996).

16. Report on Catholic-Protestant Conference at Istina, Paris, Oliver Tomkins to George Bell (September 25, 1949), vol. 103, Bell Papers, Lambeth Archives, London.

17. Nigg, *Warriors of God*, 3. See also Walter Nigg, *Grosse Heilige* (Artemis, 1946).

18. Otto Karr (ed.), *Um die Einheit der Christen* (Knecht, 1953).

19. See especially *Verbum Caro: Revue théologique et ecclésiastique*, no. 1–5.

20. Report, Pastor J. Loos (Dutch Reformed Church) to the Anglican Church's Committee on Foreign Relations (December 22, 1947), folder 202/1, files of the Church's Committee on Foreign Relations, Relations with Catholics; and letter, G. W. Broomfield (British Council of Churches) to Archbishop Geoffrey Fisher (February 8, 1946), vol. 18, Geoffrey Fisher Papers, Archives of the Church of England, Lambeth Palace, London. See also John A. Coleman, *The Evolution of Dutch Catholicism, 1958–1974* (University of California Press, 1978), 127–129. Willebrands and the foundation of the Dutch initiative are mentioned in Lukas Vischer, "The Ecumenical Movement and the Roman Catholic Church," in *The*

Ecumenical Advance: A History of the Ecumenical Movement, vol. 2: *1948–1968*, ed. Harold E. Fey (WCC, 1970), 311–352, quote from 320–321.

21. Franz Josef Schöningh, "Christliche Politik?," *Hochland* 41 (1949): 305–320. See also Gerhard Kroll, *Was ist der Staat?* (Schnell und Steiner, 1950).

22. Georg Wünsch, *Evangelische Ethik des Politischen* (Mohr, 1936).

23. Georg Wünsch, *Der Mensch im modernen Materialismus als Aufgabe christlicher Verkündigung* (Mohr, 1952), 12, 14.

24. Gerhard Kroll, *Grundlagen abendländischer Erneuerung das Manifest der abendländischen Aktion* (Neues Abendland, 1951), 135. See also Wolfgang Heilmann, "Einführung," in *Der Mensch und die Freiheit: Vorträge und Gespräche der Jahrestagung der Abendländischen Akademie 1953*, ed. Hans Asmussen et al. (Neues Abendland, 1953), 3–10, esp. 7.

25. On the Academy, see, for example, Johannes Grossmann, *Die internationale der Konservativen* (De Gruyter, 2014); Axel Schildt, *Zwischen Abendland und Amerika: Studien zur westdeutschen Ideenlandschaft der 50er Jahre* (Oldenbourg, 1999).

26. See, for example, Emil Franzel, "Portugal, der bestregierte Staat Europas," *Neues Abendland* 7 (1952): 266–277.

27. Kroll, *Grundlagen*, 135.

28. Hans Dombois, "Die Vernichtung der Freiheit im Totalitarismus," in Asmussen et al., *Der Mensch und die Freiheit*, 88–95.

29. The quote is from Konrad Adenauer, "Christian Civilization at Stake," in *World Indivisible* (New York, 1955), 13.

30. Gerhard Kroll, *Christliche Union! Bamberger Denkschrift zur Schaffung einer politischen Einheitsfront aller Christen Deutschlands* (Rems, 1946).

31. The most important work on the foundation of the CDU is Maria Mitchell, *The Origins of Christian Democracy*. On the persistence of some confessional tensions, see Martin Greschat, "Konfessionelle Spannungen in der Ära Adenauer," in *Katholiken und Protestanten in der Aufbaujahren der Bundesrepublik*, ed. Thomas Sauer (Kohlhammer, 2000), 19–34; Fabio Wolkenstein, *Die dunkle Seite der Christemokratie* (Beck, 2022), 112–118.

32. Cited in Mitchell, *Origins of Christian Democracy*, 70.

33. Patrick Major, *The Death of the KPD: Communism and Anti-Communism in West Germany, 1945–1956* (Clarendon, 1997).

34. See, for example, Joseph Hours, *MRP directions: Libres propos pour une action politique* (Imp. commerciale, 1945), 21.

35. August Edmond de Schryver, "The Christian Social Party," *Annals of the American Academy of Political and Social Change* 247 (September 1946): 5–11, here 8.

36. Cited in Pierre Letamendia, *Le movement républicain populaire* (Beauchesne, 1995), 79.

37. Cited in Carlo Invernizzi Accetti, *What Is Christian Democracy? Politics, Religion, and Ideology* (Cambridge University Press, 2019), 38.

38. Martin Conway, *Western Europe's Democratic Age, 1945–1968* (Princeton University Press, 2020), 162–197; Bruno Béthouart, "Entry of the Catholics into the Republic: The Mouvement républicain populaire in France," in *Christian Democracy in Europe since 1945*, ed. Michael Gehler and Wolfram Kaiser (Routledge, 2004), 85–100.

39. Winston Churchill, "Foreword," in *Europe Unites* (United Europe Movement, 1948), viii.

40. Cited in Marco Duranti, *The Conservative Human Rights Revolution: European Identity, Transnational Politics, and the Origins of the European Convention* (Oxford University Press, 2017), 171.

41. Ibid.

42. See, for example, Noah B. Strote, *Lions and Lambs: Conflict in Weimar and the Creation of Post-Nazi Germany* (Yale University Press, 2017), 175–196; Philip Manow, *Social Protection, Capitalist Production: The Bismarckian Welfare State in the German Political Economy, 1880–2015* (Oxford University Press, 2020), esp. 39–54. This is not to deny that the focus on confessional differences is helpful to understanding the early moments of German Christian Democracy, when Protestants spearheaded the resistance to Christian socialism. See Mitchell, *Origins of Christian Democracy*, 136–137.

43. Josef Dobretsberger, *Katholische Sozialpolitik am Scheideweg* (Ulrich Mose, 1947).

44. Walter Dirks, "Das Abendland und der Sozialismus," *Zweite Republik* (1947): 60.

45. Oscar Cole-Arnal, "The *Témoignage* of the Worker Priests: Contextual Layers of the Pioneer Epoch (1941–1955)," in *Left Catholicism 1943–1955: Catholics and Society in Western Europe at the Point of Liberation*, ed. Gerd-Rainer Horn and Emmanuel Gerard (Leuven University Press, 2001), 118–141. See also Daniela Saresella, "The Movement of Catholic Communists, 1937–1945," *Journal of Contemporary History* 53, no. 3 (2018): 644–661.

46. Hans Lutz, *Protestantismus und Sozialismus heute* (Arani, 1949), 92. On the community, see Michael Klein, *Westdeutscher Protestantismus und politische Parteien* (Mohr Siebek, 2005), 325–329.

47. Horst Symanowski, "The Missionary Responsibility of the Church in Germany," *Ecumenical Review* 1 (Summer 1949): 417–423; see also Symanowski, *Gott liebt die Weltlichen: 2 Vorträge* (Bechaug, 1956).

48. Raoul Crespin, *De protestants engagés: Le christianisme social, 1945–1970* (Les Bergers et les Mages, 1993), 17–41; Christophe Chalamet, *Revivalism and Social Christianity* (Lutterworth Press, 2017).

49. Otto Dibelius, *Volk, Staat, und Wirtschaft aus christlichem Verantwortungsbewusstsein* (Christl. Zeitschriftverlag, 1947).

50. On the impact of Mindszenty's trial, see Paul Betts, *Ruin and Renewal: Civilizing Europe after World War II* (Basic Books, 2020), 125–172.

51. Mirjam Loos, "Antikommunistische und anti-antikommunistische Stimmen im evangelischen Kirchenmilieu: Die Debatte um Wiedervereinigung, Westbindung, und Wiederbewaffung," in *Geistige Gefahr und Immunisierung der Gesellschaft: Antikommunismus und politische Kultur in der frühen Bundesrepublik*, ed. Stefan Creuzberger and Dierk Hoffmann (Schriftenreihe de Vierterljahtshefte für Zeitgeschichte, 2014), 199–213; Emma Kuby, *Political Survivors: The Resistance, the Cold War, and the Fight against Concentration Camps after 1945* (Cornell University Press, 2019), 46–77.

52. Decree of the Holy Office (July 1949), http://www.montfort.org.br/eng/documentos/decretos/anticomunismo/.

53. Mirjam Loos, *Gefährliche Metaphern: Auseinandersetzungen deutscher Protestanten mit Kommunismus und Bolschewismus* (Vandenhoeck und Ruprecht, 2020), 198–199.

54. Walter Dirks, "Der restaurative Charakter der Epoche," *Frankkfurter Hefte* 9 (1950): 942–954, here 942.

55. Joseph Höffner *Soziale Sicherheit und Eigenverantwortung* (Bonifacius-Druckerei, 1953).

56. Joseph Höffner, *Sozialpolitik im deutschen Bergbau* (Aschendorffsche, 1954), 37.

57. Joseph Höffner, *Das Ethios des Unternehmers* (Bachem, 1956).

58. Höffner, *Sozialpolitik im deutschen Bergbau*, 38.

59. Norbert Trippen, *Joseph Kardinal Höffner* (Schöningh, 2009); James Chappel, *Catholic Modern: The Challenge of Totalitarianism and the Remaking of the Church* (Harvard University Press, 2018), 200–214.

60. Johannes Messner, *Social Ethics* (Herder, 1949), esp. 697–950, quote at 869.

61. Guido Fischer, "Eigentumsformer für die Mitarbeiter der Betriebe," in *Eigentum in Arbeiterhand: Sozialreferat der Abendländischen Akademie* (Neues Abendland, 1954), 117. See also Fischer, *Christliche Gesellschaftsordnung und Sozialpraxis des Betriebes* (Kerle, 1950).

62. "Arbeitgemeinschaft der katholischen sozialen Woche," in *Sozialen Sicherung durch Neuordnung des Eigentums: Vortragsreihe der 4. Katholischen Sozialen Woche 1953 in München* (Winfried Werk, 1954), 34.

63. Hans Achinger, *Soziale Sicherheit* (Friedrich Vorwek, 1953), 45. See also Achinger, "Maximen der Rentenpolitik," *Sozialer Fortschritt* 2 (1953): 242–244; Achinger, *Wirtschaftskraft und Soziallast* (Urban und Schwarzenberg, 1948); Achinger, *Arbeit für die Jugend: Berichte über Not und Hilfe* (Stuttgart: Schwab, 1950). For analysis of Achinger's writings, see Peter C. Caldwell, *Democracy, Capitalism, and the Welfare State: Debating Social Order in Postwar West Germany* (Oxford University Press, 2019), 82–87.

64. Achinger, *Soziale Sicherheit*, 59.

65. Ibid., 139.

66. Alfred Müller-Armack, *Wirtschaftslenkung und Marktwirtschaft* (Verlag für Wirtschaft und Sozialpolitik, 1947); Müller-Armack, *Das Jahrhundert ohne Gott: Zur Kultursoziologie unserer Zeit* (Regensberg, 1948).

67. Alexander Rüstow, *Das Versagen des Wirtschaftsliberalismus als Religionsgeschichtliches Problem* (Istanbul Schriften, 1945), 459.

68. Friedrich Karrenberg, "Sozialgeschichte der insturiellen Arbeitswelt und die Chrisenheit," *Zeitschrift für Evangelische Ethik* 2, no. 2 (1958): 73–90, here 81. On the Protestant retreat from more socialist proposals in the immediate postwar years to more market-based ideas in the 1950s, see, for example, René Smolarski, *Die evangelische Kirche zwischen Mitbestimmung und Selbstbestimmung* (Mohr Siebeck, 2020), 89–270.

69. Alexander Rüstow, "Die Konfession in der Wirtschaftsgeschichte," *Revue de la faculté des sciences économiques de l'Université d'Istanbul* 3/4 (1942): 362–389.

70. Alfred Müller-Armack, "Soziale Irenik," *Weltwirtschaftliches Archiv* 64 (1950): 181–203.

71. See, for example, the records of the 1959 conference, including papers by Höffner, Rüstow, and Müller-Armack, published as *Ökonomischer Humanismus: Neoliberale Theorie, soziale Marktwirtschaft, und christliche Soziallehre* (J. P. Bachem, 1960). See also Erik von Kuehnelt-Leddihn, "Neukonservatismus und Neuliberalismus," *Neues Abendland* 11 (1956): 121–134; Erik von Kuehnelt-Leddihn, "Von der Ökonomie zur Staatsphilosophie," *Neues Abendland* 13 (1958): 267–271.

72. Cord Cordes, "Kann evangelische Ethik sich das Subsidiaritätsprinzip, wie es in der Enzyklika Quadragesimo anno gelehrt wird, zu eigen machen?," *Zeitschrift für Evangelische Ethik* 3 (1959): 145–157.

73. Hans Achinger, Joseph Höffner, et al., *Neuordnung der sozialen Leistungen* (Greven, 1955), 57.

74. Ibid., 108.

75. Karl Kummer, "Eigentum in Arbeiterhand," in *Eigentum in Arbeiterhand*, 257–261, here 258. The information about the cooperation between Müller-Armack and Knoll is from Chappel, *Catholic Modern*, 218–219.

76. ÖVP, "Was Wir Wollen" (1958), https://austria-forum.org/af/AEIOU/%C3%96 sterreichische_Volkspartei%2C_%C3%96VP/Was_Wir_Wollen_1958.

77. Dennie Oude Nijhuis, *Religion, Class and the Postwar Development of the Dutch Welfare State* (Amsterdam University Press, 2018), 71–123.

78. Laurent Ducerf, "Les démocrates chrétiens face à l'économie," in *Les "chrétiens modérés" en France et en Europe, 1870–1960*, ed. Jacques Prévotat (Septentrion, 2013),

281–290. Their background in the resistance is explored in Philip Nord, *France's New Deal* (Princeton University Press, 2010), esp. 105–116.

79. The quote is from the English translation, Joseph Höffner, *Christian Social Teaching* (Ordo Socialis, 1997), 183.

80. Hendrik van Oyen, *Der Christ und der Luxes* (Ev. Verlag, 1962). The quotes are from the English translation, *Affluence and the Christian* (Fortress Press, 1966), 11, 21.

81. Strote, *Lions and Lambs,* 194–195.

82. Jean Lacroix, *Force et faiblesses de la famille* (Éditions du Seuil, 1948); Paul Plattner, *Glücklichere Ehen* (Huber, 1950).

83. Both pamphlets are cited in Mitchell, *Origins of Christian Democracy,* 109.

84. Cited in R. E. M. Irving, *Christian Democracy in France* (Routledge, 2010), 61.

85. De Schryver, "The Christian Social Party," 10.

86. Mitchell, *Origins of Christian Democracy,* 109.

87. Helmut Thielicke, *Theologische Ethik* (Mohr, 1951). Quote is from the English translation of part 3 of the text, *The Ethics of Sex* (Clarke, 1964), 158–159.

88. Ernst Michel, *Eine Anthropologie der Geschlechtsgemenischaft* (Klett, 1948); Charlotte von Kirschbaum, *Die wirkliche Frau,* 2nd ed. (Evangelischer Verlag, 1949 [1944]); quote is from the English version, *The Question of Woman* (Eerdmans, 1996), 170.

89. Guido Groeger, *Angst und Freude der Geschlechtsentwicklung* (Laetare, 1954), 17.

90. Robert G. Moeller, *Protecting Motherhood: Women and the Family in the Politics of Postwar West Germany* (University of California Press, 1993).

91. Arthur Plaza, "From Christian Militants to Republican Renovators: The Third Ralliement of Catholics in Postwar France, 1944–1965" (PhD diss., NYU, 2008); Tjitske Akkerman, "Political Participation and Social Rights: The Triumph of the Breadwinner in the Netherlands" (in German), in *Gender, Participation and Citizenship in the Netherlands,* ed. Jet Bussemaker and Rian Voet (Routledge, 2018), 38–50.

92. On the continuity in welfare and familialism between the fascist and the postwar periods in France, see Rémi Lenoir, *Généalogie de la morale familiale* (Paris: Éditions du Seuil, 2003), esp. 241–411.

93. Elizabeth D. Heineman, *What Difference Does a Husband Make? Women and Marital Status in Nazi and Postwar Germany* (University of California Press, 1999), 136–175.

94. Franz-Josef Wuermeling, *Familie: Gabe und Aufgabe* (Luthe, 1963), 20. See also Wuermeling, "Grundlage der Gesellschaft ist die Familie," *BPIB* 21 (November 1953): 1851–1854.

95. Claire Duchen, *Women's Rights and Women's Lives in France, 1944–1968* (Routledge, 1994), 103–106; Rémi Lenoir, "Family Policy in France since 1938," in *The French Welfare State,* ed. John S. Ambler (NYU Press, 1991), 144–186.

96. Julia Lynch, *Age in the Welfare State* (Cambridge University Press, 2006), esp. 80–82.

97. Bernhard Häring, *Das Gesetz Christi* (Wewel, 1955). The quote is from the English translation, *The Law of Christ,* vol. 2 (Newman, 1967), 492.

98. Paul Althaus, *Grundriss der Ethik* (Gütersloh, 1953).

99. On the law in France, and its links to earlier Christian activism in this field, see John Phillips, "Old Wine in New Bottles? Literary Pornography in Twentieth-Century France," in *International Exposure: Perspectives on Modern European Pornography,* ed. Lisa Z. Sigel (Rutgers University Press, 2005), 125–146.

100. Cited in Dagmar Herzog, *Sex after Fascism* (Princeton University Press, 2005), 88–95.

101. Sarah Fishman, *From Vichy to the Sexual Revolution: Gender and Family Life in Postwar France* (Oxford University Press, 2017), 64; Herzog, *Sex after Fascism,* 75–77. On the adaptation of family natalism from Vichy to postwar France, see Camille Robcis, *The Law*

of Kinship: Anthropology, Psychoanalysis, and the Family in France (Cornell University Press, 2013), 17–60.

102. Julian Jackson, *Living in Acadia: Homosexuality, Politics, and Morality in France from the Liberation to AIDS* (University of Chicago Press, 2009); Samuel Clowes Huneke, *States of Liberation: Gay Men between Dictatorship and Democracy in Cold War Germany* (University of Toronto Press, 2022), chap. 2. The information on the Netherlands is taken from Dagmar Herzog, *Sexuality in Europe: A Twentieth-Century History* (Cambridge University Press, 2011), 117–118, which also provides a useful overview.

103. August Adam, *Der Primat der Liebe* (Staufen-Verlag, 1948), 9.

104. Ibid., 181.

105. Friedrich von Gagern, *Eheliche Partnerschaft* (Manz, 1955).

106. Marc Oraison, *L'union des époux* (Fayard, 1956), 88. Texts in the same spirit are Jacques Leclerque, *Le mariage chrétien* (Casternman, 1946); Eugène Masure, *Recherche de la famille* (Éditions Familiales de France, 1949). On this trend in French Catholic writings, see Anne-Marie Sohn, "French Catholics between Abstinence and 'Appeasement of Lust,' 1930–1950," in *Sexual Cultures in Europe: Themes in Sexuality*, ed. Franz Eder et al. (Manchester University Press, 1999), 1:233–254.

107. J. G. H. Holt, *Het getij: Het verband tussen vruchtbaarheid en temperatuur bij de vrouw* (Dekker & Van de Vegt, 1958).

108. Paul Tournier, *Bible et medicine* (Delachaux et Niestlé, 1953); the quote is from the English translation, *A Doctor's Casebook in the Light of the Bible* (Harper, 1954), 62–63.

109. Paul Tournier, *Le personnage et la personne* (Delachaux et Niestlé, 1954); Tournier, *Difficultés conjugales* (Fides, 1960).

110. Bernard Harnik, *Vom Sinn des Lebens* (Vadian, 1953); Harnik, *Das Ziel der Erziehung* (Vadian, 1955); the quote is from the English translation, *Toward a Healthy Marriage* (Word, 1976), 146.

111. Hendrik van Oyen, *Liebe und Ehe* (Friedrich Reinhardt, 1956), esp. 113–179.

112. Karl Barth, *Church Dogmatics III/4: The Doctrine of Creation* (Continuum, 1961), §§52–54, 125.

113. Adam, *Primat der Liebe*, 8, 20, 68–69.

114. Pierre de Locht, *L'amour dans le mariage: Perspectives chrétiennes* (Éditions Feuilles Familiales, 1956).

115. *Le sexualité*, special issue, *Esprit* 289 (November 1960): 1665–1977.

116. Harnik, *Vom Sinn des Lebens*, 149.

117. See, for example, J. Janssens, "Birth Control and Family Planning," and R. Eeg-Olofsson, "The Future of Christian Medicine," both in *The Service of a Christian Doctor in a Modern Society: Lectures Held at the First International Congress of Christian Physicians, Amsterdam, 15–19 July 1963* (Vangorcum, 1964), 80–90, 109–117. See also Max Thurian, *Mariage et célibat* (Presses Taizé, 1955).

118. Theodor Bovet, *Das Geheimnis ist Gross* (Katzmann, 1956). The quote, with slight modification, is from the English translation, *Love, Skill and Mystery: A Handbook to Marriage* (Doubleday, 1958), 41–42.

119. Ibid., 43.

120. Ibid., 54.

121. Ibid., 77.

122. Ibid., xiv.

123. Ibid., 166–167.

124. Theodor Bovet, "By Way of Introduction," *Ehe: Zentralblatt für Ehe- und Familienkunde* 1, no. 1 (1964): 1–5, here 5.

125. Theodor Bovet, "Die Eheauffassung des modernen Menschen," in *Die Mischehe*, ed. Wolfgang Sucker et al. (Vandenhoeck und Ruprecht, 1959), 59.

126. Joachim Lell, "Evangelische Mischehenseelsorge," in Sucker et al., *Die Mischehe*, 321–408.

127. Heinrich Bornkamm, *Das Verhältnis zwischen den Konfessionen im heutigen Deutschland* (Heliand, 1952), 14.

128. Kristian Buchna, *Ein klerikales Jahrzehnt? Kirche, Konfession und Politik in der Bunderrepublik während der 1950er Jahren* (Nomos, 2014), 358.

129. Henri Labouret, *Colonisation, colonialisme, décolonisation* (Paris, 1952), 19. On decolonization and its impact on Europe, see, for example, Todd Shepard, *The Invention of Decolonization: The Algerian War and the Remaking of France* (Cornell University Press, 2006); Erik Linstrum, *Age of Emergency: Living with Violence at the End of the British Empire* (Oxford University Press, 2023); Samuel Moyn, *Not Enough: Human Rights in an Unequal World* (Belknap Press of Harvard University Press, 2018), 119–145.

130. Jean Vacher-Desvernais, *L'avenir des français d'outre-mer* (Presses universitaires de France, 1962), 4.

131. Giovanni Miegge, *Religious Liberty* (United Society for Christian Literature, 1957). The text, which was solicited by the WCC and originally appeared in Italian, was translated into multiple languages.

132. The scant attention European Christians gave to Asian decolonization is registered in Justin Reynolds, "From Christian Anti-Imperialism to Postcolonial Christianity," *Journal of Global History* 13, no. 2 (July 2018): 230–251. On missionary negotiations with postcolonial states in Asia, see Bastiaan Bouwman, *From Liberalism to Liberation: The World Council of Churches and the Postwar Politics of Human Rights* (Cambridge University Press, forthcoming), chap. 2.

133. On China's expulsion of missionaries, see, for example, Albert Monshan Wu, *From Christ to Confucius: German Missionaries, Chinese Christians, and the Globalization of Christianity, 1860–1950* (Yale University Press, 2016), 220ff. On the campaign against missionaries in Guinea, see Elizabeth Schmidt, *Cold War and Decolonization in Guinea, 1946–1958* (Ohio University Press, 2007), 171–172. Christian publications on China include Barnabas [pseud.], *Christian Witness in Communist China* (Parrett and Neves, 1951); Bingwen Shen, *Chinese Communist Criminal Acts in Persecution of Christianity* (Christian Association in Free China, 1953); Roman Bleistein, *Fu-Lin und der Rote Tiger: Erzählung über das Schicksal der Christen in China* (Herder, 1956). Cimade's campaigns are chronicled in Darcie Fontaine, *Decolonizing Christianity: Religion and the End of Empire in France and Algeria* (Cambridge University Press, 2016), esp. 146–171.

134. Nicholas O. Anim, "Ghana," in *Church, State, and Education in Africa*, ed. David G. Scanlon (Teachers College Press, 1966), 165–196, here 188.

135. On postcolonial states, education, and missions, see, for example, Harry Gamble, *Contesting French West Africa: Battles over Schools and the Colonial Order* (University of Nebraska Press, 2017); Elizabeth Schmidt, *Cold War and Decolonization in Guinea, 1946–1958* (Ohio University Press, 2007), 171–172; Pascal Bianchini, *École et politique en Afrique noire* (Karthala, 2004); and the essays in Brian Stanley (ed.), *Missions, Nationalism and the End of Empire* (Eerdmans, 2003).

136. Johannes Hofinger, *Worship: The Life of the Mission* (University of Notre Dame Press, 1958), 37–38. See also Hofinger, *Der priesterlose Gemeindegottesdienst in den Missionen* (Neue Zcitschrift für Missionswissenschaft, 1956); Hofinger, *The Art of Teaching Christian Doctrine: The Good News and Its Proclamation* (University of Notre Dame Press, 1957).

137. The lecture was later published as Lesslie Newbigin, *A Faith for This One World?* (SCM Press, 1961), 9.

138. See, for example, Alioune Diop, "Peut-on dresser le Vatican les peuples de couleur?," *Présence africaine* 16 (October–November 1957): 4–7, here 4; E. Bolaji Idowu, *Towards an Indigenous Church* (Oxford University Press, 1964), 2. On Asian and African efforts to link

Christianity and support for decolonization, see, for example, Elizabeth A. Foster, *African Catholic: Decolonization and the Transformation of the Church* (Harvard University Press, 2019); Elizabeth A. Foster and Udi Greenberg (eds.), *Decolonization and the Remaking of Christianity* (University of Pennsylvania Press, 2023). The quotes are from Edwin Bruggmann, "What Future Has the Mission School?," in *Education for Reality in Africa* (Mambo Press, 1963), 64–79, here 68, 71; and Richard Dodson, "Congo-Leopoldville," in *Education for Reality in Africa*, 102.

139. Johannes Hofinger, *Der priesterlose Gemeindegottesdienst in den Missionen* (Neuen Zeitschrif für Missionswissenschaft, 1956); Walbert Bühlmann, *Afrika: Gestern, heute, morgen* (Herder, 1959), esp. 124–125.

140. Alphons Mulder, "Introduction," in *Liturgy and the Missions: The Nijmegen Papers*, ed. Johannes Hofinger (P. J. Kennedy, 1960), 18–21, here 20. The information on the Vatican and the utilization of local languages is based on the appendix to Hofinger, *Liturgy and the Missions*. The information on Protestant reforms is taken from Report of Section IV, *Report on Worship* (WCC, 1963).

141. Joseph J. Blomjous, "The Church's Mission and Ecumenical Development," *African Ecclesiastical Review* 1, no. 2 (April 1959): 254–268. See also Blomjous, "The Position of the African Layman, part 1," *African Ecclesiastical Review* 1, no. 2 (4 1959): 74–79; Blomjous, "Mission and Liturgy," in Hofinger, *Liturgy and the Missions*, 39–46. On Blomjous and his journal's considerable influence in Africa and beyond, see Adrian Hastings, *The Church in Africa* (Oxford, 1994), 568ff.

142. Blomjous, "The Church's Mission," 260.

143. Hans Burgman, "Marxism, a Fatal Cure for a Sick World," *African Ecclesiastical Review* 1, no. 1 (January 1959): 35–42; John Jordan, "Catholic Education and Catholicism in Nigeria," *African Ecclesiastical Review* 2, no. 1 (January 1960): 60–63; the quote is from H. Jowitt, "Education in Changing Africa," *African Ecclesiastical Review* 1, no. 2 (April 1959): 92–104, here 94.

144. Newbigin, *A Faith?*, 106, 111, 125.

145. Lesslie Newbigin, *Is Christ Divided? A Plea for Christian Unity in a Revolutionary Age* (London: CMS Press, 1961), 27. Similar ideas appear in Newbigin, *One Body, One Gospel, One World: The Christian Mission Today* (Friendship, 1958); Newbigin, "The Summons to Christian Mission Today," *International Review of Missions* 48, no. 190 (1959): 177–189. On Newbigin's influence, see Geoffrey Wainwright, *Lesslie Newbigin* (Oxford University Press, 2000).

146. Ben Marais, *Human Diversity and Christian Unity* (Rhodes University Press, 1958), 7–8; Jan Hermelink, *Christ im Welthorizont* (Kreuz, 1962).

147. Louis Massignon, *Les trois prières d'Abraham* (Éditions du Cerf, 1998 [1949]). On Massignon's writing, see Pierre Rocalve, *Louis Massignon et l'Islam* (Institut français de Damas, 1993); Jerrold Seigel, "The Islamic Catholicism of Louis Massignon," in *Between Cultures: Europe and Its Others in Five Exemplary Lives* (University of Pennsylvania Press, 2016), 115–151.

148. Joseph Le Guillou, "Mission et unité en perspectives protestante et catholique," *Istina* 6 (1959): 433–458, here 450. Throughout the late 1950s and early 1960s Le Guillou wrote multiple essays and booklets in this vein, which were issued in several languages.

149. Vincent J. Donovan, "The Protestant Catholic Scandal in Africa," *African Ecclesiastic Review* 1, no. 3 (July 1959): 169; Donovan further expanded on these themes in his "The Protestant-Catholic Scandal in Africa: Answer to Father Slevin," *African Ecclesiastic Review* 2, no. 3 (July 1960): 245.

150. Fridtjov Birkeli, "Die Neue Welt Asiens und Afrikas als Fragen an unsere Kirchen im Abendland," in *Lutherische Generalsynode: Bericht über die fünf Tagung der Ver-*

einigten Evangelisch-Lutherischen Kirche Deutschlands im 5 bis 9 Oktober 1959 in Lübeck (Vereinigte Evangelisch-Lutheranische Kirche Deutschlands, 1961), 39–53. For similar sentiments, see Hermelink, *Christ im Welthorizont,* esp. 100–111.

151. Report, Inventory of Institutions of Religious Bodies (October 25, 1962), folder FERES 1962/3; list, participants in the ISS-FERES Project (October 1961); History of the ISS-FERES Project (October 1964); report, Meeting of the ISS-FERES Project (January 3 and 4, 1964), all in folder Inventory 1964, box 421.450, WCC Archives; and report, Bases for Cooperation (July 1964), Executive Committee, folder 2, box 4201.2.4; report, Meeting of the Working Party between the RCC and the WCC, folder 9, box 4201.4.1; Report on the Informal Meeting of WCC/RCC Mission Staff (April 29–May 1, 1968), folder 2, box 4201.4.4; memorandum (May 1969), The Joint Working Group between the RCC and the WCC 1965–1969, folder 3, box 4201.4.0; all in WCC Archives. The meeting in Brussels is mentioned in Ruth Slade Reardon, "Catholics and Protestants in the Congo," in *Christianity in Tropical Africa,* ed. C. G. Baëta (International African Institute, 1968), 83–100.

152. Report, Consultation of the WCC and the Vatican (April 22, 1965), folder 16, box 4201.2.2; Report of the Working Party of Emergency Aid and Development Aid (January 26–28, 1966), folder 2, box 4201.5.1; letter, C. H. Hwang to Lesslie Newbigin (November 18, 1964); all in WCC Archives.

153. Report of the Working Party on Emergency Aid and Development Aid (January 1966), folder 2, box 4201.5.1; Committee on Society, Development and Peace, "Summary of SODEPAX Activities," (May 1970), folder 4, box 4201.4.7; both in WCC Archives.

154. Paul Brekelmans, report, "SODEPAX in the Rulenge Diocese Socio-Economic Development," (1969), folder Africa General, box 4202.012, WCC Archives.

155. Cited in Véronique Dimier, *The Invention of a European Development Aid: Bureaucracy Recycling Empire* (Palgrave Macmillan, 2014), 34. See also Sara Lorenzini, *Global Development: A Cold War History* (Princeton University Press, 2019), 50–64; Corinna Unger, *International Development: A Postwar History* (Bloomsbury, 2018).

156. Louis Joseph Lebret, *Suicide ou survie de l'Occident?* (Économie et humanisme, Éditions ouvrières, 1958). On Lebret and the Catholic embrace of development theory, see Giuliana Chamedes, "The Catholic Origins of Economic Development after World War II," *French Politics, Culture & Society* 33, no. 2 (Summer 2015): 55–75.

157. Egbert de Vries, *Man in Rapid Social Change* (SCM, 1961).

158. On Protestants and development, see Udi Greenberg, "The Rise of the Global South and the Protestant Peace with Socialism," *Contemporary European History* 92, no. 2 (2020): 202–219. On Christian democrats on development, see Peter van Kemseke, *Towards an Era of Development: The Globalization of Socialism and Christian Democracy* (Leuven University Press, 2006), 200–240, 262–268.

159. Report of the meeting of the Working Party between representatives of the Roman Catholic Church and the World Council of Churches (undated, likely 1966), folder 9, box 4201.4.1, WCC Archives.

160. Summary of SODEPAX activities and publications (May 1971), folder 4, box 4201.4.7, WCC Archives; Jan Sihar Aritonang and Karel Steenbrink, *A History of Christianity in Indonesia* (Brill, 2008), 844–846.

161. Brekelmans, report, "SODEPAX"; Report from Indonesia (Activity Report 1966), folder Maier, box CCPD Various Reports; both in WCC Archives; "Report of the Christian Service Committee of the Churches in Malawi," in *Development Projects: Examples of Church Involvement in Eastern Africa* (Gaba, undated). The quote is from Report, Tinka Olunide to SODEPAX (undated, probably 1964), folder Africa AACC, box 4202.012, WCC Archives.

162. Leslie Brown and Winifred Brown, *The Christian Family* (Lutterworth Press, 1959), 19; Brown and Brown, "Consultations," *African Ecclesiastical Review* 1, no. 1 (January 1959):

27–29 (and similar texts in almost all issues); Leslie Newbigin (ed.), *The All-Africa Seminar on the Christian Home and Family Life* (WCC, 1963), 18–19.

163. These and other reforms, and the debates surrounding them, are discussed in Arthur Phillips and Henry F. Morris, *Marriage Laws in Africa* (International African Institute, 1970).

164. The information on the Uganda campaign is based on Minutes, UJCC Meeting (September 6, 1963), folder 2, box 160, and Report, UJCC Conference on Alcoholism in Uganda held at Mukono (April 25, 1964), folder 3, box 162; the quotes are from the published statement that is attached to UJCC, Memorandum on Uganda Marriage Ordinance (April 29, 1964), folder 4, box 159; all in Series 5, Archives of the Church of Uganda, Office of the Archbishop, Yale Divinity School. On the formation of the UJCC, see J. J. Carney, "The Politics of Ecumenism in Uganda, 1962–1986," *Church History* 86, no. 3 (September 2017): 765–795.

165. *Unitatis redintegratio*, November 21, 1964, §3, http://www.vatican.va/archive/hist_councils/ii_vatican_council/documents/vat-ii_decree_19641121_unitatis-redintegratio_en.html. For some useful background on the secretariat and the discussions in the Vatican, see Leonard Daniel Pivonka, "The Secretariat for Promoting Christian Unity: A Study of a Catholic Response to the Modern Ecumenical Movement" (PhD diss., Catholic University of America, 1982); Jerome-Michael Vereb, *"Because He Was a German!" Cardinal Bea and the Origins of Roman Catholic Engagement in the Ecumenical Movement* (Eerdmans, 2006).

166. W. A. Visser 't Hooft, ed., *The New Delhi Report: The Third Assembly of the World Council of Churches* (New York, 1962), 151. Regarding Boegner's support for, and participation in, ecumenical dialogue, see Marc Boegner, *L'exigence œcuménique* (Michel, 1968).

167. These efforts are detailed in Willebrands to Heenan, July 8, 1966; Bea to Heenan, January 13, 1966; and Bea to Heenan, October 25, 1966; all in folder Christian Unity 1962–1967, box C15, Cardinal Hinsley Papers, Westminster Diocesan Archives, London; and the many reports of the Joint Working Group Between the Roman Catholic Church and the World Council of Churches (1965–1968), folder 1, box 4201.4.2, WCC Archives.

5. Radical Ecumenism in the 1960s and 1970s

1. Herbert Marcuse, *An Essay on Liberation* (Beacon Press, 1969), 53, 8, 26, 82, 6.
2. Ibid., 8.
3. A representative example is Ben Mercer, *Student Revolt in 1968: France, Italy, and West Germany* (Cambridge University Press, 2020). I discuss a few exceptions later in this chapter.
4. Hugh McLeod, *The Religious Crisis of the 1960s* (Oxford University Press, 2007), esp. 61–81, 196–212.
5. Dorothee Soelle, *The Silent Cry: Mysticism and Resistance* (Fortress, 2001), 294.
6. Dagmar Herzog, "The Death of God in West Germany: Between Secularization, Postfascism, and the Rise of Liberation Theology," in *Die Gegenwart Gottes in der Modernen Gesellschaft*, ed. Michael Geyer and Lucian Hölscher (Wallstein, 2006), 431–466.
7. For a partial intellectual history of the New Left, see Terence Renaud, *New Lefts: The Making of a Radical Tradition* (Princeton University Press, 2021), esp. 206–275.
8. On the link between socialism and psychology in New Left activism, see, for example, Joachim C. Häberlen, *The Emotional Politics of the Alternative Left: West Germany, 1968–1984* (Cambridge University Press, 2018). The quote is from Jake P. Smith, "Embedded Abstractions: Authenticity, Aura, and Abject Domesticity in Hamburg's Hafenstrasse," in *The Politics of Authenticity: Countercultures and Radical Movements across the Iron Curtain, 1968–1989*, ed. Joachim C. Häberlen et al. (Berghahn, 2019), 256–277, here 260.

9. Johann Baptist Metz, "Weltverständnis im Glauben: Christliche Orientierung in der Weltlichkeit der Welt heute," *Geist und Leben* 35 (1962): 165–184, here 169. See also Metz, "Für eine Theologie der Zukunft," *Neues Forum* 13 (1966): 324–328.

10. Johann Baptist Metz, "The Church in the World," in *The Word in History: The St. Xavier Symposium,* ed. T. Patrick Burke (Collins, 1966), 69–85, which also appeared in German as "Verantwortung der Hoffnung," *Stimmen der Zeit* 177 (1966): 451–462.

11. Johann Baptist Metz, "Christianity and Social Action," in *The Christian-Marxist Dialogue,* ed. Paul Oestreicher (Macmillan, 1969), 190.

12. Metz, "Christianity and Social Action," 202.

13. Johann Baptist Metz, "Christentum und Marxismus heute," in *Gespräche der Paulus-Gesellschaft,* ed. Ernst Kellner (Europa, 1966), 108–122.

14. Johann Baptist Metz, *Zur Theologie der Welt* (Matthias Grünewald, 1968). The quote is taken from the English translation, *Theology of the World* (Herder & Herder, 1969), 113.

15. Johann Baptist Metz, *Befreiendes Gedächtnis Jesu Christ* (Matthias Grünewald, 1970). See also Metz, "Erinnerung des Leidens als Kritik eines Teleologisch-Technologischen Zukunftsbegriffs," *Evangelische Theologie* 32 (1972): 338–352.

16. Johann Baptist Metz, "Politische Theologie," in *Diskussion zur "politischen Theologie,"* ed. H. Peukert (Matthias Grünewald, 1969), 267–301. The quote is from Metz, *Theology of the World,* 115.

17. For two examples out of many, see Ben van Onna, "Der Katholizismys in der spätkapitalistischen Gesellschaft," and Erik Rupp, "Der deutschen Emanzipationskatholizismus," both in *Kritischer Catholizismus: Argumente gegen die Kirchen-Gesellschaft,* ed. Ben van Onna and Martin Stankowski (Fischer, 1969), 8–43, 44–72. The dialogue between the Frankfurt School—Max Horkheimer in particular—and Christians is discussed in Pascal Eitler, *Gott ist tot—Gott is rot: Max Horkheimer und die Politisierung der Religion um 1968* (Campus, 2009).

18. See, for example, Jacques-Marie Pohier, "Unidimensionnalité du christianisme? À propos de Marcuse et de l'homme unidimensionnel," *Concilium* 6 (1971): 27–36.

19. See, for example, the articles assembled in the following issues of *Concilium:* "War, Poverty, Freedom: The Christian Response," 1966, no. 5; "Atheism and Indifference," 1967, no. 3; "Faith and the World of Politics," 1968, no. 6; "Eschatology," 1969, no. 1; "The Presence and Absence of God," 1969, no. 10.

20. David Andreas Seeber (ed.), *Katholikentag im Widerspruch: Ein Bericht über den 82. Katholikentag in Essen* (Herder, 1968), 150–160, quotation at 152.

21. Christian Schmidtmann, *Katholische Studierende, 1945–1973* (Paderborn, 2006), 316–367, quote at 358.

22. Gerd-Rainer Horn, *The Spirit of Vatican II: Western European Progressive Catholicism in the Long Sixties* (Oxford University Press, 2015), 173–185.

23. Danièle Hervieu-Léger, *De la mission á la protestation: L'évolution des étudiants chrétiens* (Éditions du Cerf, 1973), 106–121, quote at 120. See also Yves Chiron, *L'église dans la tourmente de 1968* (Artege, 2018), 35–102.

24. Jürgen Moltmann, *Theology of Hope: On the Ground and the Implications of a Christian Eschatology* (SCM Press, 1965), 16.

25. Ibid., 327.

26. References to Moltmann's participation in those conference can be found in Erich Kellner (ed.), *Christentum und Marxismus heute* (Europa, 1966); Ans J. van der Bent, *Christians and Communists: An Ecumenical Perspective* (WCC, 1980).

27. Jürgen Moltmann, *Der gekreuzigte Gott* (Kaiser, 1972). The quote is from the English translation, *The Crucified God* (Harper and Row, 1974), 320. See also Moltmann,

"Theologische Kritik der politischen Religion," in Johann Baptist Metz and Jürgen Moltmann, *Kirche im Prozess der Aufklärung: Aspekte einer neuen "politischen Theologie"* (Kaiser und Grünewald, 1970), 11–52.

28. Moltmann, *The Crucified God*, 327. See also Moltmann, "Die Revolution der Freiheit," in *Perspektiven der Theologie: Gesammelte Aufsätze* (Kaiser, 1968), 189–211.

29. Moltmann, *The Crucified God*, 320.

30. See, for example, the forum in German in *Evangelische Theologie* 27, no. 12 (1967); the roundtable in French in *Théologie de l'espérance* (Éditions du Cerf, 1970); or the Dutch collection *Discussie over Theologie can de hoop van Jürgen Moltmann* (Ambo, 1968).

31. Helmut Gollwitzer, *Die reichen Christen und der arme Lazarus* (Kaiser, 1968). Dutschke's participation in the life of the Protestant milieu is discussed in Dorothee Weitbrecht, *Aufbruch in die Dritte Welt: Der Internationalismus der Studentenbewegung von 1968 in der Bundesrepublik Deutschland* (V&R Unipress, 2012), 151–206.

32. Trutz Rendtorff and Karl Gerhard Steck, *Protestantismus und Revolution* (Kaiser, 1969). See also C. E. Braaten, "Theologie der Revolution," and Christoph Walther, "Theologie der Revolution," both *Lutherische Monatshafte* 7 (1968): 215–220, 221–224.

33. G. H. ter Schegget, *Partijgangers der Armen* (Bosch & Keuning, 1970); ter Schegget, *Klassenstrijd en staking* (Bosch & Keuning, 1974).

34. See, for example, Georges Casalis "Christianisme et revolution," *Christianisme social* 1–2 (1968): 119. See also *Christianisme social* 7–8 (1970), which was dedicated to "students of revolutionary theology" around the world.

35. Dorothee Sölle, *Politische Theologie* (Kreuz, 1971). The quote is from the English translation, *Political Theology* (Fortress, 1975), 92.

36. Evangelische Studentengemeinde an der FU Berlin, *Arbeitskreise der evangelischen Studentengemeinde an der FU Berlin im Wintersememter 1967/68* (publisher unspecified, 1968), unpaginated; Karl-Behrnd Hasselmann, *Politische Gemeinde: Ein kirchliches Handllungsmodell am Beispiel der evangelischen Studentengemeinde an der Freie Umiveristät Berlin* (Furche, 1969), 74–76.

37. See, for example, Hans Bosse, "Aggression und Emanzipation: Über den Zusammenhang von analytischer Arbeit, Gesellschaftstheorie und Strategie politischer Praxis bei Sigmund Freud, Erich Fromm, Konrad Lorenz, und Herbert Marcuse," *Verkündigung und Forschung* 14, no. 2 (1969): 68–86; Oswald Bayer, "Marcuses Kritik an Luthers Freiheitsbegriff," *Zeitschrift für Theologie und Kirche* 67, no. 4 (1970): 453–478; Theologiestudentent 1969, *Dokumente einer revolutionären Generation* (Evangelisches Verlagswerk, 1969). See also Angela Hager, "Westdeutsche Protestantismus und Studentenbewegung," in *Umbrüche: Der deutsche Protestantismus und die sozialen Bewegungen in der 1960er und 70er Jahren*, ed. Siegfried Hermle et al. (Vandenhoeck und Ruprecht, 2012), 111–130.

38. Cited in Arie Theodorus van Deursen, *The Distinctive Character of the Free University in Amsterdam* (Eerdmans, 2008), 324; on student activism more broadly, see 305–380.

39. Fédération protestante de France, *Églises et Pouvoirs* (Centre protestant d'études et de Doc, 1972). On Protestant leftist activism in this period, see Jean Baubérot, *Le pouvoir de contester: Contestations politico-religieuses autour de "mai 68" et le document "Eglise et pouvoirs"* (Labor et Fides, 1983).

40. Dorothee Sölle, *Stellvertretung; Ein Kapitel Theologie nach dem Tode Gottes* (Kreuz, 1965). The quote is from the English translation, *Christ the Representative: An Essay in Theology after "the Death of God"* (Fortress Press, 1967), 141–142.

41. See, for example, Moltmann, *Theology of Hope*, 165–167; Moltmann, *The Crucified God*, 200–220.

42. Dietrich Bonhoeffer, *Works*, vol. 8: *Letters and Papers from Prison* (Alexander Street, 2014). For a critical assessment of Bonhoeffer's reception in the 1960s, see Ernst Feil's

two-part article "Aspekte der Bonhoeffererinterpretation," *Theologische Literaturzeitung* 117, no. 1 (January1992): 1–18, and 117, no. 2 (February 1992): 81–100.

43. Johann Baptist Metz, *Reform und Gegenreformation heute* (Grünewald, 1969). See also Metz, "Braucht die Kirche eine neue Reformation?," *Concilium* 6, no. 4 (1970): 265–270.

44. Jürgen Moltmann, *Kirche in der Kraft des Geistes* (Kaiser, 1975). The quote is taken from the English translation, *The Church in the Power of the Spirit* (S.C.M., 1977), 14.

45. For their participation, see, for example, Walter H. Capps (ed.), *The Future of Hope* (Fortress, 1969); Metz and Moltmann, *Kirche im Prozess der Aufklärung*.

46. Johann Baptist Metz and Jürgen Moltmann, *Leidensgeschichte* (Herder, 1974).

47. Richard Shaull, *Befreiung durch Veränderung* (Kaiser und Grünewald, 1970); J. H. Cone, *Schwarze Theologie* (Kaiser und Grünewald, 1971); Frans van den Oudenrijn, *Kritische Theologie als Kritik der Theologie: Theorie und Praxis bei Karl Marx* (Kaiser und Grünewald, 1972); Gustavo Gutiérrez, *Theologie der Befreiung* (Kaiser und Grünewald, 1973).

48. Johann Baptist Metz, "Zu einer interdisziplinär orientierten Theologie auf Bikonfessioneller Basis," in *Die Theologie in der interdisziplinären Forschung* (Bertelsmann Universitätsverlag, 1971), 11–23, here 14. On Metz's role in the institute's foundation, see Tiemo Rainer Peters, *Johann Baptist Metz: Theologie des vermissten Gottes* (Matthias Grünewald, 1998), 83–93.

49. The event and details about its circumstances are discussed in *Christianisme social* 7–10 (1968). Ricoeur's comments on the event appear in Paul Ricoeur, "L'un des participants a l'intercelebration en rend compte," *Christianisme social* 76, no. 7–10 (1968): 424. On the evolution of Ricoeur's ecumenical thinking, see Beate Bengard, "Reception, Recognition, and Utopia: The Ecumenical Vision of Paul Ricoeur," *Ecumenical Review* 69, no. 1 (2017): 22–33.

50. Georges Casalis et al., *Die Zukunft des Ökumenismus* (Otto Lembeck, 1972). The quote is from the foreword by Günter Gassmann, 7–10, here 9.

51. Yves Congar, "Do the New Problems of Our Secular World Make Ecumenism Irrelevant?," in *Post-Ecumenical Christianity*, ed. Albert van der Heuven and Hans Küng (Herder & Herder, 1970), 11–21, here 13.

52. Mark Ruff, *The Battle for the Catholic Past in Germany, 1945–1975* (Cambridge University Press, 2017), 153–192.

53. Sölle, *Christ the Representative*, 109.

54. Jürgen Moltmann, "In Christianity," in *Christians and Jews*, ed. Hans Küng and Walter Kasper (Seabury, 1975), 66. See also Moltmann, *The Church in the Power of the Spirit*, 136–149.

55. Johann Baptist Metz, *Glaube in Geschichte und Gesellschaft: Studien zu einer praktischen Fundamentaltheologie* (Grünewald, 1978).

56. The persistent Christian ambivalence toward Jews in this period is explored in Karma Ben-Johanan, *Jacob's Younger Brother: Christian-Jewish Relations after Vatican II* (Belknap Press of Harvard University Press, 2022), 38–81.

57. Septuagintgroep, *Septuagint van Chur naar Rome: Dossiervan de solidaire priestergroepen* (Katholiek Archief, 1969), xx.

58. Septuagintgroep, *Van Rome naar Utrecht* (Katholiek Archief, 1969), esp. 17–19, here 19. See also Septuagintgroep, *Van Utrecht naar huis . . . ?* (Archief van de kerken, 1970), esp. 35–37.

59. Cited in Chris Dols and Benjamin Ziemann, "Progressive Participation and Transnational Activism in the Catholic Church after Vatican II: The Dutch and the West German Examples," *Journal of Contemporary History* 50, no. 3 (2015): 475.

60. Bernd Laeyendecker, "Septuagint: De lotgevallen van een beweging," in *Religie in de Nederlandse samenleving*, ed. Osmund Schreuder et al. (Ambo, 1990), 90–117. The motto is cited in Horn, *The Spirit of Vatican II*, 102.

61. Wolf-Dietrich Bukow, "Vorwort," in *Das Elend der sozialistischen Opposition in der Kirche: Celler Konferenz: Theologie als Gesellschaftstheorie?* (Grünewald, 1969), 9–11, here 10. See also Siegfried Baumgartner, "Reformer zwischen Revolution und Resignation: Ein Bericht über kritische Gruppen in der Kirchen" *Evangelische Kommentare* 3 (1970): 381–385. For helpful background on those gatherings, see Tobias Sarx, *Reform, Revolution, oder Stillstand? Der 68er-Bewegung an den Evangelisch-Theologisch Fakultäten Marburg, Bochum, and der kirchlichen Hochschule Berlin* (Kohlhammer, 2018).

62. Mechtild Höflich, "Zur Kritik der Praxis: Ein Gruppengespräch," in *Politisches Nachtgebet in Köln II*, ed. Dorothee Sölle and Fulbert Steffensky (Kreuz und Grünewald, 1971), 184. See also Klaus Schmidt, "Politisierung der Gewissen: Bericht über das Kölner 'Politische Nachtgebet,'" *Pastoraltheologie* 58, no. 7 (1969): 336–344, here 337.

63. Benjamin T. Shannon, "The Political Night Prayers and the Politicization of Religion in West Germany, 1968–1972" (PhD diss., University of Wisconsin–Madison, 2020). The emergence of similar initiatives elsewhere in Europe is mentioned in Maike Westhelle, "Political Ecumenism and 1968: The Political Night Prayers in Cologne," *Ecumenical Review* 70, no. 2 (2018): 283–296.

64. Michael Dohle, Dorothee Sölle, et al., "CSSR—Santo Domingo—Vietnam," in *Politisches Nachtgebet in Köln*, ed. Dorothee Sölle and Fulbert Steffensky (Kreuz und Grünewald, 1969), 13–28, here 21.

65. Martin Gentges et al., "Diskriminierungen," in Sölle and Steffensky, *Politisches Nachtgebet in Köln*, 29–46, here 43.

66. Bernhard Häring, "Routine oder prophetische Komkretion," in Casalis et al., *Die Zukunft des Ökumenismus*, 67–96, here 83.

67. Germaine Greer, *The Female Eunuch* (Macgibbon, 1970).

68. Jean-G. Lemaire and Evelyne Lemaire-Arnaud, *Les conflits conjugaux* (Sociales françaises, 1966), 46.

69. Karl Horst Wrage, *Verantwortung in der Ehe* (Mohn, 1965).

70. Catharina Halkes, *Storm na de Stilte* (Amboboeken, 1964). The quotes are from the German translation, *Frau, Welt, Kirche: Wandlungen und Forderungen* (Styria, 1967), 50.

71. Catharina Halkes and Annelies van Heijst, "New Catholic Women in the Netherlands," in *The Voice of the Turtledove: New Catholic Women in Europe*, ed. Anne Brotherton et al. (Paulist Press, 1992), 171–192.

72. Halkes, *Frau, Welt, Kirche*, 48.

73. Ibid., 73.

74. Gertrud Heinzelmann, "Zur kirchlichen Stellung der Frau," in *Wir schweigen nicht länger! We Won't Keep Silence Any Longer!*, ed. Gertrud Heinzelmann (Interfeminas, 1965), 7–20, here 8.

75. Elisabeth Schüssler, *Die vergessene Partner* (Patmos, 1964); "Der Anführer und Vollender unseres Glaubens: Zum theologischen Verständnis des Hebräerbriefes," in *Gestalt und Anspruch des Neuen Testaments*, ed. Josef Schreiner and Gerhard Dautzenberg (Echter, 1969), 262–281.

76. Elisabeth Schüssler, "Should Women Aim for Ordination to the Lowest Rung of the Hierarchical Ladder?," reprinted in Elisabeth Schüssler Fiorenza, *Discipleship of Equals: A Critical Feminist Ekklesia-logy of Liberation* (Crossroad, 1993), 30.

77. Originally published as an article, this text reappeared as a booklet in several languages. The quote is from the English translation, Kari Elisabeth Børresen, *Male-Female: A Critique of Traditional Christian Theology* (Suomen uskontotieteellinen seura, 1975), 11.

78. Elisabeth Moltmann-Wendel, *Menschenrecht für die Frau: Christliche Initiativen zur Frauenbefreiung* (Kaiser, 1974), 66–67.

79. Elisabeth Moltmann-Wendel, *Freiheit, Gleichheit, Schwesterlichkeit: Zur Emanzipation der Frau in Kirche und Gesellschaft* (Kaiser, 1977).

80. Évelyne Sullerot, "Frau und Arbeit," and Angelika Boese, "Frau und Werbung," both in *Mann und Frau: Schon Partner?*, ed. Josef Duss-von Werdt (Benziger, 1973), 51–72, 29–38.

81. See, for example, Magdalena Hartlich, "Psychologische Aspekte sexistisher Rollezwänge," *Una Sancta* (1974): 238–243, Hartlich, "Sexismus und menschliche Entwicklung: Ein soziologischer Beitrag zum Internationalen Jahr der Frau," *Vereinte Nationen* 23, no. 3 (1975): 64–68.

82. Cited in Elisabeth Moltmann-Wendel, *Autobiography* (S.C.M., 1997), 72.

83. Elisabeth Moltmann-Wendel, *Ein eigener Mensch werden: Frauen um Jesus* (Gütersloh, 1979); quotation is from the English translation, *The Women around Jesus* (1982), 9.

84. Catharin a Halkes, "Mary and Women," in *Mary in the Churches*, ed. Jürgen Moltmann and Hans Küng (Seabury Press, 1983) 66–73. See also Halkes's influential "Eine 'andere' Maria," *Una sancta* 32 (1977): 323–337, and more broadly the materials assembled in Halkes, *Met Mirjam is het begonnen* (Kampen, 1980), which was widely translated and became the most influential Catholic feminist text in Europe.

85. Moltmann-Wendel, *Ein eigener Mensch werden*.

86. Halkes, "Mary and Women," 71.

87. André Dumas, "Conference II," *Report of the Women's International Ecumenical Conference* (WCC, 1967), 69–77.

88. Tine Govaart-Halkes, "Developments in the Roman Catholic Church regarding the Question of the Ordination of Women," in *What Is Ordination Coming To? Report of a Consultation on the Ordination of Women Held in Cartigny, Geneva, Switzerland, 21st–26th September, 1970*, ed. Brigalia Bam (WCC, 1971), 30–41.

89. "Parentship," in *Sexism in the 1970s: Discrimination against Women; Report of a World Council of Churches Consultation, West Berlin, 1974* (WCC, 1975), 105–108, here 106.

90. Elisabeth Moltmann-Wendel, "New Trends in Feminist Theology," and Catharina Halkes, "Feminist Theology as a Model of Liberation Theology," both in *Consultation of European Christian Women, Brussels, 1978: The Sub-Unit on Women in Church and Society of the World Council of Churches* (WCC, 1978), 29–36, 37–40. The other topics are discussed in "Reports of the Working Groups," in the same volume, 7–28.

91. See, for example, Christine Schaumberger and Monika Maassen (eds.), *Handbuch feministische Theologie* (Morgana Frauenverlag, 1986). On the society's history, see the essays collected in Irmtraud Fischer (ed.), *Theologie von Frauen für Frauen? Chancen und Probleme der Rückbindung feministischer Theologie an die Praxis* (ESWTR, 2007).

92. Louise Janssens, "Morale conjugale er progestogenes," *Ephemerides Theologicae Lovanienses* 39 (1963): 787–826; Willem van der March, "Vruchtbaarheidregeling," *Tijschrift voor Theologie* 3 (1963): 378–413.

93. Franz Böckle, "Birth Control: A Survey of German, French, and Dutch Literature on the Question of Birth Control," *Concilium* 5 (1965): 97–129; Bernhard Häring, *Road to Renewal* (Alba House, 1966), 159–160.

94. Siegfried Keil, *Sexualität: Erkenntnisse und Mass-Stäbe* (Kreuz, 1966), esp. 206–211.

95. Karl Horst Wrage, *Mann und Frau* (Mohn, 1966), 138.

96. Paul VI, *Humanae vitae* (July 25, 1968), https://www.vatican.va/content/paul-vi/en/encyclicals/documents/hf_p-vi_enc_25071968_humanae-vitae.html.

97. There is vast scholarship on the encyclical and the responses to it. For an overview of the production of the encyclical and European responses to it, see Alana Harris (ed.), *The Schism of '68: Catholicism, Contraception, and* Humanae vitae *in Europe, 1945–1975* (Palgrave Macmillan, 2018). For Häring's campaign against the encyclical, and its broader implications for Catholic thought, see James Chappel, *Catholic Modern: The Challenge of*

Totalitarianism and the Remaking of the Church (Harvard University Press, 2018), 232–239. The quote is from Häring, *Road to Renewal,* 163.

98. Hermann Böckenförde and Bernhard Wilhelmer, "Repressive Sexualmoral, oder Wer schläft, sündigt nicht!" *Kritischer Katholizismus: Argumente gegen die Kirchen-Gesellschaft,* ed. Ben van Onna and Martin Stankowski (Fischer, 1969), 135–147.

99. Werner Simpfendörfer, *Offene Kirche—Kritische Kirche* (Kreuz, 1969), 158.

100. Jacques-Marie Pohier, "Réflexions théologiques sur la position de l'église catholique," *Lumière et Vie* 21, no. 109 (August–October, 1972): 73–107. The 1973 interview is cited in Daniela Saresella, *Catholics and Communists in Twentieth-Century Italy: Between Conflict and Dialogue* (Bloomsbury, 2019), 110.

101. Bruno Ribes (ed.), "Pour une reform de la législation française relative a l'avortement," *Études* 338 (1973): 55–84. After many responses to the forum quickly appeared in the Catholic press, Ribes followed with further reflections in his "Les chrétiens face à l'avortement," *Études* 11 (1973): 405–423.

102. Pierre de Locht hinted at those ideas in *La morale conjugale en recherche* (Casterman, 1968). On his public advocacy, see Caroline Sägesser and Cécil Vanderpelen-Diagre, "The Belgian Catholic Church and Canon Pierre de Locht on Sexuality after 1968," *Sextant* 35 (2018): 101–115.

103. Stephan Pfürtner, *Kirche und Sexualität* (Rowohlt, 1972), 214.

104. Dorothee Sölle, "Für die Bejahung des Lebens: Gegen die Bestrafung der Mutter," in *§218: Dokumentation eines 100jährigen Elends,* ed. Luc Jochimsen (Konkret, 1971), 155–159, here 155, 156.

105. See, for example, André Dumas, *Prospective et prophétie: Les églises dans la société industrielle* (Éditions du Cerf, 1972). On Dumas's advocacy for abortion rights, see Stéphane Lavignotte, *André Dumas habiter la vie* (Labor et Fides, 2020), 166–190.

106. Gyula Barczay, "Für die Fristenlösung," in *Zur Frage Schwangerschaftsabbruches,* ed. Hermann Ringeling and Hans Ruh (Reinhardt, 1974), 91–105.

107. Jacques-Marie Pohier et al., *Avortement et respect de la vie humaine* (Centre catholique des Médecins français, 1972), 222. See also the forum in "Pour une réforme de la législation française relative à l'avortement," *Études* (1973): 3–32.

108. The lectures are discussed in Ökumenischer Arbeitskreis Politisches Nachtgebet, *Ja zum Leben, Nein zu § 218* (Antoniterkirche Schildergasse, 1971). The publication is Jochimsen, *§218: Dokumentation.*

109. Jacque-Marie Pohier, *Le chrétien, le plaisir et la sexualité* (Éditions du Cerf, 1974).

110. Sölle, "Für die Bejahung des Lebens," 156.

111. Dagmar Herzog, *Unlearning Eugenics: Sexuality, Reproduction, and Disability in Post-Nazi Europe* (University of Wisconsin Press, 2018), 26–32.

112. See, for example, Robert G. Moeller, "Private Acts, Public Anxieties, and the Fight to Decriminalize Male Homosexuality in West Germany," *Feminist Studies* 36, no. 3 (2010): 528–552.

113. *Die Nieuwe Katechismus* (H. Weinmann, 1966). The quote is from the English translation, *The New Catechism: Catholic Faith for Adults* (Herder & Herder, 1966), 385. On the shift in Dutch Catholics' understanding of same-sex relations, from sin to illness, see Harry Oosterhuis, "Christian Social Policy and Homosexuality in the Netherlands, 1900–1970," *Journal of Homosexuality* 32, no. 1 (1996): 95–112.

114. Komission der Evangelischen Kirch in Deutschland, *Denkschrift zu Fragen der Sexualethik* (Evang. Pressedienst, 1971), 39–40.

115. Bernardus Witte and J. L. Grubben, *Homofilie: Informatie, onderzoek en herwaardering* (De Horstink, 1970).

116. Hélène Buisson-Fenet, *Un sexe problématique: L'église et l'homosexualité masculine en France, 1971–2000* (Presses universitaires de Vincennes, 2004). The quote is from

Jacques Perotti's introduction to the French translation of John J. McNeill's *The Homosexual and the Church* (Sheed and Ward, 1976), which appeared in French as *L'église et l'homosexuel: Un plaidoyer* (Labor et fides, 1982), ix.

117. Klaus Fitschen, *Liebe zwischen Männer? Der deutsche Protestantismus und das Thema Homosexualität* (Evangelische Verlagsanstalt, 2018), 61–74; Markus Gutfleisch, "Mit Katholikentagen die Kirche verändern," in *Augehende Saat: 40 Jahre Ökumenische Arbeitsgruppe Homosexuelle und Kirche,* ed. Michael Brinkschröder et al. (Kohlhammer, 2017), 46–55.

118. *Es gibt viele homosexuelle Christen!* (Arbeitsgruppe Homosexuelle und Kirche, 1979), unpaginated. I am grateful to the archivist at Northwestern University's library for granting me access to this pamphlet.

119. Dorothee Sölle, "Vater, Macht, und Barbarei: Feministische Anfragen an autoritäre Religion," *Concilium* 17, no. 3 (1981): 223–227, here 227.

120. Kwame Mkrumah, *Neo-Colonialism: The Last Stage of Imperialism* (Panaf, 1965); Rudi Dutschke, "The Students and the Revolution," *London Bulletin* 6 (September 1968): 4–14, here 8.

121. See, for example, Quinn Slobodian, *Foreign Front: Third World Politics in Sixties West Germany* (Duke University Press, 2012); Slobodian, "Guerilla Mothers and Distant Doubles: West German Feminists Look at China and Vietnam, 1968–1982," *Studies in Contemporary History* 12 (2015): 39–65; Christoph Kalter, *The Discovery of the Third World: Decolonization and the Rise of the New Left in France, 1950–1976* (Cambridge University Press, 2016).

122. The European left's approach to the NIEO is explored by Giuliana Chamedes, *Failed Globalists: European Socialists, the Global South, and the Struggle for Economic Decolonization* (forthcoming).

123. Dohle et al., "CSSR—Santo Domingo—Vietnam."

124. Harold Brandenburg et al., "Teufelkreis Entwicklungshilfe," in Sölle and Steffensky, *Politisches Nachtgebet in Köln,* 81–103; Sölle, *Political Theology,* 65.

125. Septuagintgroep, *Van Utrecht naar huis ...?;* Dols and Ziemann, "Progressive Participation."

126. Gustavo Gutiérrez, "Contestation in Latin America," in *Contestation in the Church,* ed. Teodoro Jiménez Urresi (Herder, 1971), 40–52, here 40.

127. Gustavo Gutiérrez, *Theologia de la liberación* (CEP, 1971). The quotes are from the English translation, *A Theology of Liberation: History, Politics, and Salvation* (Orbis, 1973), 21, 17; see 122–140 for the discussion of Metz's and Moltmann's theories.

128. Juan Luis Segundo, *The Liberation of Theology* (Orbis, 1976); Hugo Assmann, *Theology for a Nomad Church* (Orbis, 1975). For an overview, see, for example, David Tombs, *Latin American Liberation Theology* (Brill, 2002).

129. A rare exception that explores both its Catholic and its Protestant branches is Lilian Calles Barger, *The World Come of Age: An Intellectual History of Liberation Theology* (Oxford University Press, 2018).

130. Rubem Alves, *A Theology of Human Hope* (Corpus, 1969), 114–115, 23, 27.

131. José Miguez Bonino, *Doing Theology in a Revolutionary Situation* (Fortress, 1975); Julio de Santa Ana, *To Break the Chains of Oppression* (WCC, 1975); Santa Ana, *Good News to the Poor* (Orbis, 1979). Some of the figures' activities are discussed in David C. Kirkpatrick, *A Gospel for the Poor: Global Social Christianity and the Latin American Evangelical Left* (University of Pennsylvania Press, 2020).

132. Gutiérrez, "Contestation in Latin America," 45.

133. See, for example, Gutiérrez, *A Theology of Liberation,* 20–21; Alves, *A Theology of Human Hope,* 117–125.

134. Gutiérrez, "Contestation in Latin America," 51–52.

135. José Miguez Bonin, "Christian Unity in Search of Locality," *Journal of Ecumenical Studies* 6 (Spring 1969): 185–199.

136. Gustavo Gutiérrez, "The Meaning of Development (Notes on a Theology of Liberation)," and Rubem Alves, "Theology and the Liberation of Man," both in SODEPAX, *In Search of a Theology of Development: Papers from a Consultation on Theology and Development held by Sodepax in Carigny, Switzerland, November 1969* (WCC, 1969), 116–179, 75–92, quotation at 88. Some interactions between Protestant liberation theologians and the Protestant missionary world are explored in Annegreth Schilling, "Between Context and Conflict: The 'Boom' of Latin American Protestantism in the Ecumenical Movement, 1955–75," *Journal of Global History* 13, no. 2 (2018): 274–293.

137. This description is based on Sergio Torres, "Memorandum: Background of Proposed Third World Theological Consultation" (undated, probably 1979), folder I.B.2.a(1)(a), box 4, EATWOT papers, Union Theological Seminary, Columbia University (hereafter cited as EATWOT papers). There is no comprehensive history of EATWOT. For an initial and excellent sketch, see Sarah Shortall, "Decolonizing Theology: EATWOT and the Rise of Third World Theologies," in *Decolonization and the Remaking of Christianity*, ed. Elizabeth A. Foster and Udi Greenberg (University of Pennsylvania Press, 2023), 198–218.

138. Desmond Tutu, "Trends in African Christian Theology: Theology of Liberation," a paper given at a pan-African conference in Accra, Ghana (December 1977), folder I.B.2.b(2)(b), box 5, EATWOT papers.

139. Sergio Torres, Opening remarks at the pan-African conference in Accra, Ghana (December 1977), folder I.B.2.b(2)(b), box 5, EATWOT papers.

140. Tissa Balasuriya, "Introduction to the Asian Theological Conference in Sri Lanka (June 3, 1979)," Records of "Asia's Struggle for Full Humanity: Towards a Relevant Theology," folder I.B.2.c(2)(a), EATWOT papers. Balasuriya developed those ideas further in his *Jesus Christ and Human Liberation* (Quest, 1976) and his *Planetary Theology* (SCM, 1984).

141. Engelbert Mveng, "Third World Theology: What Theology? What Third World? Evaluation by an African Delegate," in *Irruption of the Third World: Challenge to Theology; Papers from the Fifth International Conference of the Ecumenical Association of Third World Theologians, August 17–29, 1981 New Delhi, India*, ed. Virginia Fabella and Sergio Torres (Orbis, 1983), 217–221, here 217. See also Mveng, "Black African Arts as Cosmic Liturgy and Religious Language," in *Africa Theology en route: Papers from the Pan-African Conference of Third World Theologians, December 17–23, 1977, Accra, Ghana*, ed. Kofi Appiah-Kubi and Sergio Torres (Orbis, 1979), 137–144.

142. François Houtart, *L'église et les mouvements révolutionnaires* (Éditions Ouvrières, 1971), 218.

143. Vincent Cosmao, "I.R.F.E.D.—Struggle for Development," *New Blackfriars* 51, no. 598 (March 1970): 125–132; *Le développement des peoples: Populorum progression* (Centurion, 1967); "Central Thrusts of the Consultation," in SODEPAX, *In Search of a Theology of Development*, 60–64.

144. Vincent Cosmao, *Développement et foi: Dieu a-t-il un sens pour les créateurs de nouveaux mondes?* (Éditions du Cerf, 1972). See also Cosmao, "Le péché du monde," *Présence Africaine Éditions* 104 (1977): 188–198.

145. Cosmao's role in translating Gutiérrez is mentioned in Guillermo Augusto Múnera Duenas, "Vincent Cosmao et la construction d'une pensée théologique transatlantique," in *Mission religieuse ou engagement tires-mondiste?*, ed. Olivier Chatelan (Arbre bleu, 2020), 117–138. His interpretation was published as Vincent Cosmao and André Rousseau, *De l'idéologie à l'apologétique: Aspects des langages de libération du militantisme catholique en France* (Centre Lebret, 1973).

146. Vincent Cosmao, *Changer le monde: Unetâche pour l'église* (Éditions du Cerf, 1979); the quote is from the English translation, *Changing the World: An Agenda for the Churches* (Orbis, 1984), 6.

147. Ibid., as well as the essays collected in Vincent Cosmao, *Nouvel ordre mondial: Dossier: Les chrétiens provoqués par le développement* (Chalet, 1978).

148. Houtart, *L'église et les mouvements révolutionnaires*, 219. For Houtart's sociological studies, see, for example, Houtart, *Church and Development in Kerala* (CRSR, 1979); Houtart, *International Responsibility for the Reconstruction of Vietnam* (CRSR, 1975).

149. Ludwig Rütti, *Zur Theologie der Mission* (Kaiser und Grünewald, 1972); Rütti, "Mission: Gegenstand der Praktischen Theologie oder Frage an die Gesamttheologie?," in *Praktische Theologie heute,* ed. Ferdinand Klostermann and Rolf Zerfass (Kaiser, 1974), 288–307; Rütti, "Westliche Identität und weltweite Ökumene," in *Ökumenische Theologie: Ein Arbeitsbuch,* ed. Peter Lengsfeld (Kohlhammer,1980), 285–296.

150. See, for example, Jacques Van Nieuwenhove, *Schul den bekering in de bevrijdingstheologie* (Relief, 1977); Van Nieuwenhove, *The Theological Project of Gustavo Gutiérrez: Reflections on Theology of Liberation* (International Center for Studies in Religious Education, 1973).

151. See, for example, the special issue on "contestation in the church" in *Concilium* 8 (1971); Marc Caudron (ed.), *Faith and Society: Act Congressus Internationalis Theologica Louvaniensis 1976* (Duculot, 1978); Norbert Greinacher and Alois Müller (eds), *The Poor and the Church* (Seabury, 1977); René Metz and John Schlick (eds.), *Liberation Theology and the Message of Salvation: Papers of the Fourth Cerdic Colloquium, Strasbourg, May 10–12, 1973* (Pickwick, 1978); Nobert Greinacher (ed.), *Evangelization Today* (Seabury, 1979); Dietmar Mieth and Jacques Pohier (eds.), *Christian Ethics and Economics: The North–South Conflict* (Clark, 1980). The quote is from Houtart, *L'église et les mouvements révolutionnaires,* 80.

152. See, for example, Georges Casalis, "The Church: A Segment of the World," in *Planning for Mission: Working Papers on the New Quest for Missionary Communities* (WCC, 1966), 122–128; as well as the statements of the Western European Working Group throughout the collection, all of which were written in 1963.

153. Georges Casalis, *Prédication, acte politique* (Éditions du Cerf, 1970); Casalis, "Liberation and Conscientization in Latin America," in Metz and Schlick *Liberation Theology,* 101–122; Casalis, "Die theologische Prioritäten des nächsten Jahrzehnts," *Theologische Practica* 6, no. 4 (1971): 316–324. The records of the symposium Casalis organized in Geneva were published as *Incommunication: A Symposium on Black Theology and Latin American Theology of Liberation* (WCC, 1973).

154. Georges Casalis, *Les idées justes ne tombent pas du ciel* (Éditions du Cerf, 1977). The quote is from the English translation, *Correct Ideas Don't Fall from the Skies* (Orbis, 1984), 32.

155. Ibid.; Casalis, "Liberation and Conscientization"; Casalis, "Nul n'a parlé comme cet homme," in *Jésus* (Librairie Hachette, 1971), 129–150.

156. Walter Hollenweger, "Blumen und Lieder," *Evangelische Theologie* 31, no. 8 (1971): 437–448; Hollenweger, *Evangelisation gestern und heute* (Steinkopf, 1973); Hollenweger, "The Aims of Evangelization," in *Evangelization in the World Today,* ed. Robert Greinacher and Alois Müller (Crossroad, 1979), 38–46.

157. Hans Jochen Margull and Justus Freytag (eds.), *Religion, Mission, Okumene* (Kaiser, 1971); Margull, *Keine Einbahnstrasse: Von der Westmission zur Weltmission* (Evangl. Missionsverlag, 1973).

158. Minutes and Report of the Assembly of the Commission on World Mission and Evangelism, in *Bangkok Assembly, 1973* (WCC, 1973), esp. 18–19, 24–25.

159. Andrew J. Kirkendall, *Paulo Freire and the Cold War Politics of Literacy* (University of North Carolina Press, 2010), 90–117.

160. This description relies on the materials relating to the WCC's Programme to Combat Racism, which are available in box 1, GB 193, World Council of Churches Archives, Ecumenical Center, Geneva, Switzerland; as well as Elisabeth Adler, *A Small Beginning: An Assessment of the First Five Years of the Programme to Combat Racism* (WCC, 1974). The quote is from *Bangkok Assembly, 1973*, 24. On the program's genesis and work in other spheres, see Claude E. Welch, "Mobilizing Morality: The World Council of Churches and Its Program to Combat Racism," *Human Rights Quarterly* 23, no. 4 (2001): 863–910.

161. Casalis, *Correct Ideas*, 172–173.

162. For a few representative examples, see Hans-Jochen Margull, *Zukunft der ökumene* (Paulsverlag, 1974); Metz and Schlick, *Liberation Theology;* Robert Greinacher and Alois Müller (eds.), *Evangelization in the World Today* (Crossroad, 1979).

163. Theo Witvliet, *De Hebreeuwse bijbel in Latijns-Amerika* (Kampen, 1979), 10.

164. This information is based on Sergio Torres, "Report, Ecumenical Dialogue of Third World Theologians: First Consultation, Kipalapala, August 1976" (undated, likely September 1976), folder I.B.2.a.(1)(c), box 4; letter, Torres to W. J. Kreeftmeijer (June 7, 1981), folder I.A.3.b(11–15); and the financial correspondence gathered in folder I.A.3.b(1–5); all in EATWOT papers.

165. See, for example, Georges Casalis and Jacques van Nieuwenhove (eds.), *Towards a Dialogue with Third World Theologians: Symposium "The Future of Europe, a Challenge to Theology," Ziest, the Netherlands, 10–14 December 1981* (EATWOT, 1981).

166. Johann Baptist Metz, "Standing at the End of the Eurocentric Era of Christianity: A Catholic View," in *Doing Theology in a Divided World: Papers from the Sixth International Conference of the Ecumenical Association of Third World Theologians January 5–13, 1983, Geneva, Switzerland*, ed. Virginia Fabella and Sergio Torres (Orbis, 1983), 85–92, here 88.

167. Peter Antes, "Das Verhältnis zu den Ungläubigen in der islamischen Theologie," in *Glauben in den einen Gott: Menschliche Gotteserfahrung im Christentum und im Islam*, ed. A. Falaturi (Herder, 1975), 117–129; Antes, "Christus und Christentum an der Sicht der grossen Weltreligionen," *Theologie und Philosophie* 25 (1976): 385–396.

168. Arnulf Camps, *Christendom en godsdiensten der wereld* (Bosch & Keuning, Baarn, 1976). The quote is from the English translation, *Partners in Dialogue: Christianity and Other World Religions* (Orbis, 1984), 90.

169. Eugene Hillman, *Polygamy Reconsidered: African Plural Marriage and the Christian Church* (Orbis, 1975), 186, 189.

170. Rudolf Bäumer et al. (eds.), *Weg und Zeugnis: Bekennende Gemeinschaften im gegenwärtigen Kirchenkampf, 1965–1980* (Missionsverlag der evgl.-luth. Gebetsgemeinschaften, 1980), 297–333; Simone Mantei, *Na und Ja zur Abtreibung: Die Evangelische Kirche in der Reformdebatte §218 StGB, 1970–1976* (Vandenhoeck und Ruprecht, 2004); Camille Robcis, "Catholics, the 'Theory of Gender,' and the Turn to the Human in France: A New Dreyfus Affair?," *Journal of Modern History* 87, no. 4 (December 2015): 892–923; Kristen Loveland, "Reproducing the Future Human: Dignity, Eugenics, and Governing Reproductive Technology in Neoliberal Germany" (PhD diss., Harvard University, 2017).

171. John R. Stott, *The Lausanne Covenant: An Exposition and Commentary* (World Wide, 1975); Congregation for the Doctrine of the Faith, "Instruction on Certain Aspects of 'Theology of Liberation'" (August 6, 1984), https://www.vatican.va/roman_curia/congregations/cfaith/documents/rc_con_cfaith_doc_19840806_theology-liberation_en.html.

172. Jacque-Marie Pohier, *Dieu fractures* (Éditions du Seuil, 1985); the quote is from the English translation, *God in Fragments* (SCM Press, 1985), 141.

Conclusion

1. Annie Ernaux, *Les années* (Gallimard, 2007). The quote is from the English translation, *The Years* (Seven Stories, 2017), 41.
2. Ibid., 146.
3. *Gemeinsame Verantwortung für eine gerechte Gesellschaft* (Evang. Kirche in Deutschland und Sekretariat der deutsche Bischofskonferenz, 2014), 20.
4. Bund der religiösen Sozialistinnen und Sozialisten Deutschlands, *Gegen den neoliberalen europäischen Mainstream! Est gibt Alternativen: Für sociale gerechtes, demokratisches und ökologisches Europa* (Bund der religiösen Sozialistinnen und Sozialisten Deutschlands, 2019).
5. Peter Beyerhaus et al., *Resist Gender Ideology!* (December 15, 2014), https://ubf.org/articledetail/12162.
6. Camille Robcis, "Catholics, the 'Theory of Gender,' and the Turn to the Human in France: A New Dreyfus Affair?," *Journal of Modern History* 87, no. 4 (2015): 892–923.
7. European Forum of LGBT Christian Groups, *For Everything Created by God Is Good, and Nothing Is to Be Rejected* (August 10, 2022), https://www.lgbtchristians.eu/wp-content/uploads/2022/11/EF-RCC-WG-Synodal-statement-2022.pdf.
8. The list of the observatory's activists and their reports can be found at https://www.intoleranceagainstchristians.eu/. Gudrun Kugler is cited in "Vienna, International Symposium at the Archbishop's Palace about Current State of Persecution against Christians across the World," *Sir Agenzia d'informazione* (November 22, 2016), https://www.agensir.it/quotidiano/2016/11/22/austria-vienna-international-symposium-at-the-archbishops-palace-about-current-state-of-persecution-against-christians-across-the-world/.
9. Statement by the Executive Committee of the ILRS (2022), https://ilrs.net/. On the history of the organization, see Robert Michael Rosso, "Religious Socialism in Post-Secular Europe," *Politics, Religion, & Ideology* 20, no. 1 (2019): 121–134.
10. Quoted in Gerard O'Connell, "Giorgia Meloni Is a Christian and Right-Wing Nationalist—How Will She Relate to Pope Francis?" (October 14, 2022), *America: The Jesuit Review*, https://www.americamagazine.org/faith/2022/10/14/pope-francis-giorgia-meloni-243965.
11. Quoted in Anthony Faiola and Stefano Pitrelli, "Tolkien's Biggest Fan? Italy's Giorgia Meloni Opens New Exhibit," *Washington Post* (November 17, 2023), https://www.washingtonpost.com/world/2023/11/16/tolkiens-biggest-fan-italys-giorgia-meloni-opens-new-exhibit/.
12. Alternative for Germany, *Manifesto for Germany* (AFD, 2016), 40.
13. The quote is from the prominent far-right German thinker Gabriele Kuby in *The Global Sexual Revolution* (Angelico, 2015).
14. Giorgia Meloni, "Speech at the World Council of Families (2019)," https://www.youtube.com/watch?v=VdfNSF-U6zc.
15. For two examples out of many, see Ugo Palheta, *La possibilité du fascisme: France, la trajectoire du désastre* (La Découverte, 2018); Matthew Karnitschnig, "Springtime for Europe's Fascists," Politico Europe, August 20, 2023, https://www.politico.eu/article/germany-fascism-populism-europe-bjorn-hocke-immigration-elections-eu/.
16. "Prime Minister Viktor Órban on the Kossuth Radio Programme 180 Minutes," May 25, 2018, https://2015-2022.miniszterelnok.hu/prime-minister-viktor-orban-on-the-kossuth-radio-programme-180-minutes-4/.

ACKNOWLEDGMENTS

Writing a book can often feel like a very solitary enterprise. So much time reading in silence in archives, thinking alone at the office, and staring at the screen, stuck in one's own head. But this book, like everything in my life, was in fact a communal endeavor. Over the long years that I worked on it, which were filled with upheavals and distractions, I benefited from the support and engagement of countless institutions, programs, and individuals. It is a relief and joy to be able to thank them all.

The beginning of this project was made possible by a Senior Faculty Fellowship from Dartmouth College, which gave me the time to conduct initial archival research in Europe. The ACLS Frederick Burkhardt Fellowship offered a year-long break from other responsibilities, which I spent at UC-Berkeley's Center for the Study of Religion. During that time I began drafting the first chapters. The rest of this book was written while teaching in Dartmouth's history department, where I was fortunate to have Bob Bonner and Cecilia Gaposchkin as chairs. Their guidance, material support, and sound advice are profoundly appreciated. A special thanks goes to Bruch Lehmann and Megan Yeo, the department's administrators. While they are always overworked and under-supported, their rare combination of warmth, professionalism, and kindness makes the history department a wonderful place to work.

Like any researcher, I am indebted to many archivists and librarians. Their tireless work cataloging materials and making them available is the precondition for historical work. My research took me to archives in Germany, Switzerland, France, Britain, and the United States, and I am grateful to the archivists who helped me find my way through the ocean of documents left by Christian organizations and individuals. Librarians were just as indispensable for the completion of this book. It could not have come together without the dedicated team at the Borrow Direct system, which helped me locate and read hundreds of Christian pamphlets, magazines, and books in multiple languages. Dartmouth's history librarian, Wendel Cox, deserves a special thank you. He not only helped me locate especially obscure and difficult-to-find sources, but also shared wise advice along the way.

Because the arguments of this book evolved slowly over the years, I was fortunate to be able to present this work in many venues. In all of them, I have benefited from collegial critique and suggestions. Thanks go to Till van Rhaden and Jennifer Evans, who invited me to test some of my earliest thoughts at Montreal's Center for German and European Studies; Or Rosenboim at Cambridge's Intellectual History

ACKNOWLEDGMENTS

Seminar; Lotte F. M. Houwink de Cate at Columbia's International History Group; Yair Mintzker at Princeton's Modern Europe Workshop; John McGreevy and Kathleen Cummings at the University of Notre Dame's Cushaw Center; Malachi Hacohen at Duke's Kenan Institute; Anna von der Goltz and Jamie Martin at Georgetown's Modern European History Seminar; Joe Blankholm at UC–Santa Barbara's Center for the Humanities and Social Change; Todd Weir at the University of Groningen; Jonathan Sheehan and Stefan-Ludwig Hoffmann at UC-Berkeley's Center for the Study of Religion and Department of History; and Ari Jaskowicz at Vanderbilt's Max Kade Center. I am also grateful to the participants in conferences and workshops at Emory, the British Academy, Oxford, Notre Dame, and Harvard for their generous feedback.

I was lucky to undertake this project with the support of incredible colleagues and friends who have read or discussed parts of the manuscript with me at varying stages. Sarah Shortall read multiple chapters and offered terrific advice; the conversations I had with her helped me think in new ways about Christian thought. Giuliana Chamedes also deserves special gratitude, for reading many pieces from this project and for encouraging me to clarify and sharpen my claims. I also thank (in alphabetical order) Daniel Bessner, Stef Geroulanos (who also generously hosted me at NYU's Remarque Institute and at Kanderstag), Martin Jay, Piotr Kosicki, Samuel Moyn, Golnar Nikpour, Justin Reynolds, Tehila Sasson, Victoria Smolkin, Danny Steinmetz-Jenkins, Albert Wu, and Gene Zubovich. The gift of their generosity has benefited my work in more ways than I can count. I'm also grateful to Daniela Blei, who as an editor provided careful and excellent writing suggestions on several chapters.

Other colleagues took on the daunting task of reading and commenting on an entire draft of this book. In 2023 the Dickey Center at Dartmouth College organized a manuscript review seminar. I cannot thank James Chappel, Liz Foster, and Sebastian Conrad enough for the care and thoughtfulness with which they read a raw and rough version of this book. Their bracing critique and insightful suggestions were enormously helpful. I'm also grateful to my amazing Dartmouth colleagues, Leslie Butler, Dave Petruccelli, and Darrin McMahon, whose kindness was matched only by their thoroughly excellent suggestions. A final thanks goes to Camille Robcis, who made time in her impossibly busy schedule to offer comments on one of the manuscript's final versions. This kind of engagement is a scholar's dream, and it helped me revise sections of this book considerably.

My editors at Harvard University Press provided support and guidance at critical moments. Andrew Kinney took interest in this project at its inception, and our conversations helped me reframe some of the contributions I intended to make with this book. During the final phases, Sam Stark shepherded the process of review and production with astounding effectiveness. His professionalism and engagement are a model, for which I cannot thank him enough.

Because I am neither European nor Christian, there are many things that I do not share with this book's protagonists. But just like them, I found the greatest source of love and stability in my family. I could write a whole book consisting solely of "thank you" typed over and over, and it would still not be enough to convey how much I owe my parents, Avner and Ofra. They have supported me in

ACKNOWLEDGMENTS

more ways than I know. The same is true for my brother, Noam, and his family, Rachel, Amos, and Beanie. Despite the ocean that separates us, their love is strongly felt. I was also fortunate to marry into a family full of inspiration and encouragement. Bob, Cathy, Chris, Jenny, Lucas, and Rose: thank you!

More than anyone, my immediate family deserves my thanks. This book's first steps took place shortly after the birth of my daughter, Ellie. In the years since, her endless curiosity and humor have been a source of hope and optimism. I began to completely reimagine this project shortly after the birth of my son, Daniel. His kindness and positivity have been contagious, offering so much comfort and joy. And finally, there is Jennie. It is impossible to put into words the gratitude I feel for her. For years she has been my most important interlocutor. She has spent endless hours discussing this book with me, edited messy draft after messy draft, and pushed me to alter disjointed and inarticulate thoughts into coherent prose. And even this is the least of it, since the life we have built together has been more than anything I could have hoped for. It is to her, and to our children, that I dedicate this book.

INDEX

Achinger, Hans, 194–197
Acker, Amandus, 102–103, 106
Adam, August, 206, 208–209, 211
Adam, Karl, 129, 134, 174, 180
Adam and Eve, 156, 209, 260
Adenauer, Konrad, 185, 186, 196
Adolfs, Robert, 235–236
Advice for Parents and Teachers about Education for Purity (Fonssagrives), 95
Affluence and the Christian (Van Oyen), 199
Africa between Yesterday and Today (Bühlmann), 216–217
African Ecclesiastical Review (journal), 217, 219, 224
African Today and Tomorrow, The (Knak), 162
Althaus, Paul, 204
Alves, Rubem, 267, 268, 269, 271
Ammende, Ewald, 131
Amrhein, Andreas, 103
Angel, Wilhelm, 192
Antes, Peter, 276–277
anti-communism, 15, 18, 122–147, 178–188; Christian efforts to overcome, 189–191, 235–236
anti-Semitism, 7, 26, 36, 41, 62, 134, 138–139, 179; Christian critique of, 167, 243–244
Anxiety and Happiness in Sexual Development (Groeger), 202
Apologetic Review (journal), 132
Aquinas, Thomas, 249, 250
Assmann, Hugo, 267
Audiganne, Armand, 44

Balasuriya, Tissa, 270
Balewa, Abubakar, 215
Balmes, Jaume, 24–25, 31, 43
Barczay, Gyula, 260
Barth, Karl, 165, 167, 208
Baudrillart, Alfred, 2, 41–42
Bäumlin, Richard, 132
Bavinck, Herman, 94
Bavink, Bernhard, 153
Bea, Augustin, 226
Beautiful Future (periodical), 131
Becking, Josef, 153–154
Beckmann, Johannes, 143
Becoming Their Own Person (Moltmann-Wendel), 254
Beerenbrouck, Charles Ruijs de, 83
Belloc, Hilaire, 124
Bérenger, René, 97, 99
Between the Nile and Table Bay (Knak), 162
Beyen, Wim, 187
Beyerhaus, Peter, 284
Bible and Medicine, The (Tournier), 207
Birkeli, Fridtjov, 220
Bismarck, Otto von, 39, 81, 100
Bloch, Iwan, 95
Bloch, Marc, 234
Blomjous, Joseph, 217–218, 219–220, 230
Bluntschli, Johann Caspar, 53
Böckenförde, Hermann, 257–258
Böckle, Franz, 236, 256
Boegner, Marc, 226
Boese, Angelika, 253
Bolanden, Conrad von, 55

343

Böll, Heinrich, 245
Bolshevism, 122, 126, 148; Christian negativity toward, 121, 123, 133, 192 (*see also* anti-communism); Nazi efforts against, 118, 127, 132
Bonhoeffer, Dietrich, 240–241
Bonino, José Miguez, 267, 268
Bornkamm, Heinrich, 212
Børresen, Kari Elisabeth, 250–251
Bovet, Theodor, 157, 209–210, 212, 253
Brasillach, Robert, 122
Brauer, Theodor, 141
Braun, Walter, 163
Brink, Heinz, 262
Brors, Franz Xaver, 54
Brown, Leslie, 224
Brucker, Joseph, 60
Brummelkamp, Anthony, 98
Brunner, Emil, 157, 173, 182, 230; anti-Semitism and, 138–139; family ethics, developing, 156, 205, 208; feminism and, 155, 205
Brust, August, 79
Bühlmann, Walbert, 9, 216–217
Buisson, Ferdinand, 40
Bunsen, Carl Josias, 52–53
Burgman, German Hans, 218
Busé, François, 82–83
Büttner, Carl, 103

Cadets of Alcazar, The (Brasillach / Massis), 122
Calvin, John, 30, 45, 146, 209
Camps, Arnulf, 277
capitalism, 25, 27; Christian ambiguity toward, 70–77, 139–145; Christian peace with, 189–199; and confessional hostility, 42–46; radical Christian critique of, 232–240
Capitalism and Socialism (Schäffle), 73
Capitalism and the Community of Labor (Perroux), 141
Carrel, Alexis, 150
Casalis, Georges, 239, 240, 242–243, 273–276
Catholica (journal), 128, 134

Catholic in the New Reich, The (Brauer), 141
Catholic Tendencies in the Evangelical Churches (Stählin), 181
Cathrein, Viktor, 4, 69
Century without God, A (Müller-Armack), 195
Chaillet, Pierre, 136
Charles, Pierre, 167–168, 169
Chiniquy, Charles, 52
Christian, Pleasure, and Sexuality, The (Pohier), 260
Christian Democratic Union (CDU), 185–186, 196–197, 201–204
Christian Feminism (Maugeret), 88
Christianity and Life (journal), 129
Christian Message in a Non-Christian World, The (Kraemer), 165–166, 169
Christ's Church and Hitler's State (Stapel), 151
Church and Revolutionary Movements (Houtart), 272–73
Church Dogmatics (Barth), 208
Churchill, Winston, 188
civilizing mission ideology, 13, 66, 213; and anti-racism, 165–169; and labor, 105–108; missionary adaption in response to decolonization, 214–217; and missions, 106–114; and racism, 160–165; and sexuality, 108–110
Civitas Humana (Röpke), 146
Class Struggle and Strike (ter Schegget), 239
Clergy and the Social Question, The (Scheicher), 72
Colijn, Hendrikus, 123
Colonial Politics and Christianity (Büttner), 103
communism, 7, 18, 20, 64; attacks on Christianity, 121–122, 191–192. See also anti-communism
Comte, Louis, 97
Concilium (journal), 236, 243, 277
Cone, James, 242
Congar, Yves, 21, 139, 243; active participation in communal life, calling for, 180–181; as anti-fascist, 119, 174; ecumenical meetings, organizing, 135–136, 182

INDEX

Congolese Woman, The (Vermeersch), 109
conscientization, 274
Constant, Benjamin, 32
Construction and Life of the Social Body (Schäffle), 73
Cordes, Cord, 196
Core Questions of the Christian World (Mausbach), 46
Corvin, Otto, 50–51
Cosmao, Vincent, 271–272, 273, 276
Courtin, René, 198
Couturier, Paul, 132
Craemer, Rudolf, 144
Crisis of Civilization (Belloc), 124
Critique of Heaven and Earth (Leeuwen), 239
Cullmann, Oscar, 182

Dahle, Lothar, 103–104
Daubanton, François, 58
D'Aubigné, Merle, 33–34
Daudet, Alphonse, 55
decolonization, 169, 176, 213, 218, 273; Christian footholds in decolonized states, 22, 265; ecumenism resulting from, 22, 177, 213–225; missionary anxieties about, 173, 213–225; radical Christian embrace of, 264–278
Defense of the West (Massis), 64, 133
De Gaulle, Charles, 136
Degrelle, Léon, 132
D'Elia, Pascal, 168
De Mun, Albert, 72, 75, 86
Denis, Jean, 141
Deraismes, Maria, 87
development, economic and social theory of, 221–222; links to gender, 224–225; missionary adoption of, 222–224; radical critique of, 265–278
Development and Faith (Gutiérrez), 271
Dibelius, Otto, 191
Diestelkamp, Leopold, 107
Diop, Alioune, 216
Dirks, Walter, 190, 192
Discovery of Russia, The (Massis), 133
Divided Christendom (Congar), 135

divorce, 12, 50, 55, 113, 120, 203, 210; doctrinal differences over, 6, 19; in Germany, 90, 127; interconfessional warning against, 84, 211; Luther's approval of, 49, 54
Dobretsberger, Josef, 190
Doctrine of Economics, The (Röpke), 145–146
Dollfuss, Engelbert, 131, 190
Döllinger, Ignaz von, 61
Dombois, Hans, 185
Doms, Herbert, 156
Donovan, Vincent, 219
Draft of a Catholic Political Program (Ketteler), 71
Drexel, Albert, 164–165
Dreyfus affair, 41–42
Drucker, Wilhelmina, 87
Dumas, André, 209, 254, 259–260
Dupanloup, Félix, 53, 54
Dupont, Joseph, 60
Dutschke, Rudi, 238, 264

Eberle, Joseph, 131
Ecumenical Association of Third World Theologians (EATWOT), 269–279
Eible, Hans, 132
Eichholz, Georg, 239
Eilers, Franz-Josef, 221
Erhard, Ludwig, 195
Ernaux, Annie, 280, 286
eschatology, 234–237, 239, 241, 267
Esprit (journal), 209
Essay on Liberation, An (Marcuse), 228–229, 266–267
Essence of the Social Question, The (Hitze), 72
Esser, Bernard Jonathan, 113
Ethos of the Entrepreneur (Höffner), 193
Études (journal), 258
Eucken, Walter, 145–146, 196
eugenics, 20, 92, 116, 148–157, 180, 261
Eugenics and Catholicism (Muckermann), 150
Evangelical Social Lexicon (Karrenberg, ed.), 195

Fallot, Tommy, 74, 95, 97
Family, The (Leclercq), 148–149, 154
Fanon, Frantz, 268, 272
Female Eunuch, The (Greer), 247
feminism, 4, 13, 151, 250, 260, 271, 278, 286; appropriation of feminist language, 65, 84, 89, 248, 251, 257; Christian antifeminism, 5, 12, 19–20, 65–66, 84–88, 90–91, 99, 102, 109, 150, 152–153, 155, 159, 176, 200–206, 209–210, 212, 263, 281, 283; equality, as seeking, 84–85, 88, 91, 148, 173, 203; in liberation theology movement, 268, 273, 276; Nazi antifeminism, 6, 20, 21, 117, 147–148, 150; New Left and, 9, 22, 264–265; radical feminism, 9, 22, 92–93, 98, 229, 251, 253; rise of feminism, 65, 87, 100, 147, 229; sexuality, seeking reform of, 91–93, 96, 99, 119, 229, 247, 256, 262; socialism, equating with, 112, 113, 219, 226
Ferrandi, Jacques, 222
First Vatican Council, 37, 38
Fischer, Guido, 193
Fischer-Dückelmann, Anna, 92
Foerster, Friedrich Wilhelm, 96–97
Fonssagrives, Joseph, 95
Forgotten Partner, The (Schüssler), 251
Foundations of Western Action (Kroll), 184–185
Frankfurt Journal (Dirks, ed.), 190
Frankfurt School, 235, 239–240
Franzel, Emil, 185
Freire, Paulo, 273–274
French Feminism (Turgeon), 89
French Revolution, 25, 122, 165, 178, 189, 195; confession and politics in wake of, 28–35; socialism, linking to, 64, 68; traumatic memories of, 50, 117
Freytag, Walter, 162–163
Froberger, Josef, 109, 111
Froment, Pierre, 41
Future of Catholic Peoples, The (Haulleville), 46

Gagern, Friedrich von, 206, 211
Galen, Clemens von, 174

Gandhi, Mohandas K., 7, 161
gender, 12, 49, 54, 124, 229, 282, 286; diverging views on, 118–119, 148, 255; in feminist theory, 89, 92–93; gendered animosities, 19, 50; gendered order, Christian efforts to solidify, 85, 90, 117, 147; gender inequality, Christian justifications for, 100, 114–115; gender norms, 3, 63, 248; interconfessional shaping of, 1, 5, 15, 16, 175–176; in missionary theory, 110, 169, 214; *Resist Gender Ideology!* manifesto, 283–284; shared understanding of, 100, 212; shift in conception of, 84, 153–155, 159, 200, 246–247, 251, 254
Gérard, Claude, 190
German Nationhood (Stapel), 150–151
German Volk and the Christian West (Hudal), 128–129
Gillouin, René, 133, 142, 152
Gladstone, William, 38–39
Gnauck-Kühne, Elisabeth, 88–89
Goebbels, Josef, 124
Gollwitzer, Helmut, 238
Görres, Ida Friederike, 211
Gounelle, Élie, 82, 191
Goyau, Georges, 46
Grave of God, The (Adolfs), 235–236
Great Refusal, the, 229, 232, 268
Great Saints (Nigg), 182
Greer, Germaine, 247, 251
Grentrup, Theodor, 109
Groeger, Guido, 202, 211
Grosche, Robert, 127–129, 134, 135
Gross, Nikolaus, 144–145
Grubben, Johannes Lambertus, 262
Gruner, Édouard, 75–76
Guardini, Romano, 187
Guizot, François, 32
Gutiérrez, Gustavo, 242, 266–269, 271, 275

Halkes, Catharina, 248–255
Hammerstein, Ludwig von, 55
Handbook to the Controversy with Rome (Hase), 38, 51
Hansen, Hubert, 111
Häring, Bernhard, 204, 243, 246, 256, 257

INDEX

Harmel, Léon, 75
Harmsen, Hans, 151
Harnik, Bernhard, 208, 209
Hartenstein, Karl, 166–167
Hartlich, Magdalena, 253
Hase, Karl von, 37–38, 51
Haug, Theodor, 154, 157
Haulleville, Prosper de, 46, 54–55
Healing of Person, The (Tournier), 157–158
Heiler, Friedrich, 83
Heinzelmann, Gertrud, 250
Heredity and Hereditary Care (Muckermann/Bavink), 153
Hermelink, Jan, 218
Herzog, Frederick, 242
Hessen, Johannes, 3–4, 9, 181
Hildebrand, Friedrich von, 156
Hillman, Eugene, 277–278
Hinschius, Paul, 38
Historical Monuments to Christian Fanaticism (Corvin), 51
History of the Reformation in Germany (Lortz), 179
Hitler, Adolf, 119, 124, 127, 129, 138, 144, 147; Catholicism and, 126, 179; foreign conquests, new attitude towards, 160–161; *Mein Kampf*, 125, 161; paternal authority and, 151; racially unity as goal, 20, 117, 179
Hitze, Franz, 72
Höffner, Joseph, 146, 192–197, 199
Hofinger, Johannes, 215–216
Höflich, Mechtild, 245
Hollenweger, Walter, 274
Holt, Johannes Gerardus Hendrikus, 207
homosexuality, 95, 147; laws against, 98, 176, 205; radical Christian embrace of, 262–263, 284, 286; threat to families, viewed as, 149, 200
Hour of Christianity (Schilling), 143
Houtart, François, 272–273
Hudal, Alois, 6, 128–129
Human Diversity and Christian Unity (Marais), 218
Human Rights for Women (Moltmann-Wendel), 252

Idowu, Bolaji, 216
Impossibility of Socialism, The (Schäffle), 74, 78
In Defense of Catholic Morality (Schilling), 142–143
indigenization, theory of, 161–168, 216–220.
Influence of Confession on Ethics (Krose), 48
Innitzer, Theodor, 131
Integral Humanism (Maritain), 135
Introduction to the Protestant Science of Mission (Daubanton), 58
Invention of Europe, The (Vesper), 132
Is Christ Divided? (Newbigin), 218
Islam, 5, 13, 215, 223; Christian hostility toward (Islamophobia), 9, 110–112, 168, 173, 276–277, 285; Christian unity against threat of, 66, 110–112, 220; communism, equating with struggle against, 122, 130; ecumenism not extended to, 177, 219; radical Christians' peace with, 276–277

Janssens, Louise, 256
Jardin, Françoise, 260
Jesuit order, 39, 60, 69, 108, 119, 122, 146, 258
Jesuits, The (Michelet), 39
John XXII, Pope, 226
Jordan, John, 218
Journal of Missionary Studies (Schwager), 59
Journal of Social Christianity (Martin/Gounelle, eds.), 191
Just-Dahlmann, Barbara, 260

Kaiser, Jacob, 186
Karr, Otto, 182
Karrenberg, Friedrich, 195
Keil, Siegfried, 256
Keller, Adolf, 170
Kellner, Ernst, 235
Kentler, Helmut, 262
Ketteler, Wilhelm Emmanuel von, 70–72, 75, 78, 86
Key, Ellen, 92
Kirschbaum, Charlotte von, 202
Knak, Siegfried, 161–163, 165, 169

INDEX

Knoll, August Maria, 198
Kraemer, Hendrik, 165–168, 169
Krafft-Ebing, Richard von, 99
Kroll, Gerhard, 184
Krose, Hermann, 48
Kugler, Gudrun, 284
Kulemann, Wilhelm, 77
Kulturkampf (culture war), 39–40, 51, 53, 61
Kummer, Karl, 197–198
Kuyper, Abraham, 75, 76, 78, 82

labor unions, 1, 2, 5; emergence of Christian, 77–78; and interconfessional cooperation, 79
Labouret, Henri, 213
Lacroix, Jean, 201
La Mauvinière, Gérald, 262
Lamennais, Felicité, 30–31
Laros, Matthias, 158
Laveleye, Émile de, 38–39, 44, 69
Lavigerie, Charles, 102, 104, 111
Law of Christ, The (Häring), 204
Lebret, Louis-Joseph, 222, 271
Leclercq, Jacques, 148–149, 151, 152, 154
Leeuwen, Arend van, 239
Le Guillou, Marie-Joseph, 219
Lell, Joachim, 212
Lemaire-Arnaud, Evelyne, 248
Lemaire, Jean-G., 248
Leo XIII, Pope, 60, 68, 73, 103
Le Pen, Marine, 285
Lévy-Bruhl, Lucien, 167
Liberalism, Socialism, and Christian Social Order (Pesch), 77
liberation theology, 230, 266–279
Liberty, Equality, Sisterhood (Moltmann-Wendel), 252
Light and Life (periodical), 258
Living Forces of the Gospel, The (Warneck), 105
Locht, Pierre de, 209, 211, 258–259
Loewenich, Walther von, 3
Lortz, Joseph, 130–131, 178–180, 181, 182
Lortzing, Johannes, 130, 131
Love in the Western World (Rougemont), 157

Lubac, Henri de, 136
Lueger, Karl, 76
Luther, Martin, 32, 69, 103, 133, 138, 209, 239; arrogance, accusations of, 29, 124; Congar on, 151, 181; divorce, allowing, 49, 54; economics, linking to, 74, 146; Germany and, 42, 64; Lortz, sympathetic view of, 130, 179; order, praise for, 33–34; principle of inquiry, establishing, 30–31
Luther in Catholics' Eyes (Congar), 151, 181
Lutz, Hans, 190–191

Mackay, Æneas, 81
Mahling, Friedrich, 89–90
Maistre, Joseph de, 29, 30
Malou Jean-Baptiste, 45
Man and Woman (Wrage), 256–257
Man in Modern Materialism (Wünsch), 184
Marais, Ben, 218
Maraval, Jean-Baptiste, 41
Marbry, Hannelore, 253
Marcel, Gabriel, 136
March, Willem van der, 256
Marcuse, Herbert, 236, 239; on the Great Refusal, 228–229, 232; Gutiérrez as inspired by, 266–267; as a New Left icon, 228, 233
Margull, Hans-Jochen, 274
Maritain, Jacques, 135, 136, 191
marriage, 27, 38, 47, 94, 150, 162, 170, 175; civil marriages, 25, 50, 54; family allowances for married couples, 149, 203; indissolubility of, 53–55; interconfessional marriages, 2, 12, 61, 158, 209, 212; interfaith marriages, 113, 212; love and fulfillment, as a site of, 25, 49, 156; main purposes of, 277–278; marriage equality, 89, 249, 283; marriage manuals, 12, 53, 92, 148, 153, 156–158, 176, 202, 206–211, 248, 256–257, 280; missions and marriage, 216, 224–225; monogamous marriage, 96, 109–110, 113, 151, 155; Nazi deemphasis on, 147, 152; sexual activity, feminists delinking from marriage, 91–92; sexuality, as the locus of, 95, 119, 206, 209, 256,

348

261; shared Christian understanding of, 12, 98, 154–155, 158–159, 226; social stability, as linked with, 51, 52–53; unmarried and married women, inequality between, 91, 99, 200, 250
Married Person, The (Becking), 153–154
Martin, François, 55
Marx, Karl, 64, 68
Marxism. *See* communism; socialism
Massignon, Louis, 219
Massis, Henri, 64, 122, 133
masturbation, 155, 157, 256
Maugeret, Marie, 88–89, 97
Maurras, Charles, 42
Mausbach, Joseph, 46, 80, 89
Mazzini, Giuseppe, 36
Meaning and Mystery of Sex, The (Piper), 157
Meaning of Life, The (Harnik), 208
Meinhoff, Karl, 111
Meloni, Giorgia, 285, 286
Menschik, Jutta, 253
Menthon, François de, 198
Mercier, Gaston, 8
Merensky, Alexander, 58, 104
Messner, Johannes, 193
Metz, Johann Baptist, 246, 249, 276; anti-Semitism, confronting, 244, 273; liberation theologians, inspiring, 266, 267; Marxism, uniting with Christianity, 234–238; Moltmann and, 237, 241–242, 279
Metzger, Max, 137
Michel, Ernst, 202
Michelet, Jules, 39
Mindszenty, József, 191
Mirbt, Carl, 57–58, 106–107, 112
Mirgeler, Albert, 134
misogyny, 110, 248, 262
Mission and Polygamy (Esser), 113
Missionary Theology (Rütti), 273
Mohammedan Propaganda and the Protestant Mission (Simon), 111–112
Moltmann, Jürgen, 240, 246, 251, 266, 267; *Christians and Jews*, 243–244; communist thinkers, in dialogue with, 237–238; social vision, sharing with Metz, 241–242, 279

Moltmann-Wendel, Elisabeth, 261; feminists, as inspiring, 253–254, 255; gender norms, questioning, 251–252
Monod, Henri, 80
Monsabré, Jacques Marie Louis, 53, 56
Montjoie, Christophe-Galart de, 29–30
Mott, John, 105
Mounier, Emmanuel, 155
Muckermann, Friedrich, 117, 131, 150
Muckermann, Hermann, 153
Mulder, Alphons, 217
Müller, Alfred Dedo, 180; as anti-Semitic, 9, 134; *Ethics*, 129, 134, 154; as pro-Nazi, 129–130, 143, 186
Müller-Armack, Alfred, 141, 195–196, 198, 199
Müntzer, Thomas, 239
Mushete, Ngindu, 269
Muslims' Christ, The (Schumann), 277
Must Russia Starve? (Ammende), 131–132
Mveng, Engelbert, 270
Mystery of God, The (Stählin), 159
Mystical Body of Christ, 128, 138, 171, 175, 179

Nacpil, Emerito, 269
Nagel, Eustachius, 112–113
Nazism, 17, 21, 120, 161, 184, 187, 200, 240; anti-Nazi interconfessional front, 137, 138, 170, 180, 181; biologism, favoring, 125, 138, 160, 163–164, 205; Catholicism, overlap with, 127–128; Christian claims of persecution under, 174, 179; Christian support for, 6, 118, 161, 169, 170, 179; corporationism, developing, 139–142, 144–145, 146; ecumenism, encouraging, 7, 20, 22, 117–118, 121–126, 130, 139, 143, 173, 186; eugenicist practices, 20, 148–157; ordoliberalism of Nazi opponents, 194–195; as racist, 20, 117, 119, 127, 129, 132, 147, 160, 163, 165, 167; rise of Nazism, 18, 116, 124, 135
Nell-Breuning, Oswald, 199
Newbigin, Lesslie, 216, 218, 219, 220, 224
New Catechism, The (Herder), 261

New International Economic Order (NIEO), 264–265, 267, 270–273
New Left, 13, 22, 228, 229, 259, 270; activism of, 230–231, 246; ecumenical efforts, 9, 23, 232–246, 278; Global South, focus on, 264–265; sexual theory, 247, 252, 255–256
New West (journal), 184
Nigg, Walter, 3, 182
Nkrumah, Kwame, 264
None Other Gods (Visser 't Hooft), 166
No One-Way Street (Margull), 274
Nyerere, Julius, 269

Ochsenbein, Ulrich, 35
Oettingen, Alexander von, 47–48
Offenbacher, Martin, 48
Ohlenmüller, Gerhard, 64
Ōkawa, Shūmei, 161
One and Holy (journal), 83
Onna, Ben van, 236
Oraison, Marc, 206–207, 209
Órban, Viktor, 286
Ordass, Lajos, 191
ordo-liberalism, 145–146, 194–196, 198
Origins of the Idea of God, The (Schmidt), 164
Österreicher, Johannes, 138
Oudenrijn, Frans van den, 242
Outline of a History of Protestant Missions (Warneck), 57
Outline of Ethics (Althaus), 204
Oyen, Hendrick van, 199, 208

Papal documents: *Casti connubii*, 150; *Divini redemptoris*, 122; *Humanae vitae*, 257; *Pastor Aeternus*, 37; *Quadragesimo anno*, 141, 146, 196; *Quod apostolici muneris*, 68; *Rerum novarum*, 73, 80, 141, 236; *Unitatis redintegration*, 226
Paris Commune, 68, 72, 117
Paul, Carl, 103
Paulsen, Friedrich, 88
Paul VI, Pope, 229, 257
Pedagogy of the Oppressed (Casalis), 273
Peers, Willy, 259

Pelletier, Madeleine, 92
Perotti, Jacques, 262
Perroux, François, 141
Pesch, Heinrich, 77, 78
Pétain, Philippe, 133–134, 142, 144, 145, 147, 152
Pfürtner, Stephan, 259
Philip, André, 188
Pieper, Josef, 140
Pierson, Hendrik, 97
Piper, Otto, 156–157
Pius XI, Pope, 14, 127, 141, 150, 164
Pius XII, Pope, 14, 192, 196, 226, 243
Plattner, Paul, 201
Pohier, Jacques-Marie, 258, 260, 279
polygamy, 66, 96; missionary anxieties about, 108–111, 224–225; radical Christians' embrace of, 277–278
Position of Women in Life, The (Mausbach), 89
Pottier, Antoine, 70
Prigent, Robert, 203
Primacy of Love (Adam), 206, 208
Prinsterer, Guillaume Groen, 34
Problems of the Modern Women Question (Mahling), 89
Probst, Maria, 205
Prolegomena of the History of Religions (Réville), 104
Protestantism and Catholicism (Balmes), 24, 26, 31
Protestantism and Socialism Today (Lutz), 190–191
Psychological Studies of State and Church (Bluntschli), 53
Public Immorality and How to Combat It (Roeren), 94
Purpose of Relationships, The (Harnik), 208

Quintessence of Socialism (Schäffle), 74

Rademacher, Arnold, 136–137, 139
Records of The Missionary Action, The (Charles), 167–168
Reformation, the, 25, 33, 59, 125, 130, 159, 179, 208; capitalism emerging from, 2,

44–45; divorce, opening the doors for, 54, 55; egalitarianism as a message of, 32, 89; as a Germanic phenomenon, 42, 46; liberation, as promising, 32, 239; revolutionary politics, associating with, 29–30, 31; Third World theology as a second reformation, 276
Reformation and Counter-Reformation Today (Metz), 241
Reformation as Religious Issue Today (Lortz), 179
Reich, Wilhelm, 232
Reunification of the Christian Churches, The (Rademacher), 137
Review of Social Christianity (journal), 74
Réville, Albert, 104, 106
Ribes, Bruno, 258
Rich Christians and Poor Lazarus, The (Gollwitzer), 238
Richter, Julius, 112
Ricoeur, Paul, 242
Riehl, Wilhelm Heinrich, 44
Ritter, Karl Bernhard, 138
Rocholl, Norbert, 156
Rocque, François de la, 133
Roeren, Hermann, 94
Rohden, Gustav von, 92–93
Röpke, Wilhelm, 145–146, 147
Rosenberg, Alfred, 124
Rösler, Augustin, 87–88, 91
Rost, Hans, 48–49
Rougemont, Denis de, 157
Roussel, Napoleon, 43–44, 45, 47, 49, 51, 52
Rouzade, Léonie, 91
Rupp, Erik, 236
Rüstow, Alexander, 195–196
Rütti, Ludwig, 273

Salleron, Louis, 188
Santa Ana, Julio de, 267
Sauer, Hermann, 130
Schäffle, Albert, 73–74, 78, 80, 81
Schebesta, Paul, 165
Schegget, Bert ter, 244
Schegget, Gijsbertus Hendricus ter, 239
Scheicher, Joseph, 72
Scherpner, Hans, 142
Schilling, Otto, 142
Schlange-Schöningen, Hans, 186
Schlesinger, Arthur, 226
Schmidt, Auguste, 87
Schmidt, Wilhelm, 163–165
Schmitt, Carl, 142, 235
Schoell, Jakob, 84
Schöningh, Franz Josef, 183
Schreiber, Wilfried, 197
Schryver, August Edmond de, 187
Schultze, Erich, 112
Schultze, Ernst, 94
Schuman, Robert, 187
Schumann, Maurice, 136
Schumann, Olaf, 277
Schüssler, Elisabeth, 251
Schutz, Roger, 136
Schwanger, Friedrich, 59–60, 107
Schwartz, Dietrich von, 107
Schweitzer, Alice, 253
Second Vatican Council, 14, 226
Secret Is Great, The (Bovet), 210–212
Segundo, Juan Luis, 267
Ségur, Louis-Gaston de, 45, 48, 49
Septuagint, 244, 266, 278
sexism, 85–91; radical Christian critique of, 228, 250–255, 263
Sexual Emancipation of Women, The (Pelletier), 92
Sexual Ethics and Sexual Pedagogy (Foerster), 96
Sexual Life of Our Time, The (Bloch), 95
Shaull, Richard, 242
Siegfried, Jules, 74, 76
Signs of the Time (Bunsen), 53
Simon, Gottfried, 111–112, 168
Simpfendörfer, Werner, 258
Sky in Us, The (Metzger), 137
Social Crisis of Our Time (Röpke), 145–146
Social Ethics (Messner), 193
socialism, 68–69; Christian alternatives to, 68–84; ecumenism as opposition to, 139–147, 189–199; radical Christian embrace of, 232–246

INDEX

Social Teachings of the Church, The (Pesch), 77
Society, Development, and Peace Committee (SODEPAX), 220–224, 269–271
Sölle, Dorothee, 231, 239, 243; *Christ the Representative*, 240; ecumenism, on the solidarity of, 263–264; night prayers, establishing, 245, 259–260; *Political Theory*, 266
Soustelle, Jacques, 136
Stählin, Wilhelm, 139, 159, 160; as anti-Nazi, 181, 185; biologism, rejecting, 137–138, 158; interconfessional relations, promoting, 15, 182, 184
Stalin, Joseph, 121, 122, 144
Stanton, Theodore, 87
Stapel, Wilhelm, 150–151, 152
Steck, Gerhard, 239
Stegerwald, Adam, 83
Steinmetz, Sebald R., 90
Stirum, Menno David van Limburg, 58
Stöcker, Adolf, 74, 76
Stöcker, Helene, 91
Subordination and Equivalence (Børrensen), 250
Sullerot, Evelyne, 253
Sully (periodical), 132, 134
Sybel, Heinrich von, 33
Symanowski, Horst, 191
System of Ethics, A (Paulsen), 88

Talma, Aritius Syb, 82
Terranova, Annalisa, 285
Theological Ethics (Thielicke), 201–202
Theology of Liberation, A (Gutiérrez), 266, 269
Thielicke, Helmut, 201–202
Tide, The (Holt), 207
Torcq, Georges, 145
Torres, Sergio, 269
Touré, Sékou, 214
Tournier, Paul, 157–158, 207–208, 209, 211
True and False Reform in the Church (Congar), 180–181
Turgeon, Charles, 89

Turman, Max, 80
Tutu, Desmond, 269
Two Sexes and God's Intention, The (Zimmermann), 156
Tzschirner, Heinrich Gottlieb, 32–33

ultramontanism, 30–31, 33–35, 37, 39, 50, 53
Union in Marital Love (Oraison), 207
Unity of Belief, The (Lortzing), 130

Vacher-Desvernais, Jean, 213
Vanistendael, August, 223
Van Nieuwenhove, Jacques, 273
Verbum Caro (journal), 182–183
Vermeersch, Arthur, 93, 109
Vesper, Noël, 132, 134
Villers, Charles de, 31–32
Visser 't Hooft, Willem A., 166, 226
Von der Heydte, Friedrich August Freiherr, 184
Vries, Egbert de, 222
Vrijburg, Jos, 244
Vuillermet, Ferdinand-Antonin, 100

Wagner, Adolph, 74, 76, 80
Warneck, Gustav, 57, 58, 101, 109
Warneck, Johannes, 105, 107–108
Weber, Ludwig, 77–78, 95
Weber, Max, 2, 44–45
Weber, Norbert, 106
Weigl, Franz, 97
Welfare and Politics (Schmitt), 142
Werdt, Josef Duss-von, 253
Westermann, Dietrich, 111, 162, 163, 169
Western Decision (Sauer), 130
We Won't Keep Silence Any Longer (Heinzelmann), 250
Wilhelmer, Bernhard, 257–258
Willebrands, Johannes, 182–183, 226
Winnig, August, 131, 139
Winter, Ernst Karl, 145
Winzen, Damasus, 128
Wirth, Joseph, 83
Wiskemann, Heinrich, 39
Witte, Bernardus, 262

Witte, Johannes, 168
Witvliet, Theo, 276
Women Question from the Viewpoint of Nature, History, and Epiphany, The (Rösler), 87–88
Worker Question and Christianity, The (Ketteler), 70, 72
World Council of Churches (WCC), 222, 226–227, 274–275, 278–279
Worship (Hofinger), 216
Wrage, Karl Horst, 248, 256–257

Wuermeling, Franz-Josef, 203
Wünsch, Georg, 8, 119, 143–144, 183–184

Young Christianity in the Upheavals of the East (Freytag), 162

Zahn, Franz Michael, 110
Zeising, Adolf, 38
Zimmermann, Franz, 156
Zuure, Bernard, 168
Zwicky, Berthold, 132